Anonymous

Biographical review:

Containing life sketches of leading citizens of Schenectady, Schoharie and Green

counties, New York

Anonymous

Biographical review:
Containing life sketches of leading citizens of Schenectady, Schoharie and Green counties, New York

ISBN/EAN: 9783337869014

Printed in Europe, USA, Canada, Australia, Japan

Cover: Foto ©ninafisch / pixelio.de

More available books at **www.hansebooks.com**

BIOGRAPHICAL REVIEW

VOLUME XXXIII

CONTAINING LIFE SKETCHES OF LEADING CITIZENS OF

SCHOHARIE, SCHENECTADY AND GREENE COUNTIES

NEW YORK

Who among men art thou, and thy years how many, good friend? — XENOPHANES

BOSTON
BIOGRAPHICAL REVIEW PUBLISHING COMPANY
1899

ATLANTIC STATES SERIES OF BIOGRAPHICAL REVIEWS.

The volumes issued in this series up to date are the following:—

I. OTSEGO COUNTY, NEW YORK.
II. MADISON COUNTY, NEW YORK.
III. BROOME COUNTY, NEW YORK.
IV. COLUMBIA COUNTY, NEW YORK.
V. CAYUGA COUNTY, NEW YORK.
VI. DELAWARE COUNTY, NEW YORK.
VII. LIVINGSTON AND WYOMING COUNTIES, NEW YORK.
VIII. CLINTON AND ESSEX COUNTIES, NEW YORK.
IX. HAMPDEN COUNTY, MASSACHUSETTS.
X. FRANKLIN COUNTY, MASSACHUSETTS.
XI. HAMPSHIRE COUNTY, MASSACHUSETTS.
XII. LITCHFIELD COUNTY, CONNECTICUT.
XIII. YORK COUNTY, MAINE.
XIV. CUMBERLAND COUNTY, MAINE.
XV. OXFORD AND FRANKLIN COUNTIES, MAINE.
XVI. CUMBERLAND COUNTY, NEW JERSEY.
XVII. ROCKINGHAM COUNTY, NEW HAMPSHIRE.
XVIII. PLYMOUTH COUNTY, MASSACHUSETTS.
XIX. CAMDEN AND BURLINGTON COUNTIES, NEW JERSEY.
XX. SAGADAHOC, LINCOLN, KNOX, AND WALDO COUNTIES, MAINE.
XXI. STRAFFORD AND BELKNAP COUNTIES, NEW HAMPSHIRE.
XXII. SULLIVAN AND MERRIMACK COUNTIES, NEW HAMPSHIRE.
XXIII. HILLSBORO AND CHESHIRE COUNTIES, NEW HAMPSHIRE.
XXIV. PITTSBURG, PENNSYLVANIA.
XXV. NORFOLK COUNTY, MASSACHUSETTS.
XXVI. NEW LONDON COUNTY, CONNECTICUT.
XXVII. MIDDLESEX COUNTY, MASSACHUSETTS.
XXVIII. ESSEX COUNTY, MASSACHUSETTS.
XXIX. SOMERSET, PISCATAQUIS, HANCOCK, WASHINGTON, AND AROOSTOOK COUNTIES, MAINE.
XXX. WORCESTER COUNTY, MASSACHUSETTS.
XXXI. BERKSHIRE COUNTY, MASSACHUSETTS.
XXXII. SOMERSET AND BEDFORD COUNTIES, PENNSYLVANIA.
XXXIII. SCHOHARIE, SCHENECTADY AND GREENE COUNTIES, NEW YORK.

NOTE.— All the biographical sketches published in this volume were submitted to their respective subjects or to the subscribers, from whom the facts were primarily obtained, for their approval or correction before going to press, and a reasonable time was allowed in each case for the return of the typewritten copies. Most of them were returned to us within the time allotted, or before the work was printed, after being corrected or revised; and those may therefore be regarded as reasonably accurate.

A few, however, were not returned to us; and, as we have no means of knowing whether they contain errors or not, we cannot vouch for their accuracy. In justice to our readers, and to render this work more valuable for reference purposes, we have indicated all uncorrected sketches by a small asterisk (*), placed immediately after the name of the subject. They will be found printed on the last pages of the book.

B. R. PUB. CO.

1336482

PREFACE.

"ONE generation passeth away, and another generation cometh"— an ancient writer thus summarizes the unending story of the life of man on the earth. Multitudes who came and went long, long ago left but scanty memorials of themselves and of their work, and these exceedingly hard to get at, necessitating in our day on the part of the heir of all the ages a new profession, requiring detective ardor and skill — that of the archæologist. With the advance of the art of living has kept pace both the study of the past and the writing of contemporary records, the present generation being especially mindful of its obligations in this respect to posterity.

For one hundred and twenty-three years has the American republic kept with open door the best and best-attended training school in the world for the development of individuals, the result being an unrivalled body of intelligent, loyal, serviceable citizens, builders and, if need be, defenders of their country.

The BIOGRAPHICAL REVIEW, of which the present issue, devoted to Schoharie, Schenectady, and Greene Counties, New York, is the thirty-third in our Atlantic Series, has for its object to preserve the life stories, with ancestral notes, of numerous representatives of the American people of to-day, well known in their respective localities — men and women of action and of integrity, helpers in the world's work — to the end that future generations may keep their memory green, may emulate their virtues, profit by their experience, and haply, with increased advantages of learning and resources, better their example.

BIOGRAPHICAL REVIEW PUBLISHING COMPANY.

OCTOBER, 1899.

AUSTIN A. YATES.

BIOGRAPHICAL.

HON. AUSTIN ANDREW YATES, one of the leading attorneys of Schenectady, served with the rank of Captain in the Civil War, and as Major of the Second Battalion, New York Infantry, was on duty with his command in various camps during the Spanish War, but is better known by the title of Judge, having been elected to that office in 1873.

He was born in Schenectady on March 24, 1836, son of the Rev. John Austin and Henrietta Maria (Cobb) Yates. The original ancestor in America was Joseph Yates, an Englishman, who emigrated in 1664 and settled in Albany. Christopher Yates, son of Joseph, and the next in this line, had a son Joseph, who was born in Albany, and settled in Glenville, N. Y., where he carried on a large plantation bordering upon the river, and owned a number of slaves.

Christopher Yates, second, son of Joseph, second, and great-grandfather of the subject of this sketch, was one of the well-to-do residents of Schenectady in his day. While serving as a Lieutenant in the Provincial army, he was wounded at the siege of Ticonderoga in the French War. He served as a Captain under Sir William Johnson in the engagement at Fort Niagara, and received from King George III. a land grant of nine thousand acres. His term of service as member of the first Provincial Congress expired just six days prior to the signing of the Declaration of Independence. Entering the Continental army as a Colonel, he served as Assistant Department Quartermaster under General Philip Schuyler, and participated in the battle of Saratoga. He reared five sons, each of whom performed some notable achievement. Joseph C. Yates, the eldest son, was one of the founders of Union College and Governor of New York, 1823-25; John B. served as Colonel of a cavalry regiment in the War of 1812, was member of Congress from Madison County, and built the Welland Canal; Henry was a State Senator from Albany; Christopher was the founder of St. George's Lodge, F. & A. M., Schenectady; and Andrew, Judge Yates's grandfather, known as the Rev. Andrew Yates, D. D., was one of the first professors at Union College.

Dr. Yates was a man of superior intellectual endowments, and was well versed in ancient and modern languages, including Holland Dutch. His professorship at Union College was productive of much benefit to that institution while in its infancy. His whole life was one of useful activity. Laboring diligently to increase the facilities for religious worship, he built thirteen churches, mostly missions of the Reformed denomination, all of which are still standing and are in a flourishing condition. He inherited considerable wealth from his father's estate. For his first wife he married Mary Austin, who was of English Puritan stock, and was a relative of the founder of Austin, Tex. Of this union there were two sons — John Austin and Andrew F. His second wife, who was formerly a Miss Hooker, of Hartford, Conn., became the mother of three children — Mary Austin, James, and Anna E. Andrew Yates also reared John Dominis, who became the consort of the Queen of the Sandwich Islands. Dr. Yates died in 1844, and his widow survived him some ten years.

The Rev. John Austin Yates, his eldest son, was born within the precincts of Union College, Schenectady, in 1801. After graduating from that institution he spent some time in Europe studying the modern languages, and spoke French and German fluently. He was afterward a tutor at Union College for some years, or until called to the pastorate of a Reformed church in Jersey City. As a pulpit orator he acquired a wide reputation. The memorable cholera epidemic of 1849 numbered him among its many victims; and his death, which occurred in Schenectady on August 26 of that year, when he was but forty-eight years old, was sincerely lamented in other localities as well as the vicinity of Union College.

In 1829 he married Henrietta Maria Cobb, an adopted daughter of his uncle, Colonel John B. Yates. He was the father of five children, namely: Henrietta Cobb, who died in infancy; Mary Austin, who married John Watkins, and died in Columbia, S.C., in 1853, leaving a family, of whom John D. and Grace S. Watkins are now living; John B., second, who served as Colonel of the First Michigan Engineers under General Sherman during the Civil War, was later a division engineer on the Erie Canal, and is now in the government service at Grosse Point, Mich.; Austin A., the subject of this sketch; and the late Captain Arthur Reed Yates, United States Navy. Captain Yates was graduated from the Naval Academy, Annapolis, in 1857, and was thus senior to Schley and Sampson. He was for some time a naval attaché in Japan. He served upon Admiral Farragut's staff during the Civil War, and received that officer's hearty commendation in recognition of his gallant conduct at the battle of Mobile Bay. He died at Portsmouth, N.H., November 4, 1892, on the eve of promotion to the rank of Commodore. The mother died in March, 1842, aged thirty-one.

Austin Andrew Yates's birth took place while his father was an instructor at Union College, and he was the second representative of the family born within its limits. He attended the public schools until entering the Schenectady Lyceum for his preparatory course, which was completed when he was but thirteen years old; and in September, 1849, he began his classical studies at Union. Leaving college in 1850, he spent two years in Western Massachusetts, where he continued his studies under the tutorship of David M. Kimball, and, passing a successful examination for the Junior class, he completed the course and was graduated from Union College in 1854. He read law in the office of the late Judge Potter, and was admitted to the bar in 1857, when twenty-one years old. During the first few years of his practice he devoted a part of his time to newspaper work, first as editor of the Schenectady *Daily Times* and later of the *Evening Star*.

Enlisting in Company H, One Hundred and Thirty-fourth Regiment, New York Volunteers, during the Civil War, he was promoted from the rank of Lieutenant to that of Captain. He was in the reserve force during the battle of Fredericksburg, and at Chancellorsville he received such severe injury to his eyes as to necessitate his discharge for disability. Re-enlisting as Captain of Company F, Fourteenth Regiment, United States Veteran Reserve Corps, he participated in some engagements near Washington, and on the occasion of a sudden attack made by the enemy under General Jubal A. Early, he assisted President Lincoln, who happened to be present, from the field. In November, 1863, he was sent with three companies to suppress a riot among the miners in Carbon County, Pennsylvania. Among the various official duties of his command after the close of hostilities was that of the execution of Mrs. Surratt and the other conspirators, which is one of the most unpleasant recollections of his military service. He was brevetted Major in 1865, and appointed Judge Advocate under Joseph Holt, Judge Advocate General, and after his discharge from the army in 1866 he resumed his law practice in Schenectady.

Politically, Judge Yates is a Republican. In 1867 he was unsuccessful as a candidate for the Assembly, owing to a factional discord in the party. He was elected District Attorney in 1868, re-elected in 1871, and in 1873 was elected Judge by a large majority. He was a candidate for the State Senate in 1885, but lacked ten votes of being elected. In 1887 he was successful in his candidacy for the Assembly, and was re-elected in 1888. Upon the expiration of his term as Judge he once more returned to his practice, and is now conducting a profitable general law business.

On December 18, 1865, Judge Yates was joined in marriage with Josephine de Vendell, daughter of John I. Yates. They have one daughter, Henrietta C.

In September, 1880, Judge Yates was commissioned Captain of the Thirty-sixth Separate Company, National Guard, State of New York, and later he was commander of the Fifteenth Battalion. In May, 1898, as Major of the Second Battalion, New York Infantry, he led his command to the field in the Spanish War, and served in camps on this side of the water at Hempstead, Lytle, Chickamauga, Tampa, Fernandina, and Camp Harden. He retired in October, having served through all the camps and service which have been the cause of such caustic criticism; and, though his regiment lost thirty-one by death, he brought home every one of his four hundred and thirty-six men alive.

Judge Yates was president of the National Guard's Association in 1890, and for a number of years Commander of the local post of the Grand Army of the Republic. He is a Master Mason, as were many of his ancestors, including his father, grandfather, and great-grandfather.

ANDREW J. GUFFIN, M.D., a successful physician of Carlisle, was born in Greenbush, Rensselaer County, N.Y., June 6, 1846, son of John and Hannah (Dings) Guffin. The Guffin family is of Scotch-Irish antecedents, and was founded in America by the Doctor's grandfather, Andrew Guffin, who was born in Newry, County Down, Ireland, in 1756.

Andrew Guffin emigrated to America when a young man, settling first in Dutchess County, New York. Later he moved to Schodack, near Nassau, Rensselaer County, where he resided until his death, which occurred in 1842. He was extensively engaged in farming. In politics he was a Whig, and his religious affiliations were with the Dutch Reformed church. In 1781 he married Hannah Ostrom, who was born in Dutchess County, New York, of German ancestry. She died in 1835, at the age of seventy-three. They were the parents of fourteen children; namely, Elizabeth, Rebecca, Andrew G., Sarah, James, John, Thomas, George, Mary, Josiah, Henry, Hannah, Elijah, and Jonas. Elijah became a teacher in an asylum for deaf-mutes. All the other sons were farmers.

John Guffin, the Doctor's father, followed agriculture in Albany and Rensselaer Counties successively until the last fifteen years of his life, which he spent in retirement as a resident of the city of Albany. He was very successful financially, owning a number of farms and other real estate. In politics he was a Republican and in his religious belief Presbyterian. He died in 1879, aged eighty years. His wife lived to the age of about eighty-two. She was the mother of four children, namely: Emma, who is no longer living; Andrew J., the subject of this sketch; Charles W., a clerk in the American Express Office in New York City; and John C., who was formerly secretary of the American Sewing Machine Company of New York.

Andrew J. Guffin, having completed his general education at the Albany Classical Institute, enlisted for service in the Civil War; and subsequent to his discharge he began the study of medicine under the direction of Dr. J. R. Boulware, a leading physician of Albany. He then took the regular course at the Albany Medical College, where he was graduated in 1868. After a year's experience as physician at the almshouse, he settled for practice in Nassau, N.Y., whence he went to Canaan Four Corners, and still later to New Canaan, Conn., from which place he removed to Clifton Park, Saratoga County, N.Y. In 1897 he came to Carlisle, where he has already built up a good practice.

Dr. Guffin is a member of the Schoharie

County Medical Society. Politically, he is a Republican, and is now serving as Health Officer. A member of the Presbyterian church, he was formerly president of the local branch of Christian Endeavor Society, and is now its treasurer.

Dr. Guffin married October 21, 1869, Vira Phillips, of Nassau, Rensselaer County, N.Y., daughter of John and Mary Phillips. Of this union was born one child, a son, John C. Mrs. Guffin departed this life in 1890. John C. Guffin was graduated from the Cobleskill High School, and is now book-keeper at William V. Downer's Life Insurance Agency.

RENWICK DIBBELL, general merchant, Tannersville, Greene County, was born at Platt Clove, in this town, July 5, 1861. His parents were Harmon B. and Deborah M. (Hummell) Dibbell, his father a native of Colchester, Delaware County, and his mother a native of Platt Clove. His grandfather, Amos Dibbell, who was a native of Holland, settled in Delaware County, New York, as a pioneer, and resided there until 1834, when he went to Platt Clove. He was a millwright by trade, following that occupation a number of years, and his death occurred at the age of eighty-four. His wife, formerly Charlotte Williams, of Colchester, died at eighty-nine years of age. They had a family of ten children.

Harmon B. Dibbell learned the trade of a millwright, which he followed at Platt Clove for a time, later moving to Kingston, where he engaged in manufacturing. Afterward he went to Elka Park, erecting there a mill, which he conducted for the rest of his life. In 1863 he raised Company E of the Fifteenth Regiment, New York Volunteers, engineer corps, and this company he commanded until mustered out at the close of the war. He was a Democrat in politics, acted as a Justice of the Peace for some time, and was a prominent man in the community. He died at the age of seventy-one. His wife, Deborah, was a daughter of Jeremiah Hummell. Her father was a farmer and an early settler of Platt Clove, where he resided until his death, which occurred when he was ninety years old. Harmon B. and Deborah M. Dibbell were the parents of six children, three of whom are living — Egbert, Renwick, and George W. Dibbell. Egbert is now residing in South Dakota. The mother still survives, and resides with her son in Tannersville.

Renwick Dibbell came to Elka Park with his parents when six years of age. He attended the common schools, and assisted his father in the lumber business until his father's death. Forming a partnership with a Mr. Goslen, he entered the contracting and building business at Elka Park, erecting a number of cottages there, also the Poggenberg Hotel, the Schoharie Mansion, and the Catherine Tower. This structure is built of stone and is fifty feet high. It is fourteen feet at the base, and has stone steps on the inside leading to the top. In 1888 Mr. Dibbell took up the profession of a civil engineer, and did considerable surveying in different parks, also laying out roads and running farm lines. In 1895 the firm purchased the store of C. F. Gray, one of the largest mercantile establishments in town, in which they carried a full stock of groceries, boots, shoes, notions, and other merchandise. This store was conducted in connection with their contracting business until October 14, 1898, when the partnership was dissolved. Since that time Mr. Dibbell has carried it on alone. Mr. Dibbell has resided here since his early boyhood, and takes an active interest in local public affairs. Through his efforts a post-office was established at Elka Park, and he has been Postmaster there for the past five years. He also succeeded in causing the extension of the telegraph and telephone lines to Elka Park and Schoharie Mansion, he being the owner of the telephone line. He has control of the switch office for the Catskill Mountain Telephone Company, and is local agent of the Western Union Telegraph Company. Having a long distance telephone, they can converse with New York, Boston, and other cities. At the present time he devotes his entire attention to his mercantile enterprise, the telegraph and telephone agencies, employing five assistants.

On October 17, 1883, Mr. Dibbell was joined in marriage with Miss Alice Bishop, of Hunter, daughter of Asa and Ann (Brown) Bishop. Her father spent most of his life as a farmer in Ulster County. He died in West Saugerties. Mr. and Mrs. Dibbell have four children — Flavius, Estella, Agnes, and Elmira.

Mr. Dibbell is a Democrat in politics. He has served on town, county, and State committees, has been a delegate to a number of county and State conventions, and was Tax Collector two terms. He is a member of the Knights of Pythias, in which he has held a number of the offices, and belongs to the Independent Order of Odd Fellows. He and Mrs. Dibbell are members of the Methodist Episcopal church.

THOMAS R. POTTER, a prosperous farmer of Glenville, Schenectady County, N.Y., was born in this town, December 2, 1837, son of Johnson and Susan M. (Romeyn) Potter. His parents were born in Saratoga County, the father in Galway, June 25, 1803, and the mother in Clifton Park, July 1, 1807. The paternal grandfather was Simeon Potter, who came to Glenville about the year 1809, and settled upon a farm in the north-west part of the township, where he resided for the rest of his life. His funeral was the first one held in the Glenville Reformed church. The maiden name of his wife was Phœbe A. Beach.

Johnson Potter, the father, came with his parents to Glenville when six years old, and was reared to agricultural pursuits. He became one of the stirring men of his day, and owned a farm of one hundred and forty-eight acres, which is now occupied by his son, Spencer S. Potter. He served as a Trustee of the town and as Commissioner of Highways. In politics he supported the Democratic party. Johnson and Susan M. Potter were the parents of

seven children, all of whom grew to maturity, and four are living, namely: Jedediah D., a resident of Chicago; Thomas R., the subject of this sketch; Spencer S., who resides at the homestead, as above mentioned; and J. Antoinette, wife of William H. Hollinbeck, of Hoffman's Ferry. The others were: Phœbe Ann, Harriet N., and Fannie E. The father died July 5, 1891, surviving the mother, who died January 20, 1885.

Thomas R. Potter acquired a district-school education. Like his ancestors he has followed agriculture with success, for many years cultivating a farm of one hundred and twenty-six acres.

Mr. Potter contracted the first of his two marriages January 6, 1861, with Jane Ann Van Wormer, who died June 9, 1893, leaving two children — Frank and Eliza J. Frank, who is in the insurance business, married Nellie F. Bennett, of Lansingburg, Rensselaer County, and has four children — Lelia B., Jennie E., Thomas R., and Henry B. Eliza J. is the wife of Elmer W. Kelderhouse, of Hoffmans, and has one daughter, Hazel L. On January 26, 1898, Mr. Potter married for his second wife Mrs. Effie C. Van Wormer, daughter of Abram S. and Bernetta M. (Dunham) Lodewick and widow of Oscar Van Wormer. Her father was a native of Schodack, Rensselaer County, and her mother of Lexington, N.Y. Mrs. Potter had four children by her first marriage, namely: Nancy B., Bessie R., and Blanche L. Van Wormer, who are living; and Jennie Inez, deceased.

Politically, Mr. Potter is a Democrat, and served with ability as Supervisor five years. He belongs to Touareuna Lodge, No. 35, I. O. O. F., and he and Mrs. Potter are members of Gold Medal Lodge, No. 554, Patrons of Industry.

GRANDISON N. FRISBIE, of Middleburg, N.Y., president of the Middleburg & Schoharie Railroad and an extensive dealer in real estate, is a native of Roxbury, Delaware County, this State, born on May 24, 1831, son of William and Marilla (Norton) Frisbie. He received a common-school education, and at seventeen years of age was apprenticed to learn the harnessmaker's trade of his brother at Fultonham. Three years later he became equal partner. Subsequently he bought out the business and conducted it alone for some time. In 1854 he began the manufacture of harnesses in Middleburg, and, being the only person engaged here in that line of industry, met with great success, and did a most profitable business. In 1867 he purchased a half-interest in the general store of Charles Earles; and some years later he bought a half-interest in the firm of W. G. Lounsbury & Co., in the hardware trade. Subsequently his two sons, Daniel D. and George D., were taken into partnership; and in time the entire management of the business passed into their hands, Mr. Frisbie himself giving his attention to real estate and insurance, which have since been his principal lines of activity. He has managed large real estate transactions, and has built a number of fine houses. His present residence, which is one of the finest in town, is one which he has remodelled.

Since March 25, 1878, Mr. Frisbie has been president and general manager of the Middleburg & Schoharie Railroad, much of whose success is due to him. This road, which was constructed under the authority of a legislative enactment of May 8, 1867, is six miles in length, and connects Middleburg and Schoharie villages. The road and trains are continued five miles farther north to a junction with the Delaware & Hudson, but the Schoharie valley road has greatly handicapped the Middleburg Company, since the latter depends upon the northern stretch as an outlet. At one time it would have been possible to purchase the Schoharie road, and Mr. Frisbie strenuously urged that this might be done, offering to make a subscription of five thousand dollars for the purpose. Since then it has been impossible to buy it. It may be interesting to review here in brief the history of the inception and growth of the Middleburg branch. When the Delaware & Hudson had been built as far as Oneonta, and the people of Schoharie had determined to connect with it there, a few prominent men of this town met at a hotel, and, after carefully considering the matter, decided that they would also make a junction at Schoharie by raising one hundred thousand dollars, half of which would be subscribed by the town and the other half by private individuals. As a matter of fact, the total capitalization, fully paid in, was but ninety-two thousand dollars. The town was bonded but comparatively little to raise the full amount of its subscription. The bonds of the company, which were placed at par (seven per cent. interest), were retired in 1893, principal and interest, by James Borst, railroad commissioner. The individual subscribers to the stock numbered about seventy-five, and included many small holders in and about Middleburg, about seventeen thousand dollars being in Albany holdings and the balance in New York. No indebtedness was incurred in the construction and equipment of the road, as one of the first resolutions passed by the directors had been that work was to stop as soon as funds were wanting. The road is now in paying condition, and shows clearly that it has been most efficiently managed. Mr. Frisbie is one of the first and largest local subscribers to the stock of the First National Bank, and from the time of its organization has been its vice-president.

In 1858 Mr. Frisbie was united in marriage with Kate Dodge, daughter of Daniel D. Dodge, late of this town. Mr. Dodge was a prominent merchant and for one year member of the State Assembly. Mrs. Frisbie departed this life in June, 1898. She was the mother of four children, namely: Daniel D. and George D., the sons above mentioned; and two daughters, Laura and Emma. Laura is now the wife of Dow Beekman, whose biography may be found on another page of the REVIEW. All these children are graduates of Hartwick Seminary in Otsego County, an institution of which Mr. Frisbie has for many years been treasurer and trustee. Mr. Frisbie and his family are members of the Lutheran church, and Mr. Frisbie is an Elder in the church. He was for several years superintendent of the Sunday-school.

HENRY T. BOTSFORD, a leading farmer of Greenville, Greene County, N.Y., was born in this town on December 18, 1845, son of Dr. Gideon and Maria L. (Tallmadge) Botsford. Dr. Botsford's grandfather, Gideon Botsford, Sr., resided in Newtown, Conn. He was possessed of liberal means, had large influence in his community, and represented his town in the councils of his State. Amos, one of his thirteen children and the grandfather of Henry T. Botsford, was born in Newtown on February 13, 1780.

Having obtained an academic education, Amos Botsford entered upon the study of medicine at the age of eighteen years, received his diploma at twenty-one years, and immediately afterward came to the new town of Greenville and settled for the practice of his profession. Dr. Amos Botsford was married on September 20, 1801, to Elizabeth Clark, daughter of Joseph Clark, of Connecticut; and his house-keeping began in what has since been known as the Ell. Knowles place. A few years after he purchased a lot and built the house in which Pierce Stevens now resides. Later he purchased of Jonathan Sherrill the lot and dwelling now occupied by his son-in-law, Dr. B. S. McCabe, and there resided until his death.

"For many years Dr. Amos Botsford was the only physician of standing or professional ability in this section of the country, consequently his services were much sought and his labors were arduous. His custom when visiting his patients was to ride on horseback. Few men possessed a finer physique than the Doctor. Of dignified appearance, he commanded the respect of all, even at first sight. He was a faithful, intelligent, and successful practitioner for over fifty years. He represented his town in the Board of Supervisors in the years 1826, 1827, 1831, 1834, and 1849. He was one of the incorporators of Greenville Academy. He was a faithful member of the Presbyterian church in Greenville, and for many years an acting Elder in it. He died on August 16, 1864. His wife died December 3, 1855.

"There were born to them two sons and two daughters. Eliza, the eldest, born June 5, 1807, was married to Charles Callender, and died April 4, 1871, leaving three children — John, Charles, and David. Of these John is engaged in the manufacture of brick in Boston. Charles (deceased) was a manufacturer of paint in Newark, N.J. David is now deceased. Clark Botsford, the second child of Dr. Amos, was born September 15, 1808. He was graduated from Union College at the age of nineteen. He then studied law, and subsequently practised his profession in the western part of the State. Mary L., the youngest child, married Dr. B. S. McCabe, and has continued to reside in the house where she was born and in which her parents died."

Gideon Botsford, third child of Dr. Amos,

and father of Henry T. Botsford, was born on June 5, 1811. He obtained a good education at Greenville Academy, and subsequently, in 1832, was graduated from the Fairfield Medical College. He began the practice of medicine with his father, and for fifty years continued to devote his entire energies to the work of the profession he so much loved. Like his father he was a man of commanding appearance and agreeable address, and like him he won and enjoyed the respect and confidence of the community. Ever active, and having in view the improvement of his native village, he never lost an opportunity to promote the public welfare. He was for many years an Elder of the Presbyterian church, of which from early life he was a faithful member. He served as a prominent member of the Board of Trustees of Greenville Academy. The Doctor's wife, Maria L., was the daughter of Dr. Henry Tallmadge, and a sister of Mrs. John G. Hart. (See sketch of John G. Hart.) Of the four children born to her, two are living — Henry T. and Anna M. Dr. Botsford was a Democrat in politics, and served the town as Supervisor for two terms.

Henry T. Botsford resided with his father up to the time of the latter's death. In 1878 he purchased of Robert Hawley a farm that he owned for eleven years, and in 1890 he bought the farm which is now his home. His house, which is the finest in the village, was begun in 1891 and completed in 1892. Mr. Botsford is one of the largest land-owners in the town. He now carries on the homestead farm of twenty acres opposite his own, the Gideon Hickock farm of one hundred acres, and the George Conklin farm of two hundred and twenty acres. He is a man of wide reading, and especially well informed on topics of public interest.

Mr. Botsford married in 1882 Mary, daughter of Thomas and Emily Robbins, and a native of Greenville. Her father was a carpenter by trade, and he also carried on a farm. He died at the age of seventy-one, having been twice married. His wife, Emily, who was born in Greenville, died in 1891. Of her two children Mrs. Botsford is the only one living. Mr. and Mrs. Botsford have one child, Frances Helena by name. In politics Mr. Botsford is a Democrat. He has dealt to quite an extent in real estate. He and his wife are members of the Presbyterian church, and he has been one of its trustees for many years.

HARMON BECKER, whose death occurred January 18, 1897, at the homestead in Cobleskill, N.Y., now occupied by Mrs. Becker and her daughters, was during his long life an esteemed citizen of this town and one of its successful farmers. He was born June 19, 1813, at Duanesburg, Schenectady County, and was a son of Nicholas Becker. He came from patriotic stock, both his paternal grandfather, Captain John Becker, and his maternal grandfather, John Ferguson, having fought as brave soldiers in the Revolutionary War, the former commanding a company of minute-men.

Nicholas Becker lived in Duanesburg some

years after his marriage to Jean Ferguson of Edinburgh, Scotland; but in 1823 he came with his family to Cobleskill, and, taking up a tract of forest-covered land, began the laborious task of clearing a farm and establishing a home.

Harmon Becker was a lad of ten years when he came here with his parents. He assisted in the pioneer labor of reclaiming a farm from the forest, and, having subsequently succeeded to its ownership, was here industriously and prosperously engaged in general farming and saw-milling to the close of his life of eighty-three years. He was a stanch Democrat in his political affiliations for the greater part of his life, and served as Supervisor two terms and as School Inspector a number of years. In his last years he voted with the Prohibition party, believing strongly in the equal suffrage plank of its platform. A valued member of the Lutheran church, he held nearly all the offices connected with that organization, and for thirty-six consecutive years was superintendent of its Sunday-school.

On January 17, 1849, Mr. Becker married Miss Julia A. Myer, who was born in Barnerville, N.Y. Her father, Stephen Myer, was of Dutch extraction. The emigrant ancestor of the Myer family came to America from Holland in old Colonial times, and was one of the original settlers of Ulster County, in this State. Mrs. Becker's paternal grandfather, Peter L. Myer, was born and brought up in Saugerties, Ulster County. Removing thence to Schoharie County, he devoted his energies to tilling the soil. His death occurred at the venerable age of ninety-one years. He, too, served with honor in the Revolutionary War. Stephen Myer continued during his life in the occupation to which he was trained, and in addition to general farming carried on a substantial business as a miller, owning and operating both a saw-mill and a grist-mill. He lived to be eighty-one years of age. His wife, whose maiden name was Elizabeth Mowers, was born in Ulster County, a daughter of Jacob Mowers. Mr. and Mrs. Stephen Myer had four children, two of whom are still living, namely: Mrs. Becker; and her sister, Sally C., who is the wife of Charles Ryder. Mrs. Myer died at the age of eighty-one years. Both she and her husband were active members of the Lutheran church, in which he filled all the offices. He was also prominent in local affairs, and for a number of years served as Highway Commissioner.

Two children were born to Mr. and Mrs. Becker — Elizabeth Jean and Mary Isadore. Mrs. Becker and her daughters live on the home farm, which they have managed with success since Mr. Becker's death. They carry on general farming, using judgment in all matters pertaining to the care of their one hundred and seventy-five acres. A part of the land is devoted to grazing, and a part to the raising of wheat, corn, and hay. They also continue the saw-mill business. Mrs. Becker and the Misses Becker are faithful members of the Lutheran church, and also of the Woman's Christian Temperance Union.

The history of the Harmon Becker homestead is unique in that for fifty-six years no death occurred on the place, either of its owners or family, or of the men or maids employed by them during that time. The carefully-kept records show that more than ninety souls lived, either permanently or temporarily, on the farm during those years.

STEPHEN A. CURTIS, an accountant in the Schenectady freight office of the Delaware & Hudson Canal Company Railway, was born on January 8, 1850, in Blenheim, Schoharie County, N.Y. That town was the native place of his parents, Stephen L. and Eliza (Maham) Curtis. His grandfather, Benjamin P. Curtis, who did garrison duty at Sackett's Harbor, N.Y., during the War of 1812, went to Blenheim from Duanesburg, Schenectady County, N.Y. Joseph Curtis, the father of Benjamin P., came from Litchfield, Conn., to New York State soon after the close of the Revolutionary War, and, clearing a farm in the wilderness, succeeded through his energy and perseverance in establishing a comfortable home. Of the children of Stephen L. and Eliza Curtis there are but two survivors: Stephen A., the subject of this sketch; and Stanley D., who is now station agent for the Delaware & Hudson River Railway at Plattsburg, N.Y. He married Harriet Gardner, and has three sons, namely: Stanley, born in 1886; Charles, born in 1889; and George T., born in 1892.

Stephen A. Curtis acquired his preliminary education in the public schools of Blenheim and Jefferson, and completed his studies at the seminary in Stamford, N.Y., where he was fitted for educational work. For a number of years he was a successful teacher in Schoharie and Broome Counties. Coming to Schenectady in 1881, he entered the freight office of the Delaware & Hudson Canal Company Railway as bookkeeper, and here after eighteen years of faithful service he remains at this day, a valuable member of their clerical force.

Mr. Curtis married Ella M. Danforth, daughter of Elijah Danforth, of Jefferson, N.Y. They have one daughter, Adeline. She is the wife of Ira Brownell, of Schenectady, and has one child, Eleanor, born in 1897.

Mr. Curtis has been quite active in public affairs, having served as Excise Commissioner and upon the board of United States Supervisors. Politically, he acts with the Democratic party. He is Past Dictator of Lodge No. 3715, Knights of Honor; is a charter member and by dispensation First Prophet of Saugh-Naughta-da Tribe, No. 123, Improved Order of Red Men. He attends the Congregational church, and is now serving as a trustee.

HON. SIMON J. SCHERMERHORN, an ex-member of Congress, one of the most prominent men of Rotterdam, N.Y., was born in this town, September 26, 1827, son of Jacob I. and Maria (Vedder) Schermerhorn. His father was born in Rotterdam in 1789, and his mother was born here in 1788. Mr. Schermerhorn is a descendant in the eighth generation of Jacob Janse Schermerhorn, who arrived from Holland about the

year 1650, and founded the family which since that date has been prominently identified with Rotterdam and vicinity. The majority of its representatives have been extensive farmers. Jacob I. Schermerhorn, the father above named, was a leading spirit in local public affairs, and served with ability as Supervisor.

Simon J. Schermerhorn acquired the usual district-school education provided for the children of his day, and he certainly made good use of his meagre opportunities. Reared a farmer, like most of his neighbors, he has followed farming with unusual success, and he still has large agricultural interests. He has also dealt extensively in broom corn, and for thirty years he was engaged in the manufacture of brooms. He has business interests in other directions, and is vice-president of the Mohawk National Bank of Schenectady.

On February 4, 1857, Mr. Schermerhorn was joined in marriage with Helen Veeder, who was born in Woestina, March 29, 1837, daughter of Harman and Eleanor (Truax) Veeder. Her father was born in Rotterdam, and her mother was a native of Schenectady. Mr. and Mrs. Schermerhorn have five children living; namely, Mary V., Sarah, Alice A., Andrew T., and Simon.

Mr. Schermerhorn's public record, which is familiar to the readers of the REVIEW, deserves more space than can consistently be allotted to a brief sketch. His efforts in behalf of improvements during his several terms as Supervisor, as well as the advance made in educational facilities while he was Commissioner of that department for this county, fully merited the hearty commendation which they received. He ably represented this district in the Assembly during the session of 1862, was a Presidential Elector on the Cleveland ticket in 1888, and as a member of the Fifty-third Congress he supported such measures as were in his estimation calculated to bestow the most benefit on the nation as a whole. Mr. and Mrs. Schermerhorn are members of the Dutch Reformed church.

JOSEPH MALCOLM, of Catskill, N.Y., head of the firm of Malcolm & Co., and one of the oldest woollen manufacturers in the State, was born in Middlebury, Vt., on August 24, 1838, son of Joseph and Harriet (Brundage) Malcolm. His paternal grandfather, James Malcolm, was a silk weaver, who lived and died in Paisley, Scotland.

Joseph Malcolm was born in Scotland, and lived there until sixteen years of age, when he came to America and found employment as a mill operative in Middlebury, Vt., where in time he worked his way to the superintendency of a large mill. Later he had a mill of his own in Matteawan, N.Y., and subsequently one in Pittsfield, Mass. He retired from business in Pittsfield, and died there at fifty-two years of age. In religious faith he and his wife were Presbyterians. Mrs. Harriet B. Malcolm was born in Cornwall, Orange County, this State. She died at the age of seventy, having been the mother of eight children. Of these, two died in infancy. William and Abraham are now deceased, and James, Joseph, Samuel, and George are living.

Samuel Malcolm resides in New York City, and James and George are in Pittsfield.

Joseph Malcolm began his working life at twelve years of age, going into a woollen-mill at Pittsfield, Mass., as a wool sorter. He had worked his way up to being in charge of the card and spinning room, when he enlisted, in 1857, in Company D of the Eighth United States Infantry, which during his connection with it was on duty at Castle Williams and at Fort Columbus, New York Harbor. Discharged in 1859, Mr. Malcolm returned to his position in the Pittsfield mill, and he subsequently remained there until some time after the breaking out of the Civil War. For one hundred days in the early part of the struggle for the Union, he was in the Allen Guard, stationed at Worcester and in Boston. On September 18, 1862, he enlisted in Company A, Forty-ninth Regiment, Massachusetts Volunteers, which left the State in November under command of Colonel William F. Bartlett, sailed for New Orleans in January, 1863, and a few months later took part in the memorable siege of Port Hudson, where occurred some of the most desperate fighting of the war. Private Malcolm, always showing his sturdy Scotch determination when duty was most perilous, was the first man to volunteer for the storming party. He doubtless inherited martial ardor, as his mother's father was a soldier in the War of 1812, and her grandfather in the Revolution. His five brothers also enlisted, and were in service from two to four years. One lost his life in the war, and one was wounded.

After being mustered out at Pittsfield, Mass., September 1, 1863, Mr. Malcolm went to Little Falls, N.Y., and was there for two years as superintendent of the Mohawk Woollen Mills. Following that he was successively superintendent in the knitting-mill at Amsterdam, N.Y., in Troy, again at Amsterdam, then in Cooperstown, N.Y., where he was both superintendent and a partner in Groat Van Brocklin's Mill. Going back once more to Amsterdam, he started a woollen industry in company with one of his present partners, Mr. Pettingill. In 1886 he came to Catskill, where he has since been most successful in the management of his woollen-mill. In this plant one hundred and seventy hands are employed, and all kinds of men's, women's, and children's underwear are manufactured. The mill is the second largest in this section.

Mr. Malcolm's first wife was before her marriage Julia Marsh. She died leaving one daughter, Hattie L., now the wife of Hamilton Jones, a plumber of Catskill, of the firm of H. T. Jones & Sons. Mr. and Mrs. Jones have one child, Dorothy. Mr. Malcolm's second wife, whose maiden name was Jennie Lewis, is the mother of one child, James L.

In politics Mr. Malcolm is a Republican. He has been a member of the Catskill Board of Education, and he takes a lively interest in all matters pertaining to the general welfare. He is a director in the Catskill National Bank, and was formerly a director in the Young Men's Christian Association. He is a Mason, having membership in the Blue Lodge of

North Hoosick and in the Royal Arch Chapter of Catskill. Of the last-named body he is a charter member, and he has served it as scribe. He is a member of the Knights of Pythias of this town; of J. W. Watson Post, G. A. R.; of the A. O. U. W.; and of the Rip Van Winkle Club. He has been delegate from the post to the State commandery, but in general has refused offices in the various fraternal organizations to which he belongs, as the demands of his business leave him little leisure. Mr. and Mrs. Malcolm are members of the Reformed church.

GEORGE HANER, M.D., an able physician and prominent citizen of Tannersville, Greene County, N.Y., was born in Prattsville, Greene County, on the 6th of August, 1847. His sole heritage was that of an unsullied name and a constitution which had been developed through generations of industrious sons of the soil. For three generations the Haners and their wives have been hard-working, persevering, and in some degree successful citizens of Greene County.

Martinus Haner, the Doctor's great-grandfather, was one of the pioneers who came to Prattsville from the more settled regions of Columbia County. He immediately engaged in peeling bark for the tanneries, which at that time formed the chief industry of the neighborhood. This pursuit he followed as long as his health permitted him to work. His son Martin continued the gathering and sale of bark, but besides this he cleared a large farm and won by his diligent application a degree of prosperity and comfort.

Martin Haner married Miss Shoemaker, a native of Columbia County, by whom he had seven children, namely: Isaac; Henry; William M., the Doctor's father; Patty M.; Elizabeth; Lavinia; and Mima Ann. Patty M. married Samuel Chamberlain, who is no longer living; Lavinia became Mrs. Spencer; Mima Ann was married to Henry Palmer; and Elizabeth became the wife of Edward Cronk. Martin Haner brought up his children in such a way as to fit them for the battle of life; and, if he did not leave them a fortune, he at least taught them to win their own way to respect and independence. His wife died at the age of fifty, but for a few years more he remained with his family, closing an honorable life, with the love and respect of all who knew him, at the age of sixty-six.

William M. Haner, like his brothers and sisters, obtained his education in the common schools of the town. In the course of time he took possession of a part of the old homestead property, which he farmed with some success until 1866, when he removed to Jewett. There he purchased a farm, but he only occupied it one year; and then selling it he removed to the town of Roxbury, near Grand Gorge, Delaware County. Here he purchased a large dairy farm, which he continued to occupy until 1895. He is now (July, 1899) seventy-six years of age, and is living with his children at Tannersville. He is a Democrat in politics, and has held office as Road Commissioner and Overseer of the Poor.

His wife, Cornelia, was a daughter of Jacob and Jennie (Stanley) Maginnes, who also were among the first settlers in Prattsville. She became the mother of eight children, four of whom are still living, namely: George, the subject of this sketch; Jennie E.; Homer H.; and Clark R. Jennie E. is the wife of Charles Voss, the genial Postmaster of Tannersville, a sketch of whom will be found elsewhere in the REVIEW. Homer has been for twenty years general agent for the Davis Sewing Machine Company, and for upward of three years he represented their interests in Australia. Clark is a book-keeper and clerk, and resides at Tannersville. Mrs. Cornelia M. Haner died on May 15, 1899, at the age of seventy-three. She was for many years a useful and honored member of the Methodist Episcopal church.

Thus it will be seen that George Haner started in life with no great advantages, but such as he had he turned to the very best account. All that the common schools of Prattsville had to give he devoured with avidity, and speedily made his way at eighteen years of age from the pupils' bench to the teacher's desk. Quiet and reserved though he was, his efficient work soon called the attention of trustees and school commissioners, and he successively and successfully taught in the schools of Red Falls, Jewett Centre, Windham, and Prattsville in Greene County, and Gilboa, Gallupville, and Middleburg in the neighboring county of Schoharie. With the power to teach came the love of and craving for more knowledge and he very soon proceeded to Fort Edward Institute, where he took an advanced course of study. A period was, however, put to his attendance at this school through lack of funds, but, nothing daunted, he turned to manual labor to supply his needs in this direction. He obtained work as a carpenter, and it was while thus engaged that a direction was given to his mind which determined his choice of a lifework. He was assisting to build a house for Dr. D. M. Leonard at Broome Centre, Schoharie County, and in discussing his future with that gentleman he was advised by him to adopt the profession of medicine. Taking this advice, he at once began his studies with Dr. Leonard, with whom he remained until he entered the Medical College of the New York University, from which he was graduated in the class of 1877. Thus equipped, Dr. Haner took up his residence in the town of Conesville, where he practised with success until 1880, when he came to Tannersville.

In 1880 Tannersville was only a small village, and the arrival of a young doctor with a university diploma and some experience was indeed an acquisition. He very speedily impressed the inhabitants with his professional knowledge and ability, and as the years have rolled along his practice has increased and his reputation as a skilful physician has continued to grow. For ten years he practised without opposition. Besides his ordinary practice he has a large clientèle among the many city boarders who visit Tannersville during the summer months, and among whom he is deservedly popular, both from a professional and social point of view. His present residence was erected in 1881, but it has been recently enlarged and beautified and made complete by a most convenient suite of offices.

In politics the Doctor is a Democrat. He has twice represented his town as Supervisor, and during the latter term was chairman of the board. The esteem of his fellow-citizens has also been manifested in his election to the office of Coroner for three terms of three years each.

His public spirit has led him to take an active interest in all that concerned the prosperity and development of the village in which he resides. He was one of the incorporators and its first president. He took measures for the laying out of its sidewalks, and was a member of the building committee which erected the first public school-building.

In 1877 Dr. Haner was united in marriage to Miss Agnes More, of Roxbury, Delaware County, a daughter of Andrew and Ann E. (Hardenburgh) More and a third cousin of the late Jay Gould. She had two sisters, Cornelia and Kate, and she has one brother, Samuel P. Kate was married to Mr. M. L. Benham. Samuel P. More is a publisher in Great Bend, Pa. Dr. and Mrs. Haner have one daughter, Helen.

The Doctor is a charter member of the Mount Tabor Lodge, F. & A. M., and belonged formerly to the Gilboa Lodge. He is a member of the County Medical Society, of which he has been secretary for three years, and also of the New York Physicians' Mutual Aid Association.

Dr. Haner is also a prominent and enthusiastic member of the Methodist Episcopal Church, and actively and generously participated in the movement which resulted in the erection of the present beautiful edifice in Tannersville belonging to that body. He worked indefatigably in the erection of the Methodist Episcopal parsonage, and to these objects combined has contributed upward of five hundred dollars.

His interest in Sunday-school work dates back to his Conesville days, when he was superintendent of the school; and ever since he came to Tannersville he has been ready with hand and brain, sympathy and purse, to advance the work of God in the church of his choice. He has held almost every office that a layman can hold, representing his brethren at both the district and annual conferences, and is at the present time a trustee.

Dr. Haner is yet in the prime of life, and if spared will be of inestimable service to the community amid which he resides.

SIMEON LAPE, a thriving general merchant of Charlotteville, N.Y., was born in the town of Summit, Schoharie County, N.Y., October 19, 1827, son of Samuel and Lana Lape. His paternal grandfather, Samuel Lape, who was the grandson of a German immigrant and the father of several children that grew to maturity, was formerly a thriving farmer of Sand Lake, N.Y. Somewhat late in life he accompanied his son Samuel to Summit, and his last days were spent in this town. He was a member of the Lutheran church.

Samuel Lape, the younger, Simeon Lape's father, served in the War of 1812. He came to Summit when a young man, and, settling here upon a farm of one hundred and fifty acres, which he afterward enlarged, he became one of the most extensive farmers in this section. Though not a seeker after place, he consented to hold some of the minor town offices. Originally a Democrat in politics, he afterward became a Republican. As one of the most active and influential members of the Lutheran church, it was generally his lot to entertain the preachers, and his family was taught to believe that religious devotion was just as necessary at home as in a place of public worship. He died at the age of seventy-three, his wife surviving him several years. They were the parents of sixteen children, of whom ten died in infancy and six lived to maturity, the latter being: Luther, Simeon, John, George, Josiah, and Elizabeth. Luther and Josiah occupy the homestead. John is a resident of East Worcester, N.Y.; and Elizabeth, who is the eldest, married Abraham Harrington, of Worcester, where she resides. George, who is living in Brooklyn, N.Y., was for a time engaged as teacher in the New York Conference Seminary and in civil engineering.

Simeon Lape was educated in the common schools of Summit. Beginning industrial life as a farmer, he followed that occupation until thirty-eight years old, when, in partnership with a Mr. Decker, he purchased the general stock of goods of the store of La Monte & Co., of Charlotteville, N.Y. This copartnership lasted but about five months, at the end of which time Mr. Decker withdrew, leaving his associate sole proprietor of the establishment, which for the past thirty-one years Mr. Lape has carried on alone. As his trade developed, he enlarged his facilities and increased his stock, and for a number of years he has transacted an extensive general mercantile business. Like his father he adheres to Republican principles; and, while he invariably has refused to become a candidate for local offices, he accepted the appointment of Postmaster, which he held in all for about twenty years.

In 1848 Mr. Lape was united in marriage with Miss Lucy La Monte, of Charlotteville, daughter of Thomas W. and Elizabeth Maria (Payne) La Monte. Mrs. Lape was a descendant of John La Monte, of Coleraine, County Antrim, Ireland. Her first American ancestor was Robert La Monte, who came to this country with his mother, the widow of John, and settled in Columbia County, this State.

Her great-grandfather, William La Monte, son of Robert, served in the Revolutionary War, and was present at the surrender of General Burgoyne. He married for his first wife Mrs. Phœbe Perkins, born Goss, and settled upon a farm in North Hinsdale, N.Y. After her death he moved into the then wilderness of Schoharie County, locating in what is now the town of Fulton, where he lived to an advanced age. Mrs. Lape's grandfather, also named William, was born in Hinsdale, January 16, 1784. When a young man he settled in Fulton, but about the year 1806 removed to Charlotteville, where he acquired possession of some seven hundred acres of land. An enterprising business man, he kept a country store, and operated saw and grist mills. Being familiar with common law, he acted as legal adviser to his neighbors, pleaded their cases in the lower courts, and was several times elected a Justice of the Peace. In his religious belief he was a Methodist. He died September 5, 1847. His wife, Jane, a daughter of Thomas Stillwell, died August 25, 1863, aged eighty years. They were the parents of six sons and five daughters, all of whom married and became the heads of families.

Thomas W. La Monte, Mrs. Lape's father, was born in Fulton, August 29, 1803. He was a prominent business man of Charlotteville in his day, and proprietor of the store which is now owned by Mr. Lape. He was also active in political and religious affairs, and was one of the founders of the New York Conference Seminary. He died June 3, 1853. His wife died April 7, 1898, aged eighty-seven years. She was the mother of thirteen children: Jacob, Lucy, Elizabeth, William and David (twins), Thomas, Jennie, George, Kate, Austin, Hannah, Maria, and Julia. All the children received a good education. Thomas was for a time engaged in teaching at the Conference Seminary, but later became a Methodist minister. George, who taught school for some time in the South, became a successful paper manufacturer and the owner of a valuable patent.

In 1850 Mr. Lape joined the Methodist church, which he has since served as steward, trustee, and superintendent of the Sunday-school, also contributing liberally to its support. Mrs. Lape died October 18, 1896, leaving no children. She was a member of the Woman's Christian Temperance Union and of the Independent Order of Good Templars.

ANDREW J. McMILLAN, who in the fall of 1898 was elected Assemblyman from Schenectady, is a thriving farmer of Rotterdam, N.Y. He was born upon the McMillan farm, a part of which he occupies, on February 9, 1856, being the only son of Andrew and Ellen (Darrow) McMillan. His father was born here on January 12, 1832, and his mother was born in Schenectady in 1832. This farm was the property of his paternal grandfather, James McMillan, a native of New Scotland, who settled here about seventy years ago, and who lived to be ninety-one years old. The maiden name of James McMillan's wife was Margaret Wingate. She died at sixty-five.

Andrew McMillan, the father, succeeded to the homestead, and is still actively engaged in its cultivation. He has made various improvements in the property, and is widely known as a practical and successful agriculturist. In politics he acts with the Republican party, and in his religious belief he is a Presbyterian. Ellen, his wife, whom he married in 1844, has had but one son, Andrew J., the subject of this sketch.

Andrew J. McMillan was educated in the district schools. As a youth he assisted his father, from whom he obtained a good knowledge of farming, and since reaching manhood he has tilled the soil upon his own account. He has at his disposal one hundred and seventy-seven acres, which he devotes to general farming, and raises excellent crops.

In November, 1882, Mr. McMillan was united in marriage with Anna L. Liddle, who was born in Duanesburg, daughter of Alexander Liddle. A sketch of her family will be found on another page of the REVIEW. Mr. and Mrs. McMillan have one son — Everett, who was born December 25, 1884.

Mr. McMillan is now in his third year as Supervisor, and is rendering efficient service in that capacity. Politically, he is a Republican. He belongs to the Independent Order of Odd Fellows, being a member of Lodge No. 171, of Mount Pleasant.

ELMER E. GOODSELL, of Hunter, station agent, telegraph operator, and agent of the American Express Company on the Stony Clove & Catskill Mountain Railroad, was born in Jewett on April 17, 1865, to Amos and Harriet (Egbertson) Goodsell. His great-grandfather Goodsell was one of the pioneer settlers of Jewett, coming to that place from the State of Connecticut. His grandfather, John Goodsell, who finished clearing the tract of land taken up by the great-grandfather and spent his life engaged in farming, died at the age of fifty-seven. John Goodsell's wife, whose maiden name was Samantha Peck, married for her first husband a Mr. Bogardus. She died at the age of fifty-four. By her second marriage she had ten children, as follows: Amos, Amelia, Mansfield, Amanda, J. Emory, Lois, Adela, Anna, Elbert, and Sarah.

Amos Goodsell was reared on a farm, and during boyhood he attended the common schools of Jewett, his native town. For over twenty years he carried on his farm in Jewett Centre. He then sold out, and since that time he has been working where he pleased. He is a Republican, and has held a number of town offices. His wife, Harriet, who died in 1884, at the age of forty-eight, was a native of Jewett, and the daughter of Jacob Egbertson, an early settler and a farmer of that place. Mr. Egbertson and his wife both died at the age of eighty-two. They had nine children; namely, John, Justus, Eliza, Sally, Tully, Caroline, Harriet, Jane, and Maria. Amos and Harriet Goodsell reared a family of three children; namely, Ella, George, and Elmer E. The daughter, Ella, is the wife of D. Clarence Gibbony, attorney-at-law, of Philadelphia; and her brother George is employed by the Missouri, Kansas & Texas Railroad at St. Louis. The parents were active members in the Methodist Episcopal Church of Jewett.

Elmer E. Goodsell received a common-school education. He then served some time as a teacher, and he subsequently attended Greenville Academy and Eastman's Business College. He was graduated at the last-named institution in June, 1888, and shortly after came to the Hunter station as assistant to Mr. Burhans, who was the agent until 1894. When Mr. Burhans left the place, Mr. Goodsell was appointed to succeed him, and in the few years he has held the position he has made himself exceedingly popular with both officials and patrons of the road. He is furnished one assistant the year through, and sometimes in the summer three. Most of the telegraphing he does himself. The Hunter station is the largest on the line, being moreover the terminal station; and Mr. Goodsell is the oldest station agent on the line as to time of service for this company.

In 1891 Mr. Goodsell was united in marriage with Anna Bell Anderson, daughter of George W. Anderson, coal and lumber dealer, whose biographical sketch appears on another page of this work. Mrs. Goodsell, who has one sister, Mabel Anderson, is the mother of two children — Marguerite and Anderson.

Mr. Goodsell is an ardent Republican, but he has refused all public offices. He is a member of Mount Tabor Lodge, No. 804, F. & A. M., of Hunter, and both he and Mrs. Goodsell are members of the Methodist church and workers in the Sunday-school. Mr. Goodsell was formerly secretary and librarian of the Sunday-school.

SEYMOUR BOUGHTON, a prominent resident of Charlotteville, was born in Summit, November 17, 1834, son of Seymour and Phœbe (Mix) Boughton. The father came here from Connecticut, settling first in Charlotteville, and later moving to Summit village, where he kept a hotel. He afterward engaged in the cooper business, and also ran a distillery.

Studying law, he was admitted to the bar in 1840, and thenceforward carried on a profitable general law business.

Actively interested in public affairs, Samuel Boughton, the elder, was elected to the Assembly on the Anti-rent ticket in 1845, was twice elected Supervisor as a Democrat, was for some years a member of the county committee, served with ability as Excise Commissioner, and was Postmaster for eight years. He was very popular with all classes irrespective of party, and his personal character was such as to fully merit the high estimation in which he was held. He was an active member of the Baptist church. He returned to Charlotteville in 1866, and died here in 1871, aged eighty-one years. Nine children were born to him and his wife, Phœbe, namely: Lucius, who died December 11, 1826; Harvey; Mary; Squire, who died December 9, 1819; Phœbe; Polly; Louisa; Harmon K., who died in 1851, aged twenty-four years; and Seymour, the subject of this sketch, he and his sister Mary being the only survivors.

Seymour Boughton after finishing his education learned the carriage painter's trade in Cobleskill, mastering it without much difficulty, as he had a natural genius for handling the brush. Engaging in business for himself, his first contract, which amounted to two thousand three hundred dollars, was tendered him by parties in Gallupville; and he subsequently enlarged his business. For many years he conducted the largest carriage-making establishment in the county. He also did most of the repairing and painting in this and the adjacent towns, and at one time he carried on two shops. Of late he has been gradually withdrawing from business, but still continues to follow his trade to some extent. Mr. Boughton's connection with public affairs began as a boy in the Assembly at Albany, and he was elected Town Clerk the year he became a voter. He afterward served as Constable two years, held some minor town offices, was elected Supervisor in 1878, re-elected in 1879, was County Clerk from 1881 to 1888, was Postmaster under Andrew Johnson and the second Cleveland administration, and has been a member of the Democratic Town Committee for many years. His political record is a most honorable one, and it is worthy of note that while some of the offices to which he was elected were hotly contested, his candidacy for a second term as Supervisor was without opposition, a fact which demonstrates the confidence of his fellow-townsmen in his ability and integrity.

Mr. Boughton contracted his first marriage with Maggie Ferguson, daughter of Thomas Ferguson. She bore him four children, namely: Arthur J., Frank, and Thomas G., none of whom are living; and Charles F., who is a painter by trade and a musician of local repute. For his second wife he married Emma Nadley, daughter of Christopher Nadley, and by this union he has two children — Edith and Horatio S. Boughton.

Mr. Boughton belongs to Jefferson Lodge, No. 554, F. & A. M., and John L. Lewis Chapter, No. 229, R. A. M.

HENRY C. VAN ZANDT, M.D., a prominent physician of Schenectady, is a native of this city. He was born on January 11, 1844, son of Gilbert and Myra (Halliday) Van Zandt. The family of which he is a representative was founded in America by Johannes Van Zandt, who came from Anheim, Holland, in 1660, and whose grave is still visible in Trinity Churchyard, New York City.

Peter P. Van Zandt, a grandson of Johannes, settled in Schenectady, and several of his descendants have won distinction in this locality. He was elected a member of the Assembly, and while in Albany he married a Miss Munson, of Schoharie. Dr. Van Zandt's grandfather was Garrett Van Zandt, who served as a soldier in the War of 1812, and was stationed at Sackett's Harbor. The Doctor's mother was a daughter of Judge Halliday, of Rochester, N.Y.

Henry C. Van Zandt prepared for his collegiate course at the Schenectady High School, and was graduated from Union College with the class of 1865. His preliminary medical studies were pursued under the direction of Dr. Vedder, of Schenectady; and after graduation from the Albany Medical School he began the practice of his profession in this city, where he has gained a high reputation. He is also engaged in the drug business, and has one of the best equipped apothecary establishments in this vicinity.

Dr. Van Zandt is a member of the surgeons' staff of Ellis Hospital, of Schenectady, also a member of the Schenectady County

1336482

H. C. VAN ZANDT.

Medical Society and of the State Medical Association. He belongs to St. George Lodge, No. 6, F. & A. M.; is a Trustee of Schau-Naugh-ta-da Tribe, No. 123, Improved Order of Red Men; and is a member of the Holland Society.

He married Hattie Hilderbrand, daughter of Henry Hilderbrand, of Schenectady, N.Y. In his religious belief the Doctor is an Episcopalian, and is a warden of Christ's Church.

THOMAS DORMADY, a retired locomotive engineer and a member of the Schenectady Board of Aldermen, was born in the town and county of Carlow, Ireland, September 10, 1827, son of Andrew and Bridget (Rice) Dormady. Coming to Schenectady with his parents when two years old, Thomas Dormady passed through the common schools of this city, and was graduated from the high school. After learning the machinist's trade in the railway shops at Albany, he followed it as a journeyman for a year, and then became a locomotive engineer on the Mohawk & Hudson River Railroad, which is now a part of the New York Central system. His first engine, which was imported from England in 1831, was originally called the "John Bull," but on being enlarged was renamed the "Rochester." For over forty years he ran a regular day train between Schenectady, Albany, Utica, and Syracuse, and in 1894 he practically retired. In 1871 he was elected to the Board of Aldermen for three years, and he was afterward re-elected for the two succeeding terms. As the Democratic candidate for Mayor in 1879, he lacked but three votes of being elected. In 1890 he was again a member of the upper branch of the city government, and in 1897 he began his fifth term in that body. The ward he represents is considered a Republican stronghold, a fact which amply attests his ability and popularity.

Mr. Dormady married Mary Sheean, a native of Troy, N.Y., a daughter of Philip Sheean (deceased). His children are: Thomas, born in 1858, a graduate of the high school and now a telegraph operator in Schenectady; Annie, a graduate of St. John's Convent School; Libbie, now the widow of J. J. Murphy; and Philip, also a graduate of the high school and at present in the employ of the city.

Mr. Dormady belongs to the Brotherhood of Locomotive Engineers, and has served as local chief of Division 83, now Division 172.

JOHN T. BENHAM, M.D., of Conesville, N.Y., one of the best known physicians in this part of the country, was born in Hudson, N.Y., October 19, 1823, son of Dr. John P. and Elizabeth (Smith) Benham. He is a descendant in the ninth generation of his emigrant ancestor, who was an Englishman, and is the fourth representative of the family in a direct line to practise medicine. The great-grandfather was Dr. Cornevius Benham, who practised in Catskill, N.Y., for many years; and his widow, who was of Dutch descent, married for her second husband Dr.

Van Buren, a relative of President Martin Van Buren. Dr. Thomas Benham, the grandfather, practised in Ashland, N. Y., where he died at the age of eighty-nine years; and two of his sons, namely, John P. and Jacob, became successful physicians.

Dr. John P. Benham, the father, resided in Hudson for many years, and then, moving from that town to Conesville, practised there for the rest of his life. He was favorably known over a wide circuit as a capable physician, whose powers of endurance were unusually vigorous; and at the time of his death, which occurred at the age of seventy-three years, he was the oldest active medical practitioner in this county. He reared two children: John T., the subject of this sketch; and Margaret E., who married Edwin H. Marshall and resides in Troy, N. Y.

John T. Benham began his education in the district schools, and advanced in learning by attending the Schoharie Academy. After working at the carpenter's trade some twelve years, he took up the study of medicine with his father, who carefully directed his preparations. He also attended lectures at Woodstock and Castleton, Vt., and at the Berkshire Medical College, Pittsfield, Mass. He subsequently spent a year at the Broadway Hospital, New York City, where he obtained much valuable experience, and returning to Conesville he entered upon the practice of his profession in company with his father. For over fifty years he has labored diligently and successfully in his calling, visiting the sick in all kinds of weather, apparently oblivious of his own health or comfort; and he is still remarkably vigorous and active.

Dr. Benham married for his first wife Rosanna Hoogland and for his second Anna M. Lader. He has two daughters by his first union, namely: Donna I., who married Oscar Mervin; and Margaret E., wife of Julian Myers.

The Doctor has always been a great reader and an independent thinker, accustomed to reason out things, as he says, for himself, even the deep questions of life. His religious opinions are liberal. Many kindly acts in the way of charity can be traced directly to him, and he is highly respected by the entire community.

J EDWARD YOUNG, one of Middleburg's literary men and the editor of the Middleburg *Gazette*, is a native of Prattsville, Greene County. He was born on January 6, 1848. His elementary education was obtained in the public schools, and subsequently he attended Roxbury Seminary, from which he was graduated. As editor of the *Gazette* he exercises a strong influence in moulding public opinion and in placing before the townspeople information which keeps them in touch with the most progressive thought of the day. The editorial columns of his paper are marked by vigorous and positive expression of opinion on all questions of national or local moment, as well as by cool and conservative criticism and level-headed judgment. He does considerable writing for other publications.

Thoroughly interested in the welfare of the

town and believing that she needs the services of her best citizens in public life, he has freely given time and effort to serve her in many ways. For two years he was Town Clerk, and for twelve consecutive years, beginning in 1881, he was village Clerk. In 1889 he represented Schoharie County in the Assembly. He was one of the most ardent workers in securing the incorporation of the village, and also of the water company. Of the last named he is now one of the directors. He is a stockholder in the First National Bank, and since 1892 has been treasurer of Middleburg Academy. He is also a member of the Board of Education. In politics Mr. Young is a most loyal Democrat, and his party has chosen him as delegate to State and county conventions, and as a member of the county committee.

On November 15, 1893, Mr. Young was united in marriage with Inez Bouck, of Conesville, a daughter of James A. Bouck. He is a prominent Odd Fellow, and is at the present time District Deputy Grand Patriarch for the Schoharie district. Canton Young, of Schoharie, of which he is a member, is named for him.

CYRUS SHOWERS, civil engineer, contractor, and builder, of Tannersville, N.Y., was born in this town, November 9, 1859, son of Isaac and Merilla A. (Loomis) Showers. He is of the sixth generation of his family in America, the line being traced back through Isaac, Japhet, Michael, John, to the emigrant progenitor, who came from Holland and settled in New Jersey, there spending the rest of his life. A more extended account of his ancestors will be found in a sketch of Isaac Showers, which appears elsewhere in the REVIEW.

Isaac Showers, Cyrus Showers's father, was born in Hunter in 1827, and spent his youth on farms in this locality. He later engaged in civil engineering, which he followed quite extensively, and became one of the largest resident land-owners in this section. He is now living in retirement. His wife, Merilla, was a daughter of Alvin J. and Harriet (Palmer) Loomis, of Windham. She became the mother of eight children, four of whom are living; namely, Cyrus, Emma, Henry W., and George Harding Showers. Emma married Edward Osborn, and resides in California. Henry W. is attending the Albany Law School. George Harding Showers is studying civil engineering at the Troy Polytechnic Institute. The others were: Jennie, who married Stephen Vining, of Windham, and died at the age of forty-one; Elmer, who died at thirteen; Isaac, who died young; and Irving, who died at the age of four years. The parents are members of the Methodist Episcopal church.

Cyrus Showers was educated in the common schools of Tannersville, and resided on the home farm of three hundred acres, of which he took entire charge at the age of eighteen. He kept fifty cows, made butter for the local market, and supplied Hotel Kaaterskill with milk for some years. At the age of twenty-five he went to Onteora Park to assist in building the cottages, and was made its superintendent. He later built a large number of houses, completing contracts amounting to one hundred thousand dollars in four years. He also built his present dwelling, and continues to follow the business of a civil engineer, displaying a marked ability for that profession. He at one time engaged in mercantile business for a short period. Politically, he is a Republican. Appointed Deputy Sheriff in 1888, he served until 1891 and again from 1894 to 1898. He was an Assessor two terms and a member of the county committee for several years. He has been secretary of the village Board of Trustees ever since its establishment, and is also a member of the Board of Health.

In 1883 Mr. Showers was joined in marriage with Lillie E. Ford, who was born in Lexington in 1863, daughter of Charles L. and Harriet (Humphrey) Ford. Her father and grandfather were both natives of Jewett; and Charles L. Ford, who at one time carried on a farm and kept a boarding-house in Lexington, moved to Tannersville, where he was similarly engaged, and still spends his summers in that village. Mrs. Showers's mother was a native of Lexington, daughter of the Rev. Eli B. and Emily (Cline) Humphrey, the former of whom was a well-known Baptist minister, and died at the age of eighty. Her grandparents had a family of twelve children, nine of whom are living, among them Hiram, Horace, Sabrina, Lucina, Susan, Harriet, Ophelia, Eudocia. The others were: Amasa, Mary, and Elizabeth. Charles L. and Harriet Ford are the parents of two children: Lillie, who is now Mrs. Showers; and Jennie E., who married Dr. Robert L. Graham, of Brooklyn, N.Y.

Mr. Showers is an active member of the Methodist Episcopal church, of which he is a steward and trustee, and he served upon the building committee which erected the new church edifice. Mrs. Showers united with the church at the age of fifteen. She is a member of the choir, and was organist for eight years.

RICHTMYER HUBBELL, M.D., an able physician and prominent citizen of Jefferson, N.Y., was born in Gilboa, Schoharie County, N.Y., February 2, 1843, son of Jacob Richtmyer and Harriet (Pierce) Hubbell. The name Hubbell, which originated in Wales, is said to have been derived from Hubba, a Danish chief who camped upon a hill. It passed through several changes, including Hubbashill and Hubhill, before the present form of spelling was adopted.

Richard Hubbell, the immigrant ancestor, of whom the Doctor is a descendant in the eighth generation, was born in Wales in 1627. He arrived in New England in 1645, and in 1647 he took the oath of allegiance to the New Haven Colonial government. In 1664 he moved to Fairfield County, Connecticut, and in 1685 became one of the original proprietors of Fairfield township. He died October 23, 1699, and his remains were interred in Stratford burying-ground, now included within the limits of the city of Bridgeport. Richard Hubbell was three times married, and was the father of fifteen children. From him the line of descent is traced directly, through Samuel,

RICHTMYER HUBBELL.

Nathan, Peter (first), Peter (second), Matthias, and Jacob R., to Dr. Richtmyer Hubbell, the subject of this sketch.

Peter Hubbell, second, the Doctor's great-grandfather, who married Sally Hurlburt, removed with his family from Connecticut to Schoharie County early in the present century. His brother-in-law, Joseph Hurlburt, built the first store in the village of Gilboa, and resided on what is known as the Dr. Fanning farm.

Matthias Hubbell, Dr. Hubbell's grandfather, accompanied his parents from Connecticut when a boy, and during his active years he was Justice of the Peace and followed general farming in the towns of Gilboa and Blenheim. He married for his first wife Sophia Richtmyer, who was of German ancestry. The grandparents were buried in the old cemetery in Gilboa village.

Jacob Richtmyer Hubbell, Dr. Hubbell's father, was a lifelong resident of this county. He died in Sharon Springs, N. Y., November 11, 1896, aged just seventy-six years, and was buried in Jefferson. His wife, Harriet, was a daughter of Benona and Betsey (Davis) Pierce, of North Blenheim. Her father was a descendant of Captain Michael Pierce, who came over from England about 1645, settled at Scituate, Mass., in 1647, and was killed in a fight with Indians in King Philip's War in March, 1676, while commanding his company. This is the line of ancestry: Captain Michael,[1] Ephraim,[2] Ephraim,[3] Mial,[4] Job,[5] Job,[6] and Benona,[7] father of Mrs. Hubbell. Benona Pierce was born in 1781, a son of Job Pierce, Jr., of Rehoboth, Mass., and died in 1855.

His wife, Mrs. Betsey D. Pierce, born in May, 1789, died in September, 1881.

Jacob R. and Harriet (Pierce) Hubbell were the parents of six children, namely: Richtmyer, the subject of this sketch; Charles B., a furniture dealer and undertaker in Jefferson; Hiram P., a physician of Stamford, Delaware County; Elizabeth, wife of J. Perry Champlin, of Ruth, Schoharie County; Sophia, who married J. E. Preston, of Sharon Springs; and Fred E. Hubbell, who died September 23, 1892, aged about thirty years.

Richtmyer Hubbell acquired his early education in the district schools and at the academy in Roxbury, Delaware County, which he attended one term. At the age of sixteen he began teaching during the winter season, his summers being devoted to agriculture; and, having taught schools in Gilboa, Blenheim, and Eminence, he in 1863 began the study of medicine under the direction of the late Dr. A. A. Wood. In the fall of that year he accompanied his preceptor to Wisconsin, where he resumed teaching for a time at Almond, Wis., and also continued his studies with Dr. Wood and Dr. Guernsey, of Almond, Wis. In 1864 he enlisted as a Corporal in Company M, First Wisconsin Heavy Artillery, of which he was shortly afterward appointed clerk, and he served until the close of the Civil War. Returning to Schoharie County after his discharge, he subsequently entered the Philadelphia University of Medicine and Surgery, from which he was graduated February 21, 1866. Borrowing the money to purchase a team and medical outfit, he began the practice of his profession in Harpersfield, Delaware County, N.Y. For the succeeding eleven years his practice, which covered a wide circuit, extending into two adjoining counties, kept him constantly driving from place to place through all kinds of weather. While residing in Harpersfield he served four terms as Town Clerk and three terms as Supervisor. On December 25, 1876, Dr. Hubbell sold his practice, together with his real estate in Harpersfield, to his brother, Hiram P., and removed to Jefferson, where he almost immediately acquired prominence as a skilful physician and surgeon. Although his practice is large and his time exceedingly valuable, he has never been known to neglect the worthy poor, believing, as he does, that life and health are as dear to them as to those who are more fortunate; and, as he himself declares, if they are unable to pay him in dollars and cents, they have more than liquidated his claim upon them by their genuine gratitude.

He has frequently held the offices of president and secretary of the Eclectic Medical Society of the Susquehannah District, comprising the counties of Schoharie, Delaware, and Otsego, and during his professional career he has directed the preparatory studies of five students, four of them becoming skilful medical practitioners and one a successful druggist. Two of the five are now deceased. In 1880 he established the Jefferson Banking House, which he carried on for two years; and, when the present bank at Stamford, N.Y., was founded, he was requested to become its president, but his professional duties prevented him from accepting the office. His hearty co-operation is always to be depended upon in forwarding all measures calculated to be of benefit to the town. He was active in securing the present water-works system, together with a public fountain, the Jefferson Co-operative Creamery, and so forth; and he is using his influence for the establishment of a union free school, with academic advantages. He is actively engaged in general farming, raises Jersey cattle, and owns about two thousand acres of agricultural property.

On April 29, 1866, Dr. Hubbell married for his first wife Amelia S. Decker, of Gilboa, daughter of Jacob Decker and a sister of William H. Decker, Supervisor of that town. She died January 19, 1889, leaving four children — Frank J., Hattie A., Benona R., and Grace Greenwood. Frank J. is a prosperous farmer of Jefferson, and Hattie A. is the wife of Charles E. Nichols, an attorney of this town. The other children reside at home. On August 27, 1890, the Doctor married for his second wife Miss Rose E. Decker, his first wife's sister. Of this union there is one son, Fred D., born July 3, 1893.

Politically, Dr. Hubbell is a Republican, a protectionist, and a firm believer in gold as a monetary standard. He belongs to the Methodist Episcopal church, and has been a member since he was sixteen years old.

GEORGE LASHER, a prosperous farmer of Duanesburg, N.Y., and an ex-member of the State Assembly, was born in this town, September 20, 1834, son of James M. and Marion (Kennedy) Lasher. The father's birth took place July 4, 1811, in a log house on the Lasher farm. This farm was cleared from the wilderness by the paternal grandfather, George Lasher, who was a native of Dutchess County, and came here in the year 1800. A sturdy, persevering man, he succeeded in overcoming the many difficulties of a pioneer's life; and he resided here until his death, which occurred August 15, 1846. He married Helen McMillan, a native of Glasgow, Scotland. In politics he voted with the Whig party. He was an active member of the Dutch Reformed church.

James M. Lasher, the father, succeeded to the ownership of the farm, which he still holds; and for many years he cultivated it energetically. Moving to Mariaville in 1862, he was engaged in mercantile business and the manufacture of lumber here in company with his son George until his retirement in 1880, since which time the store and saw-mill have been leased. Politically, he acts with the Republican party. For many years he has been an Elder of the Presbyterian church. Marion, his wife, who was born in Milton, Saratoga County, July 5, 1812, died on July 20, 1888. She was the mother of five children, namely: Anna A., who married the Rev. James W. Johnston, and died in North Carolina in 1886; Mary Helen; George, the subject of this sketch; John Kennedy, of Yonkers; and William M. Lasher, of New York City.

George Lasher began his education in the common schools, and completed his studies with a commercial course at Eastman's Business College, Poughkeepsie. At the age of twenty-one he became associated in business with his father, under the firm name of Lasher & Son, and since the retirement of the elder Lasher he has had full charge of the property, including the management of the farm, which contains two hundred acres. Mr. George Lasher is unmarried.

Since becoming a voter he has manifested a keen interest in local public affairs, and his ability displayed in various official capacities has proved beneficial to the community. He served as Justice of the Peace for several years, was Supervisor three years, and was a member of the Assembly in 1881. He is particularly interested in educational matters. In politics he is a Republican. He and his father occupy a handsome residence located upon the shores of a beautiful lake. They are highly respected members of the community. Mr. Lasher is an Elder of the Presbyterian church.

ELBERT OSBORN BRUCE, M.D., a well-known practising physician of the town of Seward, N.Y., has been located in the village of Hyndsville for nearly twoscore years, and with one exception is the oldest-established practitioner in Schoharie County. He was born in the neighboring town of Summit, December 6, 1839, a son of the Rev. Samuel and Theodosia (Harrington) Bruce.

Samuel Bruce, Sr., father of the Rev. Samuel, was born and reared in Scotland, and he lived there until after his marriage. Coming then to America with his bride, formerly a Miss Armstrong, he became a pioneer settler of Oneida County, New York, where he took up a tract of wild land, cleared a space, and erected the log house in which he made his home during his remaining days. With untiring energy and true heroism he labored to reclaim a farm from the primeval forest, and his efforts were well rewarded. He passed to the life beyond at the age of sixty-five years; but his wife survived him many years, attaining the age of ninety-five.

The Rev. Samuel Bruce was one of a family of three children. He was brought up at the old homestead, and received his early education in the pioneer schools of his district. Possessing great mental ability, he continued to add to his store of knowledge by judicious reading and studying, and for several years was employed as a teacher. He afterward settled on a farm in Summit, where he carried on general farming for some time. He also preached at Schoharie and elsewhere in this county. He was ordained as a minister of the Lutheran church, and subsequently followed his vocation in Otsego County, settling at South Worcester, where he died at the age of seventy-two years. His wife, whose maiden name was Theodosia Harrington, was a daughter of William Harrington. She survived him, passing away at the venerable age of fourscore and ten years. Of their eight children seven are now living, namely: Samuel W.; James; Elbert O.; Richard; Eli, who occupies the old homestead; Lavinia, wife of Oliver Mowbrany; and Martha, wife of Sylvester Smith, of Oneonta. Lucy Jane is deceased.

Elbert O. Bruce left home when a lad of ten years to become a pupil in the New York Conference Seminary, which he attended until it was burned, four years later. He subsequently read medicine with Dr. George H. Leonard, and in 1859 was graduated from the Castleton Medical College at Castleton, Vt. Returning then to East Worcester, Otsego County, Dr. Bruce assisted his former instructor, Dr. Leonard, a few months, and then came to Hyndsville, where he has since remained, a trusted physician and an esteemed citizen. During this time he has seen Hyndsville developed from a small hamlet of three or four houses to a flourishing village, and in its advancement and welfare he has been an important factor. He has built up an extensive practice, his ride extending twenty miles in either direction from the village; and from his first day of practice until the present date he has kept abreast with the times in regard to the progress made in the science of medicine. Through the leading medical journals he keeps informed of the new diseases and their treatments, and of the newer methods employed in curing old-time diseases of all kinds.

Dr. Bruce is a charter member of the Schoharie County Medical Society, of which he has been president three years and secretary five years, also having held all the other offices. Before his body of his professional brethren the Doctor is frequently called upon to read papers; and he has likewise contributed articles on different topics, including diphtheria and typhoid fever, to the *Medical World*. He is also a member of the New York State Medical Society, and has been a delegate three years. In politics he is a sound Democrat. He has served as Town Clerk six years; was Supervisor in 1869 and 1870; has been a member of the School Committee several years; and from 1885 until 1889, under President Cleveland's administration, he served as Postmaster. During that time he was nominated as candidate for member of Assembly, but being Postmaster he was obliged to withdraw his name. He is a prominent Mason, belonging to Cobleskill Lodge, F. & A. M., No. 394, and to Cobleskill Chapter, R. A. M., No. 229. He is a member of the Methodist church, of which he is a trustee, and for many years has been connected with its Sunday-school.

Dr. Bruce was married June 21, 1857, to Miss Cynthia Brown, the only child of Perley Brown, who was for many years a prominent man and the leading merchant of Summit. Dr. and Mrs. Brown have an adopted son, Bertie, now a pupil in the Cobleskill High School.

ROBERT SELDEN, M.D., a leading physician of Catskill, N.Y., residing at 271 Main Street, was born in Shanesville, Ohio, on August 21, 1847, his parents being Dr. Orrin G. and Catherine (Hall) Selden. His grandfather, Robert Selden, was a Scotchman, by occupation a miller. He came to this country when his son Orrin was seven years of age, and, settling in Massachusetts, worked at farming there during the remainder of his life. The maiden name of his wife was Balfour.

Orrin Selden was brought up on a farm, and followed agricultural pursuits until he became of age. His education was received in the common schools and in the academy at Haverhill. While still a young man he went to Ohio, where he taught school for some time. He subsequently studied medicine, and practised in Ohio and Wisconsin. He settled in Catskill in 1877, and here he resided until his death in 1894, one of the leading practitioners of this vicinity. His wife, Catherine, was born in Winsted, Conn. She was the daughter of Reuben Hall, a shoemaker by trade, who espoused the cause of the black man and early allied himself with the anti-slavery party. He went South, and started a school and Sunday-school for negroes at Fayetteville, but was burned out, losing all his property. He then removed to Pennsylvania and later to Ohio, where he died at the age of eighty. Orrin G. Selden and his wife were the parents of three children, of whom there are living Robert and Mary. Mrs. Selden died at the age of fifty-two. She was brought up a Methodist, but after her marriage she joined the Presbyterian church, of which her husband was a member.

Robert Selden spent his early life in Ohio. He read medicine with his father, and then took a course at the Charity Hospital Medical College, of Cleveland, from which he was graduated in 1870. He began practice at Shanesville with his father, and continued there after the latter removed to Wisconsin. Subsequently the father and son were associated in practice here until the death of the father. Dr. Robert Selden has been here since 1882. He has a very large practice and one that is constantly increasing. His patients are to be found not only in the village, but in all the outlying districts.

Dr. Selden was married in 1880 to Charlotte E. Gardiner, daughter of William H. Gardiner. She was born in Whitesboro, N.Y., where her father was a physician. Later he went to Ohio. While there he received an appointment as post surgeon for the army at Nashville, and while engaged in the discharge of the duties of that position he was attacked with cholera, which proved fatal. His wife, Emily Hull, bore him six children, of whom the living are: Mrs. Buss, of Cleveland; Mrs. Selden; and Emily H. Dr. and Mrs. Selden have two daughters — Catherine E. and Fannie, both of whom are attending school.

The Doctor is a member of the New York Medical Association, and has been its vice-president; also a member of the Greene County Medical Society, of which he has been president. He has read numerous valuable papers on medical subjects before both organizations. He has been a Mason since 1870. He holds membership in Catskill Lodge, No. 468, F. & A. M., of which he is a trustee and a Past Master; in Catskill Royal Arch Chapter, No. 285, of which he is a charter member and present High Priest; in Lafayette Commandery, K. T., of Hudson, of which he is Past Commander; in Mystic Shrine, Cypress Temple, of Albany; in the Fraternal Union of Anointed High Priests, which includes the highest officers from the various Royal Arch Chapters of the State; and in the Association of Templar Knights Commanders. He is medical examiner for a number of the largest insurance companies and for the A. O. U. W., of which he is a member and has been for several years financier. In politics the Doctor is a Democrat. He was Town Supervisor for one year. His library, of which he is justly proud, is the largest and finest private library in the county. Dr. and Mrs. Selden are members of St. Luke Episcopal Church, and he has been for a number of years a vestryman.

JOHN A. NEWELL, of the well-known mercantile firm of Potter & Newell, Main Street, Windham, Greene County, N.Y., was born in Durham, N.Y., on September 21, 1829, son of Andrus and Julia (Bushnell) Newell. His paternal grandfather, John Newell, was a native of Southington, Conn., and came to Durham among the early pioneers of that town.

Captain John Newell, as he was widely known from his rank in the State militia in the early training days, built first a log cabin and then a frame house, which he kept as a tavern for many years. He was of sturdy stock that could endure hardships without flinching, and his common sense equalled his stalwart frame. He was a militia man in the War of 1812. He lived to be over seventy years of age, and his wife also lived to be old. They reared a family of eight children.

JOHN A. NEWELL.

Andrus Newell, who was born in Durham, became a prosperous farmer on his one hundred and sixty acres. He tore down the building that his father had used as a tavern, and erected in its place the large and handsome house which is now the home of his son Charles. Like his father he was a man of sound judgment and of splendid physical strength, being hearty and hale up to the time of his death, at the age of eighty-six. He was originally a Whig in politics and later a Republican, and he held numerous offices during his long and active life. His wife, Julia, died at the age of fifty years. She was a native of Westbrook, Conn. Both were devoted members of the Congregational church. Of their ten children Louisa died at the age of twenty-seven, Zina died at the age of seventy-one, and Edwin at the age of five years. The living are: John A., Sylvia, Abby, Adelbert, Elizabeth, Charles, and Eliezur D. Sylvia is the wife of the Rev. S. H. Fellows, of Wauregan, Conn. Abby is the wife of Professor Gilbert, teacher of mathematics in the high school at Albany, N.Y. Adelbert is a prosperous farmer of Coxsackie, N.Y. Elizabeth is Mrs. Dorland A. Peck. Charles is a farmer on the old homestead, and Eliezur resides with him.

John Newell lived with his parents until he was about sixteen and a half years of age, when he came to Windham. He had received a common-school education, and upon coming here he began learning the cabinet-maker's trade with Mr. Potter, his present partner. At the age of twenty-one, having finished his apprenticeship, he went to New York City, where he worked for two years. During this time he saved a small amount of money, and at the close of his second year he received an offer from Mr. Potter to return to Windham and enter into partnership with him. This offer he accepted, and in 1852 was formed the partnership that is now the oldest in existence in this county. Since that time Messrs. Potter & Newell have built up a very large trade in Windham and the surrounding region. Both gentlemen are skilled workmen in every branch of furniture manufacturing, having made all kinds of furniture by hand. They have in past years done considerable manufacturing on their own premises, and still continue to manufacture coffins and caskets. Their trade in furniture is extensive, and as they are the only undertakers within a radius of ten miles they practically do all the business in that line hereabouts. No firm is better known in all the surrounding country than that of Potter & Newell.

In 1856 Mr. Newell married Eunice Hunt, who was born in the house in which Mr. Newell now resides. Her parents were Daniel and Mary (Rowley) Hunt, both of whom were members of the Presbyterian church. Of their family of four boys and five girls three are living and reside in Windham. Mr. Hunt was a leading man in the town and prominent in all public affairs. By occupation he was a miller, and he built the mill now standing here and the mill-race. Mrs. Hunt, who was born in Lexington, died at the age of sixty-three. Mrs. Newell died on October 10,

1898, dropping suddenly from heart disease, at the age of sixty-seven. Mr. Newell has lost his two children — Highland and Mary E. Highland Newell, who was a young man of unusual promise, died at the age of twenty-three. He was a member of the Hampden Watch Company, of Springfield, Mass., having learned the watchmaker's trade in his native place. He had been in business three years when cut down by a fatal illness. Mary E. died at five years of age.

Politically, Mr. Newell is a Republican. He has served his townspeople in the office of Collector of Taxes and as Auditor of the town accounts, and has been a candidate for Supervisor. He is a member of Mountain Lodge of Masons, No. 529, having joined shortly after the lodge was organized. His interest in Masonic affairs has been active and unremitting, and he has held nearly every office in the lodge. He was Master at the time the Masonic Temple in New York was dedicated. For nearly fifty years Mr. Newell has been an active worker in the Presbyterian church in this place, and for the last thirty years has been the leading tenor in the church choir, which is the best in any town in the county outside of Catskill. He comes of a musical family, all of them being singers. For more than a quarter of a century he has been an Elder in the church, and for nine years he served the Sunday-school as its superintendent. He can scarcely remember the time when he was not connected with the Sunday-school, either as pupil, teacher, or superintendent.

JOHN D. CAMPBELL, who owns and occupies the old Campbell homestead in Rotterdam, N.Y., was born in Albany this State, May 14, 1844, son of Daniel D. and Julia A. (Sitterly) Campbell. Mr. Campbell's father, who was adopted by an aunt, was a son of Jacob and Angelica (Bradt) Schermerhorn. Jacob was a son of Simon and Sarah (Vrooman) Schermerhorn. Simon was a son of Jacob and Margaret (Teller) Schermerhorn. Jacob was a son of Ryer and Ariantje (Bradt) Schermerhorn; and Ryer was a son of Jacob Janse Schermerhorn, the emigrant ancestor, who was born in Waterland, Holland, in 1622, and who married Jannettie Segers Van Voorhoudt.

John D. Campbell was reared in Albany, and acquired his education in the schools of that city. Since early manhood he has been extensively engaged in agricultural pursuits, and is now the owner of the Campbell homestead of three hundred acres and the Vedder farm. His place, with its Colonial brick mansion, is one of the most pretentious and attractive country seats in this section, the spacious grounds being shaded by grand old trees, thus adding to the comfort as well as the beauty of the surroundings.

On August 23, 1871, Mr. Campbell was joined in marriage with Elizabeth Clute, who was born in Schenectady, N.Y., October 30, 1848. She is now the mother of four children, namely: David, born December 3, 1873; Julia A., born June 22, 1876; John D., Jr., born March 25, 1878; and Bessie B., born August 7, 1880.

Mr. Campbell is one of the most noted agriculturists of Rotterdam, and he makes a specialty of raising thoroughbred cattle and horses. Politically, he is a Democrat, and was a member of the Assembly in 1882.

ANDREW G. BALDWIN, proprietor of one of the best dairy farms in Gilboa, N.Y., was born in Greenville, Greene County, this State, December 11, 1827, son of Harvey and Eliza (Boyd) Baldwin. His father was born in Woodbury, Conn., September 7, 1799, and his mother was born in Greenville, March 17, 1800. His paternal grandfather, Andrew Baldwin, who was a native of Connecticut, and lived there a number of years after marrying, removed with his family to Greenville, and later from there to Mount Morris, N.Y., where he died. He was an industrious farmer. He had six children, namely: Deborah, who never married; Nancy, who was the wife of Judge Reuben Hine, of New York City; Harvey; Andrew, who died while young; Hannah, who married James Conkey, of Mount Morris; and Harriet, who married William Barnes, of Monmouth, Ill.

Harvey Baldwin, father of Andrew G., was fourteen years old when his parents settled in Greenville. He remained there until 1837, when he removed to a farm in Conesville, Schoharie County, where his death occurred on December 14, 1849. He was the father of five children, two of whom are living, namely: Andrew G., the subject of this sketch; and William L. Baldwin, a lawyer of Breakabeen and ex-district attorney. The others were: Ann Jane, wife of the late Dr. E. R. Mackey, of Catskill, N.Y.; John H., M.D., who died in Olive City, Ulster County, N.Y., in 1889; and James Harvey, who died at the age of ten years. The mother died September 7, 1857.

Andrew G. Baldwin acquired his education in the schools of Greenville and Conesville. He aided in carrying on the home farm until his father's death, and continued to reside in Conesville for five or six years afterward. Coming to Gilboa in 1855, he was engaged in mercantile pursuits until 1861, when he purchased a farm, on which he lived about three years. For the past thirty-four years he has occupied a residence in the village, but still manages his agricultural property, which consists of two farms, one containing one hundred and ninety-seven acres and the other one hundred and twenty-three acres. With the aid of hired assistants he carries on general farming and dairying. He has dealt somewhat extensively in cattle, and at one time handled Canadian horses.

For more than thirty years Mr. Baldwin has served as a Justice of the Peace, and in that capacity he transacts most of the minor legal business in this vicinity. During his four years upon the Board of Supervisors he was chairman of the legislation and printing committees, and was a member of the committee on accounts of County Treasurer. He has also held other offices. He was always strongly opposed to slavery. His first Presidential vote was cast for the Whig candidate in

1852. His allegiance to the Republican party dates from its formation, when he assisted in perfecting the local organization. He has served upon various committees, and has missed but one town election since becoming a voter.

Mr. Baldwin married Charlotte E. Stryker, daughter of Peter B. Stryker, who came with his parents from New Jersey in 1785, the Stryker family being the very first to settle in this section. Mrs. Baldwin's grandfather came from Holland. Her father was quite active in public affairs, and prominently identified with the Dutch Reformed church. Mr. and Mrs. Baldwin have had five children, namely: Carrie E., who married William Hagarton, M.D., for twenty-four years a well-known physician of Gilboa; Minnie E., who married Henry Carpenter, and is no longer living; George S., M.D., who is now practising in New York City; Lewis C., a dentist, who also practises in the metropolis; and Grace A., who is studying music.

Mr. Baldwin joined the Dutch Reformed church in 1865, and during his period of membership has served as Elder, Deacon, treasurer, and superintendent of the Sunday-school.

JOHN H. GRAY, proprietor of a general store in Tannersville, Greene County, N.Y., was born in Olive, Ulster County, this State, January 13, 1853, son of Morgan and Rachel (Freileigh) Gray. His grandfather, Martin Gray, was a lifelong resident of Columbia County and a prosperous farmer.

Morgan Gray, father of John H., was born in Saratoga, and he there followed farming some years. He later came to Greene County, and remained a short time, then went to Olive in Ulster County, and in 1868 settled upon a farm in Saugerties, where he is still residing. He is now seventy-five years old, but possesses the activity of a much younger man. He is a member of the Dutch Reformed church. His wife, Rachel, was born in Saugerties, daughter of Samuel Freileigh, a prosperous farmer of that locality. She died at the age of fifty-six, having been the mother of seven children, of whom six are living; namely, Samuel M., John H., Carrie, Mary, Abbie, and Charles. Carrie married Daniel York, Mary married Orville Smith, and Abbie is the wife of Frank Smith.

John H. Gray was educated in the common schools. He assisted his father on the farm until he was thirty-one years old, when he purchased the general store conducted up to that time by his brother Samuel M., and, adding other goods, carried on the business for four years. Selling out to his brother-in-law, he came in 1890 to Tannersville, and purchasing land in the centre of the town, on the west side of Hunter Turnpike, erected his present store, in which he has carried on a profitable business ever since. The store is sixty by one hundred feet, and two stories high, the upper floor being used for storage purposes. He carries a large and varied stock, including dry and fancy goods, boots and shoes, hay and grain, paints and oils, groceries, hardware, house-furnishing goods, carpets, crockery, harnesses, robes, all kinds of patent medicines, wines, liquors, cigars, and tobacco. He also has a millinery department. He opens in April and closes January 1. With the aid of twenty-one employees, he transacts a large business, supplying all of the hotels and park resorts in this locality. He buys by the carload, and the character of his trade demands the handling of the finest quality of foreign and domestic goods. In connection with his store he carries on a well-equipped livery stable, keeping an average of thirty horses.

In 1882 Mr. Gray married Jennie Carnright, a native of Quarryville, Ulster County, daughter of Wynkoop and Abbie (Freileigh) Carnright. Her father was born in West Hadley, Ulster County. He moved from there to Quarryville and later to Malden-on-the-Hudson, where he has resided for the past twenty-five years and is general overseer on the stone dock. Her mother also was born in Quarryville. She was a daughter of Samuel P. Freileigh, a farmer of that town, who was of Dutch descent. Mrs. Carnright, who is no longer living, was the mother of two children: Jennie, who is now Mrs. Gray; and Carrie, who married James Hommul. Having a good common-school education and possessing excellent business ability, Mrs. Gray is a valuable assistant to her husband, and has a general supervision of the store. She attends to most of the buying, and gives her particular attention to the millinery department, which is well stocked with seasonable goods. Mr. and Mrs. Gray have one daughter, Maud S., aged fourteen. She is attending the academy in Kingston, and makes a specialty of music.

Mr. Gray is a Democrat in politics. He is a great lover of horses, and keeps a number of speedy animals, and Mrs. Gray is also fond of driving.

ARCHIBALD TINNING, one of the leading farmers of Princetown, N.Y., was born in Glen, Montgomery County, this State, August 6, 1824, son of James and Hannah (Bradt) Tinning. The father was born in Scotland in 1785, and in early life he followed the useful calling of a school teacher. He later kept a store on the Erie Canal, and in 1840 he settled in Pattersonville, where he ran a general store in connection with farming for eleven years. He then moved to Florida, N.Y., where he spent the rest of his life, and died in 1868. Politically, he acted in his later years with the Republican party, and in his religious belief he was a Presbyterian. Mrs. Hannah Bradt Tinning, his wife, who was born in Glen in 1795, and died in 1838, was the mother of six children, three of whom are living, namely: Archibald, the subject of this sketch; Susan, who is now Mrs. Dougal, of Glenville; and Jane, who resides in Monterey, Cal. The others were: Catharine, who became Mrs. Dorman; Margaret, who became Mrs. Brownell; and Joseph Tinning. The mother died in 1838.

Archibald Tinning was reared and educated

in Montgomery County. He began life as a clerk in his father's store, and later engaged in mercantile business on his own account. He became a property holder in Schenectady County in 1840, purchased his present farm in Princetown in 1849, and has resided here since 1850. He now owns about three hundred acres, which he uses for general farming and pasturage. He raises large and superior crops, and realizes good financial results. He keeps from twenty to thirty head of fine cattle, also raises sheep, and his stable contains some excellent horses.

In 1848 Mr. Tinning married Sarah McGee, who was born in New York City, daughter of William and Maria (Weast) McGee, who came to reside in Princetown several years prior to her marriage. She is the mother of five children; namely, James, William, Frances, Maria, and Martha. Mr. and Mrs. Tinning have eight grandchildren.

Having acquired a competency, Mr. Tinning has practically retired from active labor, and will henceforward enjoy a well-earned rest at his comfortable home. In politics he acts with the Republican party. He and Mrs. Tinning are members of the Dutch Reformed church.

Of late years Mr. Tinning has found the winters too severe, and he and Mrs. Tinning have made several journeys to California to enjoy that delightful climate, and visit friends and relatives, making his headquarters with his son William, who is a successful lawyer. He has visited the Yosemite and other natural wonders of the State, also taking great interest in the sugar beet factories and other great industries and improvements that are being carried on.

FRANK X. STRAUB, the founder and manager of the telegraph line and business in Middleburg, N.Y., is of German birth and parentage. He was born in Altheim Oberamt Horb, Würtemberg, on June 1, 1847, son of Michael and Wallpurga Noll (Von Hürrlinger) Straub. His father, who was born in Würtemberg, of an ancient and honored family, came to this country in 1851.

In the Fatherland Michael Straub had been a farmer and the owner of a large vineyard, where he manufactured wine on quite an extensive scale. He was a man of note in his native place, and esteemed by all who knew him. After coming here, he settled in Williamsburg, on the outskirts of Brooklyn, where he kept a hotel until 1863. His wife, who was one of twins, was born in 1816, and died on June 28, 1852, not long after her arrival in America. Both parents were members of the German Catholic church. Of their five children one, Rosa, is deceased. Those living are: John; Carl A., who has been for thirty-two years in the regular army; Marie S.; and Frank X., of Middleburg, whose personal history is given below.

Frank Straub received his education in a German school in Brooklyn, N.Y. He learned the machinist's trade in that city. Later he joined the Union army and was stationed at Fort Schuyler under General

FRANK N. STRAUB AND GRAND-DAUGHTER, MILDRED WELLS.

Schofield. At the close of the war he learned the barber's trade in New York City, and there worked at it for some years. Coming to Middleburg in 1868, he opened a barber shop here, and has since been in active business in this town. He has been interested in every important movement which has touched closely the welfare or progress of the town during the last thirty years.

The fire department, which is considered one of the best volunteer organizations in the State, owes him a special debt of gratitude. It was started on December 31, 1887, by a vote of the village trustees. A commodious brick engine-house was built at a cost of two thousand dollars, and a steamer and a hook and ladder company formed. Mr. Straub raised fifteen hundred dollars for the hook and ladder company, and made a personal contribution of one hundred dollars toward the steamer. He was foreman of the old Eagle engine, and was foreman of the hook and ladder company under the new organization. He has always since been connected with the fire department, and takes an active interest in all matters connected with it. He was also a pioneer mover in behalf of the water company, and together with Mr. James C. Borst laid the first line of pipe on October 26, 1894. He assisted in surveying and in making maps at the time the village was incorporated. For twelve years he had control of the telephone and of the local office of the United States Signal Service. The telegraph line, which he manages and operates, was built in June, 1889. This is patronized by all the leading business men in Middleburg, and is now regarded as an indispensable element in the transaction of daily business.

Mr. Straub was married in 1870 to Emmarette E. Gernsey, daughter of Montreville Gernsey, of this place. She was born in Middleburg. Her father is a native of this county, and her mother, whose maiden name was Alida Becker, was a native of Breakabeen. Mrs. Gernsey died at the age of thirty-six, having been the mother of nine children. Of these the following-named six are living: Mrs. Straub, Julia, Edith, Rosa, Roxy, and Lett. Mr. and Mrs. Straub are the parents of three children — Inez, Charles A., and Arthur F. The first of these is the wife of Frank Wells, a well-known druggist of Middleburg, and is the mother of one child, Mildred. Charles A., who is a graduate of the Union College of Pharmacy, is a druggist in Troy. Arthur is a baker in Albany.

Mr. Straub is a communicant of the Episcopal church and a vestryman. He was confirmed in St. Luke's Church, Middleburg, in 1869, by the Right Rev. William C. Doane. All the members of his family were baptized in the Episcopal faith. In 1886 Mr. Straub made a trip to Europe and visited his birthplace, where he was accorded a most generous reception.

Mr. Straub is a Mason, an Odd Fellow, and a member of the Columbian Literary Society and of other fraternal organizations. The following record is of interest in this connection:

He was elected Quartermaster Sergeant of Steuben Zouaves, Twenty-fifth Regiment, Company 1, in 1865; joined Good Templars, Albany, in 1867; raised to the sublime degree of Master Mason at Middleburg Lodge, No. 663, F. & A. M., in 1877; secretary of same lodge from 1881 to 1886; trustee of lodge from 1896 to 1901; elected to membership of La Bastille Lodge in 1882, and elected secretary of La Bastille Lodge in 1885; reorganized Eagle Engine Company and elected foreman of same in 1884; organized Scribner Hook and Ladder Company in 1888, and elected foreman of Scribner Hook and Ladder Company for two years; elected assistant chief of Middleburg Fire Department, and elected member of Oneongena Tribe, No. 242, Improved Order of Red Men, 1898; elected member of Middleburg Encampment, No. 129, 1894; appointed under Governor Morton Notary Public, 1895 to 1901; elected Trustee and Collector of village of Middleburg, 1897.

CHARLES E. NICHOLS, a prominent lawyer and ex-Supervisor of Jefferson, Schoharie County, was born in this town, May 2, 1862, son of Hiram O. and Elizabeth (Totten) Nichols. His great-grandfather, Ezra Nichols, who was a pioneer in Delaware County, went there from Danbury, Conn., when the grandfather, Daniel Nichols, was eight years old. The latter became a prosperous farmer in Harpersfield. He had a family of nine children, namely: Laura; Fanny; Sally; Daniel S.; Ezra; Betsey, who became Mrs. Becker Clernen; Whitman; Hannah; and Hiram O., above named.

Hiram O. Nichols, father of Charles E., formerly carried on mercantile business in connection with farming. He is now retired. His wife, Elizabeth, is a daughter of John and Amanda (Davis) Totten, of Harpersfield. They have had three children: Charles E., the subject of this sketch; Orson, who died at the age of twenty-six years; and Rollo, who is a prosperous dairy farmer in Harpersfield, is an influential member of the Republican party, and served as a Justice of the Peace.

Charles E. Nichols was graduated from the Delaware Literary Institute, Franklin, in 1882, and for a time attended Hamilton College. His law studies were completed in Schoharie, and, having been admitted to the bar in 1885, he in August of the following year opened an office in Jefferson. The skilful and energetic handling of some of his first important cases was the means of gaining a numerous and profitable clientage, and he has become a well-known practitioner before the courts of Otsego, Delaware, Greene, Ulster, Albany, and Schoharie Counties. He has figured prominently in several hotly contested suits, one of which, an action brought by certain parties for the recovery of taxes, necessarily aroused the interest of the general public; and his able management of another notable case, which had its origin in a political dispute, resulted in a victory for the local Republican organization. As one of the most able and active supporters of that party he has rendered valuable committee service, has been a delegate to various conventions, including the one which nominated Governor Black, and was a candidate for District Attorney in 1888. While holding the office of Supervisor in 1892-93, he was chosen chairman of the equalization committee and a member of the committee that erected the new almshouse, was instrumental in securing an appropriation for the repair of the fort, and rooms of the Historical Society at Schoharie. He has held other positions of trust.

Mr. Nichols married Hattie A. Hubbell, daughter of Dr. Richtmeyer Hubbell, of Jefferson. They have two children — Grace A. and Charles E., Jr.

Mr. Nichols is a member of the Delta Kappa Epsilon Fraternity of Hamilton College, and has reached an advanced degree in the Masonic order, being a Past Master of the Blue Lodge, and the only resident of this town who belongs to the Commandery and the Mystic Shrine. His lucrative practice has enabled him to amass a competency; and besides holding considerable stock in the water company, of which he is a director, he owns some valuable real estate, including agricultural property and village lots. Mr. and Mrs. Nichols are members of the Methodist Episcopal church.

WILLIAM A. WASSON, M.D., a leading physician of Greenville, N.Y., was born in 1852 in Hamburg, Erie County, this State. He is the only son of Horace and Susan E. (Oberholser) Wasson. His grandfather, John Wasson, was one of the pioneers of Hamburg, coming to that place, which lay in the old Holland patent, in 1800, at the age of nineteen. There he worked at farming during the remainder of his life, and on the homestead the succeeding generations of the family have been born. He served during the War of 1812 as a Captain in the militia. He died at the age of seventy-four. His wife, who died in middle life, was before her marriage a Miss Griffin. Of the five children born to her, two are living — Horace and Thomas, both of whom reside in Buffalo.

Horace Wasson was born on the Wasson farm in Hamburg in 1823, and was reared to farm life. In early manhood he showed marked administrative ability, and this secured his appointment to the responsible position of superintendent of the Erie County Insane Asylum in Buffalo, the duties of which he discharged in a faithful and efficient manner for a quarter of a century. The institution was a large one, having about a hundred and fifty inmates. Mr. Wasson is one of the well-known citizens of Buffalo. He gave up his position in the asylum in 1873, and has since given his attention to his personal business interests in that city. His wife, who is of German stock, was born in Otsego County. Her father, John Oberholser, who reached the advanced age of ninety-four years, was a carpenter, and worked at his trade in Lancaster County when a young man. Later he removed to Otsego County, and finally to Amherst, Erie County, where he resided until his death. He had a family of nine children. Mrs. Wasson is a member of the Church of the Disciples. She has two children: Dr. William A.; and Carrie, who is the wife of W. S. Turbett, of Buffalo.

Dr. Wasson began earning his own living in his thirteenth year, when he went to work in a broker's office in Buffalo. He was there for a year, and then became an employee in the Erie County Savings Bank for another year. Following this he attended St. Luke's School for a year, and then went to Rochester as general agent for the Knickerbocker Life Insurance Company, this being in 1867 and 1868. Subsequently he was for a year in college at Alliance, Ohio, and he then returned to Buffalo and became an assistant house physician in the Erie County Hospital. This position he held until 1872, when he was appointed house physician. While there he attended lectures at the University of Buffalo, and in 1872 received his degree from that institution. In 1873 he gave up his place at the hospital, and opened an office in Buffalo for the practice of medicine. There he remained until 1880, when he came to Greenville. He has here a large general practice, and is one of the most popular physicians of the town. His present residence, built for him in 1885, is one of the finest in the village and, indeed, one of the finest to be found in any of the villages in the county.

The Doctor was married in 1875 to Carrie E. Wooster, a native of Westerlo, daughter of Charles E. and Melissa (Hitchcock) Wooster. Her parents had a family of four children. For many years they resided here, her father being one of the well-known farmers of the town. Dr. and Mrs. Wasson have an only daughter, Alice M., who is the wife of John H. Sandford, a druggist in this town, and has a little daughter, Ruth.

Dr. Wasson is a Democrat. He is warmly interested in all public matters, but the demands of his profession prevent him from taking a very active part in political affairs. He is a member of the Greene County Medical Society, and while in Buffalo was a member of the Erie County Medical Society, and also of the Buffalo Medical Club, which has since developed into the Buffalo Academy of Medicine. The Doctor occasionally takes a rest from his professional labors by indulging his tastes as a sportsman. He is an excellent shot, and is the owner of several guns and of hunting dogs. He has been actively associated with the Masonic organization since 1877, when he joined the Queen City Lodge in Buffalo. Upon coming here he received membership in the James M. Austin Lodge, and of this he has been five years Master, and was two years District Deputy in the old Eleventh District under Grand Master William Shever and Grand Master Burnham. He has filled all the chairs in the lodge. It was at his instigation that the Greenville Royal Arch Chapter was organized, and he has been its High Priest from the start. He was a charter member of Jefferson Lodge, A. O. U. W., of Buffalo, and while in that city was examining physician of the lodge. He has held the office of trustee of the academy, and is at the present time a member of the Board of Education. He is also one of the three fire commissioners of the town and chief of the fire department.

WILLIAM T. WADDELL, Supervisor of the town of Duanesburg, N.Y., was born where he now resides, son of William and Jane (McMillan) Waddell. His father, who is still living, was born near Edinburgh, Scotland, May 5, 1815, and his mother was born in Rotterdam, N.Y., about the year 1820.

William Waddell emigrated when nineteen years old, first locating in Rotterdam, and for a time he followed the tailor's trade. Turning his attention to agriculture, he came to Duanesburg over fifty years ago, and, purchasing the farm which his son is now cultivating, he tilled the soil successfully for the rest of his active period. Jane, his wife, became the mother of two sons, namely: James McMillan Waddell, a Civil War veteran, who is now a lumberman in the West; and William T., the subject of this sketch. Mrs. Jane M. Waddell died in June, 1891. William Waddell has been a Republican in politics since the formation of the party, and in his religious belief he is a Presbyterian.

William T. Waddell was educated in the common schools. From his youth upward he has made general farming his chief occupation, having assisted his father until taking the entire management of the property. Besides the original home farm of one hundred and six acres he owns ninety-five acres of adjoining land. He raises large and superior crops, and makes a specialty of breeding full-blooded Guernsey cattle and Shropshire sheep. His industry and progressive tendencies are displayed to excellent advantage, and his farm, which is desirably located, contains good, substantial buildings.

In 1871 Mr. Waddell married for his first wife Jennie Wilkins. She died in 1873, leaving one son, Samuel W., who married Elizabeth Mead, resides in this town, and has one son. In 1875 Mr. Waddell married for his second wife Louisa Schrade, a native of Duanesburg. By this union there is one son, Harry.

Mr. Waddell has long been prominently identified with local public affairs, having served as Inspector of Elections several years, Overseer of the Poor two years, Justice of the Peace six years, while he is now serving his sixth term as Supervisor, being indorsed by both parties. In politics he is a Republican. He belongs to St. George Lodge, No. 6, F. & A. M., of Schenectady. He has held all of the important chairs of Bethany Lodge, No. 524, I. O. O. F., and is a Past Master and now secretary of Empire Grange, No. 784, Patrons of Husbandry. He attends the Episcopal church.

LEWIS SHELMANDINE, formerly a prosperous farmer and cattle dealer of Jefferson, was born in this town, July 16, 1811. He was a son of John and Lizzie (Washburn) Shelmandine and grandson of Richard Shelmandine an Englishman, who was one of the first settlers in Jefferson. Richard Shelmandine married a Miss Kniskem, of Blenheim, and resided upon a farm in this town for the rest of his life. He and his wife reared four sons and one daughter; namely, Henry, Borant, Benjamin, John, and Mary. Henry was a lifelong resident of Jefferson. Borant, who was in his younger days a hunter, later went to Oil Creek, Pa. Benjamin settled in Pennsylvania. Mary married Obadiah Ruland.

John Shelmandine, father of Lewis, was born in Jefferson, and here spent the active period of his life in tilling the soil. In 1801 he married Lizzie Washburn, of Danbury, Conn. She became the mother of nine children, namely: Kate, who is no longer living; Joseph, who died in Jefferson in 1888; Rebecca, who died in Farmington, Pa.; Rhoda, who died in Illinois; Lewis, the subject of this sketch; Daniel, who died in Blenheim; Reuben, who died in Jefferson in 1894; Sally, who died in New York; and Charles, who died in Ohio. John Shelmandine died at the age of forty-seven years, leaving his wife with a large and dependent family. She, however, was an exceedingly capable woman, and succeeded in bringing up her children. She was a member of the Methodist Episcopal church and a devout Christian.

Lewis Shelmandine was but fourteen years old when his father's death made it necessary for him to become self-supporting, and he began industrial life as a farm assistant. While still a young man he engaged in farming on his own account, and shortly after his marriage he returned to the homestead farm. His energy and thrift soon placed him among the leading dairy farmers and cattle dealers of the county, his farm in the meanwhile having been increased from about one hundred to four hundred acres. He raised, bought, and sold live stock, took many prizes at fairs, purchased premium cattle, which he sold at a profit, and became widely known as an excellent authority in all matters relating to the live-stock business. He was a progressive as well as an industrious man, and quick to appreciate every improvement in agricultural machinery, being the first farmer in Schoharie County to purchase a mowing machine. In 1856 he built a new farm residence, and in 1871 he erected a handsome house in the village, where his last days were spent.

On March 6, 1834, Mr. Shelmandine was joined in marriage with Harriet Pitcher, who was born in the town of Summit, February 5, 1813, a daughter of Horace Pitcher. Eight children were the fruit of their union; namely, Charles, Elizabeth, Phœbe A., Catharine, Sarah M., Mary, Emeline, and Rominda. Charles married Lydia Brockway, and resides in Eminence, N. Y. Elizabeth is the wife of Frank Hannay, of Eminence. Sarah M., who married David G. Proper, of Summit, died February 28, 1870. Mary first married William L. Proper, who died leaving one son, Lewis. She afterward married David S. Palmer, a resident of Jefferson. Emeline married T. O. Burnett, and resides in Summit; and Rominda married Byron Burnett, and resides in Cobleskill. Charles and Elizabeth were formerly school teachers. All the children united with the Methodist Episcopal church.

In politics Mr. Shelmandine went from the

Whig party to the Democratic party, became a Republican at the breaking out of the Civil War, and in his last days joined the party of Prohibition. He assisted in building the Methodist church at East Jefferson, of which he was for some years a steward and trustee. Benevolence was one of his leading traits, and he relieved the suffering of the poor with a willingness free from ostentation. He died March 5, 1889, surviving his wife some nineteen years, her death having occurred February 23, 1870. Mrs. Shelmandine, like her husband, was an earnest member of the Methodist Episcopal church, and both were mourned as a severe loss to the community.

HENRY F. OLMSTEAD, Catskill agent of the Greene County Bible Depository and a retired agent of the American Express Company, was born in Ridgefield, Fairfield County, Conn., November 22, 1813, son of Nathan and Martha (Watrous) Olmstead. His parents were both natives of that town, and his paternal grandfather, Jared Olmstead, followed farming there as long as he lived. Nathan Olmstead was a carpenter by trade, and besides following this mechanical calling he taught school many years. His death occurred in Ridgefield at the age of fifty-seven. He was a member of the Congregational church. His wife, Martha, who was a daughter of John Watrous, a farmer, was a member of the Methodist Episcopal church. She died at thirty-four years of age, having been the mother of seven children.

Henry F. Olmstead is now the only survivor of his father's family. In his boyhood he attended the common schools of Ridgefield, and subsequently, both prior to and after completing a course at Hilton Academy, he taught school in Norwalk. Relinquishing educational work, he went to Hudson, N.Y., to learn the trade of a hatter, and worked as a journeyman there two years. In 1842 he came to Catskill, where he continued his trade on his own account for two years, and opening a retail hat store continued it for a period of nearly twenty-five years, during the latter part of the time occupying the building in which he now has an office. For fifteen years, beginning in 1851, he conducted in addition to the other the business of the local agency for the American Express Company. In 1886 the express business had become so developed in importance that he disposed of his hat business. He continued to represent the company until December, 1880, when failing health compelled him to relinquish the arduous duties of his position. As a reward for his long and faithful service the company placed him on their emeritus list, retiring him upon half-pay. Since 1881 he has transacted a real estate business, has been the local agent for foreign steamship lines, has looked after the Clark estate, and for the past five years has been the Catskill agent for the Greene County Bible Depository. In politics he was originally a Whig, and, favoring the principles of the Republican movement, he was instrumental in organizing that party in this locality. He was Civil Justice for sixteen years, and three years Police Justice, and was noted for the impartial manner in which he disposed of all cases coming under his jurisdiction.

In 1844 Mr. Olmstead was united in marriage with Lydia H. Utley, daughter of Ralph and Sarah (Huntington) Utley. He has had two children, namely: a daughter, Mary Howard Olmstead, who is organist of the Presbyterian church, and who teaches music; and a son, Henry F., who died aged four years.

Mr. Olmstead was formerly a member of the Sons of Temperance. For many years he has been an Elder of the Presbyterian church. He is a permanent Deacon, and was superintendent of the Sunday-school for nearly twenty years. He has outlived the majority of his business contemporaries, having participated in the development of Catskill from a small hamlet to its present size. He still has in his possession the old hand sled, built by him forty-five years ago, upon which he transported the American Express packages during the early days of that company's existence.

PETER V. VAN EPS, a well-to-do farmer of Glenville, N.Y., was born in this town, November 13, 1825, son of Albert and Anna (Swart) Van Eps. The family is of Dutch origin, as the name implies. Its immigrant progenitor was Dirk Van Eps, who settled in Schenectady County as early as 1662 or 1663. Johannes Dirksie Van Eps, son of Dirk, and the next in line, was killed in the Indian massacre of 1690. He had four sons and four daughters; and Evert Van Eps, one of his sons, great-grandfather of the subject of this sketch, was twice married, and had five sons and five daughters. Johannes Baphst Van Eps, the grandfather, was born in Glenville, May 13, 1731. When a young man he located upon a tract of wild land, which he cleared into a good farm, and the rest of his active years were devoted to its cultivation. He married Anna Vedder on May 2, 1761, and had a family of thirteen children. He died January 11, 1813.

Albert Van Eps, the father, was born in Glenville, May 16, 1785. A sturdy and a thrifty farmer, he made excellent use of the resources at his command; and he resided here until his death, which occurred March 17, 1831. Politically, he acted with the Whig party. He was a member of the Reformed church. Mrs. Anna Swart Van Eps, his wife, was born in this town, January 16, 1790, and died July 22, 1841. They had nine children, four of whom are living, namely: Ann Eliza, born September 16, 1819; Sarah, born September 12, 1823; Peter V., the subject of this sketch; and Josiah, born February 11, 1828. The others were: John A., born December 14, 1813; Jacobus S., born December 24, 1815; Harmanus S., born August 13, 1817; Josias, born December 11, 1821, died in infancy; and Susanna, born June 18, 1830.

Peter V. Van Eps was educated in the schools of his native town. While still a youth he began to assist in the work of the farm; and, having succeeded to the ownership of a portion of the homestead property on coming of age, he has tilled the soil with ener-

PETER V. VAN EPS.

getic diligence and resulting prosperity for the past fifty years. His farm is situated in the fertile valley of the Mohawk, not far from Hoffman's Ferry, and in the immediate vicinity of the spot where his ancestor erected a primitive abode in the pioneer days. The region abounds in charming natural scenery, including Wolf Hollow; and the traveller who goes out of his way to ride through this picturesque ravine is amply paid for his pains. The cries of the wild beasts heard by the early settlers have given way to the more welcome sounds of implements of industry, and the valley is now dotted on either side with well-kept farm-houses.

On June 3, 1851, Mr. Van Eps was united in marriage with Mary Ann Davenport, who was born in Troy, N.Y., March 23, 1828, daughter of David Davenport. Mrs. Van Eps is the mother of three sons, of whom the following is a brief record: Jewett Edwin, born December 25, 1852, married Mary Conda, and is now cashier of the First National Bank, Schenectady; David Augustus, a prosperous farmer of Glenville, born September 15, 1854, married Annie R. Van Loan, and has two children — Jewett E. and Helen M.; and Frank Stanley Van Eps, born July 4, 1859, married Marion Bosworth, and is now a Christian Science healer in Chicago.

Owning one of the oldest farms in Glenville, Mr. Van Eps keeps up with the times in the way of improvements, and occupies a handsome modern residence. In politics he is a Republican. He is esteemed both for his manly characteristics and as a representative of one of the most highly reputable families in this section of the county. Mr. and Mrs. Van Eps are members of the Reformed church, and are socially prominent.

NICHOLAS BRADT, a prominent resident and representative of one of the oldest families of Woestina (Rotterdam Junction), N.Y., was born in this town, September 14, 1824, son of Abram N. and Maria (Vedder) Bradt. He is a descendant of Arent Andriese Bratt, or Brat, the first of the family to settle in Schenectady County, who died soon after his arrival here in 1662. He married Catalyntie De Vos, daughter of Andries De Vos, who was Deputy Director of Rensselaerwych. The first ancestor to locate in Rotterdam was Abram A. Bradt, who was an industrious farmer, and who died at Woestina. The maiden name of his wife was Sarah Van Patten. Nicholas A. Bradt, the grandfather of the subject of this biography, was born in Rotterdam, N.Y., August 15, 1773. He was in his younger days a blacksmith, but later turned his attention to farming, which he followed energetically for the rest of his active years. He was at one time Alderman from the Third Ward of Schenectady, Albany County, and also held minor offices. In politics he was a Jeffersonian Democrat. He died July 9, 1850. He married Margaret Mabee, who was born in Rotterdam in 1776, and died December 13, 1850. They were members of the Dutch Reformed church, and the grandfather was an Elder for more than twenty years.

Abram N. Bradt, the father above named, was born in Woestina, August 22, 1793. He was an able farmer and a leading citizen, serving as Supervisor in 1846 and filling other town offices. In politics he voted with the Democratic party. He was an active member and an Elder of the Reformed church. Maria, his wife, whom he married May 2, 1818, was born December 5, 1801. She became the mother of seven children, three of whom are living, namely: Jemima, who married John V. Van Patten, of Glenville; Nicholas, the subject of this sketch; and Harman Bradt, who resides in Petersburg, Va. The others were: Margaret, Simon, Sarah, and a child that died in infancy. The mother died May 12, 1833; and the father, who survived her many years, died November 5, 1878.

Nicholas Bradt was educated in the district schools of Woestina, and working with his father acquired a good knowledge of general farming. He has made agriculture a profitable employment, and since 1860 has resided on the farm of one hundred acres which he is still carrying on with energy. He also owns the homestead farm, which contains the same number of acres, and he ranks among the well-to-do residents of this section.

On September 29, 1857, Mr. Bradt was united in marriage with Hester Bradt, who was born in Rotterdam, November 13, 1834. Mrs. Bradt became the mother of seven children, namely: Helen E., born February 15, 1862; Aaron Frank, born June 29, 1865; Margaret, born October 13, 1869; Elizabeth, born June 17, 1872, now the wife of Martin H. Schermerhorn; Simon V., born January 29, 1875; Maria, who married Simon V. Veeder, and died at the age of twenty-one years; and Abram, who died at the age of twenty-four. Mrs. Bradt died May 1, 1889.

Mr. Bradt has been a Trustee of the town, was an Assessor for some time, and has rendered efficient services in other town offices. Politically, he is a Democrat. He attends the Reformed church, and his children are members.

NELSON O. GREEN, contractor and builder, of Tannersville, Greene County, N.Y., and a Civil War veteran, was born in Hunter, this county, May 25, 1844, son of Giles and Sarah (Warner) Green. His father was born in Hunter, May 23, 1800, and his mother, who was of Dutch descent, was a native of Conesville, Schoharie County. His paternal grandfather, Seth Green, who came from Connecticut, found his way here by the aid of marked trees, and was the third to settle where the village of Hunter is now located. Taking up a tract of land, he erected a log house and followed farming. He was quite prominent here in his day, and served as Justice of the Peace. He died at the age of eighty-seven. He had a large family of children, six of whom lived to be over eighty years old.

Giles Green, father of Nelson O., obtained his education in the common schools, and in his youth worked upon the home farm. Later he had one hundred and twenty-five acres of the homestead property, upon which he erected a dwelling and engaged in farming, becoming well-to-do. Besides this property he owned a number of houses in Hunter. In politics he was a Democrat. He died at eighty-nine years of age. His wife, Sarah, died at the age of eighty-four. She was the mother of four children, three of whom are living; namely, Nelson O., Emma E., and Gilbert. Emma E. Green is the widow of George Pollock, and Gilbert is a resident of this town. The parents were members of the Methodist Episcopal church.

Nelson O. Green began his education in the common schools of Hunter. He resided at the parental home until he was thirteen years old, when he went to Romeo, Mich., twenty-eight miles from Detroit, where he remained two years, attending school and following various kinds of employment. Returning East, he enlisted in 1862 in the One Hundred and Twentieth New York Regiment, with which he served three years in the Civil War. He saw a great deal of active service, and was slightly wounded. He participated in the battles of Fredericksburg, Chancellorsville, and Gettysburg — at the last-named place the regiment losing one thousand out of fifteen hundred men in a short time — the battles of Mine Run, Spottsylvania, Tolapotamie, Chickahominy, Cold Harbor, and the siege of Petersburg, where on March 25, 1863, he was taken prisoner. He was confined in Libby Prison until paroled, when he rejoined his regiment in Washington. He was made Second Sergeant, but declined further promotion, and was mustered out at the close of the war.

Upon his return he went to Saugerties, N.Y., where he was engaged in farming for two years. Later he worked in the chair factory at Susquehanna, and followed this occupation for twelve years in different towns. Coming to Hunter in 1874, he was employed in the chair factory for four years, and then turned his attention to carpentering, doing a considerable business in this line in towns along the Hudson for six years. When Onteora, Elka, and Twilight Parks were opened, he engaged in contracting for the building of cottages; and he has erected a number at each place, employing a large force of men.

In 1874 Mr. Green was joined in marriage with Alice M. Lester, of Hunter. They have had four children — Jeanette, William, Robert, and Jasper. Jeanette, who is a graduate of the State Normal School, is now engaged in teaching. Jasper died at the age of nineteen.

Mr. Green is a Republican in politics, but has declined public office. He is a comrade of A. N. Baldwin Post, No. 263, G. A. R., of Hunter, and has served as color-bearer for seven years.

GEORGE LINTNER DANFORTH, one of the leading lawyers of Schoharie County and a resident of Middleburg, was born here on July 19, 1844, son of Judge Peter and Aurelia (Lintner) Danforth. All the traditions of his family and the surroundings of his youth lent their influence in preparing him for the legal profession. His grandfather, George Danforth, who died in the South, was a lawyer of pre-eminent ability, and his father was perhaps the most eminent practitioner of law that the county has produced. His grandmother, whose maiden name was Cornelia Swart, was born in Schoharie County of Dutch parentage. One of his uncles, General George E. Danforth, acquired a high reputation in public affairs, and distinguished himself as a brigade commander in the Civil War.

Mr. Danforth's father, Judge Peter S. Danforth, lived to the age of more than threescore and fifteen years, and in his long and honorable career filled many public positions. In 1872 he was made Justice of the Supreme Court. He was a member of the Dutch Reformed church. His wife was a member of the Lutheran church until her marriage, when she united with the Reformed church. Mrs. Danforth died at the age of seventy-one. She was a daughter of the Rev. George A. Lintner, D.D., who was for many years president of the Lutheran Synod and for twenty-five years pastor of St. Paul's Lutheran Church at Schoharie, N.Y. He died at the age of seventy-five, leaving two children — Mrs. Danforth and Joseph Albert Lintner. The latter has been for many years entomologist for the State of New York. Judge and Mrs. Danforth had three children; namely, George L., Cornelia, and the Hon. Elliot Danforth. Cornelia married Isaac W. Ferris, a son of Chancellor Isaac Ferris, of New York University.

George L. Danforth, the subject of the present sketch, in his boyhood attended the common schools of Middleburg, a select school, and Schoharie Academy; and later, after continuing his studies for a while under a private tutor, he entered Rutgers College, from which he was gradated in 1863. From his early years he had spent much time in his father's office, and in reality he was in practice at the age of nineteen. At the age of twenty-one he was admitted to the bar, and since that time he has been in active practice. His clients come from all parts of the State, and he has practised in all the State courts, including the United States Circuit Court of this district. He is at the present time, with few exceptions, the oldest member of the bar in the county. He has been referee in many important cases, and counsel in a large number of cases involving intricate points of law and title to real estate, and trustee of estates in this and adjoining counties. For some time past he has been counsel in the celebrated case in the First Department known as the Coal Oil Johnny Soap Case, a suit involving hundreds of thousands of dollars. Whether as counsel for prosecution or defence, he has met with remarkable success in winning legal contests for his clients.

On December 15, 1869, Mr. Danforth was united in marriage with Anita Whitaker, a native of New York and daughter of George and Hannah (Daggett) Whitaker. Her paternal grandfather, the Rev. Jonathan Whitaker, was a Unitarian clergyman, and preached mainly in Massachusetts, where he died at the age of sixty. Among his sons were several clergymen, a judge who resided in New Orleans, and a well-known government official. Mrs. Danforth's father was engaged in mercan-

F. P. LEARD.

tile business, shipping and importing South American products. He spent the greater part of his life in New York, but died in Massachusetts at the age of fifty-four, at the home of a brother. His wife was the daughter of a wealthy ship captain and philanthropist of Edgartown, Mass. She died at the age of seventy-six years. Mr. and Mrs. Danforth have lost two children. They have one son living — Pierre W. Danforth, who is now studying law with his father, and has for some time been engaged in newspaper work. He is the youngest editor in the county, and now edits and publishes the Middleburg *Press*, a six-column quarto, which is an enterprising weekly paper.

Mr. Danforth and his family are members of the Dutch Reformed church, and Mr. Danforth has been an Elder in the church for some thirty years. He is warmly interested in Sunday-school work, and teaches the Bible class; while his wife has a class of boys. For many years he has been sent as a delegate to the General Synod. He devotes much time to literary work, frequently delivering addresses and lectures and contributing articles to newspapers and periodicals. Of fine executive ability, he readily manages the many interests which press upon his personal attention, and which would puzzle the average man to manage at all. He is a trustee of Rutgers College, and president of its alumni association, and is also president of the Schoharie County Historical Society, trustee of the Union Free School and Academy of Middleburg, director of the First National Bank, and treasurer of the Middleburg & Schoharie Railroad Company. Since the organization of the fire department, ten years ago, he has been its chief. He has given considerable attention to fraternal societies, and is an active worker in both the Masonic and Odd Fellows fraternities.

Mr. Danforth's home is the spacious mansion in the prettiest portion of the valley, where the Danforth family has lived and exercised hospitality for many years.

FRANKLIN PIERCE BEARD, M.D., of Cobleskill, Schoharie County, well known as a skilful physician and surgeon and a large real estate owner, was born November 29, 1852, in Jefferson, N.Y., a son of Jacob L. and Polly (Wilsey) Beard. He comes of pioneer ancestry, his great-grandfather Beard having been an original settler of that part of Schoharie County that was named, in his honor, Beard's Hollow. There the Doctor's paternal grandfather, John Beard, a prosperous farmer, spent his long life.

Jacob L. Beard was born and educated at Beard's Hollow; but when eighteen years old he left the ancestral farm and came to Warnerville, this county, where he served an apprenticeship at the wagon-maker's trade. After following this calling as a journeyman and also in business for himself for several years in that town, he removed to Jefferson, and in 1863 transferred his business and his residence to the neighboring village of Summit, where he was engaged in farming for a quarter of a century. In 1889 he came to Cobleskill; and from that time until his death, in 1893, he resided with his son, Dr. Beard He was a steadfast Democrat, and for a score of years served as Justice of the Peace. His wife, Polly Wilsey, who was born in Warnerville, was a daughter of Colonel Wilsey, an officer in the Revolutionary army. She bore her husband seven children; namely, David, Samuel, Rose, Franklin Pierce, Marion, Adelle, and John. The mother died at the age of sixty-eight years, in 1889. Both parents were members of the Methodist Episcopal church.

Franklin P. Beard received a practical common-school education, and in his early manhood taught in a district school five terms. Leaving home then, he turned his attention to the study of medicine, having for his instructors successively Dr. Cornell, of Richmondville; Dr. Spaulding, of Summit; and Dr. Wood, of Jefferson. He subsequently entered the Albany Medical College, from which he was graduated as a member of the class of 1875. Beginning the practice of his profession in Eminence, he continued there about two years. He then located in Summit, and for ten years ranked as the leading practitioner of that vicinity. Dr. Beard came to Cobleskill in 1886; and here, also, his eminent skill and his close attention to his professional duties has ranked him the leading physician of the county, his opinions being largely sought after in consultations extending to adjoining counties.

He is a member of the Schoharie County Medical Society and of the Cobleskill Lodge, F. & A. M. He was a Supervisor in Summit in 1882, a Coroner in Schoharie County nine years; and from October, 1895, until October, 1897, he was examining surgeon of the Pension Department.

Dr. Beard is the proprietor of two fine farms in Richmondville, this county, one in Blenheim, and one in Summit of two hundred acres, and ninety acres of land in Cobleskill. The latter has been platted and divided into building lots, a street being laid out through one portion. He has likewise valuable building property in the village, including lots on Elm Street, west of the Catholic church; and he owns a fine business block in Summit.

In April, 1873, Dr. Beard married Miss Alice D., daughter of John Chickering, of Summit, a well-known mechanic. Dr. and Mrs. Beard have five children; namely, G. Claude, John J., Leona, Mildred, and David. G. Claude, who married Lulie Kilts, is a successful agriculturist in Richmondville. John J., who was graduated from the Albany Medical School in 1897, is a physician in Sharon Springs, N. Y.

KIRBY WILBER, an enterprising merchant of Quaker Street, Duanesburg, Schenectady County, N.Y., was born in this town, September 25, 1820, son of Kirby and Mercy (Allen) Wilber. He attended school until fourteen years old, when he entered the employ of Job Cleveland as a store clerk, and remained with him two years. After a short time spent in a store at Schenectady he returned, and for the next three years worked for James E. O'Neil. In 1840 he went to Brainard Bridge, Rensselaer County, where he clerked in a general store conducted by Hastings & Smith, cloth manufacturers, for eight years, at the end of which time he purchased the stock, and for the succeeding five years carried on business in company with his brother, E. G. Wilber. Selling out his interest in 1853, he returned once more to Duanesburg; and, associating himself with his brothers in a shoe manufactory in the locality known as Quaker Street, he was for the next few years engaged in selling their products on the road. This business was started in 1845 by R. P. U. Wilber, who began making shoes for the retail trade; but five years later he established a manufactory to supply the wholesale dealers only, and continued in business until his death, which occurred in 1854. The present store of Wilber & Co. was opened in 1860, and carried on in connection with the factory until 1867, when the firm was dissolved. The business was conducted by Kirby, E. G., and Charles C. Wilber until 1874, since which time Kirby and his son Charles C. have been sole proprietors of the mercantile establishment, consisting of a well-stocked general store having a large patronage. The senior partner is one of the oldest business men of this section in point of experience, and through his ability, integrity, and other commendable characteristics he has acquired success. Aside from his mercantile business he deals quite extensively in real estate. His own residence is one of the handsomest in town.

Mr. Wilber contracted the first of his two marriages in 1843, with Lucy Ann Crego, of Chatham, Columbia County. She died in 1877, and in 1880 he married Mrs. Phœbe J. Auchampaugh, born Stevens, a native of Wright, Schoharie County. He is the father of five children, all by his first wife, namely: Ellen M., who married the Rev. Milton Tator, and died at the age of fifty-one years; Emily W., wife of Arthur D. Mead, of Schoharie; Augusta A., wife of Charles E. Hoag, of Quaker Street; Adeline C., wife of Walter Briggs, of Schenectady; and Charles C. Wilber, who is in business with his father. Mr. Wilber has ten grandchildren. In politics he is a Democrat. He is a member of the Christian church.

Charles C. Wilber was born at Brainard's Bridge, May 30, 1847, and was educated in the schools of Duanesburg. Like his father he entered mercantile pursuits when fourteen years old, and is an excellent business man. He acts with the Democratic party in politics, and served with ability as Postmaster for three years. On December 21, 1870, he married Emily Moon, who was born in this town in September, 1847, daughter of John and Emily Moon. She is the mother of one son, Archie M. Wilber, who was born March 13, 1880.

WALTON VAN LOAN, of Catskill, N.Y., publisher of the Catskill *Mountain Guide*, was born in New York City on January 8, 1834, son of Matthew D. and Julia A. (Thompson) Van Loan. His grandfather, Isaac Van Loan, a resident of Catskill, was a mason by trade, but was engaged for a long period as captain of a passenger sloop plying between Catskill and New York. Captain Van Loan died at the age of seventy-two. His wife, Jane Dies, who was born in Gilboa, died at the age of seventy-four.

Matthew D. Van Loan was one of a family of four children. He was reared in this town and educated in the common schools. In 1841 he went to New York City and opened a daguerreotype studio, being the first man in the United States to make a business of producing portraits by the new process. He continued taking pictures for ten years in New York, and from there went to Philadelphia and later to Washington, engaging in the same business. Subsequently and up to the time of his death, in 1856, he was employed in the custom-house in San Francisco. Widely known as a daguerreotype artist both in this country and abroad, he took many prizes in American cities and was given special honors in England. While in New York he had a revolving gallery in the Delmonico Building, the only one ever known. His wife, Julia, who died at the age of seventy-seven, bore him three children, two of whom are living. These are Walton and Spencer. The latter, who was a soldier in the Civil War, resides in this village. Both parents were communicants of the Episcopal church, the father being one of the vestrymen.

Walton Van Loan resided in Catskill until he was twelve years of age, and then went with his father to different cities. For a time he attended the public schools in Philadelphia. When about thirteen years of age he secured an appointment as page in the national House of Representatives. This position he held from 1846 to 1850, receiving in payment sixty dollars per month in gold. In 1852 he went to Californa via Nicaragua to join his father, and paid his own fare. He carried a letter of introduction from Daniel Webster to the custom-house officials in San Francisco, and shortly after his arrival was given a position in the custom-house. But he remained in it only a short time, leaving to go as clerk in a large book store. After four years in that business he returned to Catskill and bought out a store, which he conducted for the next twenty years, up to 1878. In that year he started his present business, which has proved to be most successful. He has issued about thirty-six thousand guide books and about fifty thousand maps of the Catskills, taking in the entire chain. He is conceded to be the most reliable authority on points concerning the geography and topography of the Catskills, and no man in the country can approach him in extent of information concerning this beautiful region. He has been to the top of nearly every peak in the entire range.

Mr. Van Loan was married in 1874 to Lucy Beach, a native of Michigan. He has now lived in Catskill for forty-three years, and in his present residence ever since 1862, when it was built. He is a member of St. Luke's Church, and has the unparalleled record of having been its treasurer for thirty years. His wife is also a member of the same church, and both are active religious workers. The society has just completed a stone edifice, which was opened on June 6, 1899. This is said to be one of the most beautiful buildings to be found on the banks of the Hudson.

FREDERICK LEROSS FRAZEE, the editor and proprietor of the *Jefferson Courier*, Jefferson, N.Y., was born in the town of Gilboa, N.Y., June 24, 1872. His father, Charles Osborn Frazee, is a much respected and well-to-do farmer.

Mr. Frazee traces his paternal ancestry back to Benoni Frazee, his great-great-grandfather, who was of Scotch descent, and who during the Revolutionary War was a resident of New Jersey and aided the patriot cause by hauling supplies for the American army. Benoni Frazee lost his little property through the worthlessness of Continental money. With his wife and eight children, he migrated, about the year 1783, to Schoharie County, then almost an unbroken wilderness, and settled on a farm one mile from the present village of Gilboa. Very soon thereafter he died, leaving his widow and children to take care of themselves.

Benjamin, the second son, who was born March 8, 1774, remained on the farm with his mother until he became a man. About the year 1797 he married Margaret Monfort, of Dutch lineage. Two years later he settled on the farm now known as the Frazee homestead, at South Gilboa. He had five children, two sons and three daughters. He died August 11, 1862, aged eighty-eight years.

Hiram, the second son of Benjamin Frazee, was born November 19, 1804, and until his death, which occurred April 2, 1850, he lived on the farm with his father. On February 13, 1833, Hiram Frazee married Phœbe H. Osborn, by whom he had five children, only two of whom survived him.

Charles Osborn, the father of the subject of this sketch and the eldest son of Hiram Frazee, was born on the ancestral farm, April 27, 1836. After the death of his grandfather he bought the place which is still his home. January 28, 1864, he married Phœbe A. Clark, a descendant of the Clark family of Blenheim. Five children were born of this union, but only two are now living, namely: Harriet Estelle, who is now the wife of John T. Shew, and lives at Harpersfield, where Mr. Shew is engaged in the mercantile business; and Frederick Leross, who is now, as above noted, in the newspaper business at Jefferson.

Frederick Leross Frazee in his early years received a good common-school education, and, entering Stamford Seminary in the fall of 1888, finished a college preparatory course of study there in 1891, receiving a regent's certificate and a diploma, which graduated him from that school. In the fall of the same year he entered Union College at Schenectady, N.Y. Here he pursued his studies for two years.

In college Mr. Frazee was popular both in society and athletics, and stood high in his class. He was a member of his class foot-ball team, and he belongs to the Greek letter society, which is one of the largest and most prosperous college fraternities in the world. On leaving college he returned to his home at South Gilboa and soon after went to the State of Illinois. In 1893 he returned to his former home, where he remained until February, 1894, when he came to Jefferson and embarked in the newspaper business.

The place then supported two newspapers, the *Courier* and the Schoharie County *Chronicle*. The former, which was an old established journal, was then edited by George M. Proper, and the latter, founded in 1891 by Albert C. Mayham and Charles H. Shutts, was the property of Mr. Shutts, who has purchased Mr. Mayham's interest in the establishment. Mr. Frazee purchased both of these newspaper plants, and, merging the *Chronicle* into the *Courier*, enlarged the same. His career as a newspaper editor has been a successful one. He receives the hearty support of the business men of Jefferson, and a good patronage from the people at large. He is not only a pleasing writer, but a practical printer as well, having learned the mechanical as well as the editorial part of newspaper work, so that he is familiar with all the details of the business. He owns one of the best equipped country offices in the State.

On July 16, 1895, Mr. Frazee assumed matrimonial responsibilities, being united in marriage with Miss Nellie Hubbell, a highly esteemed young lady of Jefferson, daughter of C. B. Hubbell.

Mr. Frazee is a member and an officer of Working Lodge, No. 554, F. & A. M., and also a church member, belonging to the Dutch Reformed church at his former home, South Gilboa. In the spring of 1899 Mr. Frazee was elected Town Clerk of Jefferson for two years by a handsome majority. He is much interested in the welfare and development of his town, is a loyal Republican in politics, and an ardent worker for his party. He possesses a genial disposition, is wide-awake and enterprising, and never can do too much for a friend.

JACOB L. KILTS, an energetic farmer of Carlisle, N.Y., was born in this town, September 2, 1846, son of William and Julia A. (Empie) Kilts. He represents the fourth generation of his family in America, being a great-grandson of Peter Kilts, who came from Germany, and settled on a farm in Stone Arabia, now the town of Palatine, Montgomery County, N.Y.

Four of the sons of Peter Kilts located in Sharon, one of the number being John, the grandfather of the subject of this sketch. John Kilts spent the active period of his life in Sharon, and died at the age of eighty-seven years. He married a Miss Smith, and his children were: William; Benjamin; Conrad; George; Kate, who married Solomon Empie; Margaret, who married David Empie; Susan, who married Gideon Empie; Sophia, who married Daniel Shafer; and Magdalene, who married Ed Pointer. Of these the survivors are: Margaret, Susan, and Sophia. All of

CHARLES DICKINSON.

the grandfather's sons reared families. They were members of the Lutheran church.

William Kilts, the father above named, was reared and educated in Sharon, his native town. He assisted in carrying on the home farm until after his marriage, when he moved to Carlisle and settled upon a farm of one hundred acres, known as the Hilsinger place, which is now owned by his son, Jacob L. He engaged in general farming and stock-raising, made a specialty of hay and grain, and realized good financial returns as the result of his industry. Politically, he acted with the Democratic party. For years he was one of the main pillars of the Lutheran church, serving as Deacon and Elder, and frequently as a delegate to the Synod. He was well informed, especially upon subjects relating to religion. William Kilts died November 20, 1890, aged seventy-five years. Julia A. Empie Kilts, his wife, was a daughter of Adam Empie. They were the parents of ten children, three of whom are living, namely: Jacob L., the subject of this sketch; Wesley H.; and Cynthia A., wife of Charles J. Warner. The mother died in 1883.

Jacob L. Kilts passed his boyhood and youth in attending the district school and assisting upon the home farm. When a young man he managed the property jointly with his brother Wesley, but later succeeded to its ownership. He has seventy acres under cultivation. Aside from producing hay and grain, he raises cattle and sheep, and has acquired a wide reputation as a stock dealer. He also deals largely in clover seeds, producing an original variety which is cleansed by machinery, and whose superiority makes it eagerly sought for by the neighboring farmers.

Mr. Kilts married Melvina Shafer, daughter of Sylvester Shafer, and has four children; namely, Beardsley W., Bertha E., Avis M., and Aurie J.

In politics Mr. Kilts is an earnest supporter of the Democratic party. He has frequently been solicited to accept nominations to town offices and to serve upon committees, but has always declined. He is a Deacon of the Lutheran church, is also a class leader, and prominenty identified with the Sunday-school.

CHARLES DICKINSON, M.D., who was for many years the leading physician in Seward valley, Schoharie County, was born in Henrietta, Monroe County, N.Y., on May 31, 1833, son of Lyman and Harriet A. (Webster) Dickinson. He is a descendant of early colonists of New England.

The first ancestor of this branch of the Dickinson family in America came from England, about 1640, and settled in the Connecticut valley. Dr. Dickinson's grandfather, James Dickinson, was born in Connecticut. He came to this State shortly after the Revolution and settled in Canaan, Columbia County. Several years later he removed to a farm in Roseboom, Otsego County, and there remained until his death, at the age of seventy-seven.

Lyman Dickinson, son of James, was born in Canaan and one of a family of seven children. He lived with his parents until he was twenty-one years of age, when he went to Henrietta, where he engaged in mechanical work for a number of years, at the same time doing some farming. He then removed to Northern Indiana, but ten years later returned to Roseboom. Some years afterward he moved to Tioga valley, and, purchasing a farm, continued to reside there until his death, at the age of eighty-eight. He attended the Presbyterian church. His wife was the daughter of Aaron Webster, and was born in Canaan, N.Y. She was of the seventh generation from the first representative of this branch of the Webster family in America. One of her ancestors, John Webster, who settled in Hartford about 1636, was the fifth Governor of Connecticut, holding the office one year, 1656-57. He afterward removed to Hadley, Mass. Her grandfather was one of the favorite scouts of General Putnam during the war of the Revolution. Her father, who was born in Connecticut, removed to Canaan and later to Roseboom. His first wife died at the age of twenty-six, leaving only one child, Charles, now Dr. Dickinson. She was a birthright Quaker. His second wife, whose maiden name was Sarah Sutphen, had five children, two of whom are living, by name Orville and Lyman D. She lived to the age of eighty.

Charles Dickinson in his early years attended the common schools and later the academy at Cherry Valley. He began the study of medicine with Dr. James E. Sutphen, of Seward, and subsequently took three courses of lectures at the Albany Medical College, from which he was graduated in 1860. Returning then to Seward, he began the practice of his profession, and remained until 1869, when he removed to Binghamton. At the end of a year and a half he came back to Seward, and has since made this the scene of his professional labors. He has now been longer in practice than any other physician in this section of the county. Dr. Dickinson is energetic and persevering in whatever he undertakes, and is able as a business man as well as skilful in his profession. During early and middle life he had a large practice, and covered a wide circle in his ministrations; but in later years he has retired to a more limited field. An untiring student through all his career, he has given attention, not simply to medical subjects, but to science and literature in general. He has now and then lectured on some scientific or literary subject; and during the summer of 1896, while he was making the tour of Europe for pleasure and study, he wrote, by request, a number of letters on his travels for the Cobleskill *Index*.

The Doctor has lived for twenty-seven years in his present house. He was married in 1859 to Celia M. France, daughter of Gilbert G. France and one of a household group of seven children. Her father was a well-known farmer of this region, where the family has been settled ever since the Revolution. Mrs. Dickinson was a member of the Methodist church. She died at the age of thirty-eight, leaving three children; namely, Everett M., Melville D., and Hattie A. All of these are graduates of Cobleskill Academy. Both sons are Knights Templar. Everett M. Dickinson has been for the last seven years a jeweller in North Adams, Mass., where he conducts a large business. He married Laura Mann, who died in 1894, and by whom he had two children — Angie and Everett. In 1895 he married Louise Tower Wallace. She had one child — Gertrude Wallace. Melville D. Dickinson studied medicine with his father, and was graduated at Albany in 1890. He was also for two years a student at Cornell University. He is now assistant surgeon of the Troy Hospital, and is physician to St. Vincent Orphan Asylum. He married Emma Cole, and has one child, Celia. Hattie Dickinson is the wife of Clarence H. Shafer, of Cobleskill. Mr. Shafer is engaged in the jewelry business.

Dr. Dickinson is a member of the Schoharie County Medical Society, has been its president, and has served as delegate to the State society. He has written and read before the society papers on a variety of medical subjects. Politically, the Doctor is a Democrat, and he has held a number of important offices in the town. As Justice of the Peace he has done a large amount of important business, and as railroad commissioner he has rendered valuable service. He was formerly a Free Mason at Cobleskill. For many years he has been a leading member of the Methodist church and for over thirty-five years a Sunday-school teacher.

ISAAC SHOWERS, a retired civil engineer, was born in Hunter, August 27, 1827, son of Japhet and Sylvia (Butts) Showers. His first American ancestor was an emigrant from Holland, who settled in New Jersey, where he spent the rest of his life, and was a farmer. The next in line, John Showers, probably came to America with his father. After residing in New Jersey for a time he settled on a farm in Albany, N.Y., where he died at an advanced age. Michael Showers, son of John and grandfather of Isaac, was a native of Albany. He worked on a farm there until reaching his majority, when he came to Great Flats (now Lexington) and built a grist-mill, which he conducted a few years. He then took up a large tract of mountain land in what is now Jewett, and resided there with his family. He died in 1819, aged forty-nine years, leaving a widow and ten children. His widow, who again married, died at the age of fifty-three years.

Japhet Showers, above named, was born in a log house on the home farm in Jewett, seven miles below where his son Isaac now lives, and always resided in that locality. He was a farmer, and fairly successful. In politics he was a Democrat, and held some of the town offices. He died at the age of seventy. His wife, Sylvia, was a daughter of Isaac Butts, a well-to-do farmer of Lexington. Her father was twice married. By his first wife he had fourteen children; and by his second wife, formerly Mrs. Ruby Bellows, of Dover, N.J., widow with four children, he was the father of seven children. Isaac Butts and his second wife both lived to be about ninety-two years old. Japhet and Sylvia (Butts) Showers had a family of eleven children, of whom four are living — Michael, Isaac, Louisa, and Caroline. Michael is married, and resides on an adjoining farm, Louisa married Beasley Teasler, and Caroline is the wife of George Benn. The mother died at the age of seventy-one. She was a Methodist in her religious belief.

Isaac Showers at the age of eight years went to live at the home of a neighbor, with whom he remained five years, and he spent another year upon a farm in the vicinity. At the age of sixteen he went to Jewett, and secured employment for six months at seven dollars per month. He next worked in a saw-mill, where he received one hundred and twenty dollars a year for ten years, and saved seven hundred dollars of his earnings. After his marriage he located on a farm adjoining his present home, which is about one and a half miles from the village of Tannersville, on the road to Jewett, first purchasing one hundred and twelve acres and later buying more land. He remained there until 1891, and from 1846 to 1879 held the agency for the Hardingburgh Land Grant, Lot 25, consisting of twenty-eight thousand acres, surveying and selling about twenty-one thousand acres during that time. In 1879 he purchased seven thousand acres lying in Ulster and Greene Counties, which he surveyed and laid out in farms. It was in a poor condition at the time he took possession, but he improved it to such an extent as to make it more desirable, and now besides a large number of farms the district contains four parks — Santa Cruz, Twilight, Sunset, and Elka — comprising in all twelve hundred acres. In 1857 he adopted the profession of civil engineering, and for the past forty years he has surveyed not only all the Hardingburgh patent, but a great many farms throughout this region. He has surveyed also land near the Hudson River in Ulster County, and has completed much work for the great quarries in that locality. He has also been called upon in many lawsuits as an expert; and, although in 1895 he was compelled on account of ill health to relinquish active work of this kind, his advice is still sought upon many important matters. In 1890 he sold the farm of two hundred and sixty-six acres adjoining his home property. He erected a new dwelling-house and other buildings upon his present farm, which contains seventy acres, used principally for dairy purposes. He also owns three other farms and outlying land, amounting in all to one thousand acres, and is one of the largest resident land-owners in the town.

In 1854 Mr Showers was united in marriage with Merilla Loomis, daughter of Alvin J. and Harriet (Palmer) Loomis, of Windham. Her father, who was a butcher in that town, died at an advanced age; and her mother, who was a native of Ashland, died at the age of forty-nine. Mr. and Mrs. Loomis had eight children, of whom five are living; namely, Addison, Merilla, Chloe, Lovisa, and Julia. Merilla is now Mrs. Showers, Chloe married Jonathan Traphagen, Lovisa is the wife of William Young, and Julia married George Goodrich. Mr. and Mrs. Isaac Showers have had eight children. The four now living are: Cyrus, Emma, Henry W., and George H. Showers. Cyrus is a civil engineer. A sketch of him appears elsewhere in the REVIEW. Emma married Edward Osborn, a blacksmith in California, and has five children. Henry W. is attending the Albany Law School, and George Harding Showers is a student at the Polytechnic Institute, Troy. The others were: Jennie, who married Stephen Vining, and died in California, leaving two daughters — Bertha and Mingie; Elmer, who died at fourteen; Isaac, Jr., who died young; and Irving, who died at the age of four years.

Mr. Showers is a Republican in politics, but has declined to serve in office. He was in 1848 a member of the Independent Order of Odd Fellows. He has been a member of the Methodist Episcopal church for fifty-five years, a class leader forty-three years, and has also been connected with the Sunday-school as teacher and superintendent. He assisted in building the churches at Tannersville and Jewett, and contributes liberally toward the support of both.

WILLIAM KOHRING, of Glenville, ex-chairman of the Board of Supervisors, was born upon the farm where he now resides, September 3, 1862, son of August and Elizabeth (Martin) Kohring. The parents, who were natives of Germany, came to Glenville about the year 1858, and settled upon a farm. August Kohring was a sturdy and industrious man, possessing the keen intelligence and ambition to advance which is characteristic of his race; and he was respected as a worthy, upright, and progressive citizen. When naturalized he embraced the principles of the Democratic party, but withdrew his allegiance on account of the slavery question, and thenceforward acted with the Republicans. In his religious belief he was a Methodist. August Kohring died July 7, 1897. His wife is still living. They reared two sons, namely: William, the subject of this sketch; and George, who died in February, 1889, aged twenty-seven years.

William Kohring began his education in the common schools and completed his studies with a two years' course at a commercial college in Schenectady. He has made agriculture his chief occupation, and is now the owner of the home farm of about fifty acres. He carries on general farming in an able and progressive manner, keeps some fine Jersey cattle, and is regarded as one of the leading farmers in this locality. In politics he is a Republican, and since reaching his majority he has taken a lively interest in local public affairs. He has served as a Justice of the Peace four years, and was Supervisor for the years 1896-97, being chairman of the board the last year.

On March 18, 1891, Mr. Kohring was united in marriage with Lillie Muller, who was born in Brooklyn, N.Y., daughter of Dedrich and Sophia Muller. Mrs. Kohring is the mother of one daughter, Lillie E., who was born December 5, 1892.

Mr. Kohring is well informed upon all the

important topics of the day, and his public services were characterized by an intelligent appreciation of the people's needs. He is a Master Mason, and belongs to St. George Lodge, No. 6, F. & A. M., of Schenectady. He is a member of the Methodist Episcopal church.

DURYEA BEEKMAN, president of the First National Bank of Middleburg, Schoharie County, N.Y., was born at Seward, this county, August 9, 1840, son of Nicholas and Alida (Becker) Beekman. Of Dutch ancestry on the paternal side and German on his mother's, he is a representative of one of the oldest and most notable families in the county.

The first progenitor of the Beekman family in this country was John Beekman, an early settler in Albany, N.Y., who later removed to a farm in the Mohawk valley. William, the next in line of descent, born in 1767, was the first Judge of Schoharie County, which position he held for thirty years. When a boy he was clerk to Colonel Marius Willet. He was appointed County Judge by Governor George Clinton, and held that office until 1833. In the years 1798, 1800, 1801, and 1802 he represented his district in the State Senate. He was married July 18, 1788, to Joanna Low, daughter of Nicholas Low, and he afterward removed to Sharon, this county. His death took place at Sharon on November 26, 1845, in the house which he had built in 1802-4, and which is still standing.

Nicholas Beekman, son of Judge Beekman and father of the subject of this sketch, was born at Sharon, N.Y., November 27, 1790. He became a prominent citizen of the town of Middleburg, where for a long period he was engaged in farming and hop-growing, being one of the first hop-growers in the Schoharie valley. He served as Supervisor and in other offices, and represented the county in the State legislature of 1841. His marriage, which occurred June 16, 1811, united him with Alida, daughter of David Becker, and their wedded life extended through a period of over sixty years. He survived his wife by two years and four days, dying January 13, 1874. Of their twelve children, six survived them.

Duryea Beekman came to Middleburg with his parents when a boy. His education was obtained in the schools of this town. Since early manhood his capacity has been demonstrated in various business enterprises, and he now holds a high position in the business community. Elected president of the First National Bank of Middleburg at the time of its organization in 1880, he still remains in office. The bank is regarded as one of the best in this part of the State, and its reputation is due in chief measure to its excellent management. Mr. Beekman was for many years secretary and is now vice-president of the Middleburg & Schoharie Railroad. He is a director of the Davenport, Middleburg & Durham Railroad Company and a director of the Merchants' and Farmers' Mutual Fire Insurance Company. In politics a Democrat, he served in the legislature of 1879, having been elected by a majority of one thousand five hundred and six votes;

and he has frequently represented his party in State and other conventions. He is a member of Middleburg Lodge, No. 663, F. & A. M.

On October 19, 1859, Mr. Beekman married Elizabeth Richtmyer, a daughter of Peter and Elizabeth Richtmyer. Mrs. Beekman's paternal grandfather, Captain George Richtmyer, a native of Germany, came to America in 1745, and settled at Hartman's Dorf, in the town of Middleburg. Captain Richtmyer was subsequently an officer in the American army during the Revolutionary War. He fought at Bemis Heights, and served with distinction in every engagement that occurred in the Schoharie valley. Mr. and Mrs. Beekman have been the parents of three children, namely: Charles, who died in infancy; Dow, of whom a separate sketch appears in this volume; and William G.

DOW BEEKMAN, of Middleburg, one of the leading lawyers and business men of Schoharie County, was born in this town, February 8, 1862, son of Duryea and Elizabeth (Richtmyer) Beekman. He comes of an old Schoharie County family, and a fuller account of his ancestors may be found in connection with the sketch of his father, Duryea Beekman, on the preceding page of this volume.

After the usual common-school course Dow Beekman prepared for college at Hartwick Seminary, Otsego County. He then entered Union College, at which he was graduated in 1884, having taken four of the most important prizes in the course. From September, 1884, until June, 1886, he was professor of mathematics at Union Classical Institute, Schenectady, N.Y., and during the same period he devoted his spare time to the study of law in the office of Judge Samuel W. Jackson, of that city. In September, 1886, he was admitted to the bar at Saratoga, and immediately began the practice of his profession in Middleburg. Since then he has built up what is probably the largest law business in this part of the county. In 1889 he was elected District Attorney of Schoharie County, receiving a majority of one thousand eight hundred votes, and during his term of office he never presented an indictment that was set aside or quashed. He has been attorney and counsel in many important cases, is attorney for the Middleburg & Schoharie Railroad Company, for the Davenport, Middleburg & Durham Railroad, and also for the corporation of the village of Middleburg. He is the possessor of an unusually extensive library.

Mr. Beekman is also a man of practical business ability. He is a director of the Middleburg & Schoharie Railroad Company, attorney and treasurer of the Merchants' and Farmers' Mutual Fire Insurance Company, and a director and secretary of the Middleburg Telephone Exchange Company. A Democrat in politics, he is secretary of the Democratic County Committee, and has delivered many addresses in different parts of the State in every Presidential campaign since he became a voter, having on several occasions been sent out by the Democratic State Committee. He has also delivered addresses on subjects foreign to politics, and his ability as a speaker has been frequently recognized by the press.

Mr. Beckman has been Master of Middleburg Lodge, No. 663, F. & A. M., for four years. In 1896 he served as District Deputy Grand Master of the Eleventh Masonic District, which comprises Delaware, Schoharie, and Greene Counties. He is now District Deputy Grand Master of the Eighteenth District, comprising Schoharie and Otsego Counties. He is a member of John L. Lewis Chapter, R. A. M. He has also been District Deputy Grand Sachem of the Improved Order of Red Men, and belongs to the Independent Order of Odd Fellows.

On June 9, 1891, Mr. Beckman married Miss Laura Frisbie, daughter of Grandison N. Frisbie, of Middleburg. Two children have blessed their union — Marjorie Elizabeth and Douw Frisbie.

THOMAS W. JERALDS, a retired business man and wealthy resident of Ashland, was born in Waterbury, Conn., August 28, 1839, son of Thomas and Mary (Brown) Jeralds. Both his father and his paternal grandfather, whose given name was Ransom, were natives of Bethany, Conn. Ransom Jeralds, however, removed from that town to Wallingford, same State, where he carried on a farm for the rest of his active period, his death occurring at the age of seventy-nine years.

When a young man Thomas Jeralds became a Methodist minister, and was attached to the New York East Conference for about twenty years. He was subsequently engaged in the silverware business at Meriden, Conn., until his retirement. He died at the age of forty-seven years. His first wife, Mary, who was a native of Burlington, Conn., died in early womanhood, leaving two children, namely: Ellen M., who married Henry Wooding, and is no longer living; and Thomas W., the subject of this sketch. For his second wife he married Betsey Parker, a sister of Charles Parker, a prominent manufacturer of Meriden and the first Mayor of that city. Of this union there were three children, two of whom are living, namely: Sarah R., who married John Ten Eyck; and Mary A., who married a Mr. Morgan, of Meriden, Conn. Mrs. Betsey P. Jeralds is still living, and is now ninety-two years old.

Thomas W. Jeralds went from the Wallingford High School to the academy in Meriden, and his studies were completed at the Ashland Collegiate Institute. Entering mercantile business in this town, he continued it in Cheshire and still later in Wallingford, where he kept a general store for some time. From Wallingford he removed to Ashland, N.Y., where he engaged in active business until his retirement in 1890, and where he still makes his home. He has business interests in various places, and his time is now devoted to the care of his investments and to the management of his fine estate in this town. This valuable property, which is known as Crescent Lawn, consists of one hundred and fifty-five acres of desirably located land, used chiefly for dairy

T. W. JERALDS.

purposes and the cultivation of small fruits, and containing two substantial residences adjoining each other.

In 1860 Mr. Jeralds was joined in marriage with Frances A. Tuttle, a native of Ashland, daughter of Albert and Aurelia Tuttle. Albert Tuttle was a well-to-do merchant and speculator. He figured conspicuously in the public affairs of this town, and held all of the important local offices. He also served as Postmaster, and while a member of the Assembly he introduced the act incorporating the town of Ashland. He was the father of five children by his first union, and by a second marriage he had two children, one of whom became Mrs. Jeralds. Mrs. Jeralds died January 9, 1898, aged fifty-eight years. She was a member of the Methodist Episcopal church and a lovely Christian lady. She left three children; namely, Caroline S., Hattie A., and John T. Caroline married Lorenzo R. Cook, of the White Sewing Machine Company, and proprietor of a large dry-goods store at Wallingford, Conn. Hattie A. married Charles C. Carroll, a jeweller of Wallingford, and her children are: Barbara J., Frances W., and Doris J. John T., who is residing in East Haven, Conn., married Berta L. Whitlesey, of East Haven.

In politics Mr. Jeralds is a Republican. He held the appointment of Postmaster both in Cheshire and Yalesville, and served with ability as Supervisor in Ashland for the years 1891-92. His interest in the welfare of Ashland began some forty years ago, when he first engaged in business; and during the period of his residence elsewhere his attachment to the place was unabated. He is a member of and a trustee of the Methodist Episcopal church, but has contributed liberally to the different churches. He takes a lively interest in Sunday-school work, and rendered valuable aid in securing and furnishing the rooms of the Young Men's Christian Association. Mr. Jeralds is an Odd Fellow, and formerly belonged to the Meriden Centre Lodge, Meriden, Conn.

MISS JANE VAN LOAN, one of the most prominent and highly respected ladies of Catskill, was born in this place, her parents being William W. and Sally (Du Bois) Van Loan.

Her grandfather, Captain Isaac Van Loan, was in his time the leading man of the town, and widely known throughout all this section of the county. He had large shipping interests, and was the owner of several sloops which ran on the river. When young he had learned the mason's trade, and always as long as he lived he took a deep interest in the welfare of mechanics, and aided them in every possible way. Nor was his helpfulness extended to this class alone. Every person deserving of sympathy was sure to find in Captain Van Loan's warm heart, which overflowed with kindness to all mankind, a fountain of consolation, and every worthy cause found in him an unfailing champion. A man of fervid religious aspirations, in the church he was a pillar of strength. He was a member of St. Luke's Episcopal Church, and many years one of its vestrymen. He took a prominent part in securing in 1801 the erection of the church edifice, which was the first in Catskill. Not only did he aid with generous contributions of money, but he gave much time and personal effort during his service as a member of the building committee. He was one of those genial and whole-hearted men who are sure to make friends wherever they go, and his death caused deep and widespread grief. He never neglected the duties of good citizenship. For many years he served the town as Road Master, and for a time was Sheriff of the county. His death occurred in 1840, at seventy-two years of age. His wife, who also died at seventy-two, was born in Schoharie. Her maiden name was Jane Dies. She was a daughter of Madame Dies, who was long the first lady in Catskill. Madame Dies lived in the beautiful, old-fashioned house that formerly stood where the Shale brick works now are. She was a daughter of Jacob Goelet, of the famous New York family of that name. Captain Isaac and Jane (Dies) Van Loan had five children.

William W. Van Loan, father of Miss Jane, received his education in the public schools of Catskill. He began his business career in the village, conducting a grocery store until 1828, when he sold it and went to New York City. There he opened a general merchandise store where the South Ferry Station now stands. In those days New York had not outgrown her early boundaries, and Canal Street was still the end of the city. Miss Van Loan remembers the old city well. In the summer of 1832 the cholera epidemic in New York drove Mr. Van Loan and his family back to Catskill, and the store and the town residence were closed. But in the fall the family returned to the city, where they remained until 1834. Mr. Van Loan then came back to his native place and went into mercantile business here in the store where Mr. Fox now is. He owned considerable land, which had been part of his father's estate. He served the town as Postmaster for some years, having the post-office where Mr. Bourke is now located. He died at the age of seventy-two. He and his wife were members of St. Luke's Church. Mrs. Van Loan was born in this village, and died here at the ripe age of eighty-four. She was a daughter of Captain Barent Du Bois, who was a lifelong resident of Catskill with the exception of the time he served in the Continental army during the Revolution. Of the children born to William and Sally (Du Bois) Van Loan, only two grew to adult years. These were Jane and Rachel. Rachel, who died in 1891, at the age of seventy-two, was the wife of John Breasted, who was prominently identified with the Alair Iron Works and with the Morgan Iron Works. He was born here, son of Peter Breasted, a painter, who was a lifelong resident in this town. John Breasted had an office in New York for some years, but later returned to Catskill, and in company with others built the Prospect Park Hotel. He was the manager of this until failing health compelled him to give up business. He died in 1884. He gave a bell for St. Luke's Church.

The Van Loan family has been identified with St. Luke's Church longer than any other family now living, and Miss Van Loan has recently shown her appreciation of the significance of this fact, as well as her affectionate veneration for her grandfather and sister, by the gift of a beautiful spire and a costly altar rail for the new church. This building is said to be the handsomest on the Hudson, and the spire, which has been erected at a cost of fifteen hundred dollars, is a masterpiece of design and construction, and greatly admired. It can be seen twenty miles down the Hudson, towering up into the blue. In it is hung the bell given by Mr. Breasted. The altar rail, which is of solid brass, is exquisitely engraved, and will be inscribed through its entire length on the front and back. On one side the inscription will be in memory of Mrs. Breasted, and on the other in memory of Captain Isaac Van Loan. It is to be made and put in at a cost of one hundred and fifty dollars.

WILLIAM S. HAMLIN, Postmaster, and general merchant, Glenville, Schenectady County, N.Y., was born in this town, February 28, 1855, son of Anson B. and Abigail (Ostrom) Hamlin. The father was born in Connecticut, September 7, 1807, and the mother was born in Glenville, April 1, 1811.

Anson B. Hamlin followed the cooper's trade in his early days; and, coming to Glenville when still a young man, he kept a hotel here for some time. He subsequently carried on a farm for a number of years, and, returning here in 1867, he was engaged in mercantile business until selling out to his son in 1882. His last years were spent in retirement, and he died May 19, 1895. He was a man of good business ability and upright character, and he gained the good will of all with whom he had dealings. In politics he was a Republican. His wife, whose maiden name was Abigail Ostrom, became the mother of ten children, five of whom are living, namely: David H.; Jewett C.; Christopher; William S., the subject of this sketch; and Clarissa. The others were: Lyman G., Oliver, Heman, Rachel A., and Betsey. Mrs. Abigail O. Hamlin died in 1889.

William S. Hamlin after attending the common schools of Glenville completed his studies with a commercial course at a business college in Troy. Beginning when twelve years old to make himself useful as an assistant to his father, he later gave his whole time to the business in the capacity of a clerk, and continued as such until becoming its proprietor. He conducts the oldest-established general store in this part of the town, keeps a large and varied stock, including agricultural implements, feed, fertilizers, and so forth, and has a numerous patronage.

On November 23, 1882, Mr. Hamlin was united in marriage with Anna Bell, a native of West Charlton, Saratoga County, daughter of George Bell.

Politically, Mr. Hamlin is a Republican. He served with ability as Town Clerk one year, and is giving excellent satisfaction as Postmaster. He has a wide circle of friends and acquaintances who appreciate his many sterling qualities, and he is a member of Touareuna Lodge, No. 35, I. O. O. F.

HENRY VAN DRESER, a prominent dairyman and poultry raiser of Cobleskill, N.Y., proprietor of Eureka Stock and Poultry Farm, was born September 4, 1839, in Schoharie, Schoharie County, a son of John I. and Anna (Warner) Van Dreser. On the paternal side he comes of substantial Dutch ancestry. His grandfather, the Rev. Henry Van Dreser, a Presbyterian minister, emigrated from Holland to New York, and for seventeen years thereafter preached in Schenectady. He married Anna Fergueson, a fair Scotch maiden, who bore him thirteen children.

John I. Van Dreser spent a large part of his early life in Schoharie, where for seven years he kept a livery stable. In 1846 he removed to Cobleskill, and, buying a large farm, was here engaged in agricultural pursuits for a number of years. When well advanced in age and unable longer to care for his property, he sold his estate, and from that time until his death, at the venerable age of eighty-seven years, made his home with his sons, J. W. and Henry. He was very successful as a farmer, and quite active in public life. He was a regular attendant at the Lutheran church, which his wife joined when a girl of sixteen. Her maiden name was Anna Warner. She was born in Warnersville, a daughter of Jacob Warner, a well-known farmer and the first dairyman in Schoharie County. The first summer that Mr. Warner made a specialty of this particular branch of industry his herd of twenty cows produced a ton of butter, which he sold in the city of New York, whither he drove with a team. This transaction attracted such attention that for many years after he was known far and wide as "Butter Jake." Of the seven children born to John I. and Anna (Warner) Van Dreser, six grew to maturity, namely: Sarah, the widow of the late Peter Shaffer; Catherine, deceased; Jacob W.; Henry, the special subject of this sketch; Mary J., wife of Clinton Tillepaugh; Emma, wife of John F. Face; and Almira, wife of Adam V. Karkar. The mother died at the advanced age of fourscore and four years.

Henry Van Dreser was reared on the home farm, and educated in the district schools. Early becoming interested in the art and science of agriculture, he decided to make farming his life occupation. In early manhood he bought in partnership with his brother Jacob the farm on which he now resides, and for several years they worked it together. In 1895 Mr. Van Dreser purchased his brother's interest in the estate, which he has since managed alone. He has added substantial improvements, including the erection of the present conveniently arranged hen-house, it being the largest in Schoharie County, and in every department has met with eminent success in his undertakings.

He served as president of the Cheviot Sheep Breeders' Association of the United States and Canada for three years. He is authority on breeds and breeding of thoroughbred cattle, and has served in the capacity of judge at the different fairs in this and other States for many years. He has been employed for the last four years by the New York State Farmers' Institute as instructor in his special lines of agriculture. He carries on general farming, but makes somewhat of a specialty of the raising of stock and poultry, and dairy products. He has served ably as president of the New York State Breeders' Association, which is devoted to the improvement of the breeding of cattle, sheep, swine, and poultry, and is a charter member of the Barnerville Grange, before which he often lectures or reads papers of interest.

Mr. Van Dreser was married October 16, 1873, to Miss Emma J. Becker, daughter of the late James Becker, who died on his farm in Cobleskill, February 16, 1895, leaving a widow and four children. Mrs. Van Dreser is a graduate of the Normal College, a woman of culture and refinement. She holds a State certificate, and prior to her marriage she taught most successfully both in Cobleskill and Albany.

JAMES STEVENS, of Greenville, N.Y., a leading insurance agent of this section of Greene County, was born on the farm where he now lives, in a house near his present dwelling-place. His family is an old one in the town, having been first represented here by his great-grandfather, Reuben Stevens, who came from Stamford, Conn., took up a tract of land, and became one of the pioneer settlers of this region.

Reuben's son Samuel, grandfather of James Stevens, was born in Stamford. After coming here he engaged in farming. He died of typhus fever when only thirty-two years of age, this being in 1813. His wife, whose maiden name was Sally Jones, was a native of Stamford. She bore him three children, all of whom are deceased. Left a widow while yet a young woman, she married a second time, and lived to be eighty-four years of age. In religion she was a zealous Baptist.

Mr. Stevens's parents were Orrin C. and Mary A. (Smith) Stevens, the father a native of Greenville. Orrin C. Stevens worked at carpentering while a young man, but subsequently he carried on the farm where his son now lives. He owned a hundred and sixty acres, and was a successful farmer. He was warmly interested in all public affairs, and held various town offices, including among others that of Supervisor. For some time he was a Justice of the Peace. In politics he was an old-time Democrat. For years he was a trustee in the Presbyterian church, and one of its most active and influential members. Valuable service was rendered by him as one of the Sons of Temperance. He lived to the age of eighty-three years. His wife, Mrs. Mary A. Stevens, who died in 1884, after a useful life covering three-quarters of a century, was born on a farm in West Springfield, being one of a family of six children. Her parents were Daniel and Sarah (Day) Smith. Of her seven children, three are deceased. One of them, a son Samuel, was Captain of Company A of the Thirty-seventh Wisconsin Volunteers in the Civil War, and lost his life in 1864, during the attack on Petersburg. The living children are: James, the subject of this sketch; Daniel, who is a physician and druggist in Nebraska; Anna, who is the wife of D. H. Smith, a dentist of Holyoke, Mass.; and Orrin C., second, who is retired from business and resides in Middleburg.

James Stevens grew up on the farm where he now resides. His education was received in the common schools, and at Greenville Academy. Throughout his active life he has devoted more or less time to agricultural pursuits, and for forty years he also did a large amount of land surveying. He has lived in the house which is now his home since 1883, when he removed here and took charge of his present farm of one hundred and thirteen acres. He carries on general farming. In 1880 he began the insurance business, being elected that year secretary and treasurer of the village fire insurance company. This office he has since held, and in the intervening years he has had the satisfaction of seeing the company constantly increase until now it carries over two million dollars insurance. In the same year Mr. Stevens received his appointment as general agent of four other fire insurance companies, and in 1893 he organized the Greene County Mutual Fire Insurance Company, of which he has since been secretary, treasurer, and general agent. This company, which does a general insurance business at sixty per cent. of stock rates, now has out over two thousand, one hundred and fifty policies in fire, representing two million, two hundred and ninety-two thousand, six hundred and seventy dollars. Its total receipts for the year 1898 were twelve thousand, five hundred dollars, and the amount of money in the treasury on December 11, 1898, was thirteen thousand, four hundred and forty-two dollars, and twenty-six cents. The agents of the company operate in Greene, Albany, Columbia, Delaware, and Schoharie Counties.

Mr. Stevens was married in 1866 to Elizabeth Sherrill, who was born in Greenville, daughter of Ezra Sherrill, a well-known farmer of this place. She is the mother of two children — Lucena and Orrin C., third. Lucena married Theodore Coonley, a farmer of this place. Orrin C., third, who is engaged in insurance in Greenville, married Arcia Cook, and has one child, James C.

Politically, Mr. Stevens is a Democrat. He has held the office of Supervisor, and from January, 1889, to April, 1893, he was Deputy County Clerk. For five years he was clerk of the Board of Supervisors. Shortly after being first elected to the office of Town Clerk, he was chosen Second Lieutenant in Company A of the Twentieth Regiment of State militia, and went South, serving for a time in the Union army. For many years he was a member of John W. Watson Post, G. A. R., of Catskill, and held the office of Adjutant in the post; but he subsequently joined the C. Swaine Evans Post, No. 580, of South Westerlo.

Mr. Stevens is a Mason, having joined the organization in March, 1858, in Cascade

SOLOMON SIAS.

Lodge, F. & A. M., of Oak Hill. In 1864 he was a charter member of James M. Austin Lodge, No. 557, of Greenville. Of this he was first Senior Deacon, for five years he was Junior Warden and Secretary, and for two years Master. He was formerly connected with the Coxsackie Royal Arch Chapter, No. 85; and upon the organization of the Greenville Chapter, No. 283, he became a charter member of that body. He has held the offices of Scribe and King. He is also a charter member of Zeus Lodge, No. 360, of the Greenville Knights of Pythias, was formerly Chancellor, and is at the present time Master of Exchequer. Mr. Stevens is a liberal supporter of the Presbyterian church, of which his family are members.

SOLOMON SIAS, principal of the public schools of Schoharie, N.Y., and one of the leading educators in the county, is a native of Danville, Caledonia County, Vt. He was born June 13, 1829. His father, the Rev. Solomon Sias, son of Benjamin and Abigail Sias, was born in London, Merrimack County, N.H. Grandfather Sias removed with his family from London to Danville, being among the pioneer farmers in that town, where he and his wife lived to a good old age. They had eight children.

Solomon Sias, Sr., grew to manhood on the paternal farm, attending school as opportunity offered. Feeling himself called to preach the gospel, and giving such proof of his calling that people heard him gladly, he became a circuit rider and later a presiding Elder, his circuit taking in at different periods Western Maine, New Hampshire, and Eastern Vermont. By himself he acquired a knowledge of Latin, Greek, and Hebrew. He was a fluent and forcible speaker, thoroughly familiar with the Holy Scriptures, a man of great resource of thought and expression. He was accustomed to ride on horseback from place to place to preach every day and evening, wherever he could get an audience. In Lynn, Mass., where he was pastor of the Union Street Methodist Church, 1815-16, he started the first Methodist Sunday-school in New England. He was sent several times as a delegate to the General Conference of the Methodist Episcopal Church, to which he belonged. He died at the age of seventy-two, a well-preserved man to the last, after thirty years of service in his Master's vineyard. He married a widow, Mrs. Amelia Rogers Hewes, the ninth lineal descendant of John Rogers, the Smithfield martyr. Mrs. Sias died at the age of sixty-seven, having reared five children, three by her first husband, Mr. Hewes, and two by her second, namely: Solomon, the subject of this sketch; and Amelia, who married Azro Mathewson.

Mr. Sias, of Schoharie, was educated at Newbury Seminary, Newbury, Vt.; at Middlebury College in that State and at Wesleyan University, Middletown, Conn., where he belonged to the class of 1852. He was an assistant teacher at Newbury Seminary as early as 1850. He received the degree A.M. from Middlebury College, Vt., and of Doctor of

Medicine from the University of Vermont at Burlington. From 1854 to 1859 he taught at Fort Edward Institute, New York, holding the chair of professor of natural science under Joseph E. King president of the Institute. Leaving Fort Edward, he accepted a call to take charge of a college for women at Bonham, Tex., where he remained conducting the affairs of the college for eight years. He then came to New York State and accepted a call to take charge of the seminary at Charlotteville. In 1874 he came to Schoharie and took the position he now holds, which, with the exception of a brief period — 1877 to 1878 — spent in Texas as president of the Soulé University at Chapel Hill, he has held continuously from that date.

The Schoharie school has greatly improved under his management, and is now a first-class high school in every respect and very flourishing. About two hundred students are enrolled and five subordinate teachers are employed. Mr. Sias is the oldest principal in active service in the county, and is among the oldest in the State as principal and teacher. He has arranged for the Schoharie school the most advanced course of any school in the county, and he always keeps up to the times in means and methods of educational work, using the latest approved text-books and reference books. His efforts are uniformly indorsed by the State regents, at whose request he has spoken upon numerous educational topics in the conventions held at the State capital. He has attended all of the meetings since 1866 and every county institute for thirty years, speaking at many of them. He has been secretary of the county institute for nearly fifteen years, has been assistant conductor one year, besides often serving briefly as assistant conductor of other institutes.

He was married July 2, 1857, to Lina Baker, daughter of Daniel Baker, of Youngstown, New York. One child was born of this union, a son named Frederick. He was educated in the Schoharie schools, then learned telegraphy at Brooklyn, N.Y., and became manager of a telegraph office. Taken suddenly ill with typhoid pneumonia, he died at the age of nineteen.

Professor Sias is a fellow of the American Association for the Advancement of Science, to which he has belonged since 1866, and for several years he was an observer for the Smithsonian Institution. He has had charge of an educational department in the Schoharie *Republican*, to which he has contributed articles that have been copied by the leading educational papers of the State, and he has been a frequent correspondent of several other journals. He is an active member of the Schoharie County Historical Society, of which he was one of the three original organizers. He was instrumental in securing the "Old Stone Fort" for the purposes of the society. He is likewise connected with the medical society of this county, having served as brigade surgeon during the Civil War. Mr. Sias was made a Mason in Connecticut, was afterward connected with the order in Vermont and later in Texas, where he was Master of a lodge. He is now a twenty-seventh degree Mason, a member of Schoharie

Lodge, No. 491, and of the chapter and council. As an Odd Fellow he belongs to Towos-scho-ho Lodge of Schoharie, has twice been Noble Grand, is now a member of Middleburg Encampment, and Past Captain of Canton Young, No. 45, of Schoharie. In politics he is a Democrat.

Mrs. Sias is a graduate of the collegiate department of Fort Edward Institute, and has taught school. Both Mr. and Mrs. Sias are members of the Methodist Episcopal church, and he has preached a great number of sermons in pulpits of Schoharie and the neighboring towns.

ANDREW G. LIDDLE, a stirring farmer of Princetown, was born in this town, February 23, 1859. Son of Alexander and Barbara (Gregg) Liddle, he comes of highly reputable Scotch ancestry, being of the fourth generation in descent from Alexander Liddle, a native of Scotland, who emigrated with his parents when a young man, and was an early settler in Duanesburg. This is the line: Alexander, Robert, Alexander, second, Andrew G.

Alexander Liddle, first, became a large land owner. The farm now owned by his grandson, Alexander, second, was a part of his estate, and he resided here until his death, which occurred in his ninety-third year. He was a member of the Reformed Presbyterian church, and a strong Abolitionist. The maiden name of his wife was Mary Gifford.

Robert Liddle, the grandfather, was born in Duanesburg, January 12, 1803. He was a prosperous farmer during his active years, and he died in Duanesburg at the age of eighty-eight. Politically, he was originally a Whig, and later a Republican. In his younger days he took an active part in military affairs, and was Captain of a local rifle company. He was an Elder of the Presbyterian church. Robert Liddle was three times married; and his first wife, Sarah Smith, a native of Princetown, became the mother of eight children, namely: Alexander; Abigail, born October 6, 1828; Mary, born August 31, 1830; Ann E., born March 3, 1834; Charles, born March 7, 1836; Thomas G., born July 18, 1838; Abram S., born June 9, 1840; and Robert W., born April 30, 1842. By his union with Sarah Robinson, his second wife, there were five children: Angus M., born January 29, 1846; Duncan N., born March 26, 1848; Jenette, born August 12, 1850; and Sarah C. and John E., twins, who are no longer living.

Alexander Liddle, second, the father, was born April 17, 1827, upon a farm adjoining the one which he now occupies. He was reared to farm life, and at the age of twenty-nine years he bought a farm in Princetown of one hundred and twenty-nine acres, upon which he resided for sixteen years, and which he still owns. He has occupied his present farm of one hundred acres in Duanesburg since 1885, and this property is provided with good buildings and is otherwise well improved. His energy and industry continue unabated, and he is highly esteemed by his fellow-townsmen. He supports the Republican party at national elections, but has never cared to hold office. Like his ancestors he is a Reformed Presbyterian in religion, and acts as an Elder of that church. Mrs. Barbara Gregg Liddle, his first wife, who was a native of Rotterdam, N.Y., died April 14, 1874, leaving two sons — Robert A. and Andrew G. Robert A. Liddle, born December 4, 1856, married Rebecca Wemple, resides in Duanesburg, and has three children — James, Barbara, and Anna. On February 9, 1876, Alexander Liddle married for his second wife Margaret Cowell, who was born in England, January 30, 1839. By this union he has one daughter, Jeannette S., who was born March 17, 1878.

Andrew G. Liddle, the special subject of this sketch, was educated in the district schools of Princetown. He has always resided upon the farm he now cultivates, which was purchased by his father in 1856, and since reaching manhood he has successfully managed the property. He raises oats, rye, corn, and hay, keeps about ten head of stock, and ranks among the leading farmers of this section of Schenectady County.

Mr. Liddle married Lillie B. DeForest, of Albany, and has three children, namely: Alexander, born July 7, 1883; Edith, born January 26, 1886; and Laura M., born May 6, 1890.

In politics Mr. Liddle is a Republican, and has served with ability as Supervisor for three years. He belongs to Farmers' Grange, No. 709, Patrons of Husbandry, and has served as Master for three years. He is a member of the South Reformed Presbyterian church.

CHARLES VOSS, merchant and Postmaster at Tannersville, Greene County, N.Y., was born in Holstein, Germany, February 14, 1849, son of Frederick and Maria (Retting) Voss. His great-grandfather, Hans Van Voss, who was a native of Holland, removed to Holstein, and after living there a short time had the name changed to Voss. He was a farmer and drover, and followed these occupations until his death, which occurred when he was sixty years old.

John Voss, grandfather of Charles, was born in Holland. He also followed farming, and was one of the largest drovers in his vicinity. He had a large family of children, among them being Frederick, Henry, Horace, Andrew, and Louisa. He died at about sixty years of age. Frederick Voss, father of Charles, was also a farmer and cattle dealer. He shipped cattle from Denmark to England, doing an extensive business in that line; and he tilled the soil of a large farm successfully until he was about sixty years old, when he retired. He then removed to Altona, near the city of Hamburg, where he died at seventy-eight. He made three visits to his son Charles in America. His wife, Maria, was a native of Holstein, where her father, Adolph Retting, followed farming, and where he died at over seventy years of age. She was the mother of eleven children, nine of whom — namely, William, Edward, Charles, Mary, Ida, Andrew, Otto, Ernest, and Theodore — are still living, four residing in America. Mary the eldest sister, married Fred Koch; Ida married a Lieutenant in the German army; Otto resides in Florida; and Ernest is in Philadelphia. Theodore is a carpenter and builder in Phœnicia, N.Y. The others were Frederick and Dora. The mother died in 1896, being over eighty years old. The parents were members of the Lutheran church.

Charles Voss spent his early years in his native town, and acquired his education in private schools. After finishing his studies he learned the trade of a miller and a cabinetmaker. He began his three years' apprenticeship at the latter at the age of sixteen, and worked as a journeyman one year. In 1869 he came to America, sailing from Hamburg and landing in New York, where he at once secured employment in a bakery. He next went to Phœnicia, N.Y., and he was employed in the Chichester Chair Factory for one year. At the expiration of that time he went to Sullivan County, Pennsylvania, and was engaged for two seasons in peeling hemlock bark. Returning to Phœnicia, he spent another year in the chair factory, and passed the next in Germany. Upon his return to the United States in 1876, he attended the Centennial Exhibition in Philadelphia, and, remaining in that city the entire summer, he was employed as conductor on the Chestnut Street line of cars. Going to Delaware County, Pennsylvania, in the fall of that year, he worked on a farm, and also ran a milk route to Philadelphia, following this occupation for two years, when he sold out and returned to Phœnicia. He later became manager of the store owned by the Chichester Chair Company, which position he occupied for nine years. Removing to Hunter, he erected the hotel known as "The Belvidere," which has accommodations for one hundred and twenty-five guests. After conducting this hotel for eight years, he sold the property. Later he repurchased it, and still owns and rents it. He owns two dwelling-houses, one of which adjoins the hotel, and is used by him as a residence. In 1892 he rented the store formerly occupied by Jacob Fromer. This he conducted for five years, when he was obliged to make an assignment; but he soon settled with his creditors, and again started in business. The building he now occupies he erected in 1894 as an annex to his large establishment, and it was used for the hardware and plumbing departments. Upon the expiration of his lease of Mr. Fromer's property, he removed the annex to its present location, where he now carries groceries and notions. The post-office is located in his store; and on July 1, 1898, he received the appointment of Postmaster for four years.

In 1880 Mr. Voss was united in marriage with Jennie E. Haner, daughter of William M. Haner, of Prattsville. Her great-grandfather, Martin Haner, who was a native of Dutchess County, moved from there to Prattsville, and was a pioneer farmer. Her grandfather, also named Martin, went from Dutchess County to Prattsville, and settled upon a farm two miles from the village on the road to West Kill. He died at the age of seventy-five. He married for his first wife Elizabeth Shumaker. They had seven children, three of whom are living, namely: Lawrence, who married Judith Spencer; William M. Haner, Mrs. Voss's father; and Jemima A., who married Henry Palmer, of Gilboa. Mrs. Elizabeth S. Haner died at the age of fifty.

William M. Haner, after cultivating a farm in Prattsville some time, moved to the town of Roxbury, where he continued to till the soil until his retirement. He is still living, and is now seventy-six years old. His wife, Cornelia Maginnis, a native of Prattsville, is a daughter of Jacob and Jennie (Stanley) Maginnis. His family consisted of eight children, four of whom are living, namely: George Haner, M.D., who resides in Tannersville; Jennie E., who is now Mrs. Charles Voss; Homer, who resides in Omaha; and Clark R., a book-keeper in Tannersville. The mother attends the Methodist Episcopal church. Mrs. Voss was educated in the common schools of Prattsville and at Jewett Academy. She is the mother of three children — Ralph, Ethel Ann, and Mollie M. Ralph is attending the high school in Hunter, and Ethel Ann has attained the highest rank in her class at school the present year. Mollie M. Voss, now a student in the Hunter High School, is considered the champion girl trick bicycle rider in the State.

Mr. Voss is a Republican in politics, and has taken an active part in public affairs. He was Supervisor in 1892 and 1893. He was greatly interested in the incoporation of the village, and was Trustee in 1897 and President in 1898. He has been a member of Kingston Lodge, F. & A. M., for over twenty-five years; is a charter member of Catskill Chapter, Royal Arch Masons, and also belongs to the Royal Arcanum. The family attend the Congregational church as well as the Sunday-school, in which Mrs. Voss is a teacher.

IRA M. TERPENING, a skilful and progressive agriculturist of Fulton, N.Y., was born July 31, 1857, in the town of Knox, Albany County, a son of Henry H. Terpening. His paternal grandfather, Moses Terpening, was born and brought up in Esopus, Ulster County, N.Y., whence he removed to Albany County, where he settled on a farm in Knox, being one of its earlier pioneers. Subsequently, coming to Summit in Schoharie County, Moses Terpening was there engaged in general farming until his decease, at the advanced age of eighty-eight years. He married a Miss Snyder, and they reared ten children.

Henry H. Terpening was educated in the district schools, and, becoming a farmer from choice, he purchased land, when a young man, in Cortland County, where he pursued his independent calling a few years. Not being very well satisfied with his prospects there, he sold out and removed to Knox, in Albany County. Several years later he purchased the farm in Fulton that is now owned and occupied by his son, Ira M., and here passed his remaining days, dying August 10, 1897, at the venerable age of ninety-one years. A man of integrity, he was highly respected by all. In politics he was an adherent of the Republican party. He married Cornelia L., daughter of Jeremiah Havens, a lifelong farmer of Jefferson, N.Y. They reared four children, namely: Ira M., of Fulton; Eunice, wife of John Feeck; Bertha, the wife of Charles Mann, of whom a brief sketch appears elsewhere in this volume; and Henry J. Both parents were members of the Reformed church, in which the father was an Elder.

Ira M. Terpening obtained a practical education in the public schools of his native town, and from his earliest youth, when not in school, assisted in the labors of the home farm. On the death of his father he succeeded to the ownership of the homestead estate of one hundred and fifty acres, and he has since managed it with signal success. He carries on general farming, including stock-raising to some extent and dairying. In politics he is a sound Republican. He is a member of the Dutch Reformed church of Middleburg, and he and his family attend also the Sunday-school connected with that church.

On January 14, 1876, Mr. Terpening married Angeline Murphy, daughter of Peter Murphy, of Fulton, and grand-daughter of Timothy Murphy, the renowned Indian scout. Timothy Murphy, born in America, of Irish parents, was one of the pioneer settlers of this section of Schoharie County, and one of the largest landholders of Fulton, owning also large tracts of real estate in South Worcester and in other places along the Susquehanna. During the Revolutionary War he rendered inestimable assistance as one of the most brave and daring scouts. His exploits, which are well-known to all students of history, won for him the name of "Murphy, the Indian Killer." At Bemis Heights his gallant conduct turned the tide of affairs and gave to General Gates the victory. At the "Middle Fort," by his cool and decisive actions, and more especially by his refusal to obey the orders of a superior officer, he saved the Schoharie garrison from falling a prey to the Red-skins. After the war he resumed the pursuit of agriculture, and remained on his farm until his death, at the age of sixty-seven years. His first wife, Margaret Feeck, was born in Fulton, on Mr. Terpening's farm, and died in this town at the early age of forty years. She left five children, of whom Peter was the youngest.

Peter Murphy inherited the ancestral homestead in Fulton and two other farms in this vicinity. These three he carried on simultaneously, and for years was one of the largest and best-known agriculturists of Fulton, where he spent his long and useful life of fourscore and four years. He was deeply interested in the welfare of his native town, which he served as Supervisor two terms, and as Collector a number of years. His wife, Catherine Borst, was born on the old Borst farm in Schoharie, one of the nine children of Peter Borst, a prosperous farmer. Mr. and Mrs. Murphy reared seven children, as follows: Marian, deceased; Helen, wife of John Follick; Margaret, who married William Wearman; Betsey, wife of Thomas Follick; Ann; Kate; and Angeline, now Mrs. Terpening.

Mr. and Mrs. Terpening have one son, C. Frederick Terpening, M.D. He completed his early education in the graded schools of Middleburg, studied medicine for a year with Dr. Rifenberg, and then entered the University Medical College, New York City, class of 1898. After receiving his diploma, he entered the Blackwell's Isle Hospital, where he will graduate in 1900.

PARKE C. LEHMAN, of the firm of Lehman Brothers, dealers in general merchandise and farming implements at Argusville, in the town of Carlisle (formerly a part of Sharon), Schoharie County, N.Y., was born in this place on April 3, 1869, son of Sylvester and Mary Ann (Lane) Lehman.

His great-grandfather Lehman came to America with Burgoyne's army, having crossed the English channel with other Germans, and joined the British soldiery before leaving England. After arriving in this country he deserted from the army, and settled in Sharon, where he was one of the first white inhabitants. It is related that he wore a metal breastplate which he brought over with him, and that this at one time saved his life by protecting him from a bullet. He remained in Sharon as long as he lived, engaged in farming. He spoke only the German tongue.

His son Benjamin, grandfather of Parke C. Lehman, was born here, and always resided here until his death at the age of eighty years. Like his father he was closely identified with the Lutheran church. He worked at his trade of carpenter, and he also farmed to some extent. He settled at what is now known as the Lehman homestead, on which his grandson Charles now resides. This property contained originally three hundred and fifteen acres. Benjamin Lehman built most of the barns and houses in this vicinity. He underwent many hardships. While working at Stone Arabia, some thirteen miles distant, he would rise early in the morning on Monday, travel the whole distance on foot, and be on hand in time for his day's work. On Saturday night he walked home again. During his absences the farm was cared for by his sons, of whom there were four. Each of these upon being married was given a plot of land and a fair start in life. Benjamin Lehman had four wives. His sons were: Stephen, who is the only one now living, Charles, Peter, and Sylvester. Both Charles and Peter were married, and the latter had a family of children. Peter died in Brooklyn, N.Y. Benjamin Lehman spoke the German language and broken English.

Sylvester Lehman, father of Parke C., was a lifelong farmer on his hundred and seventy-five acres, raising mixed crops. He was also engaged to a considerable extent in stock-raising, breeding short-horned cattle, which farmers from all the neighboring towns came to purchase. He was an ardent worker in the church, and held at one time and another nearly all the church offices. Of his family of nine children, the eldest, Jay, died in infancy. The others were as follows: Mary, who is the wife of William Crosby, M.D., of Rochester, Ind.; Charles, above named, who resides on the Lehman homestead; Jessie, who died at

THOMAS E. FERRIER.

the age of twenty-six; Romaine, who is a farmer of Sharon, N.Y.; Sylvester, Jr., who is a member of the firm of Lehman Brothers; Parke, the subject of this article; Ford, who is a student in the classical course at Penn College, Gettysburg; and Bessie G. Sylvester Lehman, Jr., married Kate Allen, daughter of James Allen, of Root, N.Y. Bessie G. Lehman was married in December, 1897, to Lewis C. Berger, of Seward, N.Y.

Parke C. Lehman in his boyhood attended the district schools in company with his brothers and sisters, and subsequently worked out at farming. After saving a small amount of money he went to Albany, where he took a course in the business college. Subsequent to that he was clerk for four years for J. P. Milligan; and at the expiration of that time, or in September, 1893, he formed a partnership with his brother Sylvester, and bought out the business of Mr. Milligan. This firm has done a most prosperous business. Their's being the only general merchandise store in Argusville, they have a large trade, and, as their business methods are prompt and thoroughly honorable, they are popular, and have the fullest confidence of their patrons. Many changes have been made in the store since Lehman Brothers took possession of it.

Parke C. Lehman was appointed Postmaster on May 6, 1898. He had previously served as Deputy Postmaster. In politics he is a Republican. Both brothers are Masons and members of Sharon Springs Lodge, No. 624. Both are active in politics, and prominent in church work. Parke C. Lehman is secretary of the Sunday school and of the church council.

Parke C. Lehman married on June 16, 1898, Miss Lilah Wemple, of Fonda, N.Y., she being a daughter of one of the first families of Montgomery County.

THOMAS E. FERRIER, one of the representative business men of Catskill, was born in the town of Warwick, Orange County, N.Y., on April 15, 1821, son of Joseph and Hannah W. (Edsall) Ferrier. According to the best information obtainable his first progenitors in this country were French Huguenots, who during revolutionary or religious disturbances in France emigrated to Ireland and thence to America.

His great-grandfather was Thomas Ferrier, who was born in 1705, and died in 1792. This Thomas removed from Connecticut to Orange County, New York, settling near Amity. His wife, whose name in maidenhood was Hester Lucky, died in 1796. Their family consisted of three daughters and one son — Sarah, Hester, Jane, and Robert. Sarah married David Perkins, Hester married Benjamin Carpenter, and Jane became the wife of William Owens.

Robert Ferrier, who was the grandfather of Thomas E., and who succeeded to the possession of the homestead farm, was born in 1762, and died in 1822. He married Mary Wilcox, said to have been of German ancestry, who was born in 1764, and died in 1836. They had a family of ten children, namely: William, born in 1786, who died in 1873; Anna, born in 1788, who died in 1858; Joseph (father of the subject of this sketch), born in 1791, who died in 1871; Thomas, born in 1793, who died in 1839; David, who was born in 1795; Hester, born in 1798, who died in 1889; Elizabeth, who was born in 1800; Robert, born in 1802, who died in 1872; Michael J., who was born in 1805; and Sarah M., born in 1807, who died in 1821, at the age of fourteen years. William married Hannah Samons, and settled at Ypsilanti, Mich. Anna married Daniel Nanny, and settled in the town of Warwick, N.Y. Joseph married Hannah W. Edsall, and settled in the town of Warwick, N.Y. Thomas married Sarah Dennison, and settled on the Ferrier homestead. David married Eliza Cain, and settled first in Yates County, New York, whence he removed subsequently to Sunbury, Delaware County, Ohio. Hester became the wife of Samuel Conklin, and settled in Yates County, New York. Elizabeth married David Carr, and settled at Wautage, Sussex County, N.J. Robert married Emily Tobey, and settled at Dundee, Yates County, N.Y. Michael J. married Mary Ann Neighbor, and went to reside at Swartswood, Sussex County, N.J.

Joseph Ferrier, who was brought up to agricultural life, settled on a farm adjoining the homestead. His wife, in maidenhood Hannah W. Edsall, was of English ancestry. They reared the following children: John M., born in 1816, married Frances Coleman in 1841, and died in 1843 as the result of an accident. Sarah M., born in 1818, who married Matthew Bailey in 1840, after his death became the wife of James Thompson in 1862, died August 10, 1899. Thomas E., born in 1821, is the subject of this sketch. Louisa, born in 1824, married Cornelius J. Jones in 1845, and after his death married for her second husband William Walling. She died in 1858. Almira, born in 1827, married Cornelius J. Laziar in 1844, and is still living. Edsall, born in 1831, married Anna M. Hummel in 1859, and is now one of the faculty of Lafayette College at Easton, Pa. Robert, born in 1835, married Cecelia D. Jones, and died in 1877.

Thomas E. Ferrier when in his fifteenth year left home and went to Edenville, where he remained two and a half years, working in a country store. He then attended the district school for a year, after which he taught school for a year at Bellvale in the town of Warwick. Then, returning home, he was employed during the summer of 1840 on his father's farm. In the fall of that year he left home for a trip through the West with the view of gaining a knowledge of the country and of possibly finding a desirable place in which to settle. Railroads were few in those days; and much or most of his journey was made by steamboat, canal, or stage. Going to Newburg, he travelled by steamboat to Albany, and thence to Buffalo by way of the Erie Canal. After spending a day or two at Buffalo and Niagara Falls, he went by steamboat on Lake Erie to Cleveland, Ohio, and thence by canal to Columbus, Ohio. Then, after staying a few days with an uncle at Sunbury, he took the stage from Columbus to Dayton, and from there travelled by canal to Cincinnati. From that place he went by steamboat on the Ohio River to Louisville, Ky., where he stopped for a few days, and then went by boat down the Ohio to the Mississippi and up that river to St. Louis, Mo., in which city he remained for two weeks. From St. Louis he went on up the river to Quincy, Ill., and after looking about in that neighborhood for a week or two he took a school in Pike County, which he taught until the following spring. He then returned home by way of the Mississippi and Ohio Rivers to Pittsburg, and through Pennsylvania and New Jersey, partly by canal and partly by rail, to New York City, and thence to Newburg by boat, arriving home in April, 1841. He then resumed work on his father's farm, following that occupation during the summer and teaching school in the winter in the neighboring school districts. In 1845, when in his twenty-fifth year, he was married to Elizabeth, daughter of John W. and Dorothy Wheeler (Rogers) Vandererf, and settled on a farm of ninety acres, adjoining his father's, which had formerly formed a part of his grandfather's homestead. Here he followed an agricultural life for twenty years. Then, selling out, he removed to Catskill, N.Y., where, in company with his brother Robert, who had preceded him to that place by about five years, he engaged in the manufacture of brick. Shortly afterward they enlarged their sphere of operations by engaging in building in Brooklyn, N.Y., Robert removing to New York to look after their interests there, while Thomas remained at Catskill to superintend the manufacture and shipping of the bricks. After the great financial panic of 1873, which proved very disastrous to their building operations, Robert returned to Catskill in very poor health, and soon afterward died. Thomas, having previously purchased his brother's interest in the brickyard and other property, continued to carry on business alone until 1882, when he took his son-in-law, Percival Golden, into partnership; and the firm has since been conducted under the name of Ferrier & Golden. Mr. Ferrier has been a director of the Catskill National Bank for the last twenty years or more, and is now vice-president of that institution. He is president of the Catskill Building and Loan Association and treasurer of the Catskill Rural Cemetery Association. He is also largely interested in the Catskill Knitting Mill, owning a three-eighths interest, which concern, one of the largest and most important in the town, gives employment to from one hundred and fifty to one hundred and sixty hands.

Mr. Ferrier is a Republican in politics. In 1885 he was elected Supervisor of the town, and, being subsequently re-elected to the same office, served therein for five years. He also was elected County Treasurer, in which office he served three years, declining a renomination on account of advancing age, he being then in his seventy-fifth year. In religion a Presbyterian, he has been for a number of years a trustee and Elder of the church of that denomination in Catskill. His reputation is that of a business man of more than average ability and of the strictest integrity, and also that of a citizen who has rendered useful service to the town and whose aid and influence can always be counted upon in favor of any practical measures for the moral or physical betterment of the community.

Mr. and Mrs. Ferrier have been the parents of three children, namely: Hannah Elizabeth, born in May, 1849, who married in 1872 Hiram W. Lane, and has one child, Herbert A. Lane, born in 1870; Willis Wentworth, born in October, 1850, who died in 1871, as the result of an accident; and Mary Wheeler, born in 1854, who married Percival Golden in 1875, and has had four children — Lizzie F. Golden, born in 1876, who died in 1885, Willis P. Golden, born in 1882, May Marshall and Mabel French Golden, twins, born in 1887.

NOAH DIBBLE WEST, a well-known apiarist of Middleburg, N. Y., is one of the largest honey producers of Schoharie County and with but two exceptions the largest in the entire State, if not in the Union. He was born March 5, 1845, in the neighboring town of Gilboa, the birthplace of his father, David West, Jr. His great-grandfather West, who came, it is believed from England, was one of the original settlers of Gilboa, whither he removed from Connecticut in Colonial times, coming here when the country was a wooded wilderness and rearing the small log cabin in which he and his family first found shelter.

David West, Sr., the grandfather of Noah D., spent the larger part of his threescore and ten years in Gilboa, where he was one of the leading farmers and a citizen of influence. Possessing considerable legal knowledge, he transacted law business to some extent for his neighbors, by whom he was highly esteemed. At his death he left his widow, whose maiden name was Rachel Ward, with four children — Orman West, Julia Ann, David, and William. She subsequently married again, and by her second husband, George Hughson, had four sons — John C., George, Cephas, and Robert. John C. Hughson left home at the early age of sixteen years, and after working out for a few years he became interested in the lumber business. He died a millionaire.

David West, Jr., was born September 27, 1813, and died June 12, 1883. He was reared on a farm, and was engaged in agricultural pursuits to a greater or less extent during his entire life. Having a natural aptitude for mechanics, he also worked at the carpenter's trade in his early manhood. Purchasing a tract of woodland, he cleared a space, on which he built his first dwelling, and in a few years he erected a fine set of other frame buildings. Thereafter he attended to the cultivation of his land until his death, at the age of sixty-nine.

He married March 20, 1840, Celinda Dibble, daughter of Noah and Abigail (Crippen) Dibble. Her paternal grandparents were Daniel and Lois (Pomeroy) Dibble, the grandmother the daughter of Daniel Pomeroy, a Revolutionary soldier. The parents of Celinda Dibble had ten children, three of whom survive, namely: Jane, born in 1820; Abigail, born in 1822; and Amanda, born in

1826. Noah Dibble, who served as a soldier of the War of 1812, was a carpenter in Middleburg, and well known throughout this section as a builder of saw-mills, which he made a specialty. He died at the age of seventy-six years. Mrs. Abigail Dibble died on September 12, 1869, aged seventy-nine years, six months, and nine days. In religion she was a Baptist. David West, Jr., and his wife, Celinda, were also members of the Baptist church. Of their union but one child was born, Noah D., the special subject of this biography. The mother was born on February 23, 1817, and died May 17, 1893, at the age of seventy-six years.

As mentioned above, Daniel Pomeroy, her grandmother Dibble's father, great-great-grandfather of the subject of this sketch, was a soldier of the American Revolution. He was under Washington, and it is related that the General on parting gave him his cane as a keepsake. This cane Daniel Pomeroy gave to his daughter Lois (Mrs. Daniel Dibble), with the request that she should hand it down to her eldest son, Noah Dibble, to be always kept in the Dibble family, held by the eldest son of each succeeding generation. From Noah Dibble the Washington cane passed to his eldest son, Ichabod Dibble, brother of Celinda; from Ichabod to his eldest son, Sylvester; and at the death of Sylvester, leaving no son, it came into the possession of his brother, Jesse Dibble, its present owner, who is a cousin of Noah Dibble West, the special subject of the present biography.

Noah D. West grew to manhood on the home farm in Gilboa. At the age of twenty he commenced teaching school, and he was thus employed in his native town for ten terms. He also assisted in the management of the home farm until attaining his majority, when he took possession of a few of its acres, and turned his attention to the culture of bees, an industry in which he had been interested from boyhood. Ten years later he bought his present farm of ten acres, located two miles from the village of Middleburg, on the road to Catskill. Here he has continued his chosen work, from year to year enlarging his operations.

After his parents' death he came into full possession of the old farm of one hundred twenty acres, formerly owned by himself and father together; and since the death of his father he has bought and now owns three adjoining farms, including in all four hundred acres. All this land, then covered by a dense forest, was once the property of his grandfather, David West.

In his five bee yards Mr. West has five hundred swarms of bees, which produce annually from eight to ten tons of honey. This he sells in the leading cities of New York and New England at the highest market price. He has made a special study throughout his life of bees and their habits, and in his efforts to obtain the best results from bee-keeping at the least possible cost he has invented and patented a spiral wire queen-cell protector and a spiral wire queen-cage, which have proved of great value. Although these inventions have been before the public but a little more than seven years, they are in demand throughout the United States, in Canada, in England — in fact, in all parts of the world; and he is carrying on a very substantial business as the sole manufacturer of these articles. For three successive years he was chosen, and paid, to act as judge on the different races of bees and of honey, bee appliances and bee literature, at the New England fairs held at Albany, on which occasions a large variety of apiarian goods was displayed and large premiums awarded. On July 11, 1899, he received the appointment of bee inspector for the State of New York.

He is a Republican and a Prohibitionist in politics and an active member of the Methodist Episcopal church, in which he has been class leader, a teacher, and the superintendent of its Sunday-school.

Mr. West married June 23, 1867, Sarah A. Haskin. She is a daughter of Joshua Haskin and a grand-daughter of Moses and Hanah (Hait) Haskin, natives of Dutchess County. Her grandparents were pioneer settlers of Broome, N.Y. They reared fifteen children, one of whom is yet living, Joshua. The grandmother was a Quaker in her religious belief. Joshua Haskin was engaged in farming in Broome until 1871, when he removed to the town of Maine, Broome County, where he has a fine farm of one hundred acres. Formerly a Democrat in politics, he has been identified with the Republican party since the Rebellion. He has served as Assessor and as Overseer of the Poor. He married Deborah A. Hughson, daughter of Nicholas and Charlotte (Duncan) Hughson, formerly of Broome, but later of Norwich, Chenango County. Mr. and Mrs. Hughson had ten children, of whom four are living, namely: Deborah A., now Mrs. Haskin; Hiram Hughson; Jane, wife of John DeMoney; and Charlotte, wife of Charles M. Markel. Of the seven children born to Joshua Haskin and his wife these five are living: Sarah A., now Mrs. West; Edwin S.; Grosvenor; Alice E., wife of Dr. Dudley; and Hiram A. All except Mrs. West reside in Broome County, and all, with their parents, are members of the Methodist Episcopal church.

Mr. and Mrs. West have eight children; namely, Orman, Ruth A., Edwin H., Elma A., David J., Alice C., Charles D., and Hattie D. The four younger are still in school. Orman M., a graduate of Middleburgh Academy and Union College, was formerly a school teacher, was graduated at the Drew Theological Seminary, and is now preaching in Port Colden, N.J. He married Dora Dorman, and they have one son, Dorman. Ruth married Delos H. Gridley, formerly a teacher, farmer, and bee-keeper, later a student at Drew Theological Seminary, now preaching at Speedsville, N.Y. They have one son, Vernon J. Mrs. Gridley was vice-president of the Women's Christian Temperance Union at Madison, N.J. Edwin H. West married Sophia M. Shafer. He was in his earlier years a farmer, interested in bee culture, also a teacher; and after his graduation from the Middleburg High School he was for a time a clerk in Schenectady, a position which he resigned to become a member of the police force in New York City. Elma A., formerly a teacher in the public schools, is the wife of Elmer B. Wood, of Broome, and has one son, Howard C. Mrs. West is a member of the W. C. T. U.; and she and all of her children are active members of the Methodist Episcopal church and of the Sunday-school, in which all the elder children have been teachers.

JOHN M. CONOVER, a descendant of an old Dutch family of repute and a representative farmer of Duanesburg, Schenectady County, N.Y., was born in Glen, Montgomery County, this State, December 26, 1839, son of George W. and Sarah M. (Radley) Conover. The father was born in Florida, N.Y., in 1812, and the mother was born in the same town in 1818. The name was originally Van Couwenhoven, and was shortened to its present form prior to the birth of the great-grandfather of the subject of this sketch. Its bearers were prominent among the early Dutch families, and contemporaneous with the Van Rensselaers, Van Beekmans, and other Knickerbockers. The immigrant progenitor was one Wolfret Garretson Van Couwenhoven, who came from Amersfoort, in the province of Utrecht, in 1630, and settled in Rensselaerwyck. He was employed by the Van Rensselaers as superintendent of farms for six years; and in June, 1636, he with others purchased a large tract of land at the western end of Long Island. His sons were: Gerrit, Jacob, Derrick, Peter, and John.

Cornelius V. Couwenhoven, the great-great-grandfather of Mr. Conover of Duanesburg, was born in 1710, and died in 1804. He had seven children; namely, John, William, Peter, Jacob, Jane, Abraham, and Isaac, the great-grandfather. Isaac Conover was born February 11, 1759. He served as a soldier in the Continental army during the Revolutionary War, and died September 21, 1845, leaving several children, among others Marcus, the grandfather, who was born in New Jersey, October 11, 1786. Marcus Conover was an early settler in Florida, N.Y., where he engaged in farming, and was a leading resident of that town. His last days were spent in Illinois, and he died in June, 1844. He married Sarah L. Schuyler, who was born February 19, 1794, and died in June, 1845.

George W. Conover, son of Marcus, was reared in Florida, N.Y., and received his business training as clerk for his uncle, John J. Schulyer. Later he was admitted to partnership, and for several years the firm carried on a general store in Amsterdam, N.Y. Relinquishing business on account of failing health, he took a protracted journey by team with Funis I. Van Derveer, through Pennsylvania, Ohio, Indiana, and Illinois, passing through Chicago when it was but a village, and driving as far West as the Mississippi River. He returned to his native State in the same manner, much benefitted in health, and, resuming mercantile business in Auriesville, Montgomery County, he remained there until 1850. Selling his store, he invested in real estate both in this State and the West, and, purchasing in 1859 the farm in Duanesburg, which his son now owns, he devoted the rest of his active period to agricultural pursuits. In politics he originally acted with the Whigs, and with the majority of that element he went into the ranks of the Republican party at its formation. George W. Conover died in 1894. On March 13, 1839, he married Sarah M. Radley, daughter of John P. and Anna (Clayton) Radley, of Florida, N.Y. Her grandfather, Philip Radley, was an early settler in that town, and he lived to reach a good old age. The Radley farm was inherited by John P. Radley, who occupied it until his death, which occurred November 27, 1862, his wife having died March 22, 1855. Mrs. Sarah Conover is still living, and resides at the homestead near the Scotch church. She reared but one son, John M., the subject of this sketch.

John M. Conover was reared and educated in Glen. At the age of twenty-one he became associated with his father in carrying on the home farm, and after his father's death the farm fell to his possession. It is one of the best pieces of agricultural property in the neighborhood. He grows all kinds of grain, cuts a large quantity of hay annually, raises some excellent cattle and horses, and displays good judgment in all his undertakings. His residence and outbuildings are exceedingly desirable.

On October 5, 1864, Mr. Conover married for his first wife Anna B. Van Vechten, who was born in Florida, N.Y., December 6, 1845. She died March 12, 1884, leaving three children, namely: Archie R., born September 23, 1866; Mabel, born May 13, 1874; and Edna, born May 20, 1877. Archie R. Conover, who was graduated from Union College in 1889, is now a lawyer in Amsterdam. He married Jessie Dougall, and has one daughter, Marion. Mabel is the wife of the Rev. F. W. McKee, pastor of the historic Scotch (or United Presbyterian) Church, Florida, N.Y.; and Edna is unmarried. On March 25, 1890, Mr. Conover married for his second wife Mary E. Smeallie, who was born in Princetown, N.Y., February 19, 1846, daughter of John and Jane (Milmine) Smeallie, the former of whom was a native of that place. Both parents were born in 1816.

Politically, Mr. Conover is a Republican. He has inherited many of the sterling characteristics of his race, whose thrifty and industrious habits made possible the development of the vast resources and wealth for which the Empire State has long been noted, and he has every reason to be proud of his origin. He is a member of the United Presbyterian Church of Florida, N.Y.

THOMAS J. KILMER, M.D., the well-known physician of Schoharie, N.Y., was born in Cobleskill, this county, November 22, 1833, son of Daniel and Maria (Shaffer) Kilmer. He is of German extraction, and a representative of the third generation of his family in this country, being the grandson of John I. Kilmer, a native of Germany, who settled in Cobleskill as a pioneer.

John I. Kilmer acquired a tract of land con-

taining five hundred acres, a considerable portion of which he cleared for agricultural purposes. Commencing his farm life in a log house, he later built a frame dwelling near the village of Barnerville; and through energy and perseverance he became one of the most prosperous farmers of Schoharie County in his day. Possessing intellectual powers of a high order, which had been developed by a good education, he became the owner of a large library, and fostered his desire for knowledge by continued reading. Being of a religious turn of mind, he united with the Lutheran church, and for years was one of its most active members. He lived to be ninety years old. He had a family of six children.

Daniel Kilmer, the Doctor's father, was a lifelong resident of Cobleskill; and, succeeding to the ownership of some three hundred acres of the homestead property, he became successful as a general farmer. He was progressive as well as energetic, and not only kept up with the times in the way of agricultural improvements, but aided in developing his neighborhood by the erection of buildings. His ability and sound judgment necessarily made him an influential factor in public affairs, and he rendered efficient service to the town as Supervisor for some time. He died at the age of fifty years. His wife, Maria, was a daughter of John I. Shaffer, who at one time owned the land which is now occupied by the village of Cobleskill. She became the mother of thirteen children, of whom eleven are living, namely: Augustus; Josiah; Margaret, wife of Elijah Griffin; Daniel A.;

Thomas J., the subject of this sketch; Andrew G.; Sylvester A.; Chauncey C.; Jonas M.; Aurelia, who married Napoleon Palmatier; and Delia, wife of David I. Boock — all of whom reside in this State. Mrs. Maria S. Kilmer lived to be eighty-three years old. The parents were members of the Lutheran church.

Thomas J. Kilmer acquired a common-school education in his native town, and subsequently taught two terms of school in Cobleskill. He assisted in carrying on the home farm for a time prior to entering upon his medical studies, which were begun at Port Crane under his brother's direction. He was graduated from the Eclectic Medical College, New York City, in 1874, and was afterward associated with his brother some seven years, at the expiration of which he came to Schoharie, where he practised successfully until 1888. Establishing the Kilmer Sanitarium, he continued in charge of that institution until failing health caused him to withdraw from its management in 1893. His success at the sanitarium, where patients are received from every part of the State, has given him a wide reputation as a skilful physician. Besides attending to his private practice, which is the largest in town, he prepares several effective remedies which have a large sale.

In 1854 Dr. Kilmer was united in marriage with Elmina Palmitier, a native of this town, daughter of John H. Palmitier. Dr. and Mrs. Kilmer have had four children — Josiah, Ira P., Julia S., and Herbert. The last-named is no longer living. Josiah and Julia S. reside at home with their parents. Ira P. married Joan Nethaway, and has two children — Stratton and Mina. Herbert, who was a railroad man, left a widow and four children — Ardah, Noah, Josiah, and Herbert.

Dr. Kilmer is a member of the Schoharie and Delaware County Eclectic Medical Society, of which for three years he has been a censor. He likewise belongs to the Masonic order. He was formerly a Deacon and a class leader of the Methodist Episcopal church at Port Crane, and the family are members of the same religious denomination in Schoharie.

HAMAN P. PETTINGILL, of the firm of Malcolm & Co., woollen manufacturers, Catskill, N.Y., was born in Florida, Montgomery County, this State, on September 25, 1847, his parents being David and Jeannette (McNee) Pettingill. His father's family is of English descent.

David Pettingill, who was born and reared in the Mohawk Valley, was one of the original promoters of the Erie Canal, and rode on the first boat that passed over the waters of the canal after its completion. He carried on farming to some extent, and also was engaged in mercantile business in Amsterdam. He spent his last years in Amsterdam, his death occurring there at the age of seventy-three. His wife, Jeannette, was one of a family of ten children. She was born in Schenectady County, this State. Her father, James McNee, was a native of Glasgow, Scotland. Immigrating to this country, he lived for a time in Schenectady County, and later in Montgomery County. He died in Montgomery County at eighty-eight years of age. His wife, whose maiden name was Maxwell, was of Scottish descent. David and Jeannette (McNee) Pettingill had eight children, namely: Agnes; Mary A., who is now Mrs. Millmine; William; Peter; Ella, who is now Mrs. Hagerman; Haman; Louisa, now Mrs. Millmine; and Anna. The mother of these children died at the age of sixty-three. Both she and her husband were members of the Presbyterian church.

Haman Pettingill attended the public schools until he was eighteen years of age, when he began learning the machinist's trade. He subsequently worked at his trade as a journeyman in Amsterdam, and later in West Albany at the locomotive works, and after that was seven years a knitter in the knitting-mill at Amsterdam. In 1882 he became a partner of Joseph Malcolm, a sketch of whom may be found in this work. The two men carried on a woollen-mill in Amsterdam for a time, and then removed to Catskill, the present company being formed. Mr. Pettingill has charge of the machinery, which has all the latest improvements. The firm manufacture men's, women's, and children's underwear, every piece produced bearing their special trademark. This mark is known to all experienced buyers as belonging only to a good class of garments. About a hundred and seventy hands are employed.

Mr. Pettingill has been twice married. The maiden name of his first wife, who was

STEPHEN L. MAHAM.

born in New York, was Margaret Morehead. They were married in 1877, and she died at the age of thirty-one. His present wife, whose maiden name was Isabel Lusk, was born in Coxsackie, being the daughter of Gilbert and Elizabeth Lusk. Mr. Lusk was for many years one of the well-known merchants of Coxsackie, and later of Catskill. Of the second union one child has been born, Charlotte.

Mr. Pettingill is a member of Catskill Lodge of Masons, No. 468. In politics he is a Republican. He is a member and trustee of the Presbyterian church, and Mrs. Pettingill is a communicant of the Episcopal church.

HON. STEPHEN L. MAYHAM, of Schoharie, former Presiding Justice of the Supreme Court, General Term, Third Department, and an ex-member of Congress, was born in Blenheim, N.Y., October 8, 1826, son of John and Betsey (Ferguson) Mayham. He represents the third generation of the family founded by his grandfather, Henry Mayham, who emigrated from Ireland in 1790.

Acquiring a tract of four hundred acres of wild land, which embraced the site now occupied by West Troy, N.Y., and the Watervliet Arsenal, Henry Mayham cleared a portion for agricultural purposes and sold the remainder. He died at the age of ninety-three. His wife's family name was Welch.

John Mayham, son of Henry, was a native of West Troy. Locating in Blenheim when a young man, he spent the rest of his life as a prosperous farmer, his death occurring at the age of sixty-five years. He took an active interest in political and religious matters, without aspiring to office, although he consented to serve as Supervisor, and faithfully performed the duties of that office for several terms. He was highly respected by the entire community. His intellectual attainments enabled him as a public speaker forcibly to discuss the important issues of the day. He married Betsey Ferguson, daughter of John Ferguson. Her father was a native of Scotland. Coming to this country, he settled at Pine Plains and later removed to Delaware County, where he died at an advanced age. John Mayham and his wife were the parents of twelve children, eleven of whom, seven sons and four daughters, grew to maturity. Five sons became professional men. Thomas Mayham, M.D., is now Mayor of Fond du Lac, Wis.; another son, who was a physician, died in that State; a third was County Judge of Fond du Lac, and is no longer living; Stephen L. is the subject of this sketch; and the youngest son, Banks, who became a noted lawyer in Southern Illinois, died suddenly at Murphysboro, Ill. The mother lived to be sixty years old.

Stephen L. Mayham grew to manhood in Blenheim. As a youth he assisted in cultivating the home farm when not pursuing his studies, and a local biographer has fittingly said that his education was acquired with a book in one hand and a plough-handle in the other. At the age of eighteen he started in life as a district school teacher. Two years later he entered the law office of Samuel Jackson, who at that time was located in Gilboa, and afterward became Justice of the Supreme Court for the Fourth Judicial District. His legal preparations were completed in the office of Love & Freer, Ithaca, N.Y.; and after his admission to the bar, in 1848, he began the practice of his profession in Blenheim. His ability as counsellor and attorney rapidly asserted itself, with the result that he soon found himself in control of a large general law business. His many qualifications, not the least among which was his personal popularity, made him especially eligible to public office; and he was not long permitted by his fellow-townsmen to devote his whole time to his private affairs.

He served as Superintendent of Schools two years and as Supervisor three years; was elected District Attorney in 1859 by a large majority, and held office two years. In the fall of 1862 he was elected to the Assembly. In 1866 he accepted as a forlorn hope the Democratic nomination for State Senator from the Fifteenth District, comprising the counties of Schenectady, Schoharie, and Delaware; and, although realizing his expected defeat, he had the satisfaction of reducing the Republican majority. In 1868 he was elected to the Forty-first Congress in the Congressional district comprising Albany and Schoharie Counties, and in 1878 was elected Representative to the Forty-fifth Congress from the Thirteenth District, including the counties of Schoharie, Greene, and Ulster. During his first term he served upon the Committees on Private Land Claims and the Expenditures of the State and Post-office Departments. In the Forty-fifth Congress he was assigned to the Committees on the District of Columbia and State Department Expenditures, and was chairman of the Subcommittee on Ways and Means. His committee work in both sessions was laborious and efficient, and his record in the national House of Representatives was irreproachable. In 1883 he was elected County Judge and Surrogate of Schoharie County, a position which he held until appointed by Governor Hill to a seat upon the Supreme Bench; and in November, 1887, the people ratified the Governor's choice by electing him for a full term. His decisions, which are carefully conceived, have been in perfect accord with legal requirements and generally sustained by the Court of Appeals.

Since 1862 the Judge has resided in Schoharie. He was president of the Board of Public Education for eight years, and was the first president of the Schoharie Valley Railroad Company. Judge Mayham's scholarly attainments and ability as a public speaker have added much to his popularity, which extends far beyond the limits of his own county. Since his retirement from the bench he has been associated with his son Claude at Schoharie in the active practice of his profession, and is often called upon to act as referee in important cases, his judicial experience having eminently qualified him for such position.

Judge Mayham married Julia Martin, a grand-daughter of General Freegift Patchin, who served in the Continental Army during the Revolutionary War. Mrs. Mayham died in 1895, aged sixty-four years. She was the mother of three sons, F. Matt, Don S., Claude B., and one daughter, Ida L., who is now the wife of George Manschaffer, of this town. F. Matt Mayham was a prominent lawyer. He died in Schoharie in 1889, aged thirty-nine years. Don S. Mayham studied law with his father; and, after serving for a time as clerk of the Surrogate Court, he entered the Albany Law School, from which he was graduated in 1888. He was admitted to the bar the same year, and practised with his elder brother until the latter's decease, when he entered into partnership with his younger brother. He was a Democrat in politics, and served as clerk of the State Senate in 1892. He married Mary B. Borst, daughter of Thomas Borst and grand-daughter of Ralph Brewster, a prominent lawyer of this locality in his day. Dying in June, 1896, at the age of thirty-three years, Don S. Mayham left one son, Stephen L. Mayham, second. Claude B. Mayham was born in Schoharie in 1868. His early education was completed at the Schoharie Academy, where he taught for two years, and began the study of law with his brother. He was graduated from Columbia College in the class of 1891, with the degrees of Bachelor of Laws and Bachelor of Philosophy, and was associated with Don S. Mayham until 1896. For a short time he was in partnership with Lyman S. Holmes, of Cobleskill, in Schoharie. While in college he was an all-round athlete and captain of the baseball team. He was also president of the leading literary society and a member of the Delta Upsilon fraternity, and he sang in the Glee Club. He takes a leading part in the literary and musical matters in Schoharie, and is one of the most popular young men in town.

ISRAEL P. UTTER, a leading farmer and representative citizen of Oak Hill, Greene County, was born in this town, on a farm near his present residence, on the second day of December, 1829. He is a son of Bani Utter, and grandson of James, the ancestor of the Utter family of this county.

James Utter was born in the State of Connecticut. He came among the early settlers to this section of New York, took up land, and built a log cabin, in which he lived for a number of years. Shortly before his removal from Connecticut, he had served in the Continental army in the Revolution. His wife, whose name was Hannah, was born in Spencer, Conn. She came on horseback through the wilds, he walking beside her. Of the eight children born to her, none are living. She died at the advanced age of ninety-five, and her husband died at the age of ninety-three. Both were lifelong Presbyterians.

Bani Utter, above named, was born in Oak Hill, not far from where his son now lives, and spent his whole life here. He helped his father build a saw-mill. This mill was carried away by rising waters, and he subsequently built another, which he operated for many years. He engaged in farming on the farm where he was born, and he helped to build the old Utter house, which, previous to its destruction by fire in 1894, was one of the landmarks of the place. Bani Utter died in the old house at the age of seventy-four. His wife, whose maiden name was Cynthia Stannard, was the daughter of Eliakim Stannard, who was a pioneer settler in Durham, N.Y., coming from Connecticut. She died at seventy-eight years of age. Of her ten children, Alfred, Ruth, and Lyman are deceased. Alfred was a soldier in the Civil War, and lost his life while in service. The living children are: Julia, now Mrs. Whitmore; Israel; Louisa, now Mrs. Taylor; Almeran; Eliakim; Adelaide; and Addison. Both parents were Methodists.

Israel Utter in his boyhood attended the common schools of his native town, and when not occupied with his lessons helped his father on the farm. Later he worked on the farm on shares for a time, but eventually he purchased the farm adjoining the one where he now lives. After having operated that successfully for a number of years, he bought his present place and built his handsome residence and the other buildings. All these are thoroughly well built, and the barns and outbuildings are thoroughly equipped for carrying on farming in accordance with the latest and most approved methods. Mr. Utter now owns the two farms, embracing about two hundred and sixty acres. He devotes his time chiefly to dairying, making butter for the New York markets.

Mr. Utter's marriage took place in 1855, his wife being Caroline, the daughter of Jacob and Hannah (Niles) Tompkins. Mr. Tompkins spent his life on a farm in this town, and died here at the age of sixty-four. He and his wife were prominent members of the Methodist church, and he held numerous official positions in the church. Mrs. Tompkins, who was born in Coeymans, N.Y., lived to be ninety-three years of age. Of the children born to her, the following-named are living: Mary, who married Rufus Gifford; Ann, who married James Gifford; William, who is in California; Sarah, who married Alexander Lounsbury; Mrs. Utter, who was born on June 12, 1834; Libby, the wife of Philo Wicks; and Niles Tompkins, who resides on the Tompkins farm.

Mr. and Mrs. Utter have had two children, one of whom died in infancy. Their daughter Alice married Elwin Haskins, only son of farmer Henry Haskins of this town. She has five children — Dora, Utter, Henry, Edison, and Paul — all of them being now in school.

In politics Mr. Utter is a Republican, as was his father before him. He takes not only a warm interest, but an active part in all matters pertaining to the welfare of the town. For nine years he was an Assessor, being three times re-elected, and for one year he was chairman of the Board. In 1881 and 1882 he was Supervisor of the town. For thirty-five years he has been a member of the Methodist church, and for the past thirty years he has been one of its trustees, a steward, and class leader. The Sunday-school has always had his warm and earnest support, and he has been both teacher and superintendent. His wife and daughter have also been workers in both church and Sunday-school, and the latter has sung in the choir and played the organ. Mr. Utter is one of the most esteemed citizens of his town.

JAMES S. STALEY, a prosperous farmer of Sharon Springs, was born in Florida, N.Y., March 20, 1825, son of Henry I. and Sarah B. (McDonald) Staley. His maternal ancestors were Irish Protestants, and his mother came to America when she was four years old. The Staleys are of Dutch origin, and the name was originally spelled Stael. The first Stael, or Staley, in America, settled in Florida, when that section of the State was mostly a wilderness, and he resided there for the rest of his life. His wife's people, who came from Germany to New Jersey, sold her for a sum sufficient to pay for their passage over, and he worked to purchase her freedom.

Jacob Staley, James S. Staley's grandfather, was a lifelong resident of Florida, and followed general farming during his active years. He had a family of six children, including Henry, Valentine, Oliver, Betsey, and two other daughters. Betsey became Mrs. Blood. Valentine and Henry succeeded to the ownership of the homestead, which contained about two hundred acres. Valentine afterward moved to Genesee, N.Y. Both the grandparents and great-grandparents were members of the Dutch Reformed church.

Henry I. Staley, James S. Staley's father, was reared at the homestead in Florida. Purchasing his brother's interest, he cultivated the property for a number of years. Selling to his brother-in-law, Mr. Blood, and coming to Sharon Springs in 1833, he bought the J. Cady farm of one hundred and fifty acres, which he occupied until his death. He was a well-known stock-raiser, owned good horses, and was noted as an excellent judge of these animals. In politics he was a Democrat. Henry I. Staley died in 1870. He was the father of ten children; namely, Jacob, Valentine, Fanny, Ann Eliza, William H., John, James S., Robert, Sarah, and Alexander. Fanny, William H., John, Robert, and Sarah are no longer living. Valentine resides at Sharon Springs; Alexander occupies the homestead; Ann Eliza is the widow of William Othman, late of Cobleskill, N.Y.; and Sarah was the wife of Peter Spraker.

James S. Staley was fitted for college at the Ames Academy, but was prevented from pursuing a classical course by an accident which seriously affected his eyesight. He was however, enabled to turn his attention to educational pursuits, and after teaching in the district schools of this locality for twelve years he went to New York City, where for four years he had full charge of Leake and Watts Orphans' School, having the aid of three assistants. That position he was forced to resign in order to undergo treatment for his eyes. Having spent nine months under the care of a skilful specialist, he returned to Sharon Springs. He continued to teach school until 1858, when he purchased the Hunt farm, which contains about ninety acres and was formerly a part of his brother Valentine's property. He was at one time quite extensively engaged in raising hops, but now devotes his attention to general and dairy farming and fruit-growing. He acquired considerable prominence in public affairs during his younger days, serving as Superintendent of Schools three years, Commissioner of Highways two terms, Railroad Commissioner three years, and Supervisor one year.

Mr. Staley married Ann E. Hodge, of the town of Canajoharie, daughter of Isaac G. Hodge. Her father was formerly a well-known figure in public affairs, and a leading member of the Methodist church, which he helped to organize. His family consisted of four sons and seven daughters. The daughters were all graduated from the Ames Academy and qualified to teach. Mrs. Staley taught school for some years before marriage. Mr. and Mrs. Staley have one son, George E. He married Minnie Snyder, daughter of Nathan Snyder, and has two children — Earl and May.

Mr. Staley belonged to a lodge of Odd Fellows that disbanded many years ago, and he has never joined another. He is a member of the Methodist Episcopal church, in which he has served as steward, class leader, and in other capacities. He is now a trustee, and superintendent of the Sunday-school, and a well-known worker in the cause of religion, temperance, and morality.

WILLIAM SALSBERGH, a prosperous agriculturist of Hyndsville, in the town of Seward, Schoharie County, was born in Wright, N.Y., October 22, 1835, in the same house in which his father, the late Philip Salsbergh, first opened his eyes to the light of this world. He is of German ancestry, being a great-grandson of Jacob Salsbergh, who emigrated from Germany to this country when a young man.

Jacob Salsbergh located in the town of Wright as one of its original settlers, and took up a homestead of three hundred acres. At the time he reared his log cabin in the little opening which he first made in the forest, there were no paths excepting the Indian trails, and the redskins and the wild beasts were his only companions. His wife, Winney, who lived to the remarkable age of one hundred and one years, was born in Germany, where she spent the first sixteen years of her life. She came to America then, poor in pocket, and for six years after her arrival in Fishkill, N.Y., worked to pay for her passage across the ocean.

John Salsbergh, the grandfather of William, was born in the little log house in the town of Wright in which his parents made their home, and on attaining his majority was given possession of a portion of the original farm. He there carried on agricultural pursuits until well advanced in years, when he came to Seward, where he died at the ripe old age of eighty-four. His wife, Margaret Sternbergh, died at the age of fourscore years. Both were members of the Reformed church.

Their son, Philip Salsbergh, was one of a family of eleven children, all of whom were brought up on the home farm, and educated in the district school. He inherited a portion of the estate, and was engaged in tilling the soil until 1840, when he removed to Seward, and, buying a farm, continued his chosen vocation until his death, at the age of eighty-five years. He was held in high respect as a man and a citizen, and was particularly active in management of the affairs of the Reformed church, in which he held all the offices. He married Catherine Woolford. Of the ten children born into their household, eight are now living, as follows: Margaret, widow of Gilbert Shank; Rebecca W., wife of Ira Frazier; John T.; Catherine M., widow of Christian Markley; William, the subject of this brief sketch; Allen; Jemima, wife of Harlem Southworth; and Amanda, wife of John Markley. The mother passed to the life immortal at the age of seventy-eight years.

William Salsbergh received a common-school education, and until his marriage worked on his father's farm. He then bought his present farm of eighty-seven acres. By dint of persevering labor and the exercise of good judgment he has made of it one of the finest-improved estates in this locality. The farm buildings are substantial and well adapted to the purposes for which they were erected. He carries on general farming with profitable results, each season raising good crops of hay and hops. At the Schoharie County Fair he has taken premiums for his exhibits. In politics he is a steadfast Republican. He is interested in all enterprises tending to benefit the town or county, but has never been an aspirant for public office. He is a liberal supporter of the Methodist Episcopal church, of which he has been an active member for years, and has served faithfully as trustee and class leader. He has also been identified with its Sunday-school, of which he has been superintendent a number of terms.

On July 2, 1856, Mr. Salsbergh married Emeline Van Tyle, who was born in Seward, one of the five children of Daniel R. and Hannah (Guernsey) Van Tyle, her father a prominent farmer, one of the most highly esteemed citizens of Richmondville. Mr. and Mrs. Salsbergh have one child, a daughter Elva. She is married to Luther Brumaguem, and has four children -- Stewart, Arthur, Ernest, and Floyd. By a former marriage to Lawyer O. Strander, Mrs. Elva Brumaguem has a son William. He has been adopted by his grandfather Salsbergh, and is now known as William Salsbergh, Jr.

MICHAEL O'HARA, farmer and boarding-house keeper at Tannersville, N.Y., was born at Croton Landing, town of White Plains, Westchester County, N.Y., February 7, 1850. His parents were John and Julia (Travers) O'Hara, his father a native of West Meath County, Ireland, and his mother of Queen's County. His grandfather, Henry O'Hara, who was a farmer, spent his entire life in Ireland.

John O'Hara came to America when about twenty years of age, arriving here during the construction of the Hudson River Railroad. He located at Croton Landing, and followed the trade of a brick-maker, which he had learned in England. At the end of twenty-five years he removed from Croton Landing to Haines Falls, settling on a farm of one hundred and fifty acres. During his latter years he conducted a boarding-house. Politically, he was a Democrat. He died at the age of sixty-nine. His wife, Julia, and four of their six children; namely, Henry, Michael, William, and Rosa, are still living, all residents of this town. The other two children were Julia and Mary.

Michael O'Hara came to Haines Falls with his parents when six years of age, and was educated in the common schools. At the age of sixteen he went to work on a farm, continuing there until his marriage in 1878, when he purchased a small farm of two acres, on which he now lives. He erected all of the buildings here, and soon began to take summer boarders. The house is located one mile from Tannersville, on the road to Haines Falls, and is about the same distance from the latter place. It is called Tannersville Cottage, is situated on an elevation twenty-two hundred feet above sea level, and commands a view of the surrounding country. There are accommodations for thirty people, the rooms being usually occupied during the entire season.

In 1878 Mr. O'Hara married Miss Ella T. Haskins, a native of Hunter, daughter of John and Mary (McGinley) Haskins. Her father, who was a native of Ireland, came to America when a young man, and locating at Jewett engaged in farming in connection with the tanner's trade. He died there at the age of eighty-two. Mr. and Mrs. Haskins had a family of twelve children, six of whom are living; namely, Rosa, Mary, Elizabeth, Catherine, Jane, and Ella T. (Mrs. O'Hara). The mother died at fifty years of age. Mr. and Mrs. O'Hara have three children — Herbert, Mary Amelia, and John.

Mr. O'Hara is a Democrat in politics. He has been on the Town Committee several years, serving as chairman part of the time, was a member of the County Committee a number of years, and a delegate to the Congressional Convention in 1898. He was Commissioner of Highways six years, being first elected in 1893, re-elected in 1894 for two years, again in 1896, and serving until 1898. The family attend the Catholic church, in which they are actively interested. Mr. O'Hara has served as a trustee, was a member of the building committee, and contributes liberally toward its support. He believes that one of the best methods of educating his children is by providing them with good books, and his home contains a well-selected library. Mr. O'Hara at one time owned the Hunter Turnpike, which was later sold to the town of Hunter and is now a free road.

JOHN A. GORDON, a prominent farmer and business man residing in Carlisle, Schoharie County, was born in Root, N.Y., February 20, 1840, son of Charles and Mary (Lyker) Gordon. The family is of Scotch origin.

Mr. Gordon's grandfather, William Gordon, came to New York from New Jersey in 1802.

JOHN A. GORDON.

Settling upon a tract of wild land in the town of Root, containing ninety-six acres, he cleared a good farm, upon which he resided for the rest of his life. He served as a soldier in the War of 1812, and for many years afterward he took an active part in military affairs. His children were: David; James; Peter; John; Charles; Gilbert; William, who died young; Lydia; Margaret. Six of his sons became prosperous farmers in this State and reared families. Gilbert Gordon was a physician, and for a number of years practised his profession in Newark.

Charles Gordon, the father of John A., was a native of New Jersey. Removing to Root with his father and the other members of the family at about the age of thirteen years, he assisted in improving the homestead, which eventually came into his possession. He dealt quite extensively in cattle and sheep, sent large quantities of wheat to the Albany market, and was known as one of the most enterprising and successful farmers of his day. At the time of his death, which occurred June 22, 1880, at the age of ninety-one years, he was one of the largest land-owners in town, his estate comprising six hundred acres. In politics he was a Democrat, but took no part in public affairs beyond casting his vote. He was an active member of the Dutch Reformed church. His wife, Mary, became the mother of nine children, seven of whom lived to maturity, namely: Margaret; Gertrude; James H.; Louisa; Elizabeth; John A., the subject of this sketch; and Jane. Margaret married Charles Grantier, and is no longer living; Gertrude is the widow of Benjamin Albaugh, and resides in Carlisle; Louisa married William Colyer, and lives in Root; and Jane is the wife of Lorenzo Gardinier, of Root. Mrs. Mary L. Gordon died September 16, 1868.

John A. Gordon was educated in the district schools of his native town. He resided at the parental home until his marriage, when he settled upon a farm of one hundred and ten acres in Carlisle given him by his father. He has since occupied a prominent place among the leading agriculturists of this town. He has increased his estate by purchasing more land from time to time, being now the owner of about three hundred acres, which he devotes to general farming. Although hop culture is largely carried on by the farmers of this locality, he has never engaged in it, as he considers the dairy business far more stable; and he realizes excellent results in that branch of agriculture. He owns a blacksmith shop and hardware store, was originally one of the principal stockholders in the cheese factory, and is now the sole owner. He also owns some valuable real estate in Argusville. As a public-spirited citizen, he takes a lively interest in all movements calculated to promote the general prosperity of the town.

Mr. Gordon married for his first wife Annah E., daughter of Martin Gardinier. She bore him three children, namely: Minnie, a graduate of the Clinton Liberal Institute, now organist at the Methodist Episcopal church; Ostrom, who died at the age of five years; and another child, who died in infancy. Minnie Gordon was married on October 26, 1898, to

Henry E. Terbush, a wagon-maker of Carlisle village. For his second wife Mr. Gordon married Sarah E. Hill, daughter of Bradford Hill, a prominent man of this section of the county. Floyd H., the only child born of this union, was drowned at the age of nine years.

A Democrat, but not an active politician, Mr. Gordon has rendered good service to the town in a public capacity, having filled the offices of Assessor and Trustee of the School District, and having acted as a Justice of the Peace for the past ten years. He is president of the Cemetery Association, was the first Master and is now a Trustee of Argusville Grange, No. 297, Patrons of Husbandry. He is officially connected with the Methodist Episcopal church, of which his wife and daughter are members.

EDWIN L. FORD, M.D., a prominent physician of Lexington, N.Y., and a veteran of the Civil War, was born on the farm where he now resides October 13, 1842, son of David and Abigail (Faulkner) Ford. His paternal grandfather, Joel Ford, who was a native of Connecticut, came to Lexington with an ox-team, bringing his wife and three children, and making his way by the aid of marked trees. He began life here in a log cabin, and after clearing a tract of land built a frame house. He was the father of thirteen children, none of whom are living.

David Ford, the Doctor's father, was a musician. He was the organizer and for fifty years the leader of Ford's String Band, and was familiarly known as "Uncle Dave." In politics he was a Democrat, and served as Tax Collector and Constable. He resided on the farm now occupied by his son, and died at the age of eighty. His wife, Abigail, was a daughter of William Faulkner, an Englishman. Her father was a shoemaker and farmer, and was prominently identified with political affairs, having been elected to Congress. Mrs. Abigail Ford died at the age of thirty-seven. She was the mother of three children, two of whom are living, namely: Edwin L., the subject of this sketch; and Jeanette, who married John P. Miller, of Jewett. The parents were members of the Baptist church.

Edwin L. Ford spent his boyhood and youth in assisting his father, and also in working by the month on farms near his home. In 1862 he enlisted as a private in Company F, One Hundred and Twentieth Regiment, New York Volunteers, for service in the Civil War. Among the engagements in which he took part were the battles of Chancellorsville, Fredericksburg, Gettysburg, and Culpepper. He was severely wounded at Gettysburg, and was in the hospital three months. When convalescent he was detailed as hospital nurse, and upon his recovery he rejoined his regiment. He was taken prisoner at Mine Run, and during his captivity was confined in Libby Prison, Belle Isle, Andersonville, Savannah, and Miller, Ga., where he was exchanged. Resuming active duty, he participated in the battle of Hatcher's Run and the siege of Petersburg, was present at Lee's surrender, and was mustered out in June, 1865. Deciding to enter professional life, he began the study of medicine with Dr. S. L. Ford, of West Kill, and later attended lectures at the Albany Medical College, from which he was graduated in 1868. Locating in Lexington, where he had already practised to some extent, he acquired a large and lucrative practice, and has faithfully discharged his duties as a physician for the past thirty years. Being the only physician in town, he has a large local field of operation, and his outside practice covers a wide circuit.

In 1872 Dr. Ford married for his first wife Frances A. Cox, of Cambridgeport, Mass., daughter of the Rev. Leonard Cox, who was a graduate of Harvard University and a Baptist minister. Mr. Cox at one time preached in Lexington, but is now a resident of Virginia. Of this union there were two children, neither of whom is living. Dr. Ford's first wife died at the age of forty, and in 1887 he married for his second wife Annie L. Dunham, of Lexington, daughter of the late Aaron B. and Mary (Bonestell) Dunham. Of this union there are two children — Edwin and Ethel.

Dr. Ford is a member of the Greene County Medical Society, and is Medical Examiner for the Phœnix, Mutual, Equitable, and other insurance companies. He belongs to the Grand Army of the Republic and the Knights of Pythias. Politically, he is a Democrat. He was Town Physician and a member of the Board of Health several years. He and his family attend the Baptist church.

WILLIAM GRANBY, a carpenter and builder of Blenheim, and at the present time a member of the Board of Supervisors from this town, was born here on November 1, 1868, son of Alexander and Julia (Kellogg) Granby.

Richard Granby, his great-grandfather, who was a native of Ireland, came to this country during the war of the Revolution, and joined the Colonial army, in which he subsequently rendered valiant service. After peace was declared, he came to Blenheim and settled on the farm about a mile from the present village, which is now owned by William Granby, his mother, brother, and his sister. Here he died in old age.

Richard's son William, first, grandfather of the present William Granby, was a native of Blenheim. He engaged in farming and in the lumber business, and also worked as a cooper. He was a very prominent citizen in the town, and served as School Overseer and in other public capacities. He was one of the leaders in the movement to build the Methodist church, and held the offices of class leader and steward in that body. His death occurred at the age of eighty-eight. His wife, whose maiden name was Susan Badgely, was a native of Coeymans. Their children were: Alexander, William, George, Jane, Ellen, and three others that died young. The mother died at the age of eighty-eight, after sixty-five years of happy married life.

Alexander Granby, father of the third William, engaged in mercantile business in early life, but later learned the cooper's business, and worked at that with farming during the remainder of his life. He was well known and highly respected in these parts, and was very successful in all his business ventures. Politically, he was a Republican, and was Town Clerk and Assessor for some years. He died at the age of sixty-five. He is survived by his wife, Julia, and their three children, namely: Arthur, who resides on the Granby homestead; Susie, who married John R. Berg, of New York; and William. Mrs. Granby is living in New York with her daughter. She was born in Carthage, Jefferson County, daughter of John Kellogg, a shoemaker and dealer of that place. Her parents had a large family of children.

William Granby, the subject of this sketch, grandson of the first William, attended the public schools of the town until about thirteen years of age, and during the next ten years gave his attention to farming. Then for some five years he worked at carpentering, though he still resided on the homestead farm. The estate originally comprised a hundred and forty acres, and of this he inherited a third. He was especially interested in dairying, finding his markets in Albany and in New York.

Mr. Granby has shown his interest in the welfare of the community by his attendance on the county conventions every year, excepting one, since he became a voter. In 1893, having been elected Town Clerk, he moved into the village, where he has since resided. He declined the nomination for the clerk's office for a second term, but became candidate for Sheriff in the county on the Republican ticket. Although defeated, he ran far ahead of the ticket, and had the satisfaction of carrying his own town, usually Democratic, by eighty-six votes. He made the greatest run ever made for the office by a Republican candidate. He has twice declined the nomination for the office of Supervisor, but in 1898 was elected to that office for a term of two years. No better representative could have been sent, and he has the hearty support of his townspeople. Mr. Granby is a member of the Odd Fellows Order, and at present Noble Grand. Shortly after he joined the organization, two years ago, he was chosen permanent secretary. As a musician, Mr. Granby has acquired considerable local reputation. For many years he has been leader of the choir at the Methodist church, and for the last five years he has been the church organist.

HENRY VAN BERGEN, the well-known miller of Coxsackie, N.Y., was born in Athens, Greene County, on December 30, 1850, son of Peter and Mary (De Griff) Van Bergen. The founder of the Van Bergen family in this country came from Holland to Albany, N.Y., in early Colonial times, and later, in 1678, with his three sturdy sons, settled in Leeds, now the town of Catskill. One of the immigrant's sons, Peter by name, was born in Albany. From him the line is through his son Henry, followed by three in successive generations bearing the name Peter, the fourth Peter being the father of the subject of this sketch. Henry, first, and his descendants above named, were all born in Coxsackie. The family is among the very oldest in Coxsackie, and all the land embraced within the town limits was at one time owned by the Van Bergens. The first Reformed church, which was built in 1740, stood on land which was the gift of one of the members of this family.

Peter Van Bergen, the great-grandfather, resided about a half mile from the present village. He died in 1854, at the age of ninety. His wife's maiden name was Woodbeck. They had a large family of children. Grandfather Peter had a brickyard near the present town of West Coxsackie, or at Lower Landing, which he carried on with great success. He was one of the leading men in the town, and a member of the Assembly in 1846. He was a stanch supporter of the Democratic party. His first wife, the grandmother of Henry Van Bergen, was an Egbertson. She bore him two children. His second wife was before marriage Christina Van Wormer. She was born in Glenville, Montgomery County. Of her six children, two are living, namely: Isaac, who resides in New York; and Christina, who is the wife of W. R. Adams, at Four Mile Point.

Peter Van Bergen, father of the subject of this sketch, purchased a farm of his own in early manhood, and later had a part of his father's farm. He lived just across the line in New Baltimore, and died there at the age of sixty-six. Like his ancestors he was an active member of the Dutch Reformed church, and one of its leading officials. His wife, Mary, who survives him, was born in Amsterdam, N.Y., a daughter of Diedrich De Graff, a farmer, who married a Miss Van Wormer, and had a large family. She is the only survivor of her father's family. Her father died at the age of sixty, and her mother at the age of seventy-five. Three children were born to Peter and Mary Van Bergen; and two, Nelson and Henry, are living, both millers in this town.

Henry Van Bergen, the special subject of this sketch, obtained his education in the common schools, and subsequently assisted his father on the home farm until the latter's death. He then came to the village and built the grist-mill, which he has since so successfully operated. It is a steam-mill, and has three runs of stone and a set of rollers. A very large custom business is here done in grinding grain, and from this mill large quantities of buckwheat flour are put into the market.

Mr. Van Bergen's marriage occurred in 1886, his wife being Phœbe J., only child of the late Captain James Delamater, for many years one of the best-known pilots on the Hudson River. She has borne him two children — Mamie and Lawrence.

Mr. Van Bergen upholds the time-honored principles of his family in his adherence to the Democratic party; but he believes in putting in office the best man, regardless of party affiliations. In 1887 and 1888 he was Supervisor in the town of New Baltimore. In 1888 he was a candidate for County Clerk, and was elected by one hundred and fifty-one votes, all the other members of the ticket being defeated by three hundred votes. After serving three years he was again nominated in 1891, and was re-elected by a thousand majority, running six hundred ahead of his ticket. Three years later, in 1894, he was again nominated, but failed of election, going down in the Democratic "land slide." In 1896 he was Presidential Elector from this district. He was on the County Committee, being its chairman in 1892, and was re-elected in the following year, but resigned. He has at different times refused the nomination both to the State legislature and to Congress. He is one of the Town Water Commissioners, and has served on the Board of Education for the last three years, having under his charge the school at West Coxsackie. He is a member of the Knights of Pythias, and he and his family are adherents of the Dutch Reformed church.

CHARLES S. BURNETT, M.D., of Summit, Schoharie County, N.Y., was born in Eminence, N.Y., September 13, 1850, son of Francis and Melissa (Germond) Burnett. Both the father's family and the mother's are of English origin. The Burnetts came here from Connecticut. Matthias Burnett, Dr. Burnett's grandfather, who was born March 8, 1778, and died April 19, 1848, was an early settler in Jefferson. After locating here he was married to Susan Guerin. She was born March 25, 1780, and she died February 27, 1844. They were the parents of nine sons and four daughters. All of the sons became prosperous farmers.

Francis Burnett, Dr. Burnett's father, was born in Jefferson, September 25, 1821. Early in life he engaged in general farming in Eminence, where he tilled the soil energetically for the rest of his active period, and he died July 7, 1890. He was the father of four children, namely: Lucetta F., who married Charles Hubbell, of Jefferson; James, who is engaged in mercantile business in Summit; Byron, a resident of Cobleskill; and Charles S., M.D., the subject of this sketch.

Charles S. Burnett acquired his early education in the schools of Eminence, N.Y. On leaving school he was employed for a time as a clerk in his brother's store, and then going to Newark, N.J., he worked at the carpenter's trade. His medical studies were begun under the direction of Dr. F. B. Beard, were continued with Dr. Bigelow, of Albany, and later at the Albany Medical School, which he entered in 1876. His expenses there he defrayed with funds saved from his earnings. He displayed such marked proficiency in his studies that when he was graduated, in 1879, he was chosen orator of his class, the majority of whose members had pursued a classical course prior to entering a professional school. Preferring a country practice, he first settled at North Blenheim, where he resided seven years, at the expiration of which time he came to Summit, succeeding to the practice of Dr. Beard. He has gained a high standing among the leading physicians in this section.

In politics he is a Democrat. In 1897 he was elected Coroner for a term of three years. He belongs to the County Medical Society,

JAMES W. WADDELL.

takes a lively interest in the advancement of science, and as a progressive, public-spirited citizen he is actively concerned in all matters relative to the improvement of this town. The residence he now occupies was erected by him in 1893.

Dr. Burnett married Nannie Buckingham, daughter of Merritt Buckingham, of Gilboa. Mrs. Burnett is a member of the Methodist Episcopal church.

JAMES W. WADDELL, former Supervisor of Duanesburg, N.Y., was born where he now resides, June 1, 1826, being the only son of David and Mary (Coie) Waddell. His father was born in the north of Ireland, August 14, 1794; and his mother was born there, February 15, 1792.

Shortly after their marriage, which took place May 23, 1816, David Waddell and his wife came to the United States, settling in Duanesburg; and about the year 1825 he bought the farm which is now owned by his son. A sturdy, industrious, and progressive farmer, he labored diligently to maintain a comfortable home for his family; and, being a worthy, upright man, he gained the sincere esteem of his fellow-townspeople. In politics he supported the Democratic party, and in his religious belief he was a Presbyterian. David Waddell died May 7, 1862, and his wife died May 7, 1871. They were the parents of eight children, namely: Ruth, born November 22, 1817; Rose Anna, born May 24, 1820; Fidelia, born July 11, 1822; Mary Jane, born February 28, 1824; James W., born, as above mentioned, June 1, 1826; Margaret, born April 3, 1829; Hannah, born March 25, 1831; and Sarah M., born September 1, 1833. Of these, four are now living, namely: Fidelia, who resides at the old homestead; Mary Jane, the wife of Thomas H. Turnbull, of Rotterdam Junction, N.Y.; James W., the subject of this sketch; and Margaret, now the widow of S. Putnam, and living in South Schenectady, N.Y. Ruth, the eldest, was the wife of Elijah Rockwell; and Hannah, the seventh child, was the wife of Dr. D. S. Kellogg.

James W. Waddell spent his early boyhood years in attending the district school and assisting his father upon the farm, and later during the winter months attended school at Charlotteville and Fort Plain Seminaries. Succeeding to the ownership of the property, which contains two hundred and thirty acres, he has improved it by erecting new buildings, carries on general farming energetically, and keeps from twenty to twenty-five head of stock.

On September 3, 1873, Mr. Waddell was united in marriage with S. Electa Howard, who was born in Duanesburg, January 27, 1843. Four children were born of this union, and two of them are living, namely: George W. H., born August 8, 1879; and William D., born May 13, 1881, both of whom are attending a business college. The others were: Mary; and another daughter, who died in infancy. Mrs. Waddell died January 26, 1899.

Politically, Mr. Waddell acts with the Democratic party at national elections. He has been Supervisor and Road Commissioner, holding each of these offices three terms and rendering capable service to the town. He takes a lively interest in the public institutions of the town, and is ever ready to aid in improving the general welfare of the community. Mr. Waddell attends the Presbyterian church.

GEORGE L. FOX, editor of the Middleburg *News*, is a native of Middleburg, N.Y. He was born on April 3, 1871, son of Lewis and Elizabeth (Wilbur) Fox. His father, who is now living retired, was formerly engaged in the paper manufacturing business in Pen Yan, and later in Baldwinsville and Middleburg. His mother was born in Schoharie. His parents had a family of five children.

Mr. Fox received his education in the common and high schools of Middleburg; and in 1888, shortly after leaving the high school, he began the publication of *The American Youth*, a monthly story paper. This was issued from Middleburg, and had a circulation in every State in the Union. The following year it was sold to a publishing house in Boston, and subsequently Mr. Fox purchased the South Orange, N.J., *Journal*, and moved it to Middleburg. Associating himself with Wellington E. Bassler, a prominent business man and a Republican, he began the publication of the Middleburg *News*, a weekly paper. At first the venture seemed most unpromising, and the field was a limited one, but the energy and perseverance with which the proprietors have worked, the fortunate methods employed by the business management, and the enterprise shown in the news columns have together united to push the paper into the front rank of Republican weeklies. It is now one of the leading news organs of the county, and has a large circulation. While its columns give ample space to events of national importance, it does not forget to emphasize matters of local interest, and is always foremost in agitating local improvements. At various times it has been designated by the Republican leaders as the organ in which the State laws should be printed.

Mr. Fox was married on October 28, 1897, to Mabel Almy. She was born in Franklinton, and is a daughter of E. C. Almy, who was formerly a farmer of that town, and is now retired and living in Middleburg. Mr. Fox is a member of Middleburg Lodge, No. 663, F. & A. M., and has held the office of Junior Deacon of the lodge. He is a member of La Bastile Lodge, No. 494, I. O. O. F., and has filled nearly all the offices in the lodge, being now Past Noble Grand. He is also a member of Oueongena Tribe of Red Men. Professionally, he is a member of the New York Editorial Association and the New York Press Association. He and his wife attend the Methodist church.

HUGH B. GARA, proprietor of the West End Hotel, Hunter, N.Y., was born in Manch Chunk, Pa., April 15, 1855, son of John and Mary (McIntire) Gara. His father was born in Ireland, and here he learned the trade of a shoemaker, which he followed as long as he lived.

Emigrating to America in 1848, John Gara settled in Mauch Chunk, and in 1855 he removed to Hunter, where his death occurred in 1859, at the age of thirty-nine years. In politics he was a Democrat. His wife, Mary, also a native of Ireland, is now seventy years old. Her father, Hugh McIntire, was a shoemaker and tavern-keeper. He came to America on a visit, and after his return to Ireland he continued in business until his retirement, when he was succeeded by his brother. Hugh McIntire had a family of seven childen. Of these the four now living are: Mrs. Gara; Joseph, who is in a post-office in Ireland; Katy, widow of Thomas Haggerty, who died in Mauch Chunk, Pa.; and Patrick, who is a hotel proprietor in Ireland. John and Mary (McIntire) Gara were the parents of eight children, of whom two are living; namely, Mary and her brother, Hugh B., the subject of this sketch, with whom she resides. The others were: Patrick, who died March 7, 1889, aged thirty-nine; John F., who died November 4, 1888, at the age of twenty-nine; Hugh, first, who died in Ireland, at seven years of age; and three children who died young.

Hugh B. Gara was brought by his parents to Hunter when six months old. He was educated in the common schools, and at the age of twelve entered the chair factory, where he was employed until eighteen. He continued to follow his trade as a journeyman one year in a chair factory in Newburg, from which place he went to New York City, and a year later became a travelling salesman in the dry-goods business. Prior to this his brother, John F., had erected the present West End Hotel in Hunter, which was opened in 1887; and Mr. Gara left the road to assist him in this enterprise, in a general way. Upon the death of his brother, Hugh took control of the house, and has since conducted it.

The West End is pleasantly located near the terminus of the Stony Clove and Catskill Mountain Railroad. It is sixty by thirty feet, with a wing twenty-eight by seventy, four stories high, and has accommodations for one hundred and thirty guests. The rooms are large, well ventilated, well furnished, and lighted with gas. The bath accommodations are ample, and the sanitary arrangements are unexcelled. The house is within easy reach of Hotel Kaaterskill and Laurel House, and of Onteora, Elka, and Twilight Parks. There is a good livery stable in connection.

On October 12, 1898, Mr. Gara was united in marriage with Mary E. O'Carroll, daughter of David and Kate (O'Neil) O'Carroll, of Dungarvan, County Waterford, Ireland. Her paternal grandfather, Michael O'Carroll, a sea captain, was also a native of that town. Her father, who was reared to sea life, became master of a vessel plying between Ireland and France, and was also engaged in trade between Cork and Liverpool. Abandoning the sea, he opened a ship-broker's office in Cardiff, Wales, and conducted that business until his death, which occurred in 1884, at the age of fifty-seven. His wife, Kate, was a sister of the Rev. Hugh O'Neil, a sketch of whom appears elsewhere in the REVIEW. She died in 1877, at the age of forty-one. She was the mother of three children. The only survivor of these is Mary E., who was educated in the Mercy Convent, Dungarvan, and is now Mrs. Hugh B. Gara. She is a fine pianist, and also received special instruction in painting and the French language. She kept house for her father until his death, and with the aid of two assistants continued his business until coming to the United States in 1886. Previous to her marriage she resided with her uncle, the Rev. Father O'Neil. Mrs. Gara is a valuable assistant to her husband, being a woman of much executive ability.

HERBERT L. ODELL, M.D., an able physician and specialist of Sharon Springs, N.Y., was born in Summit, this county, July 18, 1859, son of Isaac L. and Harriet L. (Baldwin) Odell. The family was founded in America, late in the seventeenth or early in the eighteenth century, by the great-great-great-grandfather, who emigrated from England and settled on Long Island.

Isaac L. Odell, the father, who was born in Jefferson, N.Y., in 1815, moved to Summit when a young man, and carried on quite an extensive business as a cooper. He took considerable interest in public affairs, serving as Town Clerk and in other offices. In politics he supported the Democratic party, and in his religious belief he was a Methodist. His wife, whose maiden name was Harriet L. Baldwin, was born in 1818. They were the parents of five children, namely: Daniel; George W.; Peter L.; Julia E., who married H. A. Wright, of Worcester, N.Y.; and Herbert L., the subject of this sketch. The father died in 1893, the mother's death having occurred a few months previous. Daniel, George W., and Peter L. Odell reside in Summit.

Herbert L. Odell acquired his early education in the public and select schools. His medical studies were begun under the direction of Dr. F. P. Beard, then of Summit and now of Cobleskill, with whom he remained four years. He was graduated from the Albany Medical College in 1883; and, while pursuing his course in that city, he studied with Dr. Jacob S. Mosher. Locating for practice in Hobart, N.Y., he remained there until March, 1892, when he came to Sharon Springs. During the last six years of the time spent at Hobart he was associated in practice with Dr. J. S. McNaught. While preparing for his profession, Dr. Odell made a special study of dermatology; and, since entering into practice, he has given much attention to the treatment of rheumatism, in which he is remarkably successful. During the summer a large number of patients come to Sharon Springs, in order to avail themselves of his treatment and at the same time to receive the benefits of the sulphur baths. Dr. Odell attends, also, to most of the obstetric practice in this locality. He was formerly president of the Delaware County Medical Society, is president of the Schoharie and a member of the Albany County

GARRET W. MATTICE.

Medical Societies. Progressive as well as energetic, he keeps in touch with advanced ideas by making frequent visits to the hospitals of the metropolis.

Dr. Odell and Eva L. Hoose, only daughter of Robert J. Hoose, of Hobart, N.Y., were united in marriage on May 13, 1885. They have three daughters — Grace, Eloise, and Beatrice.

Politically, Dr. Odell acts with the Democratic party. He is a Master Mason, belonging to the Blue Lodge in Sharon Springs, and is also an Odd Fellow. He is a member of the Methodist Episcopal church, of which he is now serving as steward.

GEORGE H. FAULKNER, Supervisor and Justice of the Peace, Lexington, Greene County, N.Y., was born in this town September 6, 1842, son of Alfred and Sarah (Cross) Faulkner. His paternal grandfather, William Faulkner, was a native of Liverpool, England. He came to Lexington before marriage, and, settling on a farm, engaged in its cultivation, and also followed the trade of a shoemaker. A man of considerable natural ability, in politics he was a Democrat, and represented his district in the Assembly. He married Abigail Drake. They lived to an advanced age, and had a large family of children.

Alfred Faulkner grew to manhood upon the home farm. Later he cultivated a farm of his own in Halcott, where he resided for the rest of his life, and was quite active in public affairs. His first wife, Sarah, died about the year 1845. She was a daughter of George Cross, a farmer and lifelong resident of Lexington. She had three children: Mary, who married Frank Moore, of this town; Victor, who is in Fleischmanns, Delaware County; and George H., the subject of this sketch. For his second wife he married Ann Faulkner, who at her death left two children — James and Sarah. Alfred Faulkner died at seventy-three years of age.

George H. Faulkner spent his early years with an uncle on a farm about a mile below the village, and was educated in the common schools. He followed agriculture until 1886, when he came to the village, and engaged in selling farming implements. He also transacts a great deal of legal business and has considerable practice in the minor courts.

In 1890 Mr. Faulkner married Miss Mary M. Banks, daughter of Joseph Banks, a farmer of Hardenburg, N.Y. One son, Leon, has been born of this union.

Politically, Mr. Faulkner is a Democrat. He has been Justice of the Peace since 1882. He was Justice of Special Sessions one term, is now serving as Supervisor, and has been Tax Collector two years. He is a trustee of the Baptist and Methodist churches, and Mrs. Faulkner attends the Baptist church of Lexington.

GARRET W. MATTICE, a well-known and highly respected agriculturist of Schoharie County, owns and occupies a farm on the Middleburg road in the town of Fulton, about two miles from Fultonham. He was born June 2, 1830, a son of Adam L. Mattice, and is a direct descendant of Nicholas Mattice, who emigrated from Germany in the early part of the eighteenth century and took up a tract of wild land in the vicinity of the Upper Fort, Schoharie County.

Conrad Mattice, son of Nicholas and the next in line of descent, was a lifelong resident of this part of the State. In his early manhood he located on land in Middleburg, where his son Lawrence, the grandfather of Garret W., was born.

At the time of the Revolution, Lawrence Mattice, though but a boy of sixteen, was employed at the Middle Fort, and with Murphy and other brave soldiers marched out to meet the enemy. On one of his hasty expeditions he and a companion succeeded in taking prisoner a man by the name of Adam Chrysler, whom they carried to the fort. He continued in service until the close of the war, when he settled on a farm, and from that time until his death, at the venerable age of eighty-six years, was engaged in cultivating the land. He was quite prominent in the management of town matters, and at one time was nominated to the State Assembly. His wife, Maria Brown, a native of this part of the county, bore him seven children, none of whom survive. She lived to be upward of eighty years of age, and died at the old homestead. Both she and her husband were members of the Lutheran church.

Adam L. Mattice was born September 15, 1803, in Middleburg. Following in the footsteps of his ancestors, he became a tiller of the soil. On coming of age he purchased a farm not far from the old home, and in the log house that stood in the clearing began life for himself, poor in pocket, but rich in energy, courage, and ambition. By dint of industry and economy he succeeded in paying for his land, besides which he laid up a small sum. On April 5, 1849, having sold his first estate, he took possession of the farm now occupied by his son, Garret W., and here resided until his death, July 5, 1888. A man of sound judgment and good financial ability, he became prominent in the town, and served as Highway Commissioner and Assessor for a number of years. Both he and his wife were active members of the Baptist church. He married Dinah Mattice, who was born in the town of Blenheim, a daughter of David Mattice, a prosperous farmer. They had a family of five children, three of whom survive, namely: Garret W.; Dinah, wife of Josiah Mann; and Elizabeth, wife of Peter Shaffer.

Garret W. Mattice was born in the log cabin in which his parents settled soon after marriage, and during his earlier years he assisted in the pioneer labor of redeeming a farm from the wilderness. In 1849 he came with them to his present farm, which he and a brother who died in 1877 helped to improve. From that time until the death of his father, in 1888, Mr. Mattice had the general oversight of the property, which is now in his possession. This farm contains one hundred and seventy acres of land, and he also owns a farm of one hundred acres on the road to Cobleskill.

Skilful and progressive, he has met with success as a general farmer. He raises hay, grain, and hops, is an extensive dealer in cattle, and from his small herd of cows makes a choice grade of butter, which he ships to Albany. He has made many of the most important improvements on the place, including the erection of the present commodious dwelling-house and the substantial barns and farm buildings.

In politics Mr. Mattice affiliates with the Democratic party, and besides serving as Commissioner of Highways he was Supervisor from 1896 until 1898. He is a regular attendant of the Baptist church, and in the building of the new edifice of that denomination gave material financial assistance.

On March 24, 1866, Mr. Mattice married Rachel Cowan, a daughter of James Cowan, well known in Fulton as an able farmer and lawyer. Mr. Cowan married Emeline Cary, of Schoharie, who passed to the life immortal at the age of sixty-eight years, while he attained the age of fourscore years. Mr. and Mrs. Mattice have one child living, a son, Paul B., and they have been bereft of two, namely: Eli G., who died aged three years, six months; and Ira C., who died aged four years and seven months. Paul B. Mattice after his graduation at the Middleburg High School entered Cornell University, class of 1901, intending there to fit himself for the bar. During the Spanish War he enlisted, July 17, 1898, in Company K, Two Hundred and Third New York Volunteers, and served until March 25, 1899, when he was mustered out as Corporal. On his return he again took up his studies at Cornell.

CHARLES E. NICHOLS, counsellor-at-law, and District Attorney of Greene County, and one of the best-known and most respected residents of Catskill, was born in Athens, Greene County, March 20, 1854. His father is General George Sylvester Nichols, and his mother in maidenhood was Ann Netterville Foster.

His paternal grandfather was Judge Sylvester Nichols, a native and prominent citizen of Athens. Besides carrying on a farm, the grandfather was a manufacturer of brick and lime, was also engaged in freighting on a large scale, being the owner of several vessels. He was also County Judge of Greene County for several years. He married Lucy E. Hamilton, who also was a native of Athens. She died in 1891, at the age of ninety. Seven of their children grew to maturity; namely, George Sylvester, Samuel Hamilton, William T., Elbridge, Charles P., Henry O., and Sarah.

George Sylvester Nichols, the first-named son, was born in Athens, N.Y., January 12, 1820. He attended private schools in Athens until twelve years old; and in 1832 he entered Lenox Academy, Mass., where he remained one year. In 1834 he went to Fairfield Academy, Herkimer County, N.Y., for a year; and during the year 1837 he studied at the academy in Kinderhook, N.Y., which was established by his grandfather. From 1838 to 1846 he was captain of the sloop "Science," owned by his father, carrying brick, lime, hay, and produce from Athens to New York. He was appointed Brigade Quartermaster of the Thirty-seventh Brigade of New York State Militia, and commissioned by Governor William C. Bouck on September 14, 1843; and he was appointed Brigadier-general of the Thirty-seventh Brigade by Governor Silas Wright on March 3, 1845. In 1847 and 1848 he was employed in Troy, N.Y., as superintendent of Colonel J. Hooker's docks, barges and canal boats, and general manager of his transportation line to New York. He started for California in 1849, sailing from New York on February 5 in the steamer "Crescent City" for San Francisco. After staying a month on the isthmus, in Gorgona and Panama, he left the last-named place on the steamer "Oregon" on her first trip up the coast, and, arriving at San Francisco on the first day of April, 1849, went directly to Sutter's Mill, Coloma, where he was engaged nearly two years in packing and trading. He left San Francisco for home about December 1, 1850, by steamer, going to Panama, from there crossing the isthmus to Chagres by mule and bungo, as on the trip out, and thence reaching New York by steamer about the first of January, 1851. In the spring of 1851 he was elected Supervisor of the town of Athens, and two years later was nominated by the Democratic party for State Senator for the Tenth District, which includes Greene and Ulster Counties, but was defeated by the Prohibition candidate. In 1855 he was again nominated for State Senator, this time by the American party, was elected, and

served one term. On June 8, 1860, he was appointed one of the Board of Commissioners of Excise for Greene County for three years.

When hostilities began between the South and the North, he felt that his former military training would be of value to his country, and decided to offer himself as a volunteer. On November 23, 1861, having received an appointment as Major in the Ninth New York Cavalry, and having been given his commission by Governor Morgan, he left Albany on the same day for the national capital. Upon going into active service, his bravery and ability at once became conspicuous, and his promotion was rapid. On May 30, 1863, he was made Lieutenant Colonel of his regiment, and on June 14, 1864, was commissioned Colonel by Governor Seymour. He was mustered out with the regiment at Buffalo, N.Y., on July 17, 1865. On March 13, 1865, "for gallant and meritorious services in all the cavalry engagements under General Sheridan," he was brevetted Brigadier-general of United States Volunteers.

On June 25, 1867, he was appointed by Collector H. A. Smythe Inspector of Customs in the New York Custom House, and on November 8, 1875, he was appointed, by Collector Chester A. Arthur, Deputy Collector of Customs. In 1879 he was nominated for member of Congress by the Republican party in the Fifteenth Congressional District (Ulster, Greene, and Schoharie Counties), but was defeated. In 1882 he was appointed by Secretary of the Interior, the Hon. H. M. Teller, Special Examiner in the pension office;

and in this capacity he served three years. For three years also subsequent to 1885 he held the office of County Clerk of Greene County, having been elected by the Republican party. Since 1889 General Nichols has retired from active life.

On October 7, 1845, he married Ann Netterville Foster, daughter of Captain James G. and Ann E. Foster. Mrs. Nichols was born in Athens, N.Y., and died there at the age of eighty. Her father was a sea captain, and commanded a ship that ran from New York to Liverpool, England. During the embargo placed upon American vessels by the French, he anchored his vessel in the river, a few miles below Athens, to get it in fresh water, and while there met Ann Colson, with whom he fell in love at sight. He made only one more voyage, and then married and settled in Athens, where he went into the brick-making business. This he gave up after a time, and subsequently carried on a store until his death, at the age of seventy-six. He owned a fine farm. His wife died at the age of seventy-eight, having been the mother of six children. Five children were born to General George S. and Ann N. Nichols, and four of them are living; namely, Mary, Foster, Charles E., and Arthur. Mary married Frank N. Howland, who is a member of the firm of Smith & Candee, the oldest and leading firm of dealers in lime, brick, and builders' supplies in New York City. Foster Nichols is purchasing agent for M. Guggenheim's Sons, who are among the largest smelters and refiners in the United States. Arthur Nichols is a mining operator in Leadville, Col. Mrs. Nichols was a devout Episcopalian, as is also the general; and he was formerly a member of a Masonic organization. He resides in "The Old Nest" in Athens, which has been his home for half a century.

Charles E. Nichols spent his early years in his native town of Athens, and received his early education in the district schools. Subsequently he attended the high school at Englewood, N.J., the Fairfield Seminary at Fairfield, N.Y., and the Fort Edward Collegiate Institute. Then, following the memorable advice of Horace Greeley, he went West, and was employed in the general office of the Colorado Central Railroad at Golden, Col., for about four years. Having decided to enter the legal profession, he gave his mind with ardor to the necessary studies, and was admitted to the bar in Colorado in 1880. He practised his profession in that State for about two years, during which time he also engaged to some extent in mining. Then, returning East, he was admitted to the bar in the State of New York in 1882, after which he practised law in Athens for some three years. In 1885 he was appointed Deputy County Clerk under his father, which position he held until 1889. He was then appointed Clerk to the Surrogate's Court by the present surrogate, and served until December, 1898, a period of ten years in all, when he resigned, having been elected District Attorney in the fall of that year. He still has three years to serve in this office.

Mr. Nichols was married in 1890 to Mrs.

Mary B. Willis, who was born in Connecticut, the daughter of the Rev. H. H. Bates, an Episcopalian clergyman. Her mother's maiden name was E. Samantha Bascom. Both parents were natives of Vermont. They had three children. Mr. Bates was rector of a church in Glens Falls, N.Y., at the breaking out of the Civil War; and, when one of his wardens had enlisted as a Colonel and another as a Major, he resigned his charge at their request, and went to the front as chaplain of their regiment. He remained with his regiment throughout the war, and subsequently, his health being impaired, took a small charge in Oak Hill, this county. There he died in 1868. He was an active Mason, and was buried with Masonic rites. The lodge of which he was a member erected a monument to his memory at Oak Hill, N.Y., where he was buried.

Mr. Nichols is Vice-Chancellor in the Knights of Pythias Lodge in Catskill, and Junior Sagamore of the Red Men. In 1882 he was a member of the Lodge of Knights of Pythias in Athens. He has resided in Catskill since 1890, when he removed here from Athens. He and his wife are members of the Episcopal church, which has recently erected a beautiful new church edifice. While in Athens Mr. Nichols was a lay-reader in the church there, and for three years superintendent of the Sunday-school.

RICHARD WINEGARD, a well-known miller of Hyndsville, Schoharie County, was born near this village September 19, 1845, a son of George and Eliza A. (Isham) Winegard. He is of German ancestry, and a grandson of one of the earliest settlers of this section of Schoharie County — Richard Winegard, first, who came here from Schodack, Rensselaer County.

There being no roads across the country in those early days, Grandfather Winegard made the journey hither through the unbroken woods on horseback; and, having secured a tract of land in the heart of the forest, he felled trees, and thus made an opening in which he put up a small log cabin of rude construction, with no windows, and only a blanket for a door. He was a tailor; and, in connection with clearing a farm, he worked at his trade whenever he had an opportunity. He succeeded finely at both occupations, and in the course of a few years had cleared and placed under cultivation a number of acres of land. Prudent, thrifty, and a good manager, he at length found that he was warranted in replacing the log-cabin with a substantial frame house, and in building a comfortable barn and a shed for his new wagon and farming implements. A man of intelligence and sound judgment, he became influential in the community and a leader in religious circles. He was a devout Methodist, and a regular attendant at the prayer-meetings held seven miles away, a journey that he took on horseback. He far outlived the allotted span of human life, his pilgrimage on earth extending over a period of one hundred and two years. His wife, Charity Rickart, was also of German descent. She proved herself a true helpmeet, assisting him in their early days of labor while living in the log-cabin, and training their seven children to habits of industry and usefulness. She preceded him to the better world, passing away at the age of eighty-five years.

George Winegard assisted his father in his pioneer labors, and after reaching man's estate purchased the old Peter Markle farm near by, in the town of Seward, and spent many years in improving it. He built a new dwelling, a barn, and other farm buildings, and was there engaged in agricultural pursuits several years. Subsequently coming to Hyndsville, he bought land, rebuilt the saw-mill and built a grist-mill, and during the remainder of his life was prominently identified with the highest and best interests of this little village, and was largely instrumental in its development. In politics he was, in early manhood, a stanch Whig, and later a Republican. A man of eminent piety, deeply interested in advancing the cause of religion, he was very active in the Methodist church, with which he united when young, and was for many years a class leader and one of the trustees. When its present house of worship was erected he was one of the foremost in hastening the work, and contributed fourteen hundred dollars toward the building fund. He died at the age of seventy-two years, leaving a host of friends who sympathized with the family in their great loss. His wife, whose maiden name was Eliza A. Isham, was born in this town. Her father, Benjamin Isham, was a prominent citizen and a pioneer merchant of Hyndsville. She was a woman of culture, having been educated at a New York City boarding-school. She was a distant relation of John Quincy Adams. Mrs. Winegard survived her husband, dying at the age of eighty-two years. They reared five children, namely: Emily, wife of Rector Foster; Phebe, deceased; George, deceased; Richard; and Albert.

Richard Winegard was educated in the district schools, and until he was thirty-five years old he worked with his father on the farm and in the mill. Since the death of the father he and his brother Albert have devoted their attention to the grist-mill, and, in addition to dealing somewhat in grain and feed, have carried on a very extensive business in custom grinding of corn, flour, and feed. The nine acres of land included in the original property they utilize by raising on it hay, grain, and potatoes.

Politically, Mr. Winegard is a steadfast Republican, and takes an active interest in local and county affairs. Fraternally, he is an Odd Fellow, belonging to Richmondville Lodge. True to the religious faith in which he was reared, he is a faithful member of the Methodist Episcopal church, which he has served for many years as trustee, steward, class leader, and church recorder, having taken up the work laid down by his father and successfully carried it on.

On December 23, 1874, Mr. Winegard was united in marriage to Miss Maggie J. Weidman, daughter of Nicholas and Ann (Starkins) Weidman, of Schoharie County. Mr. and Mrs. Winegard have one child, a daughter, Lottie E., wife of Benjamin F. Empie, a merchant of Hyndsville and Town Clerk of

Seward. Mr. and Mrs. Empie are the proud parents of a bright baby girl, Bernice L., born on February 2, 1899.

BARTHOLOMEW H. CLUTE, one of the representative dairymen of Glenville, N.Y., was born in Schenectady, June 24, 1831, son of Henry and Cathaline T. (Haverley) Clute. His grandfather, Bartholomew Clute, served as a soldier in the Revolutionary War. He was for some time a boatman on the Mohawk River; and on one occasion he had for a passenger the British commander, Sir Henry Clinton. The maiden name of Grandfather Clute's wife was Margaret Peters.

Their son, Henry Clute, above named, was a native of Schenectady. When a young man, he engaged in the grocery business, which he followed for the rest of his life. He died about 1835. His wife, Cathaline, was a native of Glenville. Her paternal grandfather was John Haverley, a large land-owner of this town in his day. His death occurred the same night that the subject of this sketch was born. John Haverley married Anna Adams, a representative, it is thought, of the noted Massachusetts family which has given two Presidents — John and John Quincy Adams — to the United States. Henry and Cathaline T. Clute reared four children; namely, Susan H., Christian H., Bartholomew H., and John H. B. Clute, all of whom, except Bartholomew H., are residing in Rotterdam. The mother died May, 1882. The parents were members of the Reformed church.

Bartholomew H. Clute passed his boyhood and youth in Schenectady and Glenville, and attended school in these places. His father's death threw him upon his own resources at an early age, and he began life as a workman in the broom factories of Schenectady at eleven dollars per month. In 1850 he went to Illinois, where he engaged in raising broom-corn on leased land. He also established a factory, and manufactured the first lot of Western-made brooms ever sold in Chicago. Although this enterprise proved quite successful, the gold fever soon caused him to sell out, in order to try his fortune in California. Going there by the overland route, he followed various occupations on the Pacific Coast for four years. Returning then to Schenectady County, he leased land in Glenville until 1863, since which year he has resided upon his present farm of one hundred and ten acres. He has a valuable piece of agricultural property, with good buildings and modern improvements. He keeps from twenty to twenty-five cows, and derives considerable profit from the sale of milk.

On October 20, 1858, Mr. Clute was joined in marriage with Agnes Swart, who was born in Glenville, April 13, 1832, daughter of Josias and Catharine (Vedder) Swart. Her parents belonged to highly reputable families of this county. Mrs. Clute is the mother of three children, namely: Kitte V., who is now Mrs. McCullum; Elma, who is now Mrs. Dick; and Clarence Clute.

In politics Mr. Clute is a Democrat. To

the energy and perseverance which served him so well in his boyhood days is due in a great measure the prosperity he now enjoys, his activity continuing unabated. Mr. and Mrs. Clute are members of the Reformed church.

JOHN S. CARY, a well-known resident of Braman, in the town of Cobleskill, and proprietor of one of the oldest mills in this section of the county, was born in Schoharie, in a house on the road to Howes Cave, on July 19, 1827, son of Samuel and Mercy (Swan) Cary.

His father, who was born in Stonington, Conn., was brought up in Sprakers Basin, Montgomery County, N.Y., on a farm. He also worked somewhat during boyhood at rafting on the Mohawk River, but eventually came to the farm of George Lawyer in Schoharie Court House, and during the remainder of his life was engaged in farm labor, either there or on other farms in this county, working on shares. His wife, Mercy, was the daughter of a pioneer of Knox, Albany County, who built the first mill in that region. He was a stanch patriot in Revolutionary times, and was in active service in the army throughout the war, being eleven times wounded. His wife lived to the surprising age of one hundred and three years. On her one hundred and third birthday she rode twenty miles on horseback, but the exertion was too much for her, and she died from its effects. Mrs. Mercy Cary was the youngest of quite a large family of children. Of her own children, seven in number, John S. was the youngest, and is now the only one living.

Mr. John S. Cary spent his early years at Barnerville, where he attended the public schools. After leaving school he was engaged for a time in selling dry goods and small wares along the canal, but later settled in Orleans County, where he worked for six months in a wagon-building shop. At the end of that time he came to Barnerville, and opened a wagon-maker's shop in company with Henderson Pollock. After working there for some time he hired a shop near by, and carried on wagon-making and painting and some cabinet work. Going then to Schoharie, he worked at carriage-building in the winter and at painting in the summer for a few years, and then began working as a millwright along Cobleskill Creek and the Schoharie River Valley. He built a large number of grist and saw mills, and invented a water-wheel of which he afterward constructed and put in place about two hundred in this and adjoining counties. In 1875 he came to his present mill. This he had repaired during his early millwright work, it having been built by his wife's grandfather, Peter Lowmeyers in 1790. A part of the original structure is in use yet, and is in well-preserved condition. The mill has two stories and a half. The lower floor is devoted to custom and merchant work, principally to the manufacture of rye and buckwheat flour, which is marketed in New York and in other States. There are three mill-runs, besides a "pony stone." The second floor is devoted to purifying and storing the grain, while the top floor is used for scouring and cleaning grain and for storage. This is one of the oldest mills in the section, as well as one of the largest run by water power. Mr. Cary has now been connected with milling interests for nearly half a century, probably longer than any other man now living in this region.

On the last day of January, 1849, Mr. Cary was united in marriage with Phœbe Gordon, a native of Carlisle and daughter of John Gordon, a farmer of that town, who died at the age of sixty years. Mrs. Cary was one of a family of ten children, and has herself been the mother of eight, of whom five are living. These are: Alice, Andrew, Laura, Rosalie, and Walter. The three deceased are: Harriet, who died at the age of nine years of diphtheria; Retta, who died at the age of eighteen months; and Lyman H., who died at the age of six months. Alice, who married Henry Holmes McDonald, a carpenter and contractor of bridges, has three children — Frank, John P., and Rhoda. Andrew married Cynderilla Severson, and has four children — Hattie, Foster, Daisy, and Florence. The son, Foster, is a painter and decorator in Cobleskill. Laura married Thomas Chickering, a merchant of Lawyersville. Rosalie, who married Judd Bassett, a farmer, has one child, Ralph C. Walter Cary, an engineer, married Jennie Merchant, and has two sons — Olin and Emery P.

Mr. Cary is Republican in politics. He takes a warm interest in all public matters, but has never cared to hold public office. He is a member of the Masonic lodge at Cobleskill, of De Witt Council at Albany, and of John L. Lewis Chapter at Cobleskill. He built the house in which he now resides, and two others near by which are rented to tenants; also one with a store adjoining, and owns more houses than any other man in town. In religious views Mr. Cary is a Methodist. He is connected with the Methodist church here, has been steward in the society for many years, and an active worker in the Sunday-school. Mrs. Cary likewise has been a member of the church since her early girlhood. Mr. Cary is a progressive man. He has been keenly alive to every plan promulgated for the improvement of the town, and has kept his own property in unexcelled condition. Down at the mill he has built a large wall eleven feet high, containing boulders weighing a ton, to keep the water from overflowing. His other real estate property also shows that it is constantly looked out for and never allowed to lack repairs.

LOUIS A. BOENS, proprietor of La Touraine, Tannersville, was born in the north of France, February 8, 1855, son of Augustus and Josephine (de Sainte Roch) Boens. His parents were natives of Belgium, and his father, who was a farmer, died at the age of thirty-eight. His mother was twice married, and had six children, Louis being the eldest by her second husband. Mrs. Boens came to America with five of her children. She spent her last days

HENRY S. DE FOREST.

with her son Louis, dying at the age of fifty-eight.

Louis A. Boens accompanied the family to the United States, first settling in Belport, Long Island, and a year later removing to Hunter. His training in the business of hotel-keeping was begun at the Laurel House, with which he was connected in different capacities for several years. In 1889 he completed and opened La Touraine, which was built and furnished under his personal supervision, and has accommodations for fifty guests. It is a favorite resort for New York people, and has a large patronage. The table is a special feature, and is provided with poultry raised upon the premises.

In 1886 Mr. Boens was united in marriage with Kate Askin. Her parents, John and Mary Askin, who are no longer living, had a family of sixteen children. Mr. Askin was a native of Ireland. He died at the age of eighty years. The Boens family attend the Roman Catholic church. In politics Mr. Boens acts with the Democratic party.

HON. HENRY S. DE FOREST, ex-Mayor of Schenectady and an extensive real estate dealer, was born in this city, February 16, 1847, son of O. L. and Sarah (Vedder) De Forest.

His great-grandfather De Forest and his grandfather De Forest, both of whom were named Jacob, were lifelong residents of Schenectady County. Jacob De Forest, second, was a well-to-do farmer and the father of a large family of children, one of them a son Jacob, who became a prosperous farmer, and another Martin, who acquired wealth in mercantile pursuits, and was a man of prominence in this section of the State.

O. L. De Forest, born in this county in 1806, son of the second Jacob, was a cooper by trade, and followed that business in this city successfully for a number of years, or until his death, which occurred in 1859. He served as Sheriff of Schenectady County and also as a Deputy.

His wife, Sarah, was a daughter of Nicholas Vedder, of Schenectady County, whose ancestors were among the early Dutch settlers in the Mohawk valley. Seven children were born of their union, namely: Anna, who died young; Rebecca, wife of Stephen D. Gates, of this city; Jacob, a furniture dealer, who served as Sheriff one term, and died in 1894, aged about sixty-two years, leaving a widow and five children; Ella, who married Christopher Van Slyck, and died in 1894, leaving two children; Frank V., Assistant Chief of Police; Henry S., the subject of this sketch; and Lansing, a farmer in the town of Glenville, this county. The mother, Mrs. Sarah Vedder De Forest, died in 1867, aged fifty-nine years. Henry S. De Forest attended the Union School, and completed his studies with a commercial course at Eastman's Business College, Poughkeepsie. Entering the employ of his brother-in-law, Christopher Van Slyck, a broom manufacturer, as clerk and book-keeper, he was later admitted to partnership; and after the dissolution of that firm, in 1878, he became extensively engaged in the cultivation of broom corn, which he carried on successfully for eight years. When a young man he displayed a decided preference for the real estate business, and his first land purchase consisted of two lots for which he paid one hundred dollars each. About the year 1886 he turned his attention exclusively to city property, his transactions in which during the last twelve years have amounted to two million dollars. He organized the syndicates which erected the Edison Hotel, at a cost of one hundred and eighty-five thousand dollars, and the Van Curler Opera House, completed in 1893 at a cost of one hundred and two thousand dollars, of which he is the largest individual owner. Previous to the business depression of 1893, and since 1897, he has erected many hundreds of buildings for residence and business purposes. He has laid out several thoroughfares, including Foster Avenue, named in honor of Professor John Foster, of Union College; Summit and East Avenues; and Terrace Place. These localities have been protected against the encroachments of the liquor traffic largely through his instrumentality, and his excellent judgment in regard to the real estate interests of the city has proved exceedingly beneficial to property holders. He is one of the largest owners of the Metropolitan Asphalt Pavement Company, which was organized in 1895, and which has paved the principal streets of this city in a most satisfactory manner. He is considered to-day the most extensive real estate dealer and owner in Schenectady. He is also the largest owner in the Schenectady *Daily Gazette*, the leading newspaper in the city.

Politically, he is a Democrat. He served as City Recorder four years and as Mayor for the same length of time, and deserves much credit for giving the city a sound and progressive administration. He was active in securing the erection of the new brick railway station, and an entirely new sewer system was among the number of public improvements completed during his term of office.

On September 6, 1876, Mr. De Forest married Lucy E. Van Epps, of this city, daughter of the late Harmon Van Epps. They have two daughters, namely: Beulah, a recent graduate of Lasell Seminary; and Pearl, aged eleven years.

Mr. De Forest is a director of the Schenectady State Bank. He is a Master Mason and a trustee of the Young Men's Christian Association. His business office is located at 420 and his residence at 436 State Street. As noted above, his influence and judgment have long been prominent factors in shaping the course of public improvements in this city. The fact that he began business without capital will enable those readers of the REVIEW who have hitherto been unfamiliar with his early business life to better appreciate his untiring energy and perseverance.

CHAUNCEY SMITH, of West Catskill, N.Y., dealer in coal, hay, straw, and grain, was born in Roxbury, Delaware County, this State, on July

25, 1847. His parents were Jonas M. and Deborah (Kater) Smith, both natives of Roxbury. His paternal grandfather was David Smith, a native of Scotland. Immigrating to this country, David Smith settled in Roxbury, and there made his home many years, his death occurring at the advanced age of ninety-one. His wife, Jane More, also born in Scotland, died at the age of eighty-nine. She was the mother of a large family of children, of whom the only survivor is R. B. Smith, of Cortland, N. Y.

Jonas M. Smith was reared on a farm in Roxbury. He was educated in the public schools, and he subsequently taught school for a while. Going west as far as Illinois, he lived for a time in that State, and then returned to his native town and started a variety store, which he carried on until 1863. Removing in that year to Ashland, Greene County, he engaged in farming, also devoting his energies to some extent to mercantile affairs. Subsequently he came to Catskill, where he died at the age of seventy-five. He was a man of influence, and served as Town Supervisor for four terms, as well as in other positions of trust. His wife died at the age of fifty-nine. All her four children are living. They are: Chauncey, Mary, Nettie, and Addie. Mary married William H. Tompkins, of Ashland. Nettie is now Mrs. Lewis, and Addie is Mrs. Wiers.

Chauncey Smith remained in his native town until he was seventeen years of age. Going then to Ashland, he remained there thirteen years, and at the end of that time he came to Catskill. In 1877 he was engaged in the steamboat business at the Point, and from 1878 until 1892 he was in the flour and grain business. For a part of this time, some nine years, he also carried on a mill. He met with excellent success, but finally gave up all other business interests, and has since devoted himself to his coal and grain business, which is one of the most prosperous enterprises in the town. In 1898 he erected the building which he now uses. He has both wholesale and retail trade, and is known as a man thoroughly estimable and upright.

In 1870 Mr. Smith was united in marriage with Aravesta Lewis, who was born in Durham. Eight children have blessed this union; namely, Vernon M., Howard C., Raymond E., William H., Lizzie, Robert C., Arthur, and Clifford H. Vernon M. Smith is in the real estate and insurance business in Iowa and Minnesota. He married Maud Jennings, and has one son, Chauncey Joseph. Howard C. is a dealer in horses, and resides in this town. He married Carrie Crawford. Raymond and William are in school.

Mr. Smith is a Republican. He is a member of the Water Board and of the School Board, and a trustee in the Savings Bank. He was one of the organizers of the Catskill Rural Cemetery, and is one of its trustees. He and his wife and three of their sons are members of the Methodist church. Mr. Smith is a trustee of the church, and Mrs. Smith has been a teacher in the Sunday-school. Both are earnestly interested in all efforts to promote the moral and spiritual growth of mankind.

JOHN H. STERNBERG, vice-president and director of the Sharon, Seward, and Carlisle Insurance Company, and a leading hop-grower of Seward, resides on the Lunenburg turnpike about three miles from Seward village. He was born on the Sternberg homestead in this town on April 17, 1832, son of Abraham and Anna M. (Wormuth) Sternberg, and is a representative of one of the oldest families in Schoharie County. His great-grandfather, Nicholas Sternberg, who was born in Schoharie, was a lineal descendant of Lambert Sternberg, who came to America from Germany.

Nicholas Sternberg was one of the pioneer settlers of the town of Sharon, now Seward. He cleared land and built a log cabin near the site where John H. Sternberg now lives. He became very prosperous, and a prominent man in this section, and owned a flour-mill and some three hundred acres of land.

John Sternberg, son of Nicholas, and grandfather of John H. Sternberg, was born on the homestead and reared there. The property eventually reverted to him, and he spent his life in improving it. He built the present house. A man of intelligence and sound judgment, he was highly respected by all with whom he came in contact, and he was an especially valued member of the Lutheran church, in which he held at different times all the offices. His wife, whose maiden name was Anna Shafer, was a native of this region. She died at the advanced age of eighty years. All of the eleven children born to this worthy pair grew to maturity. One of the sons, named Levi, was educated for the ministry in the Lutheran church. John Sternberg served for a time as Coroner.

Abraham Sternberg was born in the house built by his father, and was educated in the public schools of this district. He assisted his father on the farm for some time, and eventually assumed full management, carrying on general farming. He cultivated about two hundred acres of land. As a citizen he was active and well-informed, and for many years served as Supervisor, holding the office during the trying days of the Civil War. He was also Town Clerk for some years. For many years he was a trustee of the Lutheran church, and was particularly active at the time the new building was erected. He also held other offices of public trust, and was one of the first to introduce hop-growing into Schoharie County. He was also one of the original incorporators of the First National Bank of Cobleskill. His wife, Anna, who is still living at the age of eighty-one, was one of a large family of children born to Henry Wormuth, of Sharon, an early settler here, and by occupation a tanner and currier. As was her husband, she has been a lifelong member of the Lutheran church. She has been the mother of eight children, of whom there are still living — John H.; James H., who is a physician at Waterloo, N.Y.; Irving, a physician of Gouverneur, N.Y.; Henrietta, who married Barnabas Eldred; and Jerome, who is a banker in Erie, Pa. Jerome Sternberg has two sons, who are in the same bank with him.

John H. Sternberg obtained a good practical

education in the public schools near his home and at Hartwick Seminary. After completing his studies he was for some years engaged in farming on different farms away from Seward; but in 1892 he came back to his native place and settled on his present farm, where he has since been largely engaged in hop culture. He has about fifty-two acres devoted to raising this important crop. Mr. Sternberg was one of the incorporators of the Sharon, Seward, and Carlisle Insurance Company, of which he has ever since been a director and agent, and for the last six years vice-president. The company is in a very prosperous condition, and has a capital of a million and a quarter of dollars.

In politics Mr. Sternberg is a Democrat. He has been Collector of the town for some time, and for a period of eight years, beginning in 1890, he filled the office of Supervisor. He is the only man in the town who has held this important office for so long a time. Mr. Sternberg has been a lifelong member of the Lutheran church, and has officiated in all the different church offices. He is at the present time serving as a trustee of the society. He has also been warmly interested in the work of the Sunday-school, and was formerly a teacher therein. His wife is connected with the church, and has also been a worker in the Sunday-school. A number of their children are church members.

Mr. Sternberg was united in marriage on January 30, 1865, with M. Ellen Eldredge. She was born in Sharon, near Sharon Springs, daughter of Robert Eldredge, a native of Sharon Springs. Her grandfather, Barnabas Eldredge, was among the first settlers of that place, and owned nearly all of the land where the present village now stands. He kept a tavern, and was interested in the manufacture of saleratus. His seven sons, to each of whom he gave a fine farm, became prominent men in their section of the State, and some of them were well-known hotel-keepers. They were active in public affairs, and creditably perpetuated the memory of their father. Barnabas Eldredge died at the age of seventy-two. He was widely acquainted, and commanded the respect of all who knew him.

Robert Eldredge was reared in his native town. He sold the farm given him by his father, and bought another near the church in Sharon, comprising about two hundred acres, and located thereon a house and store. For twelve years he was in business there, a well-known merchant and a successful one. He was at one time judge of the county, and usually went by the name of Judge Eldredge. He was also a Justice of the Peace, and his opinion and advice were eagerly sought on important occasions. He died at the age of fifty-three. Although not connected officially with any church organization, he was a man of straightforward Christian principle, and a believer in the doctrines of the Universalist church. His wife, whose maiden name was Margaret Adams, is still living at Cobleskill, in the full possession of all her faculties at the advanced age of ninety-one years. She was born in the town of Sharon. Six of her seven children grew to maturity, and four of them are living, namely: John A.; M. Ellen; Spencer, who resides at Dwight, Ill.; and James, who is a merchant and Postmaster in California. Horatio Olcott and Elizabeth are deceased.

Mrs. Sternberg resided with her parents until her marriage. She was educated in the common schools and in Cherry Valley Academy. She has three children; namely, Howard J., Charles A., and Robert E. The first of these, who married Anna Vorhees, is proprietor of a hotel at Seward. Five children have been born to him, of whom four are living, namely: Grace A., who is with Mrs. Sternberg, and is attending school; Julia A.; George V.; and Le Ray. Charles A. Sternberg married for his first wife Lizzie Clark, who died at the age of twenty-two. He married for his second wife Mamie Clark. He is a graduate of Bellevue Hospital Medical College in New York City, and is now in practice at Gloversville, having gone to that place from Howes Cave. Robert Sternberg married Louise Snedecor. They have one child, Florence Louise, born June 17, 1898. Robert Sternberg was born in Seward and worked on the farm until he was sixteen years old. He then attended Hartwick Seminary for three years, and subsequently took a four years' course at Cornell University, graduating in 1890 with the degree of Bachelor of Laws. He then taught school in Blue Point, Long Island, for a time, and has since been appointed School Commissioner of the second district of Schoharie County, succeeding Thomas E. Finegan. He has held the office since January 1, 1893, and is regarded as one of the most efficient officers in educational work in this section of the State. He has filled in his leisure moments studying law, and was admitted to the bar in March, 1899.

JOSEPH PUTMAN, who cultivates a productive farm in Rotterdam, Schenectady County, N.Y., was born in this town May 3, 1833, son of Aaron and Nancy (Hagerman) Putman. His father was born here in 1805, and his grandfather, John Putman, was among the early residents. His great-grandfather, Aaron Putman, first, who came from Holland, settled in Rotterdam as a pioneer. All of the above-named ancestors were industrious farmers.

Aaron Putman, second, son of John, improved the farm which his son Joseph now owns, and was one of the able farmers of his day. In politics he acted with the Republican party, and was a Justice of the Peace for several years. He was a member of the Dutch Reformed church, and an earnest advocate of temperance. He died at the age of seventy-six years. Nancy Hagerman Putman, his wife, was a native of Amsterdam, N.Y, and the locality in that town known as Hagerman's Mills was named for her father. Of her children two are living, namely: John A. Putman, a real estate dealer in Brooklyn; and Joseph, the subject of this sketch. The others were: Dr. Francis D. Putman, who died at the age of twenty-three; Maggie V. Hagerman, who died November 19, 1875; Elizabeth, who became Mrs. Sauter, and died in 1897; Ernestus H., who died at the age of ten years; and two children who died in infancy. The mother lived to be eighty-two years old.

Joseph Putman acquired his education in the schools of Rotterdam and Syracuse. When thirteen years old he made himself useful about the farm, and after completing his studies he gave his entire attention to farming at the homestead. At the time of his marriage he began to work the farm on shares, and he continued to do so until his father's death, when he purchased the interest of the other heirs. He owns one hundred and twenty-five acres of desirably located land, which afford excellent opportunities for both tillage and pasturage, and, aside from raising the usual crops, he disposes of the milk of from fifteen to twenty cows.

On September 10, 1862, Mr. Putman was joined in marriage with Martha E. Shufelt, who was born in Rotterdam, September 6, 1840. Her parents, George and Pauline (Britton) Shufelt, are not living. Her father was a prosperous farmer. Mrs. Putman is the mother of two daughters — Purlie and Minnie, both of whom reside with their parents. Purlie married Van D. Sager, a building contractor, and has one son, Clinton Sager, who was born June 22, 1892. Minnie is the wife of George H. Putman, an employee at the Edison Electric Works, Schenectady, and has one son, Joseph W., who was born January 9, 1898.

Although taking a lively interest in town affairs, and supporting at the polls the candidates for local positions whom he considers most desirable, Mr. Putman has never cared to hold public office himself. In national elections he acts with the Republican party. He is sincerely respected for his sterling integrity and high moral character. He is a member of the Reformed church.

JOHN B. KNIFFEN, late a leading hop-grower of Middleburg, N.Y., and, at the time of his death, on January 25, 1899, the only hop-buyer with an office in the town, was born at New Baltimore, Greene County, on July 5, 1835. He was a son of John and Sophia (Crook) Kniffen, and descended from a line of agriculturists sprung from English stock. His first ancestor in this country came from England to a farm in New Jersey. His grandfather Kniffen removed from New Jersey to this State in early manhood, and spent the remainder of his life in New Baltimore, where he died in extreme old age, lacking only three years of having reached a full century.

John Kniffen, father of John B., was born in New Baltimore, and was there educated in the public schools. He was reared to a farmer's life, but also did some work at the stone cutter's trade. Although strong and healthy, with every prospect of a long life, he was stricken down in the fulness of manhood, and died at the age of fifty-three from typhoid fever. He was a zealous member of the Methodist Episcopal church, one of the trustees of the society, and for many years a class leader. He was a noted exhorter and a powerful man in prayer. His wife, Sophia, who died at the age of seventy-six, was also a lifelong and active Methodist. She was the mother of four sons and five daughters, and of these nine children the subject of this sketch was the latest survivor.

John B. Kniffen received a practical education in the public schools, and during vacation time worked on his father's farm, where he learned the art of successful farming. At eighteen years of age he came to Middleburg, where until he reached his majority he worked by the month on farms, and at the same time made arrangements so that he was enabled to attend school during the winter. At the age of twenty-one he purchased a farm of some forty acres, which formed the nucleus of his later splendid property of over three hundred acres. As a farmer he was very successful; and he and his son, who was in business with him for a number of years, were looked upon as two of the most progressive agriculturists in this region. The Kniffen estate embraces practically two farms, both of which are in a high state of cultivation. All the buildings on the farm upon which he lived, and also the house where his son lives, were built by Mr. Kniffen. In 1860 he began the culture of hops in a small way, being among the first here to engage in that enterprise. He constantly increased the scale of his operations, and in his later years had some fifty acres devoted to hop-growing, producing annually some one hundred and twenty-five bales of hops. In 1880 he began buying hops, and from that time on he was interested with Charles S. May, who is proprietor of one of the largest hop markets in Albany. Mr. Kniffen was the first man in Middleburg to become a buyer, and he was latterly, as before mentioned, the only one in town who had an office. He raised grain of different kinds on his farm.

Mr. Kniffen was married in 1855 to Tabitha Wormer, a native of Middleburg, and daughter of John Wormer, a successful and prominent farmer of this place. Of the four sons and four daughters born of this union, seven children are living, namely: Emery W., who was in business with his father; Erskine; Estella; Amoretta; Evelyn; Frank; and Elliot. Erskine, who married Molly Bowman, is in the insurance business connected with the Mutual Reserve Friend Association. Estella is the wife of Luther Jackson, overseer of the North Shore Road at South Schenectady, and is the mother of seven children — John, Flora, Frank, Harry, Claude, Clarence, and Ford, who is deceased. Amoretta married Charles D. Mitchell, who is in a shoe factory at Binghamton. They have a family of three children — by name, Belle, Clifford, and Forrest. Evelyn is the wife of Clarence McBain, a member of the firm of Bassler & Co., of Middleburg, and she is the mother of four children — Nellie, John, Louisa, and Alice Leona. Frank, who also is a farmer and was interested in business with his father, married Dora Crosby, and has one daughter, Delia. Elliot Kniffen resides near the old home, and is interested in bee culture, in poultry raising, and in general farming. He married Ella Van Voras.

GEORGE W. BELLINGER.

In politics Mr. Kniffen was a stanch Democrat. He was a member of Middleburg Lodge, No. 663, F. & A. M., with which he had been connected for twenty years, and he was buried with Masonic honors. He followed the religious faith of which his father was so devoted a disciple, and was one of the strong men in the Methodist church at Middleburg. He was a member of it for forty years, and his wife and nearly all of his children are members. At the time the new church edifice was erected, Mr. Kniffen contributed a thousand dollars toward its construction.

GEORGE W. BELLINGER, editor and publisher of the Cobleskill *Index* at Cobleskill, N.Y., was born in this town, December 18, 1843. His father, George Bellinger, was born, bred, and educated in Seward, Schoharie County, where he worked at farming until sixteen years old, and then learned the blacksmith's trade. When ready to establish himself permanently, George Bellinger came to Cobleskill, and was here industriously employed at his trade until his death, June 26, 1867. He married Miss Caroline Shafer, a daughter of Jacob Shafer, a prosperous farmer of this town, and a descendant of one of its earlier pioneers. Two children were born of their union; namely, George W., and a child that died when young. The mother is still living in Cobleskill.

George W. Bellinger received a practical education in the public schools of his district. Having become interested in the subject of photography when a young man, he had an opportunity to learn the art in 1865, when Mr. Oswald Burnett opened the first regular studio in the town on the third floor of the building now occupied by Charles H. Schaffer. Mr. Bellinger proved an apt pupil, and in a short time bought out his employer. Being a man of enterprise and good business ability, well endowed with artistic talent, he met with excellent success, and, having gained a wide reputation for superior skill, he won an extensive and lucrative patronage in this and surrounding towns. Removing to the present site of the dental parlors of Dr. L. T. Browne, he there carried on his work until the fire of 1873, which destroyed all of his equipments.

The following month Mr. Bellinger embarked in a new career. He bought the Cobleskill *Index*, which was established in 1865 by William H. Week and the Hon. Henry E. Abel, and during the twenty-six years that this paper has since been under his management he has kept it in a leading position among the local journals of Schoharie County. It has been greatly enlarged, its circulation increased fourfold, and its subscription rate reduced from a dollar and a half to one dollar per year. Through its columns he has been a strong advocate of all movements tending to benefit the community, and has rendered valuable aid to the Democratic party by his sound and stirring editorials. He has also been influential in establishing different organizations in the locality, among them being the Cobleskill Agricultural Society, formed in 1876, largely by his personal efforts and his "talks" on the subject in the *Index*. Mr. Bellinger was a member of this association's board of management from its inception to the year 1898, and during a like period he served without salary as its secretary.

He has also been secretary and treasurer of the Cobleskill Rural Cemetery Association six years, and has served two terms as one of the village trustees. He is prominently connected with the Farmers' and Merchants' Bank, of which he was one of the projectors, as a member of the finance committee, and is president of the Schoharie and Otsego Mutual Fire Insurance Company. In politics he has always been a loyal Democrat.

In the year 1871 Mr. Bellinger married Miss Minnie Moulton, the only daughter of the Hon. F. P. Moulton, an able and influential citizen of Montgomery County. Mr. and Mrs. Bellinger have two children, namely: Vernon M., teller in the Farmers' and Merchants' Bank; and Maud S.

HERBERT KIPP, general merchant and proprietor of the Kipp House, Lexington, Greene County, N.Y., was born in this town March 6, 1852, son of Isaac and Nancy (Van Heusen) Kipp. He is of Dutch descent. Isaac Kipp, first, his great-grandfather, was a pioneer settler of Dutchess County, New York. Benjamin Kipp, son of Isaac, first, resided in Dutchess County until twenty-one years old, when he came to Greene County. The trades of a carpenter and millwright, which he had previously learned, he followed in this locality for twenty years, or until 1802, when he purchased a farm in Lexington. Here he resided until his death, which occurred in 1837, at the age of sixty years. He married Sally Noyes, a native of New Jersey, and became the father of eleven children. The survivors of this family are: Isaac, second; and Harriet, who married a Mr. Jones, of Hartford, Conn. Mrs. Sally N. Kipp died at the age of seventy-one years.

Isaac Kipp, second, father of Herbert, was born in this town, April 12, 1818. He followed farming on the homestead until 1850, when he went to California, and was fairly successful in the gold mines on the middle fork of the American River. After spending a year there, he returned to Lexington, and remained on the home farm until 1858, when he made a trip to Pike's Peak. In 1877 he opened the general store now carried on by his son, and under the firm name of I. Kipp & Son conducted a profitable enterprise until 1887, when he disposed of his interest and went to Nebraska. The next five years he spent upon a farm in that State, and then he once more returned to his native town, where he is now residing with his son. In politics he is a Democrat. He was Supervisor two terms, and he acted as a Justice of the Peace forty years. He is a member and a trustee of the Baptist church. His wife, Nancy, was a native of Lexington, daughter of Cornelius Van Heusen, a farmer. She died at the age of sixty years, having been the mother of six children. The five now living are: Mary, who married William H. Mosher, of South Dakota; C. L.

Kipp, who is Postmaster at Lexington; Herbert, the subject of this sketch; Jennie, who married R. L. Hogaboom; and Edwin L. Kipp.

Herbert Kipp was educated in the schools of Lexington and at Eastman's Business College, Poughkeepsie. He worked on the home farm and also had charge of a stage route until 1876, when he went to Illinois and spent one year. In 1877 he, in company with his father, engaged in general mercantile business in Lexington, and the partnership continued until 1887, when he bought the elder Kipp's interest. For the next two years he was associated with his brother, C. L. Kipp, and since 1889 he has conducted the establishment alone. He occupies two floors, the main store being thirty by forty feet, with an annex forty by twelve feet, and carries a full line of groceries, boots, shoes, hats, caps, hardware, flour, grain, drugs, carpets, oil cloths, dry goods, notions, and other articles of general merchandise. In connection with his mercantile business he conducts the Kipp House, a favorite summer resort, accommodating fifty guests.

In 1881 Mr. Kipp was united in marriage with Miss Mary F. Jones, of Jewett, daughter of Benjamin Jones, a farmer, who resides with a son, and is now ninety years old. Mr. and Mrs. Kipp are the parents of three children — Pearl, Clara May, and Ralph.

Politically, Mr. Kipp acts with the Democratic party. He was Postmaster under Cleveland's first administration four years, held the same office three years during President Harrison's administration, and was Supervisor one term. He is a member of the Knights of Pythias. Mr. and Mrs. Kipp attend the Baptist church.

JOHN H. FRANCE, the representative of a pioneer family of Seward, Schoharie County, has a well-improved farm located on the road to the Seward Depot, about six miles from Cobleskill and two miles from the village of Hyndsville. He was born in Seward, March 30, 1834, and this town was also the birthplace of his father, Peter France — or Uncle Peter, as he was familiarly known.

Tracing the line back to the great-grandfather, we find a Revolutionary patriot, of whom and his family this story is told: While he was off at Schoharie defending the fort, his sons, Henry and John, who had remained at home, were taken prisoners. John was killed; but Henry, the grandfather of the subject of this sketch, fortunately escaped from his captors, and after lying in the woods for a day or two made his way home.

Henry France came to Seward in Colonial days, while yet a young man, and took up a tract of unbroken land in the depths of the forest. A few years later he removed to an adjoining farm, and was there engaged in agricultural pursuits until his death, at the age of fourscore and eight years. He united with the Lutheran church in early manhood, but was afterward an active member of the Methodist church. He was interested in the cause of temperance, and through his influence the use of liquor in the harvest field was abolished.

His wife bore him fourteen children, one of whom is now living — Gilbert, a farmer in Seward.

Peter France spent his life of seventy-four years in Seward, receiving his education in the district school, and on the home farm acquiring a practical knowledge of agriculture. On leaving the parental roof he purchased land at Seward Valley, then known as Neeley Hollow, where he spent some years. Selling that he bought the estate on which his son, John H., now resides, and from that time until his death was prominently identified with the agricultural interests of this part of the town. Possessing a good fund of general information, and being a man of sound judgment, he was often called upon for counsel and advice, and his opinions were always respected. In politics he affiliated with the Democrats prior to the Rebellion, but after that time was a stanch Republican. Influential in local affairs, he served as Overseer of the Poor and as Highway Commissioner for several years. His wife, Elizabeth Diefendorf, was born at Frey's Bush, Montgomery County, N.Y., one of the twelve children of a pioneer farmer, John Diefendorf. Both parents united with the Methodist church when young, and as true Christians exemplified its teachings in their daily lives. Both were active in church work, the father being class leader of the Seward Valley church society for many years, and their hospitable home was ever open to the ministers of the circuit. They reared three children, as follows: John H., the subject of this sketch; Emeline, wife of Sylvester Rewland, of Morrisville, N.Y.; and Louisa. The latter, who died October 17, 1892, after many years of illness, was wife of the late Norman Ottman, a graduate of the Normal School. Mr. Ottman was for some years a teacher in Seward, and afterward was here engaged as a merchant until the breaking out of the Civil War. Enlisting then as a private in Colonel Ellsworth's regiment, the One Hundred and Forty-fourth New York Volunteer Infantry, he went bravely forth to serve his country, and was killed in battle.

John H. France received a good common school education, and till he was twenty-five years of age assisted his father in farming. Then taking the farm on shares, he carried it on successfully until the death of his father, when the whole estate of one hundred and twenty acres came into his possession. He has since continued in his chosen vocation, and besides harvesting excellent crops of hay and grain each season he has raised large quantities of hops, a staple product of this region. He keeps about fifteen Jersey and Durham cows, and makes a fine quality of butter, with which he supplies private customers in Troy and Albany. His farm is well equipped with modern machinery and implements for carrying on his work; and the buildings, which were nearly all erected by his father, are kept in fine repair.

Mr. France is a Republican in politics, and has served as Inspector of Elections in his town. He is a charter member of the local organization of Good Templars, and also of the Seward Grange, P. of H., in which he has held all the offices up to Master. In the former society he was for several years the Chaplain. One of the most active and influential members of the Methodist church, he materially assisted in building the new house of worship of this denomination, and in remodelling the old one at Seward Valley. He was the first child christened in the first frame church edifice erected in this part of the country, and having joined the church at the age of sixteen, he is now, with but few exceptions, the oldest member of this locality. He has been trustee and class leader, and was for a number of years chorister of the Methodist Episcopal choir, in which he and his children sang. Since a boy of fourteen he has been connected with the Sunday-school as pupil, teacher, or superintendent, having held the latter position three terms, and during the past five years has had charge of the ladies' Bible class.

Mr. France has been twice married. On June 12, 1855, was solemnized his union with Orpha Diefendorf. She was born in Seward, a daughter of George Diefendorf, and was one of fourteen children; namely, Susan, Sylvester, Jacob, Henrietta, Salina, Jane, Judson, Orpha, Sophronia, Peter, Abraham, Wealthy, Rensselaer, and Nancy. She died at the age of thirty-four years, leaving five children, of whom the following is a brief record: Clarence L., a skilful farmer and able business man of Cobleskill, married Allie Rose, and has three children — Anson, Grace, and Harry; Emory died at the age of four years; Welton, a farmer in Seward, married Clara Hevener, and has four children — Ezra, Sadie, Norman, and Hattie; Allie May, wife of Charles Sutphen, a farmer near Richmondville, has three children — John, Emma, and Orpha; Lizzie married Jacob Van Woert, a son of the Rev. Jacob Van Woert, formerly pastor of the Dutch Reformed church. Her husband, who for several years was an instructor in the Cobleskill High School, died at the age of twenty-five years, leaving her with two children — Dora D. and Jacob H. She now lives with her father.

On June 27, 1869, Mr. France married Mrs. Sarah Wigley, who was born at Fonda, Montgomery County, N.Y., a daughter of Frederick Dockstaden, a farmer. By her first husband, Gilbert Wigley, she has one child, William Wigley, who is a fireman on the New York Central Railway. He married Ella Card, and has had three children — Willie, Bernice, and Byron, the last two being deceased.

ALEXANDER MacMILLEN, one of the most influential citizens of Carlisle, Schoharie County, was born in Bethlehem, Albany County, N.Y., on October 4, 1842, son of James and Ellen N. (Waldron) MacMillen. His great-grandfather MacMillen was a Scotch emigrant who settled in Albany. His grandfather, who resided in New Scotland, N.Y., died there at eighty-six years of age. He was a farmer and a leading politician among the old-time Whigs. He occupied prominent civil offices, such as those of Supervisor and Collector, and was one of the active and influential members of the Presbyterian church. He had a family of eleven children, seven sons and four daughters, all of whom are now deceased. They were: John, Andrew, James, Henry, Alexander, William, Aaron, Mary, Nancy, Catherine, and one whose name is not remembered. Of these, James, father of Alexander MacMillen, was the only one that settled in this county. Most of these brothers were Republicans politically, and were associated with the Presbyterian church. James, however, was a Methodist. He was a quiet, conservative man, thoroughly well-informed on the topics of the day. He left his childhood's home at about fourteen years of age, and a number of years after his marriage he came to Carlisle and bought the farm where his son Alexander, then eight years old, now lives. It was then known as the Henry Best farm. It contained, originally, a hundred acres, but since it came into possession of its present owner it has been enlarged by the addition of twenty acres. James MacMillen was married three times, and had two children --- Alexander and William. The latter enlisted in the northern army when under the age of the draft-mark, saw gallant service at Fairfax Court-house, and subsequently died of typhoid fever. He had previously worked with his father on the farm; and his death, while a severe shock to all his family, was especially affecting to his father.

Alexander MacMillen is the leading Republican in Carlisle, and one of the most prominent in the county. Somewhat singular is the fact that he has attended only two caucuses in his whole life. Three times he has been Supervisor of Carlisle, being the second Republican in this strongly Democratic town to hold that office, the other Republican holding it for only one term. Though a member of the minority party, he met with defeat only once or twice, and then by no larger majority than twenty. He has served for many years on the Republican county committee. Mr. MacMillen is the largest land-owner in town, and the wealthiest citizen of Carlisle. For the last twenty-eight years he has been a successful hop-grower, probably making a greater success of that industry than any other farmer in the locality. About a hundred acres of his farm are cleared land, and in addition to his hop crops he has raised general produce. He formerly owned three other farms, which had come to him through the foreclosures of mortgages, but these he has now disposed of. He is the largest tax-payer in Carlisle. Mr. MacMillen was a stockholder in the old bank at Cobleskill, and is a charter member, stockholder, and director in the new bank. He owns fifty shares, the largest number owned by one man. Mr. MacMillen and his wife are among the strongest supporters of the Methodist church in this place, and both sing in the choir. Mrs. MacMillen is a member of the church, and an active worker in the Sunday-school, in which she has been a teacher for many years. When the Christian Endeavor Society was started here, she became its president.

The maiden name of Mrs. MacMillen, who was married in 1864, was Eveline Bradt, and she is a daughter of William Bradt, deceased, formerly a farmer of Cobleskill. Her paternal grandfather, who came hither from Albany County, cleared the farm and built the house now standing on it. Her grandfather, James Boughton, who lived to the advanced age of ninety years, was the leading man in the Presbyterian church at Carlisle, and in his last years he sat in one of the chairs inside the altar rail. Mrs. MacMillen's father was a member of the Dutch Reformed church. He had a family of four children. Mr. and Mrs. MacMillen have one child, William A., who since attending the Albany Business College has been in business with his father. He married Ada Dockstader, and has one son, Irvin A.

FRANK AKELEY, dealer in general merchandise at West Fulton, was born here on October 20, 1851, his parents being James and Sally J. (Shutts) Akeley.

James Akeley, who was born in January, 1812, came to this town in 1840, and settled on a fine farm of about two hundred acres, near what is now his son's store, and here he remained engaged in agriculture until his death in 1861, at about the age of fifty. His wife, Sally, survived him many years, and died in February, 1898. She was the daughter of John Shutts, of Greenville, Greene County, a lifelong and prominent farmer, and also a veterinary surgeon. Her mother was of Connecticut birth. Mr. and Mrs. Shutts had a family of four children. Of these the only survivor is Mrs. Salome Hart, who resides near Greenville. Seven children were born to Mr. and Mrs. James Akeley, and all are living. They are: Edgar, who resides at Cobleskill; Emily, who is the wife of William Richards; Dr. John S., who is a physician in Ravena, Albany County; Martin A., who is County Clerk of Schoharie County; Lorenzo, farmer and Supervisor (1899); Frank, the subject of this sketch; and Mary J., who married John Hinds, of Greenville. Both parents attended the Methodist church.

Mr. Frank Akeley, after obtaining his education in the common schools of his native village and at the Normal School at Albany, taught school for a while. In 1871 he went to work in the store of M. B. Fellows, situated opposite his present place of business, and there remained until 1875, when he went to New York for a short time. Later in the same year he returned, and began teaching the school at West Fulton. During the farming season of that year, 1876, he worked for six months on a farm, but in the fall taught school at Fulton. Not long after he bought his present building, and since that time he has had a prosperous career as a merchant. He carries a large stock of goods, including groceries, boots and shoes, dry goods, ready-made clothing, underwear, glassware and hardware, patent medicines, and, to some extent, farming implements. A gradual increase of stock has made it necessary for him to have enlarged quarters; and, since starting, he has opened a second floor, so that he has now an exceedingly well-equipped business.

In politics Mr. Akeley is a Republican.

For a time he served as Assistant Postmaster. He was married in 1881 to Elmina Zeh, a native of Breakabeen, and daughter of Adam and Nancy (Shafer) Zeh. Mr. Zeh was a lifelong farmer. He had four children. After his death his widow married a second time. Mr. and Mrs. Akeley have one child, Hazel, who is at school. Mr. Akeley has served on the county committee. He is liberal in religious views, and believes in dealing with unquestionable honesty in all his business transactions.

REV. CHARLES WADSWORTH PITCHER, pastor of the Reformed Dutch church at Middleburg, Schoharie County, is one of the most able, progressive, and popular clergymen of his denomination and a highly esteemed citizen. He was born March 2, 1849, near Cohoes, Albany County, a son of the Rev. William Pitcher, whose birthplace was Red Hook, Dutchess County, N.Y. His paternal grandfather, who was an officer in the War of 1812, was a prosperous farmer and an extensive landholder at Upper Red Hook, where he died at the advanced age of fourscore years. His wife, Catherine Kipp, also attained a ripe old age. Both were members of the Dutch Reformed Church of Upper Red Hook. They had five children, none of whom are now living.

The Rev. William Pitcher was reared on the home farm, and obtained his elementary education in the district schools. He subsequently studied at Williams College and Princeton Seminary. He began his professional life as pastor of a Dutch Reformed church at Jackson, N.Y.; and three years later he assumed charge of the "Boght" church at Watervliet, three miles from the village of Cohoes. After a faithful service of thirteen years in that place he accepted a call to South Branch, Somerset County, N.J., where a church, small in numbers, had been but a short time organized. He labored there twenty-seven years, a long and successful pastorate, in which he built up a flourishing society. Going then to Greenwich, Washington County, N.Y., he there lived in retirement until his demise, at the age of seventy-three years. He was a gifted speaker, a sermonizer of especial note; and many of his pulpit discourses, published in book form, were forcible exponents of his theological belief. A man of strong personality and unusual sweetness of character, he led a pure, Christian life, and in a rare degree won the love and esteem of all with whom he came in contact. He was three times married. His first wife, Mary Ann Wadsworth, died in young womanhood, leaving one son, De Witt Pitcher, now a book-keeper in Hudson, N.Y. His second wife, Jane E. Wadsworth, sister to his first wife, was born at Bantam Falls, Litchfield County, Conn., a daughter of Henry Wadsworth, a prosperous merchant. She was a sister of the Rev. Charles Wadsworth, D.D., of Philadelphia, and James L. Wadsworth, who is now living retired from active pursuits in Darien, Conn. Of the children born of this union two are now living, namely: Charles W., the special subject of this sketch;

CHARLES W. PITCHER.

and Jane E., wife of W. B. Warner, a photographer at Northport, Long Island. The mother died at the age of thirty-six years, and the father subsequently married Mary Ann McLean.

The Rev. Charles W. Pitcher received his elementary education in the public schools of South Branch, N.J., which he left at the age of sixteen years to go to New York City, where he was clerk in a jewelry store and in a dry-goods store for four years. He then continued his studies at a select school in Neshanic, N.J., and at Rutgers Grammar School in New Brunswick, which he attended two years, and after that at Rutgers College four years and at the theological seminary two years. On January 26, 1876, having previously been licensed to preach by the Newark Congregational Association, he was ordained to the ministry at Randolph, N.Y., and at once took charge of the weak and struggling society, which in 1883 he left in a most flourishing condition, it having doubled numerically and financially under his efficient labors. The ensuing four years he was pastor of the church at Stanton, N.J., which under his guidance was wonderfully revived, large numbers being added to the organization, which increased in usefulness each year, and, according to the stated clerk of the classis to which it belongs, reached the highest degree of prosperity in its history. From 1887 until 1891 Mr. Pitcher had charge of the Kirkpatrick Memorial Church at Ringoes, N.J., where his efforts were again blessed with success. Under his fervent and eloquent preaching of the gospel, great interest was awakened; and, during a great revival that followed, sixty members were added to the church in one Sunday, forty of the converts being baptized that day. Coming from there to Middleburg, he has here been exceedingly prospered in his religious work, the church having grown as regards both its membership and its influence. A faithful and conscientious worker in the Master's vineyard, he has not only endeared himself to his immediate parishioners, but has won the respect of the entire community.

On July 14, 1875, Mr. Pitcher was married to Anna M., daughter of Abraham and Ann E. (Naylor) Amerman. Her parents were natives and lifelong residents of Somerset County, New Jersey, where the mother died when sixty years old, and the father, who was a prominent citizen of South Branch, a miller and merchant, died at the age of threescore and ten years. Mrs. Pitcher is one of a family of four children, all of whom are living, the other three being: Theodore; Elizabeth, wife of Abraham S. Beckman; and Louisa, wife of H. V. D. Van Liew. Mr. and Mrs. Pitcher have had two children, namely: Le Roy, who lived but nine months; and Anna Lee. Mrs. Pitcher, a woman of culture, is a thorough musician, being a talented singer and a fine pianist. While at Ringoes she was leader of the church choir, the organist in the Sunday-school, and one of its corps of teachers. She is a very active member of the church and of its various societies, belonging to the Christian Endeavor, the Ladies' Missionary Society, the Ladies' Aid Society, and the Woman's Christian Temperance Union. She is president of the Woman's Classical Union of Schoharie County.

The Dutch Reformed Church of Middleburg is, with possibly an exception in Albany and Schenectady, the oldest society and worshipping in the oldest building in this part of the State. This house of worship was built in 1786, and has since been kept in excellent repair. The funds for its erection were collected by committees sent through the colonies for the purpose, the struggling little society here, organized about 1730, being too poor to give much toward it. The meetings were probably held in private houses or barns until a small frame building was put up for its accommodation in 1732. That building, according to Roscoe, was dedicated in 1737. It was burned with the village on October 17, 1780, and six years later replaced by the present edifice, in which the first sermon was preached November 18, 1787, the Rev. George W. Schneider being the minister. From the time of the first regularly ordained minister of the church, Hendrick Hager, who was settled in 1713, the following have held pastorates: Fred Hager, 1720; John Jacob Ehle, 1730; Reinhardt Erickson, 1732; Michael Weiss, 1736; Johannes Schuyler, 1736-55; John Mauritius Goetschius, 1757-60; Abram Rosekrantz, 1760-65; Johannes Schuyler, 1766-79; Rynier Van Nest, 1780-85; George W. Schneider, 1785-88; J. C. Boeffel, 1788-97; Rynier Van Nest, 1797-1804; David Devoe, 1812-15; John T. Schermerhorn, 1816-27; John Garretson, 1827-33; J. B. Steele, 1834-38; Joshua Boyd, 1840-42; L. Messereau, 1842-45; Jacob West, 1846-52; I. M. See, 1852-54; E. Vedder, 1855-63; W. E. Bogardus; J. S. Scott, D.D., 1865-70; S. W. Roe, D.D., 1871-76; J. D. Gardner, 1876-80; E. N. Sebring, 1880-85; D. K. Van Doren, 1885-90; and the Rev. Charles W. Pitcher, 1891.

JOHN A. FERGUSON, one of the best-known farmers in Duanesburg, N.Y., was born in Princetown, in the same county, Schenectady, January 24, 1822, son of Duncan and Hannah Ferguson. The parents were natives of Princetown, and the paternal grandparents, John and Janet Ferguson, were natives of Scotland. John Ferguson emigrated prior to the Revolution, and he served as a soldier in that struggle. He was an early settler in Princetown, where he tilled the soil industriously for the rest of his active period, being one of the progressive farmers of his day. He and his wife lived to a good old age.

Duncan Ferguson, the father, was a lifelong resident of Princetown, and for many years he carried on general farming with prosperous results. In politics he was at one time a Whig, and later a Republican. His family consisted of eight children, two of whom are living, namely: John A., the subject of this sketch; and Duncan Ferguson, who resides at the homestead in Princetown. The others were: Thomas, Robert, Daniel, Jeanette, Ann, and Mary. The father lived to be eighty-two years old, and the mother died at about seventy-eight years old. They were members of the Presbyterian church.

John A. Ferguson was educated in the district schools of Princetown. In 1843, when twenty-one years old, he bought his first real estate, consisting of a farm of one hundred and fifty-five acres in Duanesburg, where he has since resided, and he is now the owner of other valuable lands. For a few years he was engaged in mercantile business at Esperance, Schoharie County; but general farming has been his chief occupation, and aside from growing the usual field and garden products of this locality, he raises cattle and sheep.

In 1844 Mr. Ferguson was joined in marriage with Elizabeth Humphrey, who was born in Charlestown, Montgomery County, in 1823, daughter of William Humphrey. Two daughters, Almira and Delia A., were born of this union, which lasted a little more than fifty years. Mrs. Ferguson died February 1, 1895.

Mr. Ferguson's farm contains substantial buildings. He is still cultivating it, and under his careful treatment it is made to yield large crops. His easy circumstances are the result of patient industry, and he possesses other excellent qualities which command the respect of all who know him. Politically, he acts with the Republican party. In his religious belief he is a Presbyterian.

DAVID ENDERS, a prominent and well-to-do resident of Esperance township, N.Y., was born at Schoharie Junction, September 10, 1833, son of Jacob P. and Eva (Kniskern) Enders. He is of the fifth generation in descent from Bardrum Enders, who emigrated from Holland, and, settling as a pioneer in this county, became a large land-owner. A deed for twelve hundred and seventy acres, now in the possession of Mr. David Enders, was originally conveyed from King George in 1729 to Augustus Van Cortland, who in turn transferred it to a person by the name of Holland. The latter transferred it to Mr. Dow, from whom it went to Bardrum Enders and his descendants. John Enders, son of Bardrum, reared a family of four children, one being a son Peter, who served as a soldier in the Revolutionary War. Peter Enders became the owner of all but one-seventh of his grandfather Bardrum's property, and was an extensive farmer. He had a family of two sons and six daughters, and among the latter were: Maria, who married John Enders; Christina, who married Joseph I. Borst; Nancy, who married Philip Deitz; and another, who married Harmon Beecher. The sons were: Peter I., and Jacob P., the father of David.

Jacob P. Enders followed general farming throughout the active period of his life, and like his predecessors was noted for his energy and ability. He was a member of the Dutch Reformed church, was kind-hearted and charitable, and his high character gave him considerable influence with his fellow-townsmen. In politics he was a Democrat. He was the father of nine children; namely, Peter, John, David, the subject of this sketch, Maria, Elizabeth, Christina, Eva, Katharine, and Matilda. Of the daughters four married. Peter resides in Esperance; John, who lived on the old homestead, was accidentally killed by a runaway horse.

David Enders received his education in the district schools, at the Richmondville Academy, which was destroyed by fire some nine weeks after its opening, and at the Schoharie Academy, where his studies were completed under Professor Briggs. He resided at home until after his marriage, when he purchased a piece of property known as Slingerland farm, upon which he remained nine years, and then removed to the farm where he now resides. His homestead is considered one of the handsomest in Sloansville. He takes a keen interest in the advancement of the town, and as one of its wealthiest and most public-spirited residents his aid and influence are visible in all measures instigated therefor. He served as Railroad Commissioner for fifteen consecutive years, or until the board was abolished. He was elected to the Assembly in 1896, on the Democratic ticket, and served with ability upon the Committees on Interior Affairs, Villages, and Agriculture. His interest in public affairs has in various ways proved beneficial to the community, and his well-known persistency is a sufficient guarantee that whatever he undertakes will be successfully accomplished. This was recently demonstrated by the completion of a fine new bridge over the Schoharie River at Sloansville, an improvement which was strenuously opposed by many, but through his instrumentality was finally built.

Mr. Enders married for his first wife Mary E. Larkin, daughter of Daniel Larkin. Two children were the fruit of this marriage, namely: Jacob, who died at the age of four years; and Nancy. For his second wife he married Emma Williams, daughter of Olaff H. Williams.

Mr. Enders is a Master Mason, and belongs to Schoharie Lodge, No. 492. In his religious belief he favors the Baptists, but contributes toward the support of other churches. Mrs. Enders is a Lutheran.

ELMER E. KREIGER, proprietor of a well-known restaurant in Prattsville, and a citizen prominently identified with the public affairs of this town, was born in Ashland, N.Y., March 7, 1861, son of Edward and Mahala (Benjamin) Kreiger.

His father, who is a native of Germany, was engaged in a revolutionary movement there which resulted in his being obliged in 1847 to seek refuge in the United States. Locating in Prattsville, he was in the employ of Smith & Ofler for five years, at the end of which time he moved to Ashland, where for the succeeding nine years he was engaged in farming. Next coming to Huntersfield, he continued to carry on general farming until 1888, when he retired from active labor. He is now seventy-five years old, and is residing in the village of Prattsville. His first wife, Mahala, who was a daughter of Joseph Benjamin, of Prattsville, became the mother of four children, all of whom grew to maturity. One son was accidentally killed while gunning in 1893, at the age of thirty-four years. The living are: Frank, who is residing on the farm in Huntersfield; Kate, who married Merritt Alberti; and Elmer E., the special subject of this sketch. Mrs. Mahala Kreiger died in 1863, aged thirty-six years. Edward Kreiger married for his second wife Mary Ham, by whom he has one child, a son, who is residing in this town.

Elmer E. Kreiger was educated in the public schools. He remained at home until twenty-two years old, when he became an assistant on the Stanley Hall farm, and at the end of one year was given the entire charge of that property, which contains five hundred acres. During his fourteen years as manager of this establishment he met with good financial results. After leaving Stanley Hall he bought a farm of two hundred acres in the town of Gilboa, which he sold to good advantage a year later, and, coming to Prattsville in 1894, he engaged in the restaurant business. He was also quite an extensive speculator in cattle prior to relinquishing agricultural pursuits, and in that business he became widely known throughout this section of the State. As a prominent Democrat he takes a lively interest in political affairs, and is very popular with his fellow-townsmen. He was elected to the Board of Supervisors for the years 1893, 1894, 1895, 1896, and 1897 by a large majority, and during those years he frequently acted as temporary chairman of that body.

Mr. Kreiger is unmarried. He was made a Mason at the age of twenty-two, and is now Junior Warden and a trustee of the Blue Lodge in this town. He is a director, and superintendent of grounds, of the Prattsville Agricultural and Horticultural Association, and is always ready to assist in forwarding public improvements. While not a church member, he contributes toward the support of the various denominations, and is in close sympathy with the different moral and religious societies of the village.

COLONEL ALONZO FERGUSON, of Cobleskill, N. Y., secretary of the Schoharie and Otsego Mutual Fire Insurance Company, and a veteran of the Civil War, was born in the town of Nassau, Rensselaer County, this State, on March 19, 1820, son of German and Elizabeth (Sliter) Ferguson. His parents were both natives of Nassau. One of his great-grandfathers, a German of the name of Sornberger, was a pioneer settler of Dutchess County. His paternal grandfather was Jeremiah Ferguson, and his maternal grandfather, John Sliter, both of Nassau, and the latter a Revolutionary soldier and pensioner.

In 1826, about three years after the death of his wife Elizabeth, which occurred when their son Alonzo was only three and a half years old, he came to Cobleskill. Here he spent the rest of his life, and died at the age of seventy-six. In religion he was a Methodist.

Colonel Ferguson was only six years old when his father came to Cobleskill. Here, up to his fifteenth year, he received what little education the common schools of that day afforded in winter, and in summer he was employed on farm work. At the age of seventeen he was apprenticed to learn wagon-making, and for the succeeding nine years he worked at that trade. At twenty-six he entered a village store at Carlisle as clerk, and there remained for a year. In the spring of 1847 he became a partner of the late Charles Courter at Cobleskill, continuing the connection until 1851, when he engaged in the hardware business at Cobleskill on his own account. This he carried on for four years, and at the end of that time sold out to the late Charles H. Shaver. In 1850 and 1851 he was Clerk of the town of Cobleskill. In 1855 he removed to the city of Buffalo, and in 1862 entered the government service in the commissary department of the army.

He was ordered to duty in Kentucky, and followed the army to Pittsburg Landing. Having contracted a fever, he was obliged to return north about the first of June, but shortly after was commissioned Adjutant by Governor Morgan to organize the quota of the Twentieth Senatorial District of New York under the call of President Lincoln for three hundred thousand volunteers, and he immediately reported to Colonel Richard Franchot at Mohawk, Herkimer County, where camp was established. This was early in July, 1862, and on the twenty third of the following month the One Hundred and Twenty-first Regiment went to the front with one thousand and ten men. A second regiment being needed to complete the quota, at the earnest request of the war committee, he was again assigned by the governor to the task, and on October 15, 1862, the One Hundred and Fifty-second Regiment was mustered into service, thus completing the enlistment of more than two thousand men within the space of three months. Governor Morgan commissioned him Lieutenant Colonel of the One Hundred and Fifty-second Regiment, and on October 21 he left with his command for the front. In January of the following year he was promoted to the rank of Colonel. He was with his regiment at the siege of Suffolk, Va., under General Peck, in April and May, 1863, and from there was ordered to the Peninsula, thence to Washington, and thence, in July, on to New York to suppress the draft riots. His was the first volunteer regiment to arrive in that city. Order being restored, he was directed by General Canby, who was in command at New York, to proceed to Schenectady and be present there during the enforcement of the draft. He was then ordered back to New York, where his command remained on detached duty until October, when he was ordered to join the second corps of the Army of the Potomac. About the first of December the Colonel was obliged to resign on account of impaired health, not being willing to remain in the service unless he could perform active duty.

Returning North he engaged in business in the city of New York, and subseqently in the State of Florida. In 1876 he served as a member of the State Senate of Florida, being sent from the first district of that State. He was at the capital when the arguments on the

ANDREW J. VANDERPOEL.

Tilden and Hayes returns were made, knew the officials who canvassed the returns, and learned from the lips of the secretary of State all that related to the question. Returning in 1879 to his old home, he here engaged in the hardware business, but later sold out and started an insurance business. In this line he has been very successful, having been agent for most of the standard companies. In October, 1895, he organized the fire insurance company of which he is now secretary. During his recent residence here he has been chairman of the Republican county committee for four years, and for two years he was a member of the state committee.

Colonel Ferguson was married in March, 1847, to Mary Courter, of this town. She was born in Schoharie, and died in 1859, at the age of thirty-two, leaving two children: Charles, who is now a travelling agent in the West; and Sarah, who died at the age of thirty-three. The latter was the wife of Frank M. Goodrich, and the mother of two children, one of whom is living. The Colonel was married in April, 1865, to Libbie M. Pegg, a native of Springfield, Otsego County, and daughter of George A. Pegg, a well-known hotel-keeper of that town. By this marriage there is one son, Howard P., who is now in business with his father. He was for six years in New York as a hotel clerk.

The Colonel is a member of Cobleskill Lodge, No. 394, F. & A. M., having joined in 1865. He takes an active interest in town affairs. Colonel and Mrs. Ferguson are members of the Lutheran church, of which he has been an Elder for a number of years, being also treasurer of the society.

CAPTAIN ANDREW J. VANDERPOEL, dealer in ice, a highly respected citizen of New Baltimore, N.Y., was born in this town on May 7, 1838, his parents being Andrew and Jane (Van Slyke) Vanderpoel. His grandfather, also named Andrew, was a native of Columbia County. He spent his life there engaged in farming, and died there at the age of fifty-eight. His wife, whose maiden name was Elizabeth Smith, was born in Connecticut. None of their seven children are living. Her death occurred at the age of seventy-eight. She was a member of the Methodist Episcopal church, and had a brother who was an Elder in that church.

Andrew Vanderpoel, the second, father of the subject of this sketch, came to New Baltimore when a young man, purchased a farm here, and subsequently engaged in farming until about the age of sixty years when he retired and moved to New Baltimore village, and at the age of seventy-nine he died. He was a Deacon in the Dutch Reformed church and for many years an Elder. In politics he was first a Whig and later a Republican. He was a man of sound judgment, and his advice and counsel were sought by many. His wife, Jane, was born in this place; and was a daughter of Tunis Van Slyke, a farmer and large land-owner. She was one of a family of eight children. Of the six born to her, four are living, namely: Tunis, who resides in New Baltimore; Andrew J.; Peter, who is in Massachusetts; and Mrs. Alida Mead of this town. The mother died at the age of ninety years.

Captain Vanderpoel in his boyhood attended the district school, and at the age of twenty studied for a time in Claverick Institute. He began his working life on his father's farm, and subsequently went into business, forming a partnership with a Mr. Smith under the firm name of Smith & Vanderpoel, and for six years carrying on a general merchandise store. At the end of that time he disposed of his interest in the business to Mr. Holmes. A little later he started a coal yard in New Baltimore, also entered the ice business, also ran boats to New York. He then bought back his interest in the store from Mr. Holmes, retaining it until 1880, when he sold it to Mr. Nelson. During the next six years he was captain of the "City of Hudson," the day boat which ran from Catskill to Albany. While occupying this position he removed his family to Catskill, where he continued to reside until 1887, when he returned to this town. After he left off running the "City of Hudson," he was engaged in the transportation of freight to New York, but in 1897 his dock buildings burned, and he discontinued the freight trade. Since then he has carried on an ice business, housing twenty-six thousand tons of ice a year and disbursing it in large quantities in New York at wholesale. In 1890 the Captain bought his present beautiful estate, which is a fine farm devoted principally to fruit orchards. It is known as the Dr. Cornell homestead, and overlooks the gliding Hudson.

Captain Vanderpoel has been twice married, the first time, in 1869, to Elizabeth Randall, and the second time in 1882 to Ella Jennings. The first Mrs. Vanderpoel was a Nova Scotian by birth. She died at the age of thirty-nine, having been the mother of five children, namely: Weston R. and Frank, who are in California; Martha and Margaret who are in New Jersey, and Andrew, also in California. The second Mrs. Vanderpoel was born near Durham. Her father, Daniel D. Jennings, was a well-known hotel-keeper in his native town of Cairo. He died when his daughter Ella was a young girl. His second wife, Eleanor Souser, a descendant of the noted Salisbury family which came from England, was born in Jefferson in the town of Catskill. She bore him four children, of whom there are living: Peter, of New York; Irving, a Catskill lawyer and bank president; and Mrs. Vanderpoel. Captain and Mrs. Vanderpoel have one child, Peter Jennings, now eleven years of age. They lost two little sons — John Benham, at two years of age; and Worthington, who died an infant.

The Captain is a Republican; but he refuses to accept nomination for public office, though frequently asked to do so. He is a Mason, being formerly associated with Ark Lodge of Coxsackie and at present a member of Social Friendship Lodge of New Baltimore. Of the latter he is a charter member, one of three, and since its organization has been treasurer of the lodge. Mrs. Vanderpoel is a member of the Dutch Reformed Church of Catskill.

WILLIAM HENRY DECKER, Supervisor of the town of Gilboa, Schoharie County, N.Y., and by occupation a dairyman and fruit-grower, was born in Gilboa on November 12, 1846. His parents were Jacob and Betsy Ann (Shew) Decker, and his paternal grandfather was Tunis Decker, whose immigrant progenitor was one of a colony of Dutch emigrants who settled in Deckertown, N.J., and Columbia County, New York.

Tunis Decker was born in 1765 in Columbia County, and lived there for some time. He came eventually to Gilboa, and purchased a tract of three hundred acres, part of which estate is where his grandson William now resides. Although ostensibly a farmer, he was a man of varied talents, and could turn his hand to almost any kind of work. He came here in 1833, and died some twenty years later, in his eighty-ninth year. His remains were the first to be carried into the Shew Hollow Methodist church for funeral services. No other place seemed so fitting as the church for which he had worked and sacrificed, and to whose interests he was so thoroughly devoted. His wife, whom he had married shortly after the Revolution, survived him some years, dying at the age of eighty-eight. Of their family of twelve children three died in infancy. The nine that continued life's journey were: Cornelia, Jacob and Sophia (twins,) Polly, Catherine, Susan, Eliza, Cornelius, and George. Eliza Decker died on Long Island of yellow fever. Tall stature was a family characteristic. The three sons became farmers, and each upon settling in life for himself was given a hundred acres of land from the paternal estate. Cornelius died in New London, Wis. He had three sons, only one of whom is living. This one and William Henry Decker are the only living male descendants of Tunis Decker bearing his name. George had two sons, but both are deceased.

Jacob Decker, who was born June 30, 1811, at Conesville, Schoharie County, N.Y., and died in Gilboa, N.Y., on Christmas Day, 1879, was a carpenter, and followed his trade for twenty-two years, being considered one of the most skilled workmen in these parts. He lived with his parents until his marriage, and then settled on the lot his father gave him, living first in the log house on the premises which became the birthplace of the subject of this sketch and most of his brothers and sisters. Later Jacob Decker built a large house. He was a Republican from the formation of the party, and a leader in all local affairs. He was deeply interested in the progress of the church, and was one of those who helped build the Methodist church edifice at Shew Hollow. He was class leader for fourteen years. Indeed, this family has been and still is noted for its liberal support of all religious organizations both in a moral and a financial way. Jacob Decker's wife, Betsy Ann, was a granddaughter, on her mother's side, of Captain Hagar, who won renown during the days of the Revolution by his valiant service in behalf of the colonists. His brother Joseph was shot during the war, and his father was carried a prisoner to Canada, and detained there until the end of the struggle. One of three pewter plates, the history of which is connected with the Revolution, is still preserved in Mr. Decker's family. They were thrown into a well by the wife of Captain Hagar just before the house was burned by Brant's Indians and Tories, and they were taken from the well at the close of the war. Mrs. Betsy Ann Decker died at eighty years of age, on March 12, 1894. She was the mother of the following-named children: Marietta; S. Amelia; Martha A.; Francelia; Rozella; Almira, who died at the age of six years; Helen, who died young; William H.; and two elder sons, who died young. Marietta married David Simonson, and resides in Hobart, N.Y. Amelia married Dr. R. Hubbell, of Jefferson, N.Y., and died in 1889. Francelia is the wife of William R. Ladd, of Bangor, Me. Rozella is the second wife of Dr. R. Hubbell, of Jefferson, N.Y.

William Henry Decker is a man of fine physique, and in his prime was known as the strongest and most active man in this section. He has been known to lift twelve hundred pounds dead weight. He early engaged in blacksmithing, for which he seemed so well adapted by nature, and in wood working and repairing. His motto was, "Do it right and you won't have to do it over again"; and, as this sentiment found constant expression in all work that he did, he had no difficulty in securing the best trade in his line in this vicinity. But after twenty years of mechanical labor he was attacked by rheumatism, and it became necessary for him to make a change in this business. He therefore confined himself to farming on his two hundred and thirty-eight acres, devoting his attention chiefly to dairying and fruit-growing. His dairy of sixty milch cows is one of the largest in town, and is composed of excellent stock. He has about six hundred apple-trees. He is one of the five directors in the creamery company at South Gilboa, and previous to its incorporation was one of the committee that built the creamery and carried on the business. This creamery, which is one of the most expensive in this vicinity, cost, with buildings and equipment, seven thousand dollars.

Politically, Mr. Decker is a strong Republican. He has attended many conventions, and every year since he became a voter has taken an active part in election and nomination of officials. With the exception of one year, when he was sick, he has always been present at town elections. He has held the offices of Collector, Road Commissioner, Poormaster, Assessor, Constable, and, indeed, every office in the town except those of Town Clerk and Justice of the Peace. If he lives till the end of his present term he will have been Supervisor of his town five years. Every nomination has come to him unsolicited. While he was serving as Road Commissioner thirty bridges were repaired in one season, but expenses were kept at a minimum. In 1896 he was elected Supervisor for two years; in 1898 he was re-elected, for one year, as the unanimous choice of both parties; and in the early part of the present year, 1899, he was re-elected for two years. His opponent at his first election was Stephen Wildsey, who had been on the board twice before.

Mr. Decker has been twice married, his wives being sisters, daughters of Hiram Brown, of Dutch descent. Mr. Brown is living, but his wife died in April, 1896. They were the parents of two sons and three daughters, namely: Eliza; Reuben; Jacob, who resides in Gilboa; Addie; and Angie. Addie Brown, to whom Mr. Decker was married first, died in her thirty-fourth year, on November 21, 1889. She was the mother of five children, and is survived by three; namely, Lizzie E., Zanah, and Arthur B. Willie J. died at two years of age, on November 2, 1880; and Inza died at four years of age, on October 22, 1884. Mr. Decker's present wife was before marriage Angie Brown. Mr. Decker is a member of the Shew Hollow Methodist Episcopal Church. He has always been a temperate man in every way, using neither tobacco nor intoxicants of any kind. His genial temper and hearty good humor make him a general favorite, and his jovial laugh is a pleasant sound to hear.

WILLIAM D. SHAFER, M.D., a rising young physician of Oak Hill, town of Durham, N.Y., was born in Cobleskill, Schoharie County, March 16, 1870, son of Daniel G. and Mary J. (Van Volkenberg) Shafer. His paternal grandfather, Daniel Shafer, was a lifelong resident of Cobleskill, where he cultivated a farm during his active period, and died at the age of eighty years.

Daniel G. Shafer, Dr. Shafer's father, acquired a good education in the common schools and at Charlotte Academy. For many years he was associated with his brother-in-law. He finally purchased a piece of agricultural property of one hundred and thirty acres, situated near Mineral Springs, upon which he spent his last years, and where his widow, Mrs. Mary J. Shafer, still resides. In politics he was a Democrat. Mrs. Shafer's father, Hiram Van Volkenberg, was a farmer of Schoharie County. She is the mother of two children: William D., the subject of this sketch; and Mary, wife of Jesse Shafer of Mineral Springs.

After attending the common schools and the high school of Cobleskill, William D. Shafer began the study of medicine with Dr. Allen of that town, and later attended the New York Eclectic College, from which he was graduated in 1892. He began the practice of his profession in New York City, and went from there to Livingstonville. Since July, 1896, he has been the only physician at Oak Hill, and his practice, which has already assumed large proportions, extends into Schoharie and Albany Counties, necessitating long tedious rides in all kinds of weather.

In 1892 Dr. Shafer was united in marriage with Jessie Dillenbeck, daughter of Jonas Dillenbeck, a druggist of Cobleskill. They have one son, Rudolph.

Politically, Dr. Shafer acts with the Democratic party. He served as Coroner in Schoharie County, resigning that office when he removed from Livingstonville. He is treasurer of the Lyman Tremaine Lodge, No. 265, I. O. O. F., Oak Hill, and a member of the Middleburg Encampment. He is medical examiner for the New York Life and Prudential Insurance Companies; also for the Masonic Life Association of Western New York, and formerly belonged to the New York Eclectic Society. He attends the Episcopal church, of which Mrs. Shafer is a member.

REV. HUGH O'NEIL, pastor of St. Mary's Church, Hunter, N.Y., and of St. Francis de Sales Church, Platerkill, was born in Dungarvan, County Waterford, Ireland, May 18, 1838, son of Patrick and Ellen (McSweeney) O'Neil.

The first of the family to settle in Waterford was his great-grandfather, Hugh O'Neil, who went there from Shaw's Castle, County Tyrone. Edward O'Neil, his grandfather, was born in Kilkenny, and was a farmer. Patrick O'Neil, his father, who was born in Waterford and was a farmer in early life, later engaged in the bakery business in Dungarvan. He was also a spirits merchant, and before the advent of railroads he ran a line of carriages known as post coaches. He was a great admirer of Daniel O'Connell, and while taking an active part in electing a member of parliament he contracted an illness which caused his death at the age of fifty-two years.

Patrick O'Neil was a highly respected citizen and an able supporter of the church. His wife, Ellen, was born in Tipperary in 1796, daughter of Thomas McSweeney. During the Rebellion of 1798 her parents took refuge in a town in the county of Waterford. She was the mother of eight children, of whom the subject of this sketch and his sister Margaret are the only survivors. Margaret, now Mrs. O'Callahan, resides with her brother in Hunter. She has a daughter who is the Assistant Reverend Mother in the convent at West Troy. One of Father O'Neil's brothers, Edward, was educated in St. John's College, Waterford, from which he was graduated in 1852. He was ordained to the priesthood, and sent to Manchester, England, where he became a Canon, and served in that capacity until his death, which occurred in 1892, at the age of sixty-seven.

Hugh O'Neil began his education in a classical school, prepared for college under private tutors, and in 1858 went to Allhallows College, where he was graduated in 1860. His theological studies were pursued at Waterford and at St. Mary's College, Oscott, England, where he was a fellow-student with the late King Alphonso of Spain and with the father of the late General Garcia, the Cuban leader. He was ordained a priest of the Roman Catholic Church, February 9, 1867, and his first appointment was to St. Barnabas Cathedral, Nottingham, England, where he remained nine months. His next charge was at the village of Ilkeston, now a city, where his duties required him to cover a circuit of forty-five miles; and during his labors there, which extended through a period of eleven years, he erected a church and a school building and developed the parish into a highly prosperous condition. The routine work which he accomplished unaided is now performed by eight priests. At his own request he was transferred to the village of Hathersage, Peak of Derbyshire, famous as the home of Robin Hood, and with the assistance of the Duke of Norfolk he repaired and opened an ancient church built previous to the Reformation.

At the expiration of four and one-half years he came to the United States on a leave of absence, arriving in New York in 1882, and, subsequently deciding to remain this country, he severed his connection with his English parish and accepted an assignment to a mission church in Philadelphia. At the request of the bishop of Indianapolis he went to St. Patrick's Church in that city. After that he was again stationed in Philadelphia for a short time, and then became attached to the diocese of Albany, and was assigned to St. Mary's Church in Troy. In 1887 he came to Hunter as pastor of St. Mary's Church.

The arduous duties of a widely distributed district, which included villages and settlements within a radius of fifty miles, were zealously and energetically performed by him for five years, or until his circuit was divided, since which time the concentration of his labors has enabled him to accomplish results far more visible in their effects. Beside effecting the enlargement and improvement of St. Mary's Church, he erected St. Francis de Sales Church in Platerkill in 1891. At both of these churches he officiates the year round, celebrating two masses each Sunday during the summer season, besides holding week-day services whenever occasion demands. He formerly conducted service regularly at the hotel Kaaterskill during the season, but these he was obliged to relinquish on account of his increasing labors elsewhere. He has earnestly endeavored to promote the spiritual welfare of his widely-scattered flock, and the zeal he displays in conducting the affairs of his pastorate has gained for him the good will of the entire community. He organized the Sacred Heart and Rosary societies, and he takes a lively interest in the work of the town improvement society, of which he is a member. At the earnest request of the people of Lexington he aided in securing the erection of a church in that village; and he has also repaired St. Henry's Church, located between Ashland and Prattsville.

Father O'Neil began to interest himself in political affairs shortly after his arrival in this country, and in 1884 he headed a committee who, at the Fifth Avenue Hotel, New York City, presented the late Hon. James G. Blaine with a gold-headed cane. He is a naturalized citizen of the United States, and supports the Democratic party.

JOHN G. EMPIE, who has been actively identified with the agricultural interests of the town of Seward, Schoharie County, for more than thirty years, is the owner of a well-improved farm lying about one mile from the village of Hyndsville. He was born in Sharon, N. Y., January 5, 1836, a son of Peter Empie, Jr. He is of French and German ancestry, and the descendant of one of the earliest settlers of Schoharie County his great-grandfather, John Empie, having removed in early manhood from Stone Arabia, Montgomery County, to the town of Sharon. A hard-working pioneer, John Empie cleared a farm from the wilderness, and there passed the remainder of his life.

Peter Empie, Sr., grandfather of John G., spent his seventy-seven years of life on the old homestead in Sharon, Schoharie County, working as a farmer through boyhood, early manhood, and old age. He cleared off wood, cultivated the soil, and in course of time erected substantial frame buildings in place of the original log house and barn. His wife, Katie Lehman, was born in Sharon. She was a daughter of John Lehman, whose father was one of the original settlers of that place. Of their eight children, none survive.

Peter Empie, Jr., son of Peter, Sr., was born and brought up on the old farm in Sharon, and received his education in the pioneer schools of his day and generation. Following in the footsteps of his ancestors, he chose farming as his life occupation, and on reaching manhood purchased land near the parental estate, and was there successfully engaged in his independent calling until his decease, at the venerable age of eighty-three years. He was a Democrat in politics, greatly interested in public affairs, and served his fellow-townsmen as Assessor for a number of years. Both he and his wife were members of the Reformed church. He married Maria Empie, who was born in Sharon, a daughter of a later John Empie than the pioneer. Peter and Maria Empie had seven children; namely, Norman D., Jane E., John G., Peter H., Anna S., Harvey L., and Dewitt C.

John G. Empie acquired a practical education in the common schools of Sharon and at the Carlisle Seminary. He subsequently taught school several terms, both in Sharon and Seward, but in 1867 gave up his position at the teacher's desk to take possession of his present fine estate of one hundred acres, which was formerly known as the Falk farm. From year to year he has made marked improvements on the place, having erected within the last quarter of a century all the buildings that are now on it and cleared off much of the wood. He has a large part of the land under cultivation. He carries on general farming in all its branches, and in past times he raised vast quantities of hops, which proved a valuable crop.

In politics Mr. Empie affiliates with the Democratic party. He has served acceptably in various local offices, including those of Supervisor, Commissioner of Highways, and trustee of his school district. He has also been secretary and trustee of the People's Cemetery Association of Sharon ever since its organization in 1867.

On June 30, 1858, Mr. Empie married Miss Nancy C. Borst, who was also born in Sharon, as was her father, Peter G. Borst, a lifelong farmer of that place. Mr. and Mrs. Empie have two children — the Rev. Alfred R. and Edward J. The Rev. Alfred R. Empie was graduated from Hartwick Seminary, and is now preaching in Maryland, Otsego County, N.Y. He married Miss Anna Skinner, and they have

ALONZO WAKEMAN

one child, Lillian. Edward J. Empie married Miss Anna Nellis, and is the father of two children — Everett and Nancy Ella. Mr. and Mrs. John G. Empie are members of the Lutheran church, in which he has been Deacon, Elder, and secretary.

ALONZO WAKEMAN, for many years one of the leading farmers of Lawyersville, Schoharie County, was born October 23, 1810, in this town, and here spent his entire life of nearly seventy-eight years, his death occurring on August 31, 1888. He was of patriotic Revolutionary stock, his paternal grandfather, Gershom Wakeman, a native of Fairfield, Conn., having served as an officer in the war for American independence.

Gershom Wakeman was a farmer by occupation. He was among the very first to enlist in the Colonial forces, and was killed in one of the early battles of the war. His wife, Elizabeth Downs, was born in Fairfield County, Connecticut, daughter of David Downs and the descendant of one of the earliest settled families of that county. She died not very long after her husband's death, leaving seven children: namely, Abigail, Abel, Gershom, Dolly, Amelia, Isaac, and Seth B., the latter of whom was the father of Alonzo Wakeman.

Seth B. Wakeman was brought up on a farm. In early manhood he learned the carpenter's trade, which he subsequently followed many years in Lawyersville, where he was one of the first settlers. He erected the house now occupied by his son Alonzo's widow, the residence of Stanton Courter, of Cobleskill, and several business houses of this locality. He bought a farm of two hundred acres near the village and also other land in town; and for some years prior to his death, at the age of eighty-two years, was successfully engaged in general farming. He likewise carried on an extensive business as a manufacturer of lumber, being the owner of a saw-mill. His first wife, Clara Nichols, a native of Fairfield County, Connecticut, died in early womanhood, leaving him five children, namely: Horace; Alonzo, the special subject of this sketch; Horatio; Maria; and Charles. In religion, both parents were of the Universalist faith. After the death of his first wife Seth B. Wakeman married Sarah Wheeler, also of Fairfield County, Connecticut.

Alonzo Wakeman in 1878 bought the valuable farm of two hundred acres, on which his daughter Emma now resides, and until his death, as above mentioned, was recognized in the community as one of its foremost agriculturists. Strictly honest and upright, he was influential in the neighborhood, and, as a Notary Public, for many years transacted a good deal of business. In politics, he was an ardent supporter of the principles of the Republican party, but persistently refused to accept all offices, even that of president of the National Bank, of which he was one of the founders and for many years a director.

Mr. Alonzo Wakeman's first wife was Miss Catharine Stall, daughter of Mr. and Mrs. Peter Stall, of Sharon, Schoharie County, N.Y.; she lived ten months after their marriage, her death occurring in 1834 at the age of nineteen years and eleven months. In June, 1838, Mr. Wakeman married Mary O'Dell, who was born September 26, 1815, in Redding, Conn., daughter of Dr. Joseph O'Dell. Mrs. Wakeman is of French ancestry, her great-grandfather O'Dell, one of the first settlers of Norwalk, Conn., having emigrated to that town from France in Colonial days. Nathan O'Dell, her grandfather, was a prosperous farmer and a lifelong resident of Norwalk, Conn. His wife, Mary Burritt, bore him fourteen children, all of whom grew to maturity and married. Joseph O'Dell, having received his early education in the common schools, pursued the study of medicine, at first with one of the local physicians, Dr. Jesse Shepard, and afterward in New York City. On graduating, he located first as a practitioner in Dover, Conn., whence he removed to Redding, Conn., where he continued actively engaged in the practice of his profession. At the age of thirty-one years he died in Charleston, S.C., while there for the benefit of his health. His wife, Lucy Wakeman, was born in Fairfield, Conn., a daughter of Gershom Wakeman, second, who was an uncle of Alonzo Wakeman. Gershom Wakeman, second, married Sibbell Bradley, of Fairfield, Conn., and Lucy was their only daughter. They were very prominent members of the Congregational church.

Mr. Alonzo Wakeman is survived by his wife and four children; namely, Emma, Clara A., Ella, and Sarah W. Emma J. married Solomon Larkin, a farmer, who died in 1897, leaving her with one child, Charles W. Larkin; Clara A. is the wife of Romeyn Brown, a hardware merchant of Oneonta, and the mother of three children — Wakeman, Floyd, and an infant (deceased); Ella is the wife of George Story, a carpenter; and Sarah W. is the wife of Daniel J. Gannon, who is her third husband. Mrs. Wakeman and all her family except one are valued members of the Lutheran church.

ANDREW J. KLINE, proprietor of a well-stocked general store in Pattersonville, Schenectady County, N.Y., was born in this place, November 1, 1850, son of Joseph and Janet (Staley) Kline. His father was born in Aiken, Montgomery County, in 1818, and his mother was born in Princetown, this county, in 1823. Grandfather Kline was an early settler in Montgomery County, and there carried on general farming for the rest of his active period.

Joseph Kline was reared on his father's farm. At the age of eighteen he came to Pattersonville, then called Hoffman's Ferry, and for a number of years he kept a grocery store. Removing to Swartztown, N.Y., he carried on the same business in connection with a hotel, and also cultivated a farm. His activity continued until a few years prior to his death, which occurred at the age of seventy-five years. His wife died at seventy. She was the mother of six children, namely: Geroe G., who died at the age of forty-six years; Andrew J., the subject of this sketch; Oliver S.; Jennie M., who is now Mrs. Herrick; Harriet A.; and Ella, who is now Mrs. Gregg. Mrs. Janet Kline was a member of the Reformed church.

Andrew J. Kline was reared and educated in Swartztown. When a young man he began business as a dealer in farm produce along the Erie Canal, and was thus engaged for twelve years. Since 1886 he has been located at his present place of business in Pattersonville. His store, which is one of the leading sources of supply in this section, is well stocked with agricultural implements, fertilizers, and general merchandise.

In 1877 Mr. Kline was united in marriage with Henrietta Sterling, of Florida, N.Y., daughter of Winslow Sterling. Mrs. Kline is the mother of three children; namely, Jessie R., Bertha H., and Boyd J.

Politically, Mr. Kline is a Democrat. Able, energetic, and conscientious, he has secured a firm foothold in business through his own exertions, and he fully merits the high esteem accorded him by his fellow-townsmen.

JOHN ROE, senior partner in the firm of J. & E. Roe, general merchants of Greenville, N.Y., was born in Wisconsin on October 16, 1849, son of William P. and Marietta (Newman) Roe. His paternal grandfather, William Roe, was a farmer by occupation. He liked to go from place to place, and lived successively in Athens, Greenville, and Cairo, owning farms at different times in each of these places in Greene County. He died at Cairo at the age of eighty-four. His wife Jane, who was before her marriage a Barker, was born in Greenville, and belonged to one of the old pioneer families.

William P. Roe, son of William and Jane, was born in Athens, N.Y., and reared to farm life. He lived for a time in Wisconsin, where he was interested in speculating and in farming, and held the office of Town Supervisor. Later he returned to New York State, settled in Greenville, and died here at the age of seventy-eight. He was County Superintendent of the Poor for three years. In politics he was a Democrat. His wife, Marietta, was a native of this place, and died here at the age of fifty-two. She was the daughter of Alva Newman, and one of a family of six children. Her father was a Greenville farmer, but he removed from Greenville to Wisconsin, and died there at the age of seventy. Mrs. Marietta N. Roe was the mother of six children. Of these five are living, namely: John, the subject of this sketch; Jasper, a farmer; Annis, who married Charles Roe; Ella, who married Charles Coonley; and Edgar, who is a member of the firm of Roe Brothers. Both parents were Baptists.

John Roe came with his father and mother to this town when eight years old, and worked with his father until twenty-six years of age. In the winters of 1871, 1872, and 1873 he taught school in Greenville, and one winter he attended the Poughkeepsie Business College. Then, at the age of twenty-six, he formed a partnership with M. P. Blenis, which continued for twelve years, or until the time of

Mr. Blenis's death. For the first year they operated a general store located opposite Mr. Roe's present stand, moving across the street at the end of that time. Upon the death of Mr. Blenis, Mr. Edgar Roe bought out his interests, and the firm assumed its present name. There is only one store in town larger than this. A full line of general merchandise is carried, including dry goods, groceries, boots and shoes, crockery and glass ware, carpets and oil-cloths, hats and caps. One clerk is employed. Mr. Roe has now been in business over twenty-three years, and is one of the oldest merchants here. He is known through all the country side, and enjoys the esteem of every one.

In 1878 Mr. Roe married Arvillia Deyo, a native of Durham, and daughter of Milo Deyo, now the popular blacksmith of Greenville. Of this union four children have been born, by name Milo B., Ford, Mary, and John.

In politics Mr. Roe is a Democrat. He has given valuable service to the town in numerous public positions. In 1890, and the four succeeding years, he was Supervisor, and in 1894 and 1895 he was chairman of the board. He has been a member of the Board of Education ever since it was organized. While chairman of their board in his last term the Supervisors presented him with a very fine easy chair, this being an expression of their appreciation of his services while a member of the body. In 1897 he was elected Superintendent of the Poor, to serve until 1900. Mr. Roe makes a most efficient manager for the almshouse. Under his care the place is kept in the best of repair, and everything about it is neat and orderly, while the health and comfort of the seventy inmates is carefully looked after.

Mr. Roe is a prominent Mason, being connected with James M. Austin Lodge, F. & A. M., and Greenville Royal Arch Chapter, No. 283. He has held all the offices in the lodge, having been warden, deacon, master for two years, and secretary six years. His membership in the lodge dates back twenty-five years. He is a charter member of the chapter, and has always been its treasurer. He is frequently sent by his fellow-townsmen as delegate to county conventions, and is a member of the Town and County Committee. No worthy object fails to receive his warm and active support, and he is often the originator of plans, the carrying out of which proves to be a benefit to the town and the community.

FRANK L. CASPER, manufacturer of extension tables and the patentee of table supports for drop-leaf tables, in the town of Cobleskill, Schoharie County, has a large and finely equipped plant at Howe's Cave, not far from the railway station of that village. He was born October 10, 1857, in the town of Cobleskill, and is the only surviving son of George Casper, a well-known business man of this section of the county. He is of German and Scotch descent, and the representative of a pioneer family of Schoharie County, his paternal grandfather, whose name was Peter, having been an early settler of this town. Peter Casper was a farmer and the owner of a good homestead, which he managed successfully until his death, at the age of threescore years. He and his wife, whose maiden name was Margaret Herron, were among the leading members of the Reformed church. They reared a large family of children.

George Casper left the home farm on becoming of age, engaged in business for himself as a miller, purchasing a clover-mill and a saw-mill, and afterward a planing-mill and a cider-mill, all of which, with the exception of the first named, he is still operating with success. With true German thrift he saved each year a portion of his earnings, and soon erected the house in which he is now living. He has also accumulated some other property. A strong Democrat in politics, he takes an intelligent interest in local matters, and has served his fellow-townsmen in various ways. He has held different offices in the Reformed church, of which he and his wife are active members, and for a number of years has been Elder of the church. He married Emeline Berner, who was born in Barnerville, this county, a daughter of John J. Berner. Of their five children three are now living, as follows: Ella, wife of Sylvester Mann, of Howes Cave; Alice, wife of Harvey Boorn; and Frank L. John P. Casper, who was preparing for the ministry at Rutgers College, died at the age of twenty-three years, and a daughter, Ida, wife of Ira Rickard, died on March 13, 1899.

Frank L. Casper in his boyhood and youth acquired a practical common-school education, and until attaining his majority assisted his father in the care of his different mills. Desirous, then, of turning his natural mechanical ability to some good account, he began the manufacture of furniture on a small scale, and succeeded so well that in the course of a few years he was forced to build an addition to the shop in which he had started his operations. He subsequently leased the main building of the old Braman woollen factory, and, erecting near by a drying kiln, a finishing-room, and a wareroom, has here since 1882 devoted his entire time to the making of extension tables. His plant is furnished with the latest improved and approved machinery, much of which he designed and made in his own factory, this being, with a single exception, the only one of the kind between Binghamton and Albany. He employs a large force of men all the time in order to meet the demands of his customers in the six New England States, New York, and Pennsylvania, his tables being sold on their merits His trade, already large, is constantly increasing, orders being daily received from firms in different parts of the Union. His factory and residence are both warmed by steam heat and lighted throughout by electricity.

Mr. Casper is a steadfast Prohibitionist in politics, and labors hard to advance the temperance cause. He is an active member of the Reformed church, in which he has served as Elder and treasurer, and has also held other offices. He has been connected with the Sunday-school for many years, much of the time being its superintendent or the teacher of the Bible class.

On March 5, 1879, Mr. Casper married Miss Belle Becker, daughter of Francis Becker, a prominent manufacturer of Schoharie County, owning and operating mills at Central Bridge, Galupville, and Berne. Mr. and Mrs. Casper have two children — Le Roy and Le Grand, the eldest a pupil in the Cobleskill High School, class of 1899. The younger son will enter Cobleskill High School the coming fall.

WILLIAM H. STEWART, proprietor of the Stewart house in Athens, N.Y., and a representative citizen of this place, was born in Jacksonville, now Earlton, in the town of Coxsackie, Greene County, on December 8, 1849, son of William C. and Margaret (Hardick) Stewart. William C. Stewart, who was born in Coxsackie, was a lawyer by profession, and practised in his native town for over a quarter of a century. He was a leading man there, and for a number of years was justice. In his later life he made his home with his son William. His death occurred in 1884, at the age of sixty-eight. He was a Republican in politics. His wife was born in the town of Athens, and died in Earlton at the age of sixty-three. She was the daughter of Jacob Hardick, who carried on farming on what was known as the Hardick farm. She bore her husband six children, only two of whom are living; namely, William H. and his sister, Lucy J. The latter, who now resides in McHenry, Ill., is the wife of Isaac Wentworth, formerly of Athens, Greene County, N.Y.

William H. Stewart's early years were spent in Jacksonville in the town of Coxsackie, and he attended the public schools there until he was fifteen years of age. He then went to work as errand boy in the store of Daniel Whiting, who dealt in general merchandise, and also carried on a brick manufactory and a wood yard. Young Stewart rose from the humble position of errand boy to that of clerk, and in this capacity worked for Mr. Whiting some ten or twelve years. Subsequently to that he was clerk for a year in the Wormer House, now the Arlington House, of Athens, and at the end of that time, in 1875, he purchased his present property. The small house then standing on the lot was torn down, and the finely appointed Stewart house of to-day erected in its place. The building is three stories high, and is fitted with all modern improvements, such as steam-heating apparatus, electricity for call bells and for lighting, hot and cold water and sanitary bath tubs. Besides the main house, Mr. Stewart owns the three adjoining houses and the dock where the ferry boat from Hudson lands. He has accommodations for about fifty guests, and as a landlord is deservedly popular. He has always taken an active part in politics, and has been trustee of the village a number of years and also school trustee.

Mr. Stewart was married in 1877 to Ida Hollenbeck, who was born at Guilderland Centre, in Albany County, daughter of Garret

GEORGE W. ANDERSON

and Harriet (Van Valkenberg) Hollenbeck. Her father, who was a farmer, died when only forty years of age. Her mother, who was born in Albany, is still living, being now sixty-nine years of age. Of Mrs. Hollenbeck's three children, Mrs. Stewart is the only one living. Mr. and Mrs. Stewart have one child, Hattie W., who lives with them. They lost a son, Wilfred D., at the age of ten years.

Mr. Stewart is a member of Custer Lodge of Odd Fellows, No. 508, and of the Knights of Pythias, No. 129, of Athens. He has served several years as a member of Mackawack Hand Engine Company, but is now exempt from duty with that company, though he is an active member of the Hook and Ladder Company, which is said to be one of the finest in the State. He is also a member of the Horse Thief Detective Association, and one of its riders. He is the oldest hotel man in this town, and with one exception the oldest in the county. His wife and daughter attend the Reformed church. In connection with his hotel Mr. Stewart carries on a livery, which is one of the best in the town.

GEORGE W. ANDERSON, the leading business man of Hunter, Greene County, N.Y., dealer in wood and coal and building supplies, and proprietor of the Central House, was born in New Sharon, Monmouth County, N.J., May 12, 1850, his parents being Jacob and Matilda (Brown) Anderson. His grandfather Anderson resided in Perrineville, N.J., in which town Jacob was born in 1814. His grandmother, whose maiden name was Mary Baldwin, was the daughter of Thomas Baldwin. Her father lived to the advanced age of ninety-three. She died at the age of fifty, having been the mother of five children.

Jacob Anderson was a carpenter and builder by trade, and for thirty-five years carried on business in Hightstown, Mercer County, N.J., where he was a prominent citizen. The last years of his life were spent on a farm. In politics he was a Republican. He was an active member of an Odd Fellows organization. His death occurred in 1890, at the age of seventy-six. His wife, Matilda, who was born in Hightstown in 1824, and died in 1896, was the daughter of Captain George W. Brown, who commanded a company of militia stationed at Sandy Hook in the War of 1812. Both Jacob Anderson and his wife were members of the Methodist church. Of their family of five sons and two daughters, only one, a son Jacob, is deceased. The living are: Abijah A., William W., George W., Carrie M., Thomas B., and Lilly B. Carrie married John W. Brown, and Lilly is the wife of Bills Flock.

George W. Anderson lived with his parents and attended the common schools until he was about sixteen years old, when he began life for himself. At first he worked on a farm, and then he learned the carpenter's trade. His brothers, it may be mentioned, are also engaged as carpenters and builders. He worked at his trade in Hightstown, Freehold, New Brunswick, and Newark, N.J., and at College Point, Long Island. Coming to Hunter in

1876, Mr. Anderson worked for four years as a wheelwright, but at the end of that time engaged in the building business. His success has been remarkable. He has seen the town double in size since he came here, and has himself put up the more important of the new buildings. He built the Methodist church and the Kaatsberg Hotel, remodelled the Hunter House, built the church and the chair factory at Edgewood, and many houses in Hunter, Edgewood, and Tannersville. During busy seasons he employed thirty hands, carrying on the largest contracting business anywhere in this section. During a number of years he has supplied large quantities of lumber to other builders, and for some time he was the only lumber dealer in five towns of this section. He is consequently widely known. Mr. Anderson's house, which is one of the finest in the village, was built by him, as was also the building in which his office is now located, and which was from 1880 to 1887 used as a sash and blind shop. Since 1884 Mr. Anderson has done little or no building, but has given his time and attention to the management of his large lumber yard and carriage repository. In connection with this he does a large business in coal, wood, and grain, and carries a line of paints, oils, and hardware supplies, and all kinds of building material used by both carpenters and masons. He is the only coal dealer in Hunter, Windham, Ashland, or Jewett.

Mr. Anderson was married in 1872 to Julia E. Lake, daughter of Hiram and Bathsheba (Lounsberry) Lake. She was born in Freehold, N.Y. Her father, who was a farmer, died at the age of sixty, and her mother died at the age of fifty-three. Of their two children, Hiram and Julia E., Mrs. Anderson is the only one living. Mr. Lake was twice married. By his first wife, formerly Julia Rockwell, of East Durham, N.Y., he had two sons — James M. and Charles E., the latter now deceased. Mr. and Mrs. Anderson have two daughters, namely: Mabel, who is yet in school; and Anna Bell, who is the wife of Elmer E. Goodsell, telegraph operator and agent on the Stony Clove & Catskill Mountain Railroad. (See biography on another page.) There are three grandchildren — Marguerite, Anderson, and Vera.

Mr. Anderson has always shown a vital interest in all public affairs since first he came to Hunter. He has served the town in the office of Assessor for three years, as Commissioner of Streets, as trustee and clerk of the School Board, as one of the Trustees of the village, and is at the present time a member of the Town Committee. His political affiliations are with the Republican party. He and his family are members of the Baptist church, but they attend the Methodist church in Hunter, Mr. Anderson being a trustee of the church and treasurer of the board. He can always be depended upon to work for any good cause in the church as well as outside. He was one of the projectors of the Maplewood Cemetery Association, and for many years has been its president. Fraternally, he is a member and treasurer of Mount Tabor Lodge, No. 807, F. & A. M., and of Mountain Chapter,

R. A. M. He was one of the charter members of Catskill Chapter at Catskill.

JARED VAN WAGENEN, a well-known and prosperous agriculturist of Lawyersville, Schoharie County, owning and occupying the valuable estate known as Hillside farm, was born January 13, 1835, near Sharon Hill, in the neighboring town of Seward. Son of Rynear Van Wagenen, he is of Dutch ancestry, being a lineal descendant of Aart Jacobsen Van Wagenen, who emigrated from Wageningen, Holland, a town not far from the Rhine, to Bergen, N.J., in 1650, and whose name, with that of his wife, Annetji Gerrits, was recorded as a member of the Dutch church of Kingston, Bergen County, June 24, 1661.

Conrad Van Wagenen, grandfather of Jared, was born January 15, 1752, in Somerset County, New Jersey, whence in early manhood he removed to Charleston, Montgomery County, N.Y., as one of its earliest settlers. He took up unimproved land, and, having cleared a portion of it, devoted himself to general farming, in conjunction with which he operated a small tannery. He subsequently came to Schoharie County, and, buying a farm near Sharon Hill, resided there until his death, at the venerable age of ninety years. Tradition says that he was present as a guard at the execution of Major André on October 2, 1780, at Tappan.

Rynear Van Wagenen with his numerous brothers and sisters was brought up on a farm, spending his earliest years in Charleston, N.Y., and completing his education in the district schools of Sharon, whither he accompanied his parents when a boy. On reaching man's estate he bought land in Cobleskill, where for a number of years he was engaged in farming. His death occurred at the home of his son Jared, in the seventieth year of his age. He was quite active in local matters, serving his fellow-townsmen in various offices besides that of Justice of the Peace, which he held several terms. In politics he was a strong adherent of the Democratic party. His wife, Emily Goodyear, was born on Hillside farm, then owned by her father, Jared Goodyear, who was born and reared in Hampden, Conn. Mr. Goodyear on removing to New York became a pioneer settler in a small town near Ithaca, which was named Goodyears. On account of malaria he left that place, and coming to Schoharie County bought two hundred acres of woodland in Cobleskill, and here spent the remainder of his life. He erected a log house for his first dwelling, and then began the improvement of his property. He cleared a considerable tract of his land, and, being an energetic, progressive man, he was very successful not only as a farmer, but as one of the most popular tavern-keepers of this vicinity. Four sons were born to Mr. and Mrs. Rynear Van Wagenen, and three of them survive, as follows: Jared, of Lawyersville; Albert, of Boston, Mass.; and James, who resides with his brother Jared. Both parents were members of the Reformed church.

Jared Van Wagenen lived at home until

nine years old, when he became an inmate of the household of his uncles, Willis and George Goodyear, who brought him up, their home being the farm where he now resides. He attended the district school and assisted in the farm labors until the death of his uncles, and since that time has had entire charge of this magnificent farm of two hundred and fifty acres, one of the finest in its improvements of any in this section of Schoharie County. He makes a specialty of dairying, keeping a herd of thirty or forty cows, and manufactures a fine grade of butter, which he sells to special customers in this vicinity. A few years ago Mr. Van Wagenen built his large barn, three stories in height, one hundred and thirty by eighty-seven feet, with all modern equipments, including an engine and two silos of two hundred tons capacity.

He has been an active member of the Cobleskill Agricultural Society; also of the New York State Agricultural Association; and is vice-president of the Farmers' and Merchants' Bank. In politics he is a loyal Democrat, and has been Supervisor of the town two years. He contributes liberally toward the maintenance of the Dutch Reformed church, of which he and his family are members, and in which he has held many of the offices.

On November 18, 1858, Mr. Van Wagenen married Loraine McNeill, the only child of Mr. and Mrs. Brazillia McNeill. Her mother is still living, a capable woman of eighty-six years. Mr. and Mrs. Van Wagenen have one son living; namely, Jared, Jr., born May 14, 1871; and have been bereft of one, Albert, who died at the age of fifteen years. Jared Van Wagenen, Jr., obtained his elementary education in Lawyersville, and after his graduation at the Cobleskill High School took the Bachelor's degree in 1891, and the Master's degree in 1896 at Cornell University, where he has since taught in the Dairy Department. He is now assisting his father on the home farm. He married Magdalena Lamont, the only child of E. W. Lamont, a prominent farmer of this town. Two children have been born of this union; namely, Sarah Lamont and Loraine McNeill.

RUDOLPH BESTLE, M.D., a leading physician and surgeon of Hunter, N.Y., was born in Troy, this State, on August 20, 1866, his parents being John and Wilhelmina (Shutheis) Bestle. His father, who was of German birth, came to Troy, N.Y., before marriage, and engaged in the restaurant business. He died when only thirty-four years of age. He and his wife were members of the Presbyterian church. Mrs. Bestle also was born in Germany, being one of a family of several children. She is still living at Kingston, this State. Her father, who was a druggist and medical practitioner, lived to the advanced age of ninety-eight years. Of her eight children, four are living, namely: George, who resides in New York; Henrietta, who married William Weston, of Rondout; August; and Rudolph, the special subject of this biography.

Rudolph Bestle received his elementary education in the common schools, and at the age of eighteen began the study of medicine with Dr. McLane, a leading physician of Troy, and Dr. O'Conner of the Troy Hospital. He subsequently entered the Albany Medical College, and was graduated at that institution in 1888, at twenty-one years of age, standing high in his class. He immediately began the practice of his profession in Troy, but eighteen months later removed to Burke, in Franklyn County, N.Y., where he remained for the next six years. He then came to Hunter, where he has since been in practice. He is a general practitioner, and also a surgeon of unusual skill, having performed many difficult operations. During his two years in the Troy Hospital, and for several months while he was in the New York Polyclinic, he had a large amount of valuable experience in attending cases of appendicitis, and in his subsequent practice he has had remarkable success with the many cases of that nature brought to him for treatment.

Dr. Bestle is a member both of the Greene County Medical Society and of the Medical Society of Northern New York. He is also a member of the Sixth Separate Company of militia of Troy, and of the Arba Reed Steamer Company of that city. Fraternally, he holds membership in Frontier Lodge, F. & A. M., of Chateaugay. In politics the Doctor is a Republican, and in religious faith an Episcopalian, being connected with St. Paul's Episcopal Church of Troy. Although he has been in Hunter a comparatively short time, he has already built up a large practice, and is very popular both socially and professionally.

WELLINGTON E. BASSLER, one of the leading business men of Middleburg, N.Y., was born on August 19, 1848, son of David and Augusta (Tibbits) Bassler. His paternal grandfather was Henry Bassler. He was born in Knox, Albany County, and spent his early years in that place. After his marriage he came to Huntersland, this town, and settled on what is now known as the Bassler homestead, where he spent the remainder of his life, and where he died at the age of forty-four. His wife, whose maiden name was Mary Saddlemyer, was also a native of Albany County. She lived to reach the age of eighty-nine. Of the ten children born to her, five are living, namely: Amanda, who married Resolved Macomber; Amaziah; Eliza Ann, who married Peleg Cook; Sylvester, who occupies the old homestead; and Lucy, who married Salem Smith, and resides near Rensselaerville, Albany County.

David Bassler, who was born in Huntersland, March 22, 1822, and died September 13, 1893, was reared on the home farm, and up to 1859, with the exception of one year, was engaged exclusively in agricultural work. In 1860 he went into mercantile life in Huntersland; and in 1869 he bought the Luther Vroman store in Middleburg, at the corner of Main Street and Railroad Avenue, and thus became the proprietor of what to-day, under the efficient management of his successors, is one of the leading stores in town. David Bassler's wife, to whom he was married in October, 1847, was the daughter of Harry and Betsy (Styles) Tibbits, of Huntersland, early residents of the town. Mr. Tibbits lived to be eighty-five years of age, and Mrs. Tibbits lived to be sixty. Mrs. Augusta T. Bassler, who died on September 7, 1880, at the age of fifty-two, was one of four daughters born to her parents. She was a member of the Christian church at Huntersland. Her children were: Wellington E. Bassler; Ida, who married Peter Wormer; and Ella, who married George B. Hyde, of Middleburg.

Wellington E. Bassler was educated in the public schools, and at Starkey Seminary, from which he was graduated in June, 1869. Following this he was clerk in his father's store for two years, and then in 1871 he was admitted to a half-interest in the business, which assumed the name of D. Bassler & Son. In April, 1875, John H. Cornell bought the elder Mr. Bassler's interest, and the firm name was changed to Bassler & Cornell. On January 1, 1880, Mr. Cornell retired. In 1887 Mr. Bassler took into partnership two of his clerks, C. L. McBain and George B. Wheeler, and the firm name has since been W. E. Bassler & Co.

Mr. Bassler is a wide-awake man, and is interested in varied enterprises of a progressive character. He is a warm-hearted Republican, and has been connected with the Republican County Committee for some time, six years as its chairman, and a number of years as secretary of the committee. On April 1, 1889, he assumed the duties of Postmaster of Middleburg. He held this position five years, and in that time he greatly improved the postal service of this town, had the satisfaction of seeing the office raised from the fourth class to the third class list, and the position of Postmaster made a salaried one. Since then the salary has been increased by five hundred dollars. Mr. Bassler was nominated for the Assembly in 1894, and again in 1896, and in both instances ran ahead of his ticket by hundreds of votes. Since 1894 he has been president of the Mutual Fire Insurance Association, which was formed that year by the business men of Middleburg, to embrace Schoharie, Otsego, and Albany Counties, Chenango and Montgomery Counties having been added since. This association has met with remarkable success, and does a very large amount of business. Mr. Bassler is also a director in the Oak Hill and Middleburg Local Exchange Telephone Companies; a director of the First National Bank of Middleburg; director of the Middleburg and Schoharie Railroad; and president of the board of trustees of Starkey Seminary, which position he has held since 1881. He was a trustee of Middleburg Academy for six years, and for four years of the time president of the board. Ten years ago he founded the Starkey Seminary Monthly, of which he was the editor until 1897. Mr. Bassler is an active worker in the Reformed church, and since 1884 has been superintendent of its Sunday-school. From 1882 to 1888 he was secretary of the County Association of Sunday-schools, and subsequently for five years he was president of the association. Since 1893 he has been president of the Schoharie County Bible Society.

Mr. Bassler's store is in a most prosperous condition. Four assistants are employed in its management; and since it is one of the old-established business enterprises in this region, and has always maintained its early reputation for honest dealing and high grade goods, it has the confidence and the patronage of the public.

Mr. Bassler has seen many and important changes in Middleburg since he first began business here. The handsome school-house has been built, many of the big business blocks have been erected, and a water supply system has been introduced into the town. He himself has aided in many of the more noteworthy improvements. On January 1, 1890, he associated himself with Mr. G. L. Fox in founding the Middleburg *News*, a paper advanced in rank and one now growing steadily in favor, as well as one which bears the distinction of being the first Republican paper in this end of the county.

In 1874 Mr. Bassler was united in marriage with Alida, only child of Hezekiah Manning, and a native of this place. Mr. Manning was born here, and spent his entire life engaged in farming. He died in 1889. His wife, whose maiden name was Maria Beekman, was born in Sharon. She resides with Mr. and Mrs. Bassler. Since his marriage Mr. Bassler has made his home at the old Manning homestead, which is a very attractive place just outside the village, the house being sheltered by tall elms and stately pines, surrounded by extensive grounds, and guarded by the dark-browed, lofty cliffs which stand as venerable sentinels at the eastern portals of the Schoharie Valley. Mr. Bassler is a great fancier of poultry, and has model poultry yards, where he raises many fancy breeds, such as Leghorns, Plymouth Rocks, and Light Brahmas. He makes a feature of egg-producing poultry, and ships eggs West as far as Colorado, and South as far as Maryland. He is also a fancier of Holstein cattle.

JOHN A. MYERS, a veteran agriculturist of Seward, N.Y., living about two miles from the village of Hyndsville, was born in this town, March 27, 1819, a son of Philip P. and Catherine (Strobeck) Myers. His paternal grandfather, Peter Myers, came from Dutchess County to Schoharie County at an early period of its history, and for a short time lived in Seward. He removed from here to Otsego County, and, purchasing land near the town of South Valley, improved a farm, on which he resided many years. He finally returned to Seward, and died at the home of his son, Philip P. He was twice married, and by his second wife, who was the grandmother of John A., had five children.

Philip P. Myers, son of Peter, was reared to farming pursuits, and soon after his marriage settled on the Myers homestead, now owned and occupied by his son, John A. Here he toiled with persistent energy to clear and improve a farm, and was numbered among the respected and successful farmers of the neighborhood. His death occurred at the age of threescore years and ten. He was a strong supporter of the principles of the Democratic party, but never aspired to political office. His wife, Catherine, was born in Seward, being one of the six children of John A.

Strobeck, a prominent pioneer farmer of the town, and one of its most esteemed citizens. Mr. Strobeck as a young man served in the war of the Revolution, and in one of its battles was severely wounded. He attained the advanced age of eighty years. Philip P. and Catherine S. Myers reared six children, two of whom are living, namely: John A., the first-born; and Catherine, residing in East Worcester, being the wife of Abraham Smith, who is her second husband.

John A. Myers was educated in the district school. For three and one-half years after his marriage he lived on the old home farm with his parents, subsequently lived for a year with his father-in-law, and then rented a farm on shares for four years. Having accumulated some money, he next bought a farm of one hundred and nine acres on Winegard Hill, where he lived for eighteen years, when he sold that and purchased a larger farm, of one hundred and forty acres, which he carried on two years. Returning then to the old homestead, he took charge of it until the death of his father, and after that event he bought out the other heirs, and has since been its sole possessor. This place contains one hundred and twenty-five acres of land, most of which is under cultivation; and he has also another estate near by of one hundred and twenty-two acres, which he rents by the year. He has practically given up the management of his property to his son Peter, who lives with him, and they are carrying on general farming and dairying with signal success, and are also engaged to some extent in manufacturing lumber.

In politics Mr. Myers is identified with the Democratic party, but has persistently refused to accept all offices excepting those of Highway Commissioner and Collector of Taxes, both of which he filled a short time. He is an active member of the Methodist Episcopal church, of which he has been trustee and steward, and has been connected with the Sunday-school.

On May 28, 1839, Mr. Myers married Emily B. Youngs, who was born in Seward, a daughter of Adam Youngs, formerly a well-to-do farmer and lumber manufacturer, he having been owner of the saw-mill now operated by Mr. Myers and his son. Mr. and Mrs. Myers have had nine children, six of whom grew to mature years, namely: Adam, a physician in Buskirk, Rensselaer County, who married Mary Diefendorf, and has two children — Victor and Ralph; Millard, deceased, who married Hannah Shear, and had one child, Emily; Elmira, the wife of Harvey Oliver, a farmer; Peter, who lives on the home farm, married Mary Marks, and has three children — John D., Howard C., and Dewey Willard; Lorenzo, the oldest child, who died leaving a widow, whose maiden name was Lottie M. Simmonds, and one child, Lewis; and Julia, who died at the age of eighteen years.

F REDERICK EISENMENGER, Police Justice, Schenectady, N.Y., was born in this city, March 21, 1849, son of Ferdinand and Wilhelmina (Laman) Eisenmenger. The

FREDERICK EISENMENGER.

parents were born in Germany, the father about the year 1827.

In 1846, having acquired a good education and mastered the machinist's trade, he came to the United States, intending to engage in business. Instead of adhering to his original plan, he entered the employ of the Schenectady & Utica Railway Company, with whom he remained about sixteen years. In 1862 he enlisted as a private in Company K, One Hundred and Thirty-fourth Regiment, New York Volunteers, with which he served in the Civil War until fatally wounded in May, 1864, his death occurring on June 16 of the same year. Mrs. Wilhelmina Eisenmenger, his wife, was left with two children: Pauline, who died in 1865, aged five years; and Frederick, the subject of this sketch. The mother died in 1886, at the age of sixty-eight.

On August 11, 1862, Frederick Eisenmenger, when but thirteen years old, joined the same regiment in which his father enlisted, and was enrolled in the ranks of Company B, being one of the youngest volunteers to enter the service. He was detailed to serve at division headquarters under Major-general John W. Geary, commander of the Second Division, Twentieth Army Corps, and afterward Governor of Pennsylvania. While in front of Atlanta he received a severe wound in the jaw, and he was mustered out with his regiment in June, 1865. In 1868 he began a four years' apprenticeship at the machinist's trade in the Schenectady Locomotive Works, and he completed the term. Feeling the need of a better education, he studied nights, and while still employed at the works he began to read law under the direction of Judge Yates. He practised his profession until May 2, 1882, when he was appointed Police Justice. The duties of this position he has performed with marked ability for over sixteen years. His present term will expire in 1900.

In September, 1874, Judge Eisenmenger married Louisa, daughter of the late Louis Pepper, of this city. They have two children, namely: Frederick, who was graduated from the high school in 1893, and is now in the experimental department of the General Electrical Works; and Clara, now a student at the high school.

Judge Eisenmenger belongs to St. George Lodge, No. 6, F. & A. M.; is Past Commander of Horsfall Post, No. 90, G. A. R.; and president of the One Hundred and Thirty-fourth Regimental Association. He is a member and has been an official of the Methodist Episcopal church. His residence at 105 Union Avenue was built by him in 1887, and he purchased for his mother the house in which she spent her last years.

WILLIAM W. BURGETT, M.D., of the village of Fultonham, one of the foremost physicians and surgeons of Schoharie County, was born in Fultonham, May 14, 1860. He is the son of Charles S. and Julia A. (Teller) Burgett, and is a lineal descendant in the sixth generation of one of two brothers who came from Holland to America in the early part of the eighteenth century and settled on Manhattan Island. They bought land, and afterward leased one hundred acres near the present site of Trinity Church in New York City, for a term of ninety-nine years. Both married, and both had sons in the Revolutionary army. "Burghardt," the original spelling of their surname, was retained until within a comparatively few years.

Millbury Burghardt, or Burgett, the next in line of descent, was a pioneer of Schoharie County, and the founder of the family in Fulton, where he reared his eight children, one of whom, Millbury, was the succeeding ancestor. Storm Burgett, son of Conrad Burgett, was the Doctor's grandfather. He was born in Fulton, and there he lived and died. He owned the farm now in the possession of Mr. C. E. Markham, of whom a brief sketch may be found on another page of this volume. He was a wagon-maker and carpenter by trade, occupations at which he worked in conjunction with farming, and was well known as one of the most industrious and thrifty men of the community. To Storm Burgett and his wife, whose maiden name was Sally Banner, six children were born, three of whom are living; namely, Charles S., Lydia, wife of Timothy Becker, and Peter.

Charles S. Burgett was born in Fulton, August 30, 1831, and spent his earlier years on the home farm. He subsequently learned the blacksmith's trade, at which he continued to work until 1866, when he bought the hotel which he has since managed successfully. He is a stanch Democrat in politics, but has never been an aspirant for official honors. Both he and his wife are members of the Lutheran church. In 1851 he married Julia A. Teller, who was born August 4, 1832, in Fulton.

Her father, Cornelius Teller, spent the entire sixty-one years of his life in this town, being engaged during his active period in agricultural pursuits on a small farm that he had bought near his boyhood's home. He was one of the leading Democrats of this vicinity, and served as a Tax Collector two terms in the earlier part of this century, when the entire receipts for the year were but one thousand one hundred dollars, against the eight thousand dollars collected in 1898. His wife, Lavinia Vroman, was a daughter of Martin Vroman, a lifelong farmer of what is now the town of Middleburg; and Lavinia Vroman's mother, the grandmother of Mrs. Charles S. Burgett, was before marriage a Miss Zeie, who was born in Middleburg in Colonial days, and from the age of seven to fourteen years, during the entire period of the Revolution, lived in the Upper Fort. Cornelius Teller's father, William Teller, was born in Schenectady, N.Y., whence he came when a young man to this county, and in 1800 settled in the town of Middleburg, where he lived until his death, at the age of forty-two years. He was a shoemaker by trade. After coming here he married Maggie Feeck, the descendant of one of the original settlers of this part of the county. She survived him, living to the age of fifty-six years. Both were active members of the Reformed church. They reared eight children.

Of the five children born of the union of Charles S. and Julia A. (Teller) Burgett, three are still living; namely, Marion, the Doctor, and Laura. Marion, after the death of her first husband, Frank P. Haynes, married Warren P. Hollenbeck, a prominent farmer in the town of Broome, N.Y. Laura married first Harland Haynes, of Fulton, who died leaving her with one child, Marion Harland. She is now the wife of F. J. Graham, a shoe dealer of New York City, and has one child by this marriage, Mildred. Both parents are members of the Lutheran church.

William W. Burgett obtained the rudiments of his education in the public schools of Fultonham, and was further advanced in learning by a course of study at the high school under Professor Sias, of whom a biographical sketch appears elsewhere in this REVIEW. A short time he spent as a clerk in the store of H. T. Kingsley, and he taught school one term in Fulton. Going then to Schoharie, he read medicine two years with Dr. Layman, after which he entered the medical department of the University of New York City, from which he received his degree of Doctor of Medicine in March, 1882, at the age of twenty-one years. In addition to the regular curriculum of the university, he took special clinical examinations at Bellevue Hospital under Professor William H. Thompson, while at the same hospital he received private instruction in physical diagnosis from Professor Alfred L. Loomis, in operative surgery from Professor J. W. Wright, and in urinary analyses under Professor John C. Draper. Returning to Fultonham immediately after his graduation, Dr. Burgett here began the duties of his profession, and has since built up a large and successful patronage as a general medical practitioner. In 1884 he erected his present residence in the village, and also a substantial barn on the same lot. He has served a number of terms on the local Board of Health, and for six years has been County Coroner. Politically, he is a sound Democrat. He is a member of the Schoharie County Medical Society, of which he has been vice-president and president. He is also a member of Middleburg Lodge, No. 663, F. & A. M., and is at present Master of Fultonham Grange, No. 809.

On September 25, 1883, Dr. Burgett married Miss Maggie E. Schaeffer, who was born in Fulton, daughter of Hendrick Schaeffer, a retired farmer of Fulton. Among the pioneer settlers of the town of Schoharie was Christian Schaeffer, one of the largest landholders of that locality, whose son, Jacob Henry, born in Schoharie in 1808, was the grandfather of Mrs. Burgett. Grandfather Schaeffer was a lifelong agriculturist of Schoharie, where he spent his eighty-eight years of earthly existence, and was one of its most esteemed citizens. He was a Republican in politics, and served as an Overseer of the Poor. He contributed liberally toward the support of the Lutheran church, of which he was one of the oldest and most influential members. His wife, Ann Alida Groesbeck, who died at the age of eighty-four years, bore him ten children. Hendrick Schaeffer married Helen Borst, a native of Middleburg, and a daughter of Peter H. Borst, the representative of an early family of Schoharie County, and himself one of the most wealthy and prominent of its farmers. He was a member of the Lutheran church, and his death, at the age of sixty-five years, removed from that organization one of its substantial supporters. His wife, Nancy Effner, a lifelong resident of Middleburg, died in 1861. Mr. and Mrs. Hendrick Schaeffer reared four children, of whom three are living, as follows: Charles, a farmer in Schoharie; Alida, wife of Seneca Haynes; and Maggie E., now Mrs. Burgett. Peter, a carpenter, died at the age of thirty-five years.

Dr. and Mrs. Burgett have two children, namely: William Layman, who was named for one of the Doctor's early preceptors; and Charles Leland. Dr. Burgett is an elder and one of the trustees of the Lutheran church, and Mrs. Burgett also is an active church member, and for many years has been a teacher in the Sunday-school.

WILLIAM H. MEAD, M.D., the veteran physician and surgeon of Windham, Greene County, N.Y., was born in Jewett, this county, on April 6, 1833, to Stephen and Caroline (Hosford) Mead. His great-grandfather Hosford, whose Christian name was Gideon, was a prominent farmer and land-owner in Farmington, Conn., and Dr. Mead has in his possession some of the ancestral deeds bearing the seal of King George.

Philip Mead, the Doctor's paternal grandfather, was born in Dutchess County, New York, and grew up on a farm. He removed to Jewett when his son Stephen was five years old, finding his way hither by following marked trees. He lived first in most primitive fashion in a log hut, but in time cleared a goodly tract of land and erected a commodious frame house. He was a lifelong farmer. After spending some years in Jewett, he went to Cayuga, near Weedsport, where he resided until his death, at sixty years of age. The maiden name of his wife was Hannah Townsend. They had a large family of children.

The Doctor's father, Stephen Mead was born in Dutchess County, and reared to farm life. When he became of age he purchased a farm in Jewett, where he spent the remainder of his life, and where he died at the age of eighty-six. He followed agriculture and lumbering, and did a large business in selling bark to tanners. He and his wife, Caroline, were members of the Methodist Episcopal church. Mrs. Mead died at the age of sixtynine. She was the daughter of Joel and Maria Hosford, farmer folk of Jewett. Her father died at the age of eighty-four, and her mother, who was of Dutch descent, died while quite a young woman, although she lived to bear four children. Stephen and Caroline Mead were also the parents of four children, three of whom are living, namely: Dr. William H., of Windham; Dr. J. H. Mead, of Hunter, a sketch of whose life is to be found on another page; and Adeline, who married Alanson Woodworth, of Hunter, whose biography also appears in this volume.

William H. Mead's early life was spent on

his father's farm in Jewett. He attended the common schools of the town, and later became a teacher in them and in the schools of Hunter. After teaching for several years he took up the study of medicine with his brother Joel, then settled in Hunter, and he subsequently attended the Albany Medical College. After his graduation in 1868 he began practice in Ashland, where he remained until 1879, when he came to Windham. He has now been in continuous practice here for thirty years, and, barring one or two exceptions, is the oldest medical practitioner in service in the county. He has given much attention to surgery, and has performed some remarkable operations, his skill being known throughout the county. His career as a general practitioner has also been a distinguished one.

In 1856 Dr. William H. Mead was united in marriage with Matilda Winter, daughter, and one of a number of children, of Moses Winter, a farmer of Jewett. Mrs. Mead died November 26, 1896. Of the three children born to her, one died at the age of ten months, and another at the age of five years. A daughter, Eugenie, is living. She is the wife of Emery A. Hill, a well-known Windham farmer, and has two children — Blanche and William Henry.

Dr. Mead is a stanch Republican. His first Presidential vote was cast in 1856, and he has voted every election since with the exception of one. He has held a few minor offices in the village, but in the main has refused public office. He is a member of the Masonic fraternity in this town, and was elected Junior Warden within two weeks after joining the organization. He has been a member of the Greene County Medical Society ever since it was started, twenty-five years ago. His church connections are with the Methodist society of this place, of which also his wife was a member. For many years he was steward in the church, but within a short time he has tendered his resignation of that office. For many years, too, he was a teacher in the Sunday-school and chorister of the church. During their residence in Ashland Mrs. Mead also was a teacher. Throughout his long and useful life the Doctor has been a promoter of every good and philanthropic cause, and has been actively interested in every effort to promote the well-being of his fellows.

JOHN ROSSMAN, M.D., a prominent physician of Schoharie County and a resident of Middleburg, was born in the town of Fulton on March 8, 1847, his parents being George and Marietta (Beard) Rossman. His first ancestors in this country came from Germany, and were among the early settlers of Columbia County, New York. His grandfather, whose name was Christopher, was born in that county, and lived there during early life. Before the birth of his son George, Christopher Rossman removed to Schoharie County and settled in Summit, where he passed the remainder of his life. In politics he was a Republican, and both he and his wife were members of the Methodist church. Mrs. Rossman, whose maiden name was Lana

Mickel, was born in Schoharie of an old family. She was the mother of fourteen children, all of whom grew to maturity. They were named as follows: George, Mary, John, Betsy, William, Christina, Nathaniel, Phœbe, David, Lucy, Charles, Huldah, Jane, and Cassie.

Dr. Rossman's father was born in Summit, received his education in the common schools there, and subsequently removed to Fulton, where he bought a farm and resided until his death, at the age of forty-seven. Politically, George Rossman was at first a Republican and later a Democrat. For twenty-two years he served as a Justice of the Peace. He was twice married. His first wife, Marietta, who died when their son John was four years of age, was born in Richmondville. She was a daughter of Jacob Beard, and one of a family of four children. Her father was a farmer of that town, and subsequently of Fulton. Late in life he removed to Geneseo County, where he died at the advanced age of ninety. Mrs. Marietta B. Rossman was the mother of two children. Her daughter, Louise, is deceased. The second wife of George Rossman was before her marriage Marcia Holmes. She also was born in Fulton, of one of the old families. She died at the age of forty.

John Rossman in his boyhood and youth secured a good common-school education in the public schools, which he attended both summer and winter. In 1865 he began to read medicine with Dr. J. D. Wheeler, of Middleburg, and in 1868 he was graduated at the Philadelphia University of Medicine and Surgery. He began practising with Dr. Wheeler, but at the end of a year went to West Fulton and started an independent practice. Three years later he returned and again engaged with his former partner, but after a year of joint work the two doctors severed their connection, and since then Dr. Rossman has worked alone. He has built up a large general practice, and is now the oldest physician in town in point of service.

The Doctor married his first wife, Mary, the daughter of Cornelius Bouck, in 1869. She died at the age of twenty-eight, leaving three children — Marietta, Anna A., and Charles H. Marietta married M. J. Vroman, and is the mother of three children — Cecil, Lena, and Marguerite. Anna is the wife of Dr. Simpkins of this town. Charles married Agnes McLean, and has one child, Marion, by name. The Doctor's second wife, whose maiden name was Lizzie B. Smith, is a native of Middleburg, and the daughter of Silas Smith. She is a member of the Episcopal church, but an attendant of the Reformed church.

For the past fifteen years Dr. Rossman has been Health Officer of the town, holding his office by annual re-elections. He is an active and influential member of the Schoharie Medical Society, and was secretary of the Board of Pension Examiners for the county. He is a Democrat, but never an office-seeker; in fact, he has never been willing to accept public office, except in cases where it has seemed plainly his duty to do so. He is a member of Middleburg Lodge, No. 663, F. & A. M.; of John L. Lewis Chapter, No. 229; of St.

George's Commandery, No. 37; La Bastile Lodge, No. 494, I. O. O. F.; and Middleburg Encampment, No. 129. In the Blue Lodge he has held all the offices, having been Master for two years, and secretary and Junior Warden for the same length of time each. He is Past Noble Grand of the Subordinate Lodge of this district, and Past Chief Patriarch of the Encampment, and was District Deputy for two years. For seven years he has been president of the Middleburg Cemetery Organization.

SYLVESTER B. SAGE, of Catskill, dealer in carriages and harnesses, and present member of the New York Assembly from Greene County, was born in Prattsville on September 8, 1836, son of Hart C. and Clarissa H. (Van Luven) Sage.

The founder of the Sage family in America is said to have been David Sage, who came to New England in 1652, and settled at Middletown, Conn., where he died in 1703, aged sixty-four years.

David Sage of a later generation, grandfather of Mr. Sage, of Catskill, was one of the early settlers of Broome, Schoharie County, N. Y., and resided on a farm there throughout the greater part of his life.

Hart C. Sage, son of the second David here mentioned, was brought up on the farm in Broome, but after his marriage came to Catskill. Here he remained two years engaged in mercantile business, and at the end of that time went to Prattsville, where he carried on a store. He died at the age of thirty-six. In early life he taught school for several terms. He was prominent among the Odd Fellows, and after he went to Prattsville he built a hall there for the organization. He was a member of the Presbyterian church, and conformed his daily life and walk to his professed beliefs. His wife, Clarissa, who shared his religious faith, was born in Broome. She was a descendant of one of the early settlers there, and one of a large family of children. She died at seventy, having been the mother of five children, namely: Osmar C., who is now deceased; Omar V.; Sylvester B.; H. Clarence; and Hart C., Jr., also deceased. Omar V. Sage is a well-known public man. He was Clerk of Greene County for two terms, and member of the New York Assembly two terms, and for the past five years he has held the important position of Warden of Sing Sing Prison. H. Clarence Sage is a professor of music, residing in New York City.

Sylvester B. Sage when a lad of eleven years lost his father, and at a very early age he was obliged to shift for himself. After working in Prattsville for a time as clerk in a store, he was in business there down to 1869. He then sold out his trade and stock and came to Catskill, and for eleven years, from 1869 to 1880, conducted a grocery here. In 1880 he received an appointment as under sheriff, and this office he filled in an entirely acceptable manner for three years. At the end of that time he opened his present business, which has since proved to be such a success. In his extensive warerooms on Main Street are to be found vehicles of all kinds, harnesses, whips, and general horse and carriage furnishings. He does a larger business in this line than any other firm between Albany and New York. He makes many of the harnesses he carries in stock, and sells many at wholesale, keeping five harness-makers employed the entire year. All wagons and carriages to be found in his repository are built by the best manufacturers. He employs fourteen men in the store, and sells at both wholesale and retail. He is among the oldest business men on the street, and, with two or three exceptions, the oldest in the town.

In politics Mr. Sage is a Democrat. He held the office of Town Collector for a year, and that of Police Justice for six years, and was then appointed Under Sheriff. He has also been on the Board of Education several years, and was clerk of the board during the greater part of his period of membership. In 1897 he was elected to the Assembly, receiving three thousand, eight hundred and sixteen votes, against three thousand, four hundred and fifty-three for John B. Logendyke. During that year he was a member of the Committees on Internal Affairs and Villages. In 1898 he was again elected to the Assembly, against D. G. Green, of Coxsackie, and is now serving on the Committees on General Laws and Revision, the two best in the House.

Mr. Sage married, in 1861, Alice, daughter of Darius W. Smith, proprietor of a sale stable in 24th Street, New York. Of this union two children have been born — Francis V. and Clarence B. The latter is in business with his father. Mr. Sage's business is located in one of the handsomest blocks in Catskill, and his residence, purchased in 1872, occupies one of the most sightly spots in the town.

Mr. Sage is a member of Catskill Lodge, No. 468, having joined many years ago. He held the office of Clerk for a long time, but has declined all other offices. He is at the present time vice-president of the Catskill Driving Park Association, and president of the Mountain Dew Brewery, and a director in both organizations; also a member of the Executive Committee of the Retail Carriage Dealers' Protective Association, which is a national organization. In 1895 he was president of the association. Mr. Sage and his family are all members of the Presbyterian church. He is one of Catskill's most progressive and most highly respected citizens.

CHARLES E. WEIDMAN, M.D., the well-known medical practitioner of Gallupville, in the town of Wright, his native place, was born on November 8, 1870, his parents being Daniel and Louisa (Vroman) Weidman. His grandfather, Peter I. Weidman, who was born in Middleburg, was a farmer by occupation, and there spent the early part of his active life. Later he lived in the town of New Scotland for ten years, and at the end of that time came to Wright, where he died at the age of seventy-five. Peter I. Weidman's wife, the Doctor's grandmother, Edith Houghtaling, a native of New Scotland, Albany County, is still living on the old farm. All her life she has been

CHARLES E. WIIDMAN

a devoted member of the Lutheran church. Of the five children born to her, only one is living.

Daniel Weidman, son of Peter I., was reared on a farm, and received his education in the common schools. He spent the later years of his life on the old homestead, his death occurring at the age of fifty-two. In politics he was a stanch Republican, as his father before him had been. He was a leading agriculturist of his town and an active member of the Lutheran church.

Dr. Weidman's mother, who was the daughter of Albert Vroman and one of a family of eleven children, was born in 1846, in the town of Guilderland, in Albany County, this State. Her father was a speculator in farm produce. Her mother, whose maiden name was Van Aurnum, is still living. Besides the Doctor, Mrs. Weidman had two children, namely: Austin J.; and Edith, who is the wife of Charles S. Young. Mrs. Weidman died in 1889 at the age of forty-three. Both parents were members of the Lutheran church, and the father had held the office of Deacon as well as others of less importance.

The boyhood of Dr. Weidman was spent on the home farm. He attended the common schools and Hartwick Seminary, graduating from the last-named institution in 1891. Subsequent to this he taught school in Gallupville for two years. He pursued the study of medicine in the Albany Medical College, was graduated in 1895, and since that time has been located here. He has demonstrated his fitness for the profession in which he has engaged, and has built up a flourishing practice, his ability being recognized by all who have had occasion to call upon him. Although he has been here but a comparatively short time, he has won many friends professionally; and his services are in requisition, not only in the village, but also in the outlying districts.

Dr. Weidman was married in the fall of 1896 to Minnetta C. Barringer, who was born in Germantown, Columbia County. She is the daughter of John I. Barringer, a druggist of Hudson, formerly of Germantown, and one of a family of three children. In politics, the Doctor is a Republican. He has served on the town Republican committee, and has been candidate for Coroner. He has held a number of offices on the election board, among these being that of ballot clerk. In 1898 he was elected Supervisor of the town of Wright, and in 1899 was re-elected for two years. Professionally, he is a member of the Schoharie County Medical Society. He is a member of Orion Lodge, No. 624, Independent Order of Odd Fellows; is Past Grand, and has been through all the other chairs. Mrs. Weidman is a member of the Presbyterian Church of Waterford.

ROBERT ELLIOTT, whose death occurred on January 6, 1899, was for many years a representative citizen of Hunter, N.Y., being well known in the third quarter of the century as a general merchant, and later as the builder and proprietor of the Kaatsberg. He was of Scotch Irish parentage, and was born on June 24, 1822, in

Ireland, where his father, whose name was Thomas, spent his entire life engaged in agriculture.

Thomas Elliott and his family were stanch members of the Presbyterian church, and he was an Elder for many years. He lived to be eighty years old. His wife, Jane McLane Elliott, was of Scotch descent, and one of a large family. She was the mother of the following-named children: Robert; John, who lives in Kansas; Thomas, Jr., also in Kansas; Samuel, Harriet, and James, all three deceased; Helena and Jane, who are living in Ireland; and Adam, who went to Australia. James Elliott was educated for the Presbyterian ministry at Belfast. He subsequently taught in Canada.

Robert Elliott inherited from his parents those sterling qualities which ever characterized his dealings, and which were such potent factors in shaping his successful business career. He was educated in the national schools of Ireland. At the early age of eighteen years he took the place of a professor in one of those schools, and performed the duties of the position for six months in a highly creditable manner. At the end of that time he set sail for America. He soon obtained a position in a tannery, and after a short time he entered the employ of Mr. Edwards, who belonged to the prominent Hunter family of that name, and who was descended from the Jonathan Edwards family of Massachusetts. Mr. Elliott kept books for Mr. Edwards until that gentleman died, and he then entered the employ of his brother, Colonel William W. Edwards, with whom he came to this town in 1848. Colonel Edwards carried on a large tannery here, and Mr. Elliott had charge of the accounts of the concern until his employer went out of business.

In 1853 Mr. Elliott opened a general store, and for the next twenty-five years he conducted a large and successful business. At the end of that time he sold out, and later bought the lot upon which he erected the beautiful Kaatsberg. This fine house he built in 1883 — the finest house in Hunter village. He ran this as a summer boarding-house up to 1897, when he gave up the management to his son, Robert G. Elliott. All built under Mr. Elliott's supervision, it is a monument to his thoroughness and is admired by every one.

In 1855 Mr. Elliott married Mary A. Caldwell, a lady of Canadian birth. Of the six children born of this union, four are living; namely, Helena, Elmore E., Clara, and Robert G. Elmore E., who is a prominent physician in Catskill, married Mabel Sanderson, a daughter of Judge Sanderson, of Catskill, and has two sons — John Sanderson and Robert Caldwell. Clara resides with her mother. Helena is the wife of Dr. C. P. McCabe, of Greenville. Of her three children one is living, a daughter Dorothy.

JEREMIAH DUNCKEL, who resides on his farm in the town of Seward, about a mile from the village of Hyndsville in Schoharie County, is living retired from active pursuits, enjoying the fruits of his earlier years of toil. He was born April 7, 1821, in Canajoharie, N.Y., a son of George G. Dunckel, and the descendant of a pioneer settler of that town.

His great-grandfather, Dunckel, whose name was Peter, emigrated from Germany in Colonial times. Peter Dunckel took up a large tract of unbroken land in Canajoharie, and, erecting a small log cabin in the woods, settled there with his wife and children. He was an industrious, hard-working man, and while clearing a farm for himself he assisted in the upbuilding of the town. His son George, who was the grandfather of Jeremiah Dunckel, the subject of this brief sketch, enlisted as a soldier in the Revolutionary army, and at the battle of Cedar Swamp was unfortunate enough to lose an eye.

George Dunckel was born in Germany, and spent the first ten years of his life in the Fatherland. Coming then to New York with his parents, he performed his full share of the pioneer labor of redeeming a homestead from the forest. When, on the death of his father, the farm came into his possession, he continued the improvements already begun; and prior to his death, which occurred at the age of eighty-four years, he had a fine set of frame buildings on the place, which was one of the best in its appointments of any in the neighborhood. Six children were born to him and his wife, Elizabeth Countryman. She, too, lived to an advanced age. Both were active members of the Lutheran church.

George G. Dunckel, son of George, grew to manhood on the ancestral farm in Canajoharie, where from his youth up he was familiar with its daily labors. He subsequently became sole owner of the homestead property, and was there prosperously engaged in agricultural pursuits until 1848. Selling out at that time, he came to Seward, and, having purchased the farm now owned and occupied by his son Jeremiah, he carried it on until his decease, at the age of seventy-seven years. A man of energy and intelligence, he was a valued member of the Democratic party, and for a number of terms served wisely as Assessor and Highway Commissioner. He was a Methodist in his religious belief, and an active member of the church of that denomination. He married Maria Cook, daughter of John R. Cook, a farmer and blacksmith of Canajoharie. They had a family of eleven children, three of whom are now living, namely: Jeremiah, the fifth-born; Levi, who lives at Central Bridge; and Sophronia, widow of Austin Lory, late of Hyndsville.

Jeremiah Dunckel obtained his early education in the common schools, and under the instruction of his father became well versed in farming pursuits. When the family came to Seward he accompanied them, and, remaining an inmate of the household, assisted in the management of the new farm. This valuable estate of two hundred acres he now holds in his own name, having purchased the interest of the remaining heirs. In its care he has shown excellent judgment and skill. He has carried on general farming to advantage, devoting a part of the land to raising hops, a profitable crop in this section of the State, and has also met with success as a dairyman. He has sometimes had as many as forty cows in his herd, and his butter has always met with a ready sale. Of recent years he has relegated the management of the estate to his eldest son, Lucius Dunckel.

On October 5, 1843, Mr. Dunckel married Lana A., daughter of Sylvanus Nestle, a well-known tailor of Sprout Brook, N.Y. She died at the age of sixty-one years, having borne him four children. Of these two are dead, namely: Esther, who married Anson Hynds; and Helen M., who married Irving Schoolcraft. The two now living are Lucius and George. Lucius, born April 6, 1846, has spent his life on the home farm, of which he has had full charge since 1882. He is a Democrat in politics and has served as school trustee. In 1869 he married Adelaide Lory, daughter of John Lory, of Seward. They have one child, Lottie Ann, who married Clark Bouton, Postmaster and merchant at Hyndsville, and has two children — Edna Belle and J. Leroy. George, a resident of Cobleskill, married Angerilla Falk. They had five children: Jerry; Ann; Una and Ula, twins; and Oscar, who died at the age of nineteen years. After the death of his first wife, Mr. Dunckel married Henrietta Young, who was born in Seward township, where her father, Jeremiah Young, a farmer of Seward township, but a native of Onondaga County, died aged seventy years. Her mother, whose maiden name was Caroline E. Weatherwax, was born in Rensselaer County. She died in 1892, aged eighty-one years, leaving seven children out of a family of ten born to her and her husband. Mr. and Mrs. Young were members of the Lutheran church.

Mr. Dunckel is a stanch Jeffersonian Democrat, dyed in the wool. He has taken an active interest in advancing the welfare of the town and county, but has invariably refused public office, although he has served as trustee of the School Board. He was one of the originators of the Cobleskill Agricultural Society, and has been among its most active and valued members. Mrs. Dunckel is a member of the Methodist church.

JAMES B. DALEY, of Prattsville, attorney-at-law and a Civil War veteran, was born in Ohio, township of Richfield, March 7, 1845, son of Daniel and Mary Ann (Champlin) Daley. His paternal grandfather, Joseph Daley, and his great-grandfather, Obadiah Daley, were lifelong residents of Columbia County, New York, and the latter was the son of Joseph Daley, first, who came from New England to Chatham, N.Y., where he cleared a farm. Joseph Daley, second, Mr. Daley's grandfather, was a prosperous farmer, and noted for his physical strength and power of endurance. He married Hannah Son. Her father was an early settler in Columbia County, and she inherited a part of the Son farm. The grandparents died at the age of eighty years. They reared a large family of children, and none are now living

Daniel Daley, James B. Daley's father, followed the blacksmith's trade in Chatham for a time, and moving from there to Lebanon Springs, N.Y., he carried on the wagon-making business for some years, finally retiring to a farm in Chatham, where he died at the age of seventy-seven. He was widely known among Odd Fellows, having been a member of that order for many years; and he also had a large number of friends and acquaintances outside of that fraternity. His wife, Mary Ann, was born in Chatham, daughter of William and Mary (Kenyon) Champlin. Her father, who came to this State from Rhode Island, taught school in New York City prior to settling upon a farm in the town of Chatham. He had a family of six children. Daniel and Mary Ann Daley were the parents of ten children, six of whom are living; namely, William C., George, James B., Henry, Sarah, and Charles. William C. and George Daley are practising law in Chatham, and a sketch of each will be found in the BIOGRAPHICAL REVIEW of Columbia County. James B. is the subject of this sketch; Henry is a lawyer residing in Coxsackie, N.Y.; Sarah is the widow of Nathan C. Hagerborn, late of Stillbrook, N.Y.; and Charles is residing at the homestead in Chatham. The mother died at the age of seventy-two years. The parents were Baptists. They were highly esteemed for their many excellent qualities, and obituary notices of each were published in the county newspapers.

Having supplemented his common-school studies with a course at the Lebanon Springs Academy, James B. Daley turned his attention to educational pursuits, teaching schools in Columbia and Rensselaer Counties, New York, and in Berkshire County, Massachusetts. His law studies were pursued in the office of his brother George, and after his admission to the bar in 1872, he began the practice of his profession in Prattsville. In the spring of 1873 he returned to Chatham, where he was in business one year, at the end of which time he removed to Windham, Greene County, and for the succeeding eight years was a member of the firm of Daley & Talmadge, who transacted an extensive general law and real estate business. After the dissolution of that partnership he once more returned to Prattsville, where he has practised continuously to the present time. His Civil War services were performed in Company B, Ninety-first Regiment, New York Volunteers, with which he participated in a number of engagements, including the battle of Five Forks; and he witnessed the surrender of General Lee at Appomattox Court House.

In June, 1878, Mr. Daley was united in marriage with Lucy Tyler, who was born in Roxbury, Delaware County, daughter of Henry and Deborah (Hull) Tyler. Her father was a wealthy farmer. He eventually removed from Roxbury, his native town, to Prattsville, where he spent the rest of his life. Henry Tyler died at seventy-three, and his wife died at seventy. They reared three children: Lorinda, who married John Erkson, a leading merchant of Prattsville; Lucy, who married Mr. Daley; and Annie, who married Homer B. Van Cott, of Norwich, N.Y. Mrs.

Daley was a graduate of the Fort Edwards Institute, and prior to her marriage she taught music at the institute in Ellenville. She died in 1896, aged forty-six years. As a member of the Methodist Episcopal church she took an active interest in religious work, and was sincerely respected for her estimable character and rare intellectual qualities. She left four children; namely, Mamie, Emma, Ethel, and James, aged respectively sixteen, fourteen, twelve, and ten years.

Politically, Mr. Daley is a Republican. He has served with ability as a trustee of the village and of the Cemetery Association for a number of years, and acts as a notary public. His literary talents are highly appreciated in Prattsville and vicinity, and his frequent contributions to the various county papers upon different subjects are widely read. His more notable writings are: a series of articles describing his war experience, published in the Catskill *Examiner;* another series devoted to Western life, printed in the Hunter *Phœnix,* and a number of articles upon legal subjects, which have been bound with the law journal for preservation. Mr. Daley attends the Methodist Episcopal church.

HON. JOHN A. GRISWOLD, of Catskill, N.Y., ex-Congressman and former Judge and Surrogate of Greene County, was born in Cairo, this county, November 18, 1822, son of Stephen H. and Phœbe (Ashley) Griswold. He is a representative of the Griswold family of Connecticut, an account of whom appeared in the *Magazine of American History* in 1884. His father was born in Greene County, New York, February 26, 1793; and his grandfather, Jeremiah Griswold, came to Catskill from Connecticut about the year 1800, accompanied by his family.

Jeremiah Griswold, who was a prosperous farmer, lived to an advanced age. He married Mary Hill, whose birth took place either in Massachusetts or Connecticut in December, 1753. She served the patriot cause during the Revolutionary War by making cartridges for her brothers. She died December 8, 1841.

Stephen H. Griswold, Judge Griswold's father, studied law, but did not enter into practice, preferring instead to engage in agricultural pursuits. He owned a good farm in Cairo, where he resided until his death, which occurred June 14, 1844. As a stanch supporter of the Democratic party he took an active interest in the political affairs of his day, and was universally esteemed for his upright character. He was a Free Mason, and in his younger days was identified with the local Blue Lodge. He and his wife, Phœbe, were members of the Methodist Episcopal church. Mrs. Griswold was a native of Catskill, where her father, John Ashley, was an industrious farmer. She became the mother of ten children, five of whom are living, namely: John A., the subject of this sketch; Miles, who resides in one of the Western States; Addison, a well-known lawyer of Catskill; Alonzo, who is residing on a farm in Jesup, Ia.; and Marion, who is a banker in Ohio. The others

JOHN A. GRISWOLD.

were: Mary, Stephen, Emily, Jerome, and Mahala. Stephen, who entered the Union army as a surgeon early in the Civil War, was captured by the enemy at the first battle of Bull Run, and died in prison. Jerome, who was a druggist in Kansas, was killed by Confederate raiders under Quantrell. Judge Griswold's mother died June 13, 1877, aged seventy-two years.

Having pursued his preliminary studies in the public schools, John A. Griswold became a pupil at the academies in Prattsville and Catskill, concluding his attendance at the latter at the age of sixteen. After teaching for a time, he applied himself to the study of law with his uncle, Addison C. Griswold, and Richard Corning, the latter a brother of Erastus Corning, of Albany. Subsequently he continued his preparations in Syracuse, N.Y., and was admitted to the bar as an attorney and counsellor of the State in 1848. Commencing the practice of his profession alone, he was later associated with Addison Griswold until elected District Attorney in 1857, and afterward he was for some time in company with Rufus W. Watson. He ably performed the duties of District Attorney for three years, winning in that capacity a high reputation; and his able handling of several important cases, both as a public and private practitioner, caused his elevation in 1864 to the position of Judge and Surrogate of Greene County. His four years' service upon the bench was extremely creditable to himself as well as beneficial to the community; and in 1868 he was elected to a seat in Congress by the Democratic party, defeating Thomas Cornell, of Rondout, by a majority of five hundred votes. His work in the national House of Representatives was characterized by a thorough understanding of the principles of federal government and a clear conception of the many important questions submitted for legislation; and, when a convention was decided upon for the purpose of revising the Constitution of the State of New York, he was again called into service as a delegate from his district. In 1876 he was a delegate to the National Convention which nominated Samuel J. Tilden for President. He has also rendered his share of service in town affairs, serving as a Supervisor in 1872; and his interest in the welfare of the community in which he lives was not eclipsed by the higher public duties to which he has been called.

In 1857 Judge Griswold married Miss Elizabeth M. Roberts, a daughter of the late William Roberts, who was a prosperous farmer of Cliftondale, Ulster County, this State. Mrs. Griswold died November 8, 1896, aged sixty-six years. Judge Griswold resides in what is known as the Cornwall house, situated on an estate commanding a view for twenty miles around of the varied and picturesque scenery for which the Catskill region is noted. He has survived all of his former legal contemporaries in this section, but is still upon the active list; and, if not as young in years as his personal appearance would indicate, his mental capacity retains its accustomed vigor, and his strong, manly character is as much appreciated to-day as it was during the period of his public services. He is a Master Mason, and was formerly a member of the Catskill Lodge, No. 468. In his religious belief he is an Episcopalian.

WILLARD T. RIVENBURG, M.D., a well-known medical practitioner of Middleburg, N.Y., was born in the village of Chatham in Ghent, Columbia County, this State, on November 25, 1863, son of J. Morgan and Charlotte (Tipple) Rivenburg. As his name indicates, he is of Dutch ancestry, although his family has been settled in New York for many years.

His grandfather, Henry Rivenburg, was born in Columbia County, and there spent his entire life. He helped in clearing a part of the farm which he occupied and carried on. The Doctor's father was an agriculturist, and was a man highly respected in his town. He was killed by the cars at the age of thirty-seven. His wife, who was born in Otsego County, was descended from Revolutionary stock. She was also related to Walter Gunn, who with his wife was in the mission field in India, under the auspices of the Lutheran church. Both parents were members of the Reformed church at Ghent. Of their three children, two grew to maturity. These are the Doctor and John Rivenburg, Superintendent of Poor for Columbia County and a coal dealer at Ghent.

Dr. Rivenburg was educated at the Boys' Academy, Troy, the South Berkshire Institute, Mass., and the University of Buffalo, from the last named of which he received the degree of Doctor of Medicine in 1885.

While in college he was president of the Alpha Omega Delta Society, and his society sheepskin bears his own official signature as such. He was the founder of the college society known as the "Secret Seven." Dr. Rivenburg first settled for practice at Blenheim, but after a short stay there he came, in 1887, to Middleburg, where he has won a position of influence. He covers a wide area in his professional visits, and receives calls for consultation from physicians residing twenty-five miles distant.

The Doctor was married on October 14, 1891, to Belle Stanton, a graduate of the Albany Female Academy and a daughter of John Stanton, who was a merchant, and later railroad station agent of this town. She was born on the homestead of her grandmother, not far from here, and is descended from one of the oldest and most honored families in this region. Among her ancestors was brave General James Dana, who was immortalized by Washington in his first general order immediately following the battle of Bunker Hill, where Dana, then Captain, commanded a company of the Connecticut line of Continental troops.

Dr. Rivenburg is a physician of the county almshouse. He has served as president and vice-president of the Medical Society of Schoharie County, and is now medical examiner for several well-known insurance companies, chief of which are the Mutual Life of New York, the North-western, the Penn, the Brooklyn, the Nederland, the Manhattan, the Bankers', and the United States Accident.

In 1886 he took a post-graduate course at the College of Physicians and Surgeons in New York. He is a charter member of the John M. Scribner Hook and Ladder Company, and for five years was in active service, since which time he has been on the reserve list. Fraternally, he is Master of Middleburg Lodge, No. 663, F. & A. M.; and Past Sachem of Oneongena Tribe, No. 240, I. O. R. M. He is treasurer of the Village Corporation; also a trustee of St. Mark's Evangelical Lutheran church, and assistant superintendent of the Sunday-school.

DANIEL W. JENKINS, agent of the D. & H. Railroad at Central Bridge, Schoharie County, N.Y., was born in Glen, Montgomery County, on September 27, 1846, son of Nathaniel and Eleanor (Shannon) Jenkins. His great-grandfather Jenkins, who was a Welshman by birth, came to this country and settled on Long Island, where he died. At the time the British invaded the island he was made a prisoner of war. After the close of the Revolution the family removed to Duanesburg, Schenectady County, this State. William, one of the sons and grandfather of Daniel W. Jenkins, was born on Long Island, but spent the last years of his life in Montgomery County, where he died in old age.

Nathaniel Jenkins, son of William by his second wife, was born in Montgomery. He was reared on a farm, and received his education in the public schools. He was one of a large family of children, only two of whom are now living, both physicians and prominent in their professions — namely, Thomas, residing at Vandalia, and George, at Kilbourn City, Wis. Nathaniel was very successful in his farming, and was highly respected by all who knew him. He died at the age of eighty-two. His wife, Eleanor, who died at the age of eighty, was born in Prattsville. Both were members of the Society of Friends.

Daniel W. Jenkins received a practical common-school education, and on September 15, 1863, at the age of seventeen years, entered the employ of the Albany & Susquehanna Railroad Company. This road has since become a part of the D. & H. C. Company system. Mr. Jenkins's father was agent at Quaker Street (now Delanson), and at that time the equipments of the ticket office were carried in a tin box, and the way bills were made out on a board that was set up in the embankment. The road then ended at the Schoharie Creek, near the present Schoharie Junction. Mr. Jenkins has since seen it advanced all the distance to Binghamton. There was only one train per day, as against fifty per day at the present time, and most of the modern improvements have been added since then. Mr. Jenkins succeeded his father as agent at Quaker Street, and in 1868 became the agent at Central Bridge, where he has since remained. He has now two assistants. He is the youngest of seven children, the others being: De Witt C., at Syracuse; Zerah and William A., at Delanson; Mrs. Lottie Christman, of Iowa; Mrs. Colonel Coryell, whose husband is an ex-paymaster of the D. & H. Road; and Mrs. M. S. Hoag, of Albany. In addition to his duties as station agent, Mr. Jenkins does a large business in handling coal, lumber, hay, and straw.

As a business man Mr. Jenkins is known as a "hustler." Whatever he finds to do he does with all his might, and, as a rule, successfully. Recognizing his superior business qualifications, the Board of Trustees of the Schoharie County Agricultural Society elected him president of the society, which position he has held for the past eight or ten years. As a representative of this organization he has been one of the leading spirits in the State organization of county societies, serving on the Executive Committee; and for the past few years he has been vice-president of the society, frequently visiting Albany during the legislative sessions in the interests of agricultural societies generally.

In politics Mr. Jenkins is a stanch Democrat, and has frequently attended county and State conventions as a representative of his party. In the winter of 1889 he accepted the nomination for Supervisor of the town of Schoharie. At the succeeding town meeting he was elected, and he has served the town continuously since then as Supervisor, having been elected three times without opposition. He was chairman of the board for the years 1893, 1896, and 1897, and at the spring meeting held May 2, 1899, was again honored by being unanimously elected chairman for the ensuing two years. As Supervisor he has exerted a powerful influence. He was largely instrumental in effecting a settlement of the suits brought against the county by several towns of the county (including the town of Schoharie), when the law went into effect requiring the amount raised by taxation of the railroads in towns having a bonded railroad debt to be deposited with the county treasurer as a sinking fund with which to meet the bonds when due. In this settlement the town of Schoharie received its full share — in fact, more than she had reason to expect. As a member of the county board he has looked carefully after the interests of the county, believing liberality without extravagance in the care of county property to be a benefit in the long run, and firmly advocating the policy of the county paying its debts instead of paying interest on old claims. He is always foremost in any movement which contemplates the interests of his town, and more than once has contributed of his means for such a purpose.

On September 9, 1869, Mr. Jenkins was united in marriage with Harriet L. Rosekrans, daughter of Charles Rosekrans, of Jonesville, Saratoga County.

Mr. Jenkins is identified with the order of Masonry, being a thirty-second degree Mason; and he has many social ties in Schoharie County. He belongs to Schoharie Valley Lodge, No. 491; John L. Lewis Chapter of Cobleskill; Temple Commandery of Albany, a noted commandery in the State; to De Witt Clinton Council of Albany; and to Cypress Temple of the Mystic Shrine, of the same city. He is also a member of Wellington

Lodge, No. 731, I. O. O. F., of Central Bridge. He is an attendant and liberal supporter of the Lutheran church.

CHARLES FOWLER, proprietor of the Fowler House, Prattsville, was born in Lexington, Greene County, N.Y., September 15, 1845, son of David S. and Agnes (Muir) Fowler.

The Fowler family is of English origin. There were several immigrants of this name in New England in early Colonial times. It is said that William Fowler, who arrived in Boston in June, 1637, and the next year went to New Haven, was the ancestor of most, if not all, of the Fowlers, of Connecticut.

Silas Fowler, great-grandfather of Charles Fowler, was a native of Connecticut. After his marriage he came to New York State, and settling in Lexington, now Jewett, resided there until his death, which occurred at the age of eighty-four years. He was a Revolutionary soldier from this State, and a memento of his services in the shape of a flint-lock gun taken by him at the battle of Bunker Hill is now owned by his grandson, Addison Fowler, of Lexington, N.Y. He reared a family of eight children.

Silas Fowler, second, Charles Fowler's grandfather, was three years old when his parents moved to Lexington. He remained at the homestead until after his marriage, when he purchased a farm near by, and tilled the soil industriously for the rest of his life. His wife, whose maiden name was Hannah McLane, is a native of Livingston, N.Y., a daughter of George McLane. Her father followed the shoemaker's trade in connection with farming. She became the mother of nine children; namely, Charles, Rachel, David S., Louise, Elizabeth, Minerva, Silas, Addison, and Julia. Charles, Rachel, and Silas are no longer living. Elizabeth married Addison De Voe. Minerva married Henry Moore, of Milford, Michigan. Silas Fowler, second, died at the age of seventy-four years, and his wife lived to be ninety-six years old. They were both members of the Dutch Reformed church.

David S. Fowler, Charles Fowler's father, was born in Lexington, February 24, 1818. Beginning life for himself upon a leased farm, which he afterward purchased, he resided in his native town until 1875. He then removed to Prattsville, where he bought a farm and carried it on for two years, at the end of which time he retired and purchased a residence in the village where he is still living. Mr. Fowler, who is unusually active, both physically and mentally, for one of his years, remembers when deer roamed fearlessly over the town of Lexington. He has witnessed the growth of Prattsville from a struggling little settlement, and saw its founder, Colonel Pratt, set out many of the shade trees that now adorn its main thoroughfare. He was in his younger days interested in military affairs, serving as an officer in a local artillery company. He has a distinct recollection of the days when slavery was permitted in this section. Later he belonged to the famous

Know-Nothing party. He has voted the straight Democratic ticket for sixty years. David S. Fowler contracted the first of his two marriages in 1841 with Agnes Muir, a native of Scotland, who died in 1873; and for his second wife he married Laura Goodsell, whose ancestors came from Connecticut. He is the father of three children, all by his first union; namely, Mary, Charles, and Agnes. Mary married A. Beckwith, a prosperous farmer of Lexington. They have one daughter, Ada, who is the wife of George Raeder, and has one son, Charles. Agnes married Alonzo Johnson, of Lexington, and her children are: Charles, May, and Willie.

Charles Fowler acquired a common-school education in his native town. He was reared to agricultural pursuits, and assisted his father in carrying on the homestead farm until the latter's removal to Prattsville, when he took charge of the property which he managed for five years, or until it was sold. Coming to Prattsville in 1880, he in March of that year bought a half-interest in the Prattsville House, in the management of which he was associated until July, 1882, when he sold out. He immediately purchased his present property, which, after repairing and refurnishing, he opened as the Fowler House. Here he has ever since entertained the travelling public in a most hospitable manner. The Fowler House provides ample accommodations for fifty guests. It occupies a sightly location on the banks of Schoharie Creek, in a region noted for its beautiful and varied scenery. Its sanitary and other conveniences for the health and comfort of its patrons are unsurpassed, and a first-class livery stable connected with the house affords excellent facilities for driving over the surrounding country.

In 1871 Mr. Fowler was joined in marriage with Mary Coggshall, of this town. She was born in Rensselaerville, daughter of Asa and Mary (Joyce) Coggshall, the former of whom was a native of Gilderland and a schoolmaster by occupation. Asa and Mary Coggshall had a family of ten children, nine of whom are living; namely, Harvey, George, Origen, Sarah, Samuel, Asa, Mary, Julia, and Aletta. Sarah married E. P. Churchill, of Prattsville, and Aletta married Dwight Miller. Mr. and Mrs. Fowler have one daughter, Edith, who completed her education at the Stamford Seminary.

In politics Mr. Fowler is a Democrat. Though frequently solicited to become a candidate for public office, he invariably declines. Mrs. Fowler and her daughter are members of the Methodist Episcopal church.

MRS. JULIA A. WILSON, one of the best known temperance workers in Jefferson, Schoharie County, N.Y., was born in this town in January, 1828, daughter of John and Laura (Hamilton) Nichols. She is of New England ancestry on both sides. Her great-grandfather Nichols, whose name was Daniel, was a resident of Western Massachusetts. Her grandfather, Ezra Nichols, came to New York from Williamstown, Mass., settled as a pioneer at North

Harpersfield, Delaware County, N.Y., and through energy and perseverance became the owner of a good farm containing about two hundred acres. He resided in that town for the rest of his life. Ezra Nichols married Elizabeth Knapp, of Danbury, Conn., and his children were: Daniel, John, Clemon, Eli, Sarah, and Chloe. Daniel died in Harpersfield; Clemon died in Jefferson, at the age of ninety-four years; Eli died in Madison, Ohio; Sarah became Mrs. Knapp; and Chloe became Mrs. Dixon.

John Nichols, Mrs. Wilson's father, was born on April 18, 1787, and was five years old when his parents removed to Delaware County. During his early years he resided for a while in Dutchess County. He settled in Jefferson in 1818, having resided with his father for some time previous to coming here. When his farm was ready for permanent occupancy he went to Connecticut for his bride, with whom he began life in a new house and on a new farm. His industry and thrift enabled him to accumulate a large amount of property, and this he divided among his children, his real estate alone amounting to twelve hundred acres. John Nichols lived to be ninety-five years old. He was fond of reading, and was a good mathematician. He also possessed considerable musical ability, and taught a singing-school in his neighborhood for a number of years. Charitable and affectionate in his disposition, he was considerate of the feelings of others. His firm belief in the immortality of the soul was the result of long and patient study of the Bible. In politics he was a Republican. His wife, Laura, who was a native of Danbury, Conn., became the mother of seven children, namely: Susan, born in 1822; Franklin, born in 1824; Wesley, born in 1826; Julia A., the subject of this sketch, born in January, 1828; Clara E., born in 1832; Cynthia L., born in 1834; and George H., born in 1836. Susan, who died in 1845, was the wife of Joseph Hallenbeck, a farmer. Franklin, who settled as a farmer in Altona, Knox County, Ill., married Margaret Multer. Their children are: Walter, now residing at the old homestead in Altona, Ill.; George, a farmer of Summit, N.Y.; Nathan and Irving, who live in Illinois. Wesley died in 1834. Clara E., who is a graduate of Musicdale Seminary, Salem, Conn., and was for some time engaged as a teacher of music at Level Green Institute, near Suffolk, Va., and at Goldsboro College, N.C., was married in 1857 to the Rev. John Q. Evans, of Harpersfield, N.Y. Mrs. Evans has two children, Thomas D. and Florine, both of whom possess remarkable musical talent. Mr. Evans died in 1895 at Larned, Kan. Cynthia L. Nichols, who is unmarried, resides in Jefferson. George H. married Maria Titus, and has three children — John, Clara E., and Fred, all of whom are married.

Julia A., now Mrs. Wilson, was graduated from the New York Conference Seminary, Charlotteville, in 1852. She studied painting in Cobleskill, N.Y., and, having completed her preparations for educational work, she went to Suffolk, Va., where she taught painting at a young ladies' seminary, and was at one time its principal. She afterward taught French and mathematics at the Goldsboro (N.C.) College, remaining there until compelled by failing health to return North, when she relinquished her work with reluctance. She married Henry Wilson in 1855, and has resided in Jefferson continuously to the present time. She has had two children, neither of whom is living. Mrs. Wilson is one of the most active members of the Woman's Christian Temperance Union in Jefferson, having served as recording secretary and as corresponding secretary, also as a delegate to several State and county conventions. She is a charter member of the local lodge, Independent Order of Good Templars, in which she is a Past Vice-Templar, and is its treasurer at the present time. She belongs to the Patrons of Husbandry, and is Chaplain of the local grange. Mrs. Wilson is an active member of the Presbyterian church, and for years has devoted a great deal of her time to Sunday-school and other religious work.

WILLIAM LAUDER CAMPBELL, Chief of Police, Schenectady, N.Y., was born near Gatehouse, Kirkcudbrightshire, Scotland, February 2, 1844, son of William and Susan (Lauder) Campbell. The family for many preceding generations consisted of industrious farming people, and some of its representatives were overseers on large estates. The grandfather, also named William Campbell, was a native of Perthshire, and spent the greater part of his life as a farm overseer in Kirkcudbrightshire, in the south of Scotland. He married a Miss Campbell, who, though not a near relative, belonged to Clan Campbell, and in all probability was a descendant of the same stock. The grandparents reared four sons and four daughters. Two of the latter married well-to-do husbands, and were left widows with means. Coming to America with their children in 1855, they purchased fine farms in Prescott, Canada, opposite Ogdensburg, N.Y., and became affluent. One was the widow of William Black, and the other of David McKinnon.

In 1857 William Campbell, the father of William Lauder, sailed from Wigton with his wife and six of his children, for Liverpool, where he embarked for the United States on board the ship "William Tapscott," Captain William Bell. Arriving at New York, August 17, 1858, after an eight weeks' passage, they were met at Castle Garden by two other members of their family, James and Mary, who had preceded them a year before. The parents settled first at Bay Side, Long Island. They had ten children, two of whom died in Scotland; and Charles, aged nine, and Robert, aged one year and six months, died of scarlet fever while on the passage over, and were buried at sea. The living are: James, a farmer and landscape gardener, who married a Miss Palmer, and resides at Hartford, Conn.; Mary, who married John Dillen, a farmer, and resides at Choptauk, Caroline County, Md.; William L., the subject of this sketch; Susan, who married Robert Hemmens, an Englishman, and a moulder by trade, residing in Schenectady;

Jessie, wife of James Myers, a contractor and builder at Schenectady, N.Y.; and Margaret, who is the widow of James Macgregor, late Paymaster's Clerk in the United States navy, is now living in Baltimore, Md., and has one daughter. James Campbell, who is now residing at Hartford, Conn., was supervising agent and landscape gardener for the Morgans of New York for seventeen years, and was employed in the same capacity by the Garretts of Baltimore, Md., having charge of their entire estate, amounting to three thousand acres, with several assistant superintendents under him. The father died in 1894, aged nearly eighty-three years, surviving the mother, who died in 1890, aged seventy-seven.

William L. Campbell obtained his elementary education in Scotland, where (as well as in the United States, after his arrival here) he attended both the day and night schools. Having acquired a good knowledge of landscape gardening from his father, and receiving from the latter his full liberty some years previous to his majority, he entered the employ of Andrew Boardman, of Poughkeepsie, N.Y., where he remained seven years, supervising the laying out of that gentleman's gardens, roads, lawns, and pleasure-grounds, having previously attended school and worked with his father, at Flushing, Long Island. He followed landscape gardening until joining the Schenectady police force in 1869, and during his residence in Poughkeepsie he drove the first stake in laying out the grounds of Vassar College. From his boyhood he has taken a lively interest in out-door games, and he was known in his youth as a good all-around athlete. Coming to Schenectady in 1868 solely for the purpose of attending a supper given by the St. Andrew's Society, he was induced to locate here, and on August 3, 1869, was appointed a patrolman on the capitol police force in this city. That body was disbanded eleven months afterward, and going to Saratoga he was for the succeeding three months in charge of a force whose duty it was to patrol the streets and watch private property, he having been the first uniformed police officer to do duty in that village. Returning to this city after spending the summer months in Saratoga, he again in September, 1870, joined the regular Schenectady police force as a patrolman; was advanced on June 1, 1872, to the position of assistant to Charles H. Willard, whom he succeeded as chief on July 6 of the same year. He has held that office ever since, a period of twenty-seven years, having acted chief from July 6 to December 3, 1872, when he received regular appointment — longer than that of any other chief or superintendent of police in the State of New York, and, as far as known, in the United States.

On January 10, 1872, Mr. Campbell was joined in marriage with Harriet S. Orr, of Saratoga, N.Y. They have had two sons, one of them, Bertie, died at the age of one year. William Alexander Campbell, who was graduated from Union University in 1897, and after studying law at the law school of the same university, where he graduated June 26, 1899, and was admitted to the bar July 13, 1899, is, like his father and grandfather, unusually well-developed physically. He is proficient in athletic sports, and a champion bicycle rider and lawn tennis player.

Mr. Campbell belongs to the Masonic Order, the Elks, the Knights of Pythias, and the Foresters.

In his report as chief of police of the city of Schenectady for the year ending November 30, 1898 — an interesting and valuable document, betokening a clear head and an earnest purpose - Mr. Campbell recommends that the penal ordinances, so far as they relate to peace and good order, together with the sanitary rules and regulations of the city, be printed in pamphlet form the size of a pocket diary and placed in the hands of the newsdealers for sale; that police officers and city officials be provided with copies; and that pupils in the schools should be instructed as to their duties in observing ordinances. He would have even the smallest child thus led to see that a policeman is his servant and not his master. Following the adoption of this plan, he sagely thinks that "another generation would see the number of policemen in cities reduced to one-half the ratio per thousand inhabitant now employed, and in this way our citizens would become more nearly self-governing."

WILLIAM H. ALBRO, of Middleburg, Schoharie County, N.Y., is of English, Welsh, and Holland ancestry. On the paternal side he is a descendant of John Albro, who was born in Aldboro, England, in 1617, and who married in 1647 Doratha Potter, widow of Nathaniel Potter.

In 1634, at the age of seventeen years, John Albro embarked in the ship "Francis" from Ipswich, England, for Boston. In 1638 he went with William Freeborn to Portsmouth, R.I. In 1639 certain lands at Portsmouth, R.I., were granted to said John Albro and others, by the king of England, on condition that they build upon those lands within one year — which they did. And upon the lands thus acquired John Albro and his descendants lived for nearly two hundred years. In 1644 this John Albro was a Corporal in the Colonial militia, rising successively in after years to be Lieutenant, Captain, and Major. In 1649 he was chosen to view cattle, to be clerk of weights and measures, and member of Town Council. In 1660 and 1661 he was a commissioner, and member of a committee to receive contributions for agents in England. In 1666 he was appointed with two other persons to take areas of highways and driftways not set off. In 1670, with three other persons, he loaned the colony of Rhode Island seven pounds on account of the town of Portsmouth. From 1671 to 1686, with the exception of a few years in the seventies, he was an Assistant, a town officer. In 1676 he with three other persons was appointed a committee for the care and disposal of powder for the supply of Portsmouth. He was also a commissioner to order watch and ward of the island. This was during King Philip's War. He was also a member of the court-martial at Newport to try certain Ind-

WILLIAM HENRY ALBRO.

ians. In 1677 he was a member of a committee in the matter of injurious and illegal acts of Connecticut. In 1679 he was one of the members of a committee to draw up a letter to the king of England, giving an account of the territory of Mount Hope and of their late war with the Indians. He was also appointed with one other person a committee to lay out the western boundary line of the colony. In 1685 he, Major John Albro, Assistant and Coroner, summoned a jury in the case of an Indian found dead on clay-pit lands. The verdict of the jury was "That the said Indian being much distempered with drink, was bewildered, and by the extremity of the cold he lost his life." In 1686 he was a member of Sir Edmund Andros's Council, and was present at their first meeting at Boston, December 30, 1686. In 1697 he was allowed twenty shillings for his expenses for going to Boston. He died December 14, 1712. His will, dated December 28, 1710, was proved in 1713. By it he divided a considerable amount of real and personal property among his sons and daughters and their children. He was buried in his own orchard. His children were: Samuel, Elizabeth, Mary, John, and Susannah.

John Albro, second, who is in the direct line of descent to the subject of this sketch, married Mary Stokes, April 27, 1693. In 1677 he and others granted five thousand acres of land to be called East Greenwich, upon which land so granted stands the present town of East Greenwich, R.I. He died December 4, 1724. His son, John Albro, third, who was born August 23, 1694, married Ruth Lawton, November 25, 1725. He had a son John, fourth, sometimes called Jonathan, who was born January 2, 1734, and married Sarah Taber, October 21, 1759. This fourth John Albro was a private in Captain Benjamin West's company, Colonel John Topham's regiment of Rhode Island troops, during the Revolutionary War, from March 16, 1778, to February 20, 1779. John, fourth (or, as he was more commonly called, Jonathan) Albro, had a son Isaac, who was born at Portsmouth, R.I., September 3, 1765. Isaac Albro married Sarah Bliss, whose ancestors were English and Welsh. She was a daughter of William Bliss, whose father, Josiah Bliss, was the son of John and Damaris (Arnold) Bliss, the latter a daughter of Benedict Arnold, who was one of Rhode Island's earliest and best governors. John Bliss was an Ensign in the Continental Army in 1667, also a Deputy. In 1696 he was a Major for Rhode Island. Governor Arnold, his wife's father, built as a wind-mill for grinding grain, it is now said, the Old Stone Tower, which for a great many years has been one of Newport's greatest curiosities to visitors, and which for a long time was supposed to have been built by the Northmen, or Norsemen, who landed on the coast of New England before the discovery of America by Columbus.

About the year 1800 Isaac Albro and family moved from Portsmouth, R.I., where for nearly two centuries his ancestors had lived, to the town of Berne, Albany County, N.Y. About the year 1785 John Bliss, who was a brother of Sarah Bliss, wife of Isaac Albro, removed from Portsmouth to Greenfield, Saratoga County, N.Y., seven miles from Saratoga Springs. In the month of February, 1801, John Bliss walked all the way from his home in Greenfield, Saratoga County, N.Y., to Newport, R.I., to submit to the ordinance of baptism. John Bliss had twelve sons and four daughters. One of the sons, Isaac Bliss, was the father of P. P. Bliss, the author of the Gospel Hymns, and a singer and musical composer of world-wide reputation, who met a violent death December 29, 1876, by a railroad accident at Ashtabula, Ohio. Isaac Albro was a prosperous farmer. He died November 12, 1838, having survived his wife Sarah about thirty-three years.

Their son, Benjamin Albro, who was born December 25, 1802, married Mary E. Bassler, of Middleburg, Schoharie County, N.Y., January 17, 1838. She was born July 25, 1818, and died February 7, 1884. Her ancestors originally came from Holland, and previous to the Revolutionary War settled in the towns of Berne and Knox, Albany County, N.Y. In early life Benjamin Albro taught school in Albany and Schoharie Counties, and afterwards in Wayne and Cayuga Counties, New York. He was engaged in mercantile business for some years, was Town Superintendent of common schools of the town of Middleburg, and for the last forty-five years of his life he lived upon a farm near the village of Middleburg. He was an honored member of the Middleburg Methodist Episcopal church for seventy-three years, and was noted for his integrity and character. He died February 10, 1895, aged ninety-two years.

Benjamin Albro and Mary E. Albro, his wife, had a son, William Henry Albro, the subject of this sketch, who was born in the town of Middleburg, Schoharie County, N.Y., on September 8, 1840. He obtained his elementary education in the district and select schools of the town, was fitted for college at Charlotteville Seminary and Fort Edward Institute, and he attended and was graduated from Union College at Schenectady, N.Y. He taught several terms in the district schools of the town. Afterward he read law in the office of W. H. Engle, Esq., of Middleburg, during the years 1864 and 1865, and was admitted to practice as an attorney and counsellor-at-law of this State at a general term of the Supreme Court held at the capitol in the city of Albany, N.Y., on December 8, 1865. On January 1, 1866, he formed a partnership for the practice of law with the said W. H. Engle, which continued until February, 1874, when it was dissolved by mutual consent. He then opened an office in the village of Middleburg, where he has been engaged in the practice of law up to the present time.

On October 31, 1867, William Henry Albro married Elizabeth Dodge, daughter of the late Daniel D. Dodge, of Middleburg, N.Y., now deceased. Three children were the fruit of this union, namely: Willie D. Albro, who was born January 29, 1870, and who died of scarlet fever April 14, 1872; Arthur D. Albro, who was born October 29, 1871, and who died November 28, 1893; and Grace D. Albro, who was born May 5, 1874.

Mrs. Elizabeth Dodge Albro was born in the

town of Middleburg, Schoharie County, N.Y., on September 7, 1837, and died February 8, 1892. She was a most excellent wife and mother, and was held in high esteem by all who knew her. Her death caused as much genuine sorrow as that of any other person ever did in the community in which she was known and had lived. In every true sense of the term she was of the noblest and best type of women. Her husband, the subject of this sketch, and their daughter, Grace D., are all of the family who now survive her. The son, Arthur Dodge Albro, a bright and promising young man, who had just entered upon business life, survived his mother only about two years. Since the death of mother and son, the father and daughter live together in the old home and constitute the remnant of what was once a prosperous and happy family.

Upon Arthur's death his business came into the hands of his father; and since then, in addition to his general law practice, the subject of this sketch has been conducting a large and successful mercantile business. His store is one of the largest in the county, carrying a large stock of drugs, groceries, and miscellaneous goods. His law office contains one of the largest and best-selected law libraries in the county. He has been fairly successful as a lawyer, and also as a business man. He has held some official positions, among them that of School Commissioner of First Commissioner District of Schoharie County, during the years 1879, 1880, and 1881. He was elected to that office by a majority of two hundred and eighteen votes at a time when there was a natural political majority of about five hundred against him. He points with pride to the record which he made while holding that office. No paper sent by him to the office of the State Superintendent of Public Instruction was rejected or sent back to him for correction, and no request was ever made by him to the superintendent that was not cheerfully and promptly granted.

The subject of this sketch is a member of the Masonic fraternity; also of the Methodist Episcopal church, of which he has been a trustee for many years, and in which he has held other positions of trust. He was virtually the founder of the Union Free School and Academy at Middleburg, N.Y., and was the first president of the Board of Education of that institution. His daughter Grace was one of the first graduates of this institution.

The Albro family, of Aldboro, England, of which the original John Albro was a member, had a coat-of-arms, a record of which may be found in the public offices of London at the present day. From the facts aforesaid, it clearly appears that Mr. Albro is a lineal descendant in the seventh degree of John Albro, of Aldboro, England, born 1617; that he is also a lineal descendant in the sixth degree of Benedict Arnold, Governor of Rhode Island for three terms, beginning in 1663, and who built Newport's Old Stone Tower; and that he is related in the sixth degree to P. P. Bliss, author of Gospel Hymns and a celebrated musical composer. He takes pride in tracing his ancestry back through the centuries and to and through families in whose veins flowed some of the purest and best of English, Welsh, and Holland blood.

EDWIN D. HAGER, a general merchant of Blenheim, Schoharie County, is prominently identified with the leading interests of this section of the State. He was born May 31, 1847, in Middleburg, N.Y., a son of Daniel J. Hager, and the lineal descendant, we are told, of one of four brothers who came from Holland to America in the seventeenth century, and assisted the settlement of eastern New York.

His paternal grandfather, Jacob Hager, was for many years an extensive farmer in Fulton, whence he and his wife, Cathern Feeh, removed with their twelve children to Oeland, Orleans County, N.Y., where both died when well advanced in years. The grandfather was active in local affairs in both counties in which he resided, and in both he owned and cleared large tracts of land. Six of his children subsequently returned to Schoharie County, and for a time lived in Breakabeen. They were: Tunis, Jacob, John, Daniel J., Jane, and Margaret, none of whom are now living.

Tunis Hager married Rebecca Becker, and settled in Sharon Springs. Jacob married, and removed to Albany, and in 1849 he went with the gold-seekers to California. Returning from the Pacific Coast to Schoharie, he kept the public house known as the Wood House a few years, after which he conducted a hotel that occupied the site of the present capitol building in Albany, and then coming back to this county he farmed it in the town of Esperance until his decease. John went with his brother Jacob to California, came back with him to Schoharie, and after his marriage made a second trip to the Golden Gate. Returning East, he went into the livery business with Jesse Mills in New York City. In a short time he sold out to his partner, and opened a livery on his own account at 896 Broadway, and at the St. Nicholas Hotel, where he carried on a thriving business some years. Retiring then from the livery, he bought a beautiful farm in Rhinebeck, whither he removed with his wife and three sons, and there lived until his death, at the age of threescore and ten years.

Daniel J. Hager was born in Fulton, September 5, 1811. He learned the shoemaker's trade in his native place, and after his marriage, at the age of twenty-one, he continued to work at it first at Middleburg, then at Breakabeen, and finally in Blenheim, where he passed his last years, dying September 18, 1871. He was a loyal Republican in politics, and as a soldier in the Union army he participated in several of the battles of the Civil War. He married Eliza C. Zelie, who was a native of Fulton, being the eldest of a family of nine children — Eliza C., Lias, Christina, David, Jane, Ephraim, Harriet, Andrew, and Margaret — born to Peter Zelie, whose wife was before marriage a Miss Vroman. (Further ancestral history may be found on another page of this work, in connection with the sketch of Luther Zelie.) Mrs. Eliza C. Zelie Hager was born November 10, 1816, and died

October 10, 1874. She had five children, namely: Mary C., wife of George Becker, the representative of an old family of Schoharie County; William S., a farmer in Blenheim; Peter Z., a farmer in Oswego County; Edwin D.; and Harriet A., wife of Peter Burgett, of Schoharie County. Both parents were members of the Methodist Episcopal church of Middleburg, in which the father held various offices.

Edwin D. Hager attended the district schools in his youthful days, and until he was sixteen years old he remained at home with his parents. He subsequently worked out by the day, sometimes as a farm laborer, for two years, after which he was employed by his brother-in-law as a clerk in Breakabeen for three years. The ensuing year he was engaged in the mercantile business for himself in Blenheim. He then sold out, and for two years was employed as a clerk or a teacher. In 1868 he went to Catskill, where he remained a year, when he returned to Blenheim, and for a year was here a clerk in a general store. Going then to Middleburg, Mr. Hager was with J. Nevill three years, and then, in partnership with the late Silas Sweet, he bought out the store of John Hager, in Blenheim, and carried on a successful business until the death of Mr. Sweet, three years later. The following spring he sold out the business, and the next year purchased a half-interest with Seneca West, and later formed a copartnership with Ira Haverly, to whom, at the end of four years, he sold out. Two years later Mr. Hager purchased the building which he is now occupying, and put in a new and complete stock of merchandise. He has now one of the largest stores in this section of the county, and carries the finest stock of goods in his line. Being one of the oldest merchants in this locality, and with two exceptions the oldest in the county, he is well known, and it is safe to say no man has a better reputation, or is more highly esteemed in business and social circles.

Mr. Hager is a strong silver man in politics, and takes a prominent part in local affairs. For eighteen consecutive years he was a member of the county committee, and was a regular attendant at all conventions. In 1882 he served as a delegate to the State convention held in Syracuse, and in 1883 as a delegate to the Congressional convention. He has served as Supervisor of the town four terms, in 1878, 1879, 1882, and 1883; and in 1884 he was appointed Postmaster by President Cleveland, a position to which he was again appointed in 1892. He is one of the trustees of the school district, and a stockholder in the Blenheim Creamery Company, of which he has been president since its incorporation. Fraternally, he united with the Middleburg Lodge, F. & A. M., in 1870, and is also a member of the Middleburg Lodge, I. O. O. F.

On November 16, 1876, Mr. Hager married Nellie E. Beckwith, of Springfield, Mass., daughter of Calvin and Lucy B. Balton Beckwith. Mr. and Mrs. Hager are the parents of three children, namely: Clyde L., who died at the age of twenty-two months; Eugene B., born August 28, 1877; and Florence A., born July 20, 1882. Eugene B. Hager, who was educated in the graded schools, was formerly employed as clerk in Brooklyn and New York City, but is now in business with his father. He married, December 15, 1897, Margie Dibble, who was born March 8, 1878, in Middleburg, a daughter of —— ·—— and Elizabeth (Dexter) Dibble. Mr. Hager and all his family attend the Methodist Episcopal church.

AMBROSE R. HUNTING, a prominent citizen of Schoharie, N.Y., residing on the Hunting homestead, was born in this town on September 14, 1833, son of Joseph and Mary A. (Chesebro) Hunting.

The first of his family in this country was John Hunting, who came from England in August, 1638, and settled in Dedham, Mass. He was one of the founders of that town, and an Elder in the church there for many years. He had a son named John, of whom little is known, and a grandson, Nathaniel, who was graduated at Harvard College, and subsequently preached to the church in East Hampton, N.Y., for fifty-seven years.

The fourth in line, Nathaniel Hunting, second, was educated for the ministry, but poor health compelled him to give up his beloved profession, and devote himself to agriculture. His son, Joseph Hunting, was a sea captain. After this Joseph came two others of the same name. The first of these, who was the grandfather of Ambrose R. Hunting, was the first Hunting to come to Schoharie. He came hither from Long Island in 1791, accompanied by his mother, and settled on the farm which has since been in the possession of his descendants. He was a shoemaker by trade, but was engaged more or less in farming and in mercantile affairs.

The third Joseph Hunting, father of Ambrose R., was born in Schoharie in 1805, and resided in the town throughout his life. He was known as a man who attended strictly to his own affairs and caused no annoyance to other persons by interference. He never brought suit against any one, was never sued, and never called upon to serve as a witness. In politics he was a Democrat. He was a leading member of the Methodist church, and for more than forty years a class leader. His wife, Mary, was born in Knox, Albany County, the daughter of Peleg Chesebro, a cooper and farmer. Her grandfather, Christopher Chesebro, who was a carpenter by trade, fought in the Revolution. He lived originally in Stonington, Conn., but removed thence to Knox in 1791.

Ambrose R. Hunting was reared on the paternal homestead, and attended the public schools until he was seventeen years of age. He then was sent to Schoharie Academy for two terms, and afterward to the New York Conference Seminary at Charlotteville. After studying there for two years, he was prepared to enter the Junior class at Union College, Schenectady; but, his family being opposed to the profession he had chosen, he yielded to their wishes and withdrew from school. After

HIRAM RIFENBARK

teaching for several terms he returned to the farm and began devoting himself to agriculture.

Mr. Hunting has been a loyal member of the Methodist church for fifty years, and has held every position in the church to which a layman is entitled, except that of lay delegate to the general conference. In politics he is a Democrat. He has held the office of Supervisor for four years, that of School Commissioner for two terms, and for a year he was a member of the Assembly. Fraternally, he is connected with Schoharie Valley Lodge, No. 491, F. & A. M.; and John L. Lewis Chapter, No. 229, R. A. M.

Mr. Hunting was first married on April 14, 1859, to Amanda Severson. Two sons were born of this union: William J., who died in 1875; and Edwin F., who is a graduate of the Albany College of Pharmacy, and is now a successful druggist in that city. On June 5, 1869, Mr. Hunting was married to Mary M. Northrop, who was born in Berne, Albany County, the daughter of Asa T. and Ann E. Northrop. By this second marriage there is one child, Florence A. She has received a musical education at Claverack Institute.

HIRAM RIFENBARK, a representative citizen of the town of Summit, residing in the village of Charlotteville, was born in Summit on April 30, 1839, his parents being Aaron and Mary (Banks) Rifenbark.

The family is of German origin, and Mr. Rifenbark's great-grandfather spelled his name Rifenbarck. The grandfather, Henry Rifenbark, came from Columbia County in 1802 or near that date, and settled about two miles east of Summit village. There he owned a whiskey still, a store, and an inn or tavern. He was a man of influence and of considerable property, and his tavern was often the gathering place of important assemblies. Town meetings were sometimes held there. His brother Peter was a clergyman of the Dutch Reformed church. Henry Rifenbark's wife was a daughter of Caleb Clark, who was captured by the British and Indians during the Revolution, and carried to Canada. There Mr. Clark was kept at Fort Niagara under guard, but was sent out every day with other captives under a guard of Indians to chop wood in the forest. The Indians, believing that it was impossible for them to escape, often left them alone during the day, returning for them at night. Mr. Clark and his fellow-prisoners, however, with sturdy pioneer determination, resolved to make an effort to regain their freedom. Accordingly, one morning after their captors had left them, they started on snow-shoes for the Mohawk River, carrying the food that had been measured out to them for their mid-day meal. For many days this was all the food they had. At length, at the end of a week, he and his companions came to a deserted and tumble-down hut in the Mohawk Valley, where they found some mice. These they were forced to eat to keep themselves from starving. They finally reached home in safety, but Mr. Clark always felt exceedingly bitter toward the British. Henry Rifenbark and his wife had seven children, three sons — Harry C., Aaron, and Ebenezer — and four daughters — Julia Ann, Hattie, Harriet, and Caroline. All of the boys became farmers.

Aaron Rifenbark, who was born in Summit in 1804, and died in 1883, was a leading citizen here and a prominent man in the Democratic party. He was twice married, the first time to Mary Banks and the second time to her sister Catharine. The first wife died in 1848 and the second in 1895. The six children — William H., John, who is deceased, Hiram, Ebenezer, Permelia, and Hettie — were the fruit of the first marriage. The first-named of these, who resides in Hobart, Ind., is a leading Republican there, and in 1897 and 1899 was a member of the Indiana legislature. He is prominent in business circles and as a Grand Army man. In the year 1898 he was engaged in building county roads. In 1893 he exhibited at the World's Fair steel neck yokes and whiffletrees manufactured by the company of which he was president. Ebenezer Rifenbark resides at Summit. He fought for the Union in the Civil War, and was wounded at Gettysburg. Permelia is the wife of Winthrop D. Gallup. Hettie married P. P. Gordon, M.D., of Hobart, Ind., and died in 1892.

Hiram Rifenbark received his education in the public schools of Summit and at Charlotteville Seminary. At the age of seventeen he engaged to work on a farm seven months for sixty-five dollars. Mr. H. Masters, his employer, who was away from home much of the time, told him one day to sow a piece of land to buckwheat, putting in two bushels of seed. This was new work to Rifenbark. He began sowing broadcast, and soon found that he had put half the seed on a quarter of the land. He then sowed the remainder of the seed more sparingly, making it cover the other three-fourths of the land. He watched the growth with interest, but before harvest time the cows got into the field and ate up the grain, thick and thin. He lost not a day in that seven months. In the winter he attended school, and the next seven months he worked for a farmer in Fulton, his only holiday being the Fourth of July, which he insisted on keeping. The next winter he taught school four months at ten dollars a month. April 1 of his nineteenth year found him engaged to a farmer in Summit seven months at eleven dollars a month. This summer there was not a day of lost time, the man for whom he worked giving him the Fourth of July. The following winter he again taught in the same district where he taught the first term, but with an increase of two dollars a month in his wages. He continued to teach school winters after this until he was married and settled on the farm, teaching one term in the winter, while on the farm, at two dollars a day. When twenty years old he worked seven months at Richmondville, driving team for the iron foundry at twelve dollars a month. The next spring he began working at carpentry, continuing for three summers under a boss, and after that time he took jobs for himself till he purchased his father's farm of ninety-six acres in 1868. Four years later he sold the farm, and bought the property, including the store now belonging to Levi J. Lincoln in Charlotteville, N.Y. After conducting a general merchandise business there for ten years, he sold the property, and, buying a vacant lot, built the residence he now occupies and the store across the street, where he conducted business for twelve years. He then sold the goods to Kingsley & Griffin, to whom he rented the store. Since that time he has been selling agricultural implements and fertilizers, and looking after business for himself and others. Mr. Rifenbark is a strong Democrat. He has shown a warm interest in political matters ever since he became a voter. He has been on the Town Committee a number of times, on the School Board several terms, in 1865 Town Clerk, and much of the time since 1870 Notary Public. He has also served two terms as a Justice of the Peace, and has done a large amount of business settling estates and drawing contracts. He has served as executor of a number of the wills filed in this town, as he is known to have an excellent knowledge of technical law points. From 1888 to 1890, inclusive, he was Supervisor of Summit. His record as Supervisor is marked primarily by a strong effort to secure an honest and economical expenditure of the public funds. Fearless and daring in his personal expression and effort when he believed himself laboring in a worthy cause, he met with some opposition, but in the main won a loyal recognition from his constituents. He broke up abuses in the county relating to the housing and feeding of vagrants, secured action by the governing board that caused the removal of all luxuries from the county prison, and worked hard for a reduction of expenses in every way. He served on the Committee on Sheriffs' Accounts, on public and other buildings, and on the Committee on Legislation.

Mr. Rifenbark married Amelia Burnett, daughter of Colonel George O. Burnett, who was prominent in the militia. Mrs. Rifenbark attended Charlotteville Seminary, and subsequently taught school for ten terms before her marriage. She is active in church work, and when the Good Templars and the Woman's Christian Temperance Union were in existence here was one of their earnest supporters. Mr. Rifenbark was also connected with the Good Templars, being Chief Templar. He has been clerk of the Baptist church at Summit, a member of the ministerial committee, trustee, and for years superintendent of the Sunday-school. He is the teacher of the Bible class. He is strictly temperate in all things. His early life taught him the value of money, and he then acquired the habits of industry and economy which are still characteristic of him. He is a liberal contributor to every good cause, but never upholds extravagance or waste.

MICHAEL LACKEY, Jr., real estate and insurance broker, a well-known business man of Greene County, is a resident of Tannersville, where he was born on November 24, 1860, son of Michael and Catherine (Burke) Lackey. His parents are still living, and make their home with him.

His paternal grandfather, Thomas Lackey, who was born in Ireland, went to England in 1821, and resided there until 1829, when he emigrated to America, and, settling in New York City, followed the trade of a cabinet-maker. In 1835 Thomas Lackey retired from active business pursuits and came to Tannersville, where he resided with his son, the elder Michael, until his death, which occurred in 1853.

Michael Lackey, Sr., father of the subject of this sketch, was born in Ireland, May 18, 1815. He came to America with his parents when fourteen years old, and was educated in the night schools of New York City. He learned the trade of a house painter, which he followed there for a time and then removed to Tannersville, where he continued in the same occupation. He also kept a country tavern in the old stage times when Tannersville was a hamlet called Greenland. He is a Democrat in politics, and has held offices. His wife, whose maiden name was Catherine Burke, is a native of Ireland. They have had four children, two of whom are now living; namely, Michael, Jr., and his sister, Lizzie P. The latter is the wife of Michael B. Dolan.

Michael Lackey, Jr., acquired his education in the common schools of Tannersville. At the age of fifteen he went to New York City, and entered Ehrich's dry-goods store on Eighth Avenue, where he kept the country order books for one year. He then engaged in the ice cream and confectionery business at the corner of Eighth Avenue and Fifty-ninth Street. Returning to Tannersville later, he taught school until 1883, at the same time studying law and becoming a practitioner. In 1875 he purchased a farm of one hundred acres in Hunter known as Onteora Glen, which he conducted with his other business until 1892. From May 10, 1891, to October 20 of that year, he was proprietor of a laundry, having an exclusive contract for Onteora Park, including thirty cottages and a large inn; and he was ably assisted in this work by his wife. He moved from his farm in 1892, renting it until 1896 when he exchanged that property for the half-way house on the road to Hunter, and removed to the village of Tannersville. Soon after his return he erected a dwelling-house, office, and store, the latter of which is well stocked with stationery, school supplies, sporting goods, and other merchandise, and is carried on by his wife. He does quite a business in the buying of Christmas-trees for the New York market, shipping from six to ten carloads annually. In 1893 he engaged in the real estate business. He erected a large building which he rents. He makes collections for many concerns through the county, and was appointed assignee for Willsey & Fromer, one of the largest firms in this vicinity. As local representative of several large insurance companies, he has secured some of the principal risks in the town. He has a great deal of law practice in the minor courts.

In 1883 Mr. Lackey was united in marriage with Julia Weller, daughter of Thomas Weller, formerly an inn-keeper in Birmingham, England. They have five children— Robert E., Charles H., Edward W., Mary L., and Clara E.

Politically, Mr. Lackey is a Democrat. In 1889 he was appointed Deputy Sheriff, holding that office three years; and he was a candidate for Supervisor in 1891. He was appointed Postmaster in 1893, and held that position until 1898, giving general satisfaction. He has been Counsel for the village corporation ever since its organization, has acted as notary public for the past fourteen years, and is frequently called upon to address political meetings. He is a member of the Knights of Pythias, and Past Chancellor of the local lodge.

STEPHEN LOUDON, a retired farmer of Fulton, Schoharie County, was born in the town of Blenheim, N.Y., February 16, 1821, son of John and Sarah (Tinkelpaugh) Loudon.

John Loudon was born in Delaware, where he grew to man's estate on the parental homestead. Choosing farming as his life occupation, he moved to Schoharie County, which was then in its primitive wildness. He took up a tract of land in Blenheim, at a time when there were very few clearings in that locality or in the county, and there partly improved a farm. Disposing, however, of his newly acquired land in Blenheim, he bought land in the neighboring town of Gilboa, and was there engaged in his independent calling until his death, at the venerable age of eighty-three years. His wife, whose maiden name was Sarah Tinkelpaugh, died at the age of fifty-nine years, having borne him ten children. Four of the nine are still living, namely: Mary, wife of John Mattice; Stephen; Libby, wife of Jacob I. Coons; and Nancy. Both parents were members of the Baptist church.

Stephen Loudon, by persevering industry and wise economy, accumulated considerable property, and while yet a young man purchased a farm in Breakabeen, which he afterward sold, and bought a large farm on Bouck's Island, adjoining the Governor Bouck homestead. Upon that farm he resided until 1894, when he bought his present home property, which is managed by his son-in-law, C. E. Markham, in connection with his own farm. Mr. Loudon has always been deeply interested in the welfare and advancement of the town of his adoption. In politics he is a firm supporter of the principles of the Democratic party.

On August 31, 1846, Mr. Loudon married Lavinia Whaley, who is a native of Dutchess County, New York, and is the only living child born to the late Daniel and Sarah (Carpenter) Whaley.

Mr. and Mrs. Loudon have three daughters, namely: Caroline, wife of Prof. C. E. Markham, teacher and farmer of Fulton; Emma, wife of George Coykendall; and Mary, wife of Peter E. Schoonmaker, both of whom are successful business men in Kingston, N.Y. These daughters are all graduates of the State Normal School, and were all of them teachers in their younger days. Mr. Loudon is a member of the Baptist church, and Mrs. Loudon belongs to the Reformed church.

JACOB FROMER, one of the most successful business men in Tannersville, N.Y., was born in Wittenberg, Germany, October 14, 1849, son of Daniel and Mary (Liepold) Fromer. His father, who also was a native of Wittenberg, emigrated to the United States in 1853. After his arrival in this country Daniel Fromer followed the trade of a chair-maker for a time, and then turned his attention to farming, first in Jewett and later in Tannersville, where he died at seventy-two. His wife, Mary, who was a native of Germany, was the mother of six children, namely: Mary; Rosa; John, first (deceased); Daniel, Jr.; Jacob; and John. Mary married Leonard L. Woodard. Rosa became the wife of Clarence Willsey. John keeps a boarding-house. Daniel, Jr., is proprietor of a hotel. Mrs. Mary L. Fromer died at the age of seventy-one. The parents were members of the Presbyterian church.

Jacob Fromer acquired his education in the schools of Jewett, and worked on the home farm until he was nineteen years old, when he went to the oil regions of Pennsylvania, going thence to West Virginia, and later entering mercantile business in Parkersburg, Va. Disposing of his establishment there at the end of eighteen months, he came to Hunter, where he engaged in the express business and also ran a stage to the Catskill. He abandoned this enterprise at the expiration of a year and a half, and again entered mercantile business, carrying on a general store under the Cascade House for the same length of time. He next erected a building sixty by sixty feet, and three stories high, adjoining his present office, and, putting in a stock of general merchandise, carried on business until 1892, when he sold out. He started in a small way, but as his trade increased he was forced to enlarge both his stock and floor space in order to meet the demands of his patrons. He transacted a business amounting to over one hundred and twenty-five thousand dollars annually, and employed twelve assistants. In 1893 he made a trip to Florida, and upon his return in 1894 opened a sale and livery stable here and another at Elka Park, Hunter, both of which he has since conducted successfully, also doing quite an extensive business in the selling of carriages, sleighs, robes, and harnesses. He keeps twenty horses, and at times has as many as thirty for livery purposes. In connection with this he is engaged in the real estate and insurance business, and besides his stable and office he has erected several dwelling-houses.

In 1875 Mr. Fromer was united in marriage with Susan Showers, a native of Hunter, daughter of Michael Showers, a farmer of that town. Her parents had a family of six children, four daughters and two sons. Mrs. Fromer's sisters are all married.

Mr. Fromer is a Republican in politics. He was Supervisor continuously from 1893 to 1899, having with a few exceptions served longer than any other member of the board; and during his term of office he succeeded in reducing the taxes. He was largely instrumental in securing the incorporation of the village, and was trustee a number of years. He and Mrs. Fromer are attendants of the Methodist Episcopal church, and contribute to the support of other denominations.

SOLOMON KELLEY was born February 14, 1823, on the farm in Princetown, N.Y., on which he now resides, he being the owner thereof and devoting his energies to its improvement and cultivation. His parents were Solomon and Grace (Wingate) Kelley. His father was born in Rotterdam, N.Y., and his mother in Princetown. His paternal grandfather was William Kelley, a Scotchman, whose occupation was that of a miller and a farmer. He was an early settler in Rotterdam, but afterward resided in Princetown and in Duanesburg, and died in Mariaville.

Solomon Kelley, the elder, learned the carpenter's trade, which he followed for several years. Settling upon new land in Princetown when a young man, he cleared the farm which is now owned by his son, and erected the buildings. An industrious farmer and a citizen of worth, he gained the good will of his neighbors by his many sterling qualities. In politics he voted with the Whig party, and in his religious belief he was a Presbyterian. He was the father of ten children, five of whom are living, namely: Solomon, the subject of this sketch; Robert; John; Samuel; and Grace. The others were: William, Andrew, Sally, Jane, and Mary A.

Solomon Kelley was reared at the homestead and educated in the district schools. He has always resided at his birthplace, and succeeding to its ownership he has made general farming a profitable employment up to the present time. He is still smart and active, with the ability to perform a day's work which would tire many younger men, his early vigor giving no sign of decay. In politics he is a Republican. He attends the Presbyterian church.

When twenty-seven years old Mr. Kelley married for his first wife Evelyn Love. His present wife was before marriage Nancy Gregg. By his first marriage he has one son, William, who is living at home.

JAMES H. FLANAGAN, a prosperous farmer of Tannersville, N.Y., and a veteran of the Civil War, was born in New York City, February 14, 1842, son of Matthew and Margaret (Olwell) Flanagan. He is a descendant of the O'Flanagans of Ireland. His great-grandfather Flanagan was named Thomas, and his grandfather was Patrick O'Flanagan.

Matthew Flanagan, son of Patrick, emigrated to America when a young man, first settling in New York City. After his marriage he came to this locality, where he worked in a tannery for some time, and then purchased a farm. Politically, he was a

Democrat. He died at the age of sixty-eight. His wife, Margaret, was a native of Ireland. She was a daughter of John Olwell, a farmer, who emigrated to the United States, and spent his last years on a farm in the vicinity of Tannersville. Matthew and Margaret Flanagan were the parents of ten children, seven of whom grew to maturity, and five are now living; namely, James H., Patrick, Alice, Kate, and Rose. Patrick lives in Newark, N.J. Alice married John Hoolahan, and resides in Brooklyn. Rose married Patrick Gillooly, and is also residing in Brooklyn. The mother died at the age of fifty-six years.

James H. Flanagan came to Tannersville with his parents when very young, and attended the common schools. At the age of twenty, in 1862, he enlisted in Company G, Fourteenth United States Infantry. In the second battle of Bull Run he was severely wounded in the leg, and he lay upon the field for ten days unattended. He was then taken to Washington, and after being in various hospitals was discharged in 1863. Upon recovering from the effects of his wound he re-enlisted in the Cavalry, Independent Corps, and was stationed on the frontier, where he served three years. He was mustered out as a Corporal. Returning to Tannersville, he worked on his father's farm for two years, at the end of which time he went to Wisconsin, and from there to St. Clair County, Illinois, where he remained one and a half years. He then returned East, and, again settling in Tannersville, has followed farming with good results ever since. His property originally consisted of one hundred and fifty acres, but he disposed of one hundred acres to good advantage. In politics he is a Republican, and served as Excise Commissioner some time.

In 1876 Mr. Flanagan married Miss Mary E. Smith, of Brooklyn, daughter of Patrick Smith, a member of the police force of that city. They have four children — Eileen, Fairie, Una Eideen Desmond, and Oscar. Eileen and Fairie are now preparing themselves for educational work.

Mr. Flanagan is a comrade of A. N. Baldwin Post, G. A. R. He is an earnest advocate of temperance, and has rendered valuable service to the community in that direction. The family attend the Roman Catholic church. Mr. Flanagan from childhood has shown a marked liking for literature, and he has a fine library containing books by some of the very best authors. He is also very fond of music, and has a choice collection of instrumental and classical musical works.

JOHN BRADT, a retired farmer of Rotterdam, was born in this town, October 6, 1839, son of Aaron I. and Eliza C. (Vedder) Bradt. The parents were natives of Schenectady; and the father was a prosperous farmer of Rotterdam, where he spent the greater part of his life. He died at the age of fifty-eight years, and his wife lived to be ninety-one. They were the parents of five children, two of whom are living, namely: John, the subject of this sketch; and Aaron

JOHN BRADY

B., who resides in Schenectady. The others were: Francis, Hester, and Helen.

John Bradt acquired his education in the common schools of his native town. After the completion of his studies he assisted his father in carrying on the home farm, thereby obtaining a good knowledge of agriculture; and in early manhood he and his brothers, Aaron B. and Francis, purchased their sister's interest in the old homestead farm, which contained about one hundred and sixty acres, located along the banks of the Mohawk River. This they carried on successfully together till Aaron sold his interest. After that the farm was managed by John and Francis until 1889. In that year Mr. John Bradt retired, and built a handsome residence in the village, which he has since occupied, the industry displayed during his long period of activity having placed him in easy circumstances. It is interesting here to note that the ancestral farm has been handed down from his grandfather to the fourth generation, being now owned by Mr. Bradt's nephew, Aaron J. Bradt, son of Francis above named.

On December 28, 1871, Mr. Bradt was united in marriage with Eleanor Dorn, who was born in Princetown, August 3, 1847, daughter of Alexander and Harriet Dorn. Her father, who was a stirring farmer of Duanesburg, died at the age of sixty-one years. He was an active member of the Dutch Reformed church and for more than forty years an Elder. Mrs. Dorn is still living, and resides in Duanesburg.

In politics Mr. Bradt is a Republican, but takes no part in public affairs beyond casting his vote. He has been a Deacon of the Reformed church for the past eight years, and Mrs. Bradt is a member of the church.

BENJAMIN I. TALLMADGE, the well-known attorney and counsellor-at-law of Windham, N.Y., is a native of New Baltimore, Greene County, and was born on November 1, 1869, his parents being Thomas D. and Helen (Raymond) Tallmadge. Thomas D. Tallmadge's paternal grandfather, who was a leading farmer of Greene County, died before Benjamin I. was born.

Thomas D. Tallmadge spent his life on a farm until he was a middle-aged man, when he opened a general merchandise store. After carrying that on for several years, he removed with his family to Albany, his son Benjamin being then about fourteen years old. Later Thomas D. Tallmadge removed to Oneonta, where he for a time conducted an ice business and afterward a market. He retired from business in Oneonta, and subsequently resided there until his death, in June, 1893, at the age of sixty-three. He was stanchly a Democrat, but never took an active interest in local politics. His wife, Helen, was the daughter of John G. and Elizabeth Hinman Raymond, of Coxsackie. Mr. Raymond, who had resided in New Baltimore previous to coming to Coxsackie, was a large real estate owner. He died at Coxsackie in his seventy-ninth year. Of his seven children one son, Wallace W., who is a merchant, resides at Coxsackie. Both he and his wife were Presbyterians. Thomas D. and Helen Tallmadge were the parents of eleven children, all of whom are living. They are as follows: Raymond, who is book-keeper and general manager for Van Slyke & Horton, of Albany; Alice A.; Josiah C., an attorney at Catskill; Elizabeth; Edward C., who is in the employ of the John G. Myers firm in Albany; Matilda, who is the wife of the Rev. Samuel W. Eaton, pastor of the Methodist Episcopal church at Patter, Pa.; Thomas D., an artist residing in New York City; Caroline; Benjamin I.; Mae; and R. DeWitt, who was a member of the First New York Volunteers in the late war. The mother of these children is still living in Oneonta, and her four daughters reside with her. She and her two youngest daughters are members of the Baptist church, while Alice and Elizabeth are connected with the Methodist church. The family is remarkable for its musical ability, and all four of the daughters have sung in church choirs. Edward C. Tallmadge also, who is a member of the First Reformed Church, has sung in the choir. He is likewise a member of the Consistory.

Benjamin I. Tallmadge resided with his parents until he was about sixteen years of age. After attending the public schools of New Baltimore, he began a special course in Windham preparatory to studying law, which enabled him to secure what is known as a law student's certificate from the Board of Regents in Albany. He entered the office of his brother, the Hon. J. C. Tallmadge, who was then practising in Windham, and there he remained until his admission to the bar in 1893. Immediately upon his admission to the bar he formed a partnership with his brother, under the firm name of J. C. & B. I. Tallmadge, and this continued until February, 1897, since which time he has been in business alone.

The Hon. Josiah C. Tallmadge, who is now a leading attorney in Catskill, began his practice in Windham in 1875, having previously studied here with his uncle, Eugene Raymond, who started in practice here over forty years ago. From 1890 to 1893 the Hon. J. C. Tallmadge was District Attorney of Greene County, and during that time was engaged in some notable criminal trials. He was one of the attorneys in the Loring Robertson case, which is one of the most celebrated, not only in the county, but in the State. His success in winning this for his client won for him great praise. Tallmadge brothers were for several years the only attorneys in Windham.

Mr. Tallmadge was married in 1894 to Rose B. Graham, who was born in this town, the daughter of Lucius S. and Phœbe (Bump) Graham, the father a well-known shoe dealer. Both Mr. and Mrs. Graham are deceased, the former at the age of sixty-nine and the latter at the age of fifty-five. They were active members of the Episcopal church. Their four children are: Mrs. Tallmadge, who is the eldest; Ella, who married L. H. Townsend; Margaret R.; and Edwin. Mr. and Mrs. Tallmadge have one child, a daughter Dorothy, aged two years.

Mr. Tallmadge is, as was his father, a

Democrat, but he does not engage actively in politics. He is a Mason and member of Mountain Lodge, No. 529. Both he and his wife are members of the Presbyterian church, and he is treasurer of the Board of Trustees, leader of the choir, and an active worker in the Sunday-school. Mrs. Tallmadge is the church organist. Mr. Tallmadge was one of the organizers of the Windham Water Company, and he is now secretary and treasurer of the organization and one of its directors.

ALBERT CHASE, a well-known farmer of Hensonville, was born in Lexington, January 4, 1819, son of Benjamin and Lydia (Skiff) Chase. The family is of English descent. Thomas and Aquila Chase, brothers, emigrated from England, and were living at Hampton, N.H., as early as 1640. A few years later Aquila removed to Newbury, Mass. "A large majority of the Chases of the United States," some one has said, "are his descendants." Thomas Chase married Elizabeth Philbrick, and had five sons. The fourth son, Isaac, removed to Edgartown, Martha's Vineyard, Mass. He was twice married, and had a number of children.

Benjamin Chase, the father above mentioned, was a son of Zephaniah Chase, and both were natives of Martha's Vineyard. Zephaniah Chase, the grandfather of the subject of this sketch, came to Lexington as a pioneer. He cleared a large tract of land, and spent the rest of his life there, dying at the age of eighty.

Benjamin Chase resided on the home farm for some years. Later he purchased a farm near by, where he spent the rest of his life. His death also occurred at eighty years. When a young man he was an officer of the militia. His wife, Lydia, who, like himself, was a native of Martha's Vineyard, became the mother of ten children, nine of whom grew to maturity, and two are now living, namely: Albert, of Hensonville; and Ira, who resides in Jewett. The others were: Benjamin, who lived in Lexington, and died aged ninety-three; Elizabeth, who resided on the old homestead, and died at eighty years of age; Lydia, who married Orin Burgess, of Hunter, and died at the age of sixty; William, who died in Ohio at eighty; Lucinda, who married Mathias Chittenden, and resided in Callicoon, Sullivan County, where her death occurred when she was sixty years old; Mary, who became the wife of Samuel Cook, of Sidney, Delaware County, and died at the age of sixty; and Sarah, who became Mrs. Peleg Chamberlain, resided in Michigan, and died at the same age. The mother died in 1827, at the age of fifty.

Albert Chase in his early childhood attended the common schools of Lexington. He resided at home until the death of his mother, when, a lad of eight years, he went to live with an uncle in Jewett, about two miles below Hunter village. At the age of twenty he returned to Lexington and learned the carpenter's trade, which he followed for about twenty-five years, becoming one of the largest contractors in this section of the county. He erected many private residences, business blocks, mills, bridges, and other structures, employing a number of men. He came to Hensonville in 1845, when this village was in its infancy, and did an extensive business here, erecting many of the present buildings. Purchasing a saw-mill in 1863, he carried on a large lumber business for some years. He removed to his present farm, consisting of three hundred acres, in 1858, erected his dwelling-house and other buildings, and, relinquishing his contracting business a few years later, gave his principal attention to farming. Since 1880 his son, De Mont, has had charge of the cultivation of the home acres. Mr. Chase and his son have purchased two additional farms, one being devoted to dairy purposes, and they keep twenty-seven cows, mostly Jerseys.

In 1844 Mr. Chase was united in marriage with Miss Laura O. Woodworth, of Windham, daughter of Abner and Betsey (Judson) Woodworth. Her father, who was a native of Cherry Valley, and followed farming during his active period, spent his last days in East Jewett, dying at the age of eighty-two years. Her mother, who was born in Windham, died at the age of forty-eight. Mr. and Mrs. Woodworth reared a family of six children. Of these the three living are: Laura, who is now Mrs. Chase; Lucius, who resides in Hunter; and Lucinda, who is the wife of Dr. Mead. Mr. and Mrs. Chase have had five children — Sophronia, Lydia, Abner, Emery, and De Mont L. Chase. Sophronia died of diphtheria at the age of seventeen. Lydia, who is no longer living, married Cyrus Bloodgood, clerk of Catskill County. Abner died at the age of two years. Emery, formerly a member of the law firm of Hallock, Jennings & Chase, later Jennings & Chase, was elected Judge of the Supreme Court in 1896. He married Mary Churchill, daughter of the proprietor of St. Charles Hotel, of New York, and has two children — Jessie C. and Albert W. Chase. De Mont L. Chase is now associated with his father in carrying on the farm. He has served as Supervisor and Tax Collector. He married Josephine Osborn, daughter of Elbert Osborn, of Brooklyn, and has two children — Leona L. and Elbert O. Chase.

Mr. Chase is a Republican in politics. He has been Overseer of the Poor, and has acted as Justice of the Peace for four years. He is connected with the Order of Good Templars, also with the Sons of Temperance, and has filled some of the important chairs in these societies. He is a member of the Methodist Episcopal church, of which he has been trustee, steward, and class leader for many years. He has also been district steward, was a member of the building committee which erected the new church, and served as trustee of the parsonage. He was formerly superintendent of the Sunday-school, and Mrs. Chase was a teacher.

WILLIAM S. VANDERBILT, a representative citizen of the village of Greenville, was born in New York City on February 10, 1845, his parents being William S. and Susan A. (Wright) Vanderbilt. He belongs to a family that has for many years been prominent in Rockland County. His

WILLIAM S. VANDERBILT.

great-grandfather settled in Clarkstown, in that county, when a young man, and resided there on a farm during the remainder of his life. His grandfather, Isaac Vanderbilt, was born in Clarkstown, and spent his life there engaged in agricultural pursuits.

William S. Vanderbilt, Sr., son of Isaac and father of the subject of this sketch, was also born on the homestead, but at the age of fifteen he left the parental roof and learned the merchant tailor's trade. At twenty-one he began business for himself in New York City, and subsequently for twenty-seven years conducted it most successfully. His store was at 416 and later at 408 Broadway, and his was one of the best-known tailoring establishments in the city. He died on February 13, 1864, being only forty-eight years of age. His wife, Susan, who died in 1893, at the age of sixty-nine, was born in Greenwich village, now a part of New York City, and spent the whole of her life in the great metropolis. She was the daughter of Charles S. Wright, who was for many years one of the most influential members of the School Board of Trustees of the Ninth Ward in the city of New York, and for a long time its chairman. At one time Mr. Wright was waited upon by a committee to see if he would accept the nomination to the legislature. Mr. Wright declined the honor. He lived, about 1824, in the house in Greenwich village which his father had built. It was then out in the country, and the canal wound its sluggish way through what is now Canal Street.

William S., Sr., and Susan Vanderbilt, had eight children, of whom four are now living; namely, William S., Oliver DeGray, John, and Mrs. George W. Vanderhoef. Mrs. Vanderbilt, after the death of her first husband, married Andrew Hoogland, a prominent and well-to-do citizen of New York, and one of the best-known members of the New York Produce Exchange. Mr. Hoogland was born on May 20, 1815, and died in 1879. He was a director in the Corn Exchange Bank, and of the New Amsterdam Insurance Company, and for many years a member of St. Andrew's Curling Club, its president in 1873 and 1874, and at one time president of the National Curling Club. He also represented the St. Andrew's of New York City at the national convention at Toronto in 1873. To the last-named club he gave a fine flag. He held membership in the Dutch church, and was one of its active and liberal supporters. At one time he was a member of the Seventh Regiment of militia, and later a member of the Victorian Association.

William S. Vanderbilt, the subject of this sketch, lived in New York City until 1871, when he took up his residence in Greenville. He boarded in different families for a number of years, but in 1888 began buying land, and the following year built his present handsome residence. He owns a number of fine farms, including what are known as the Lewis Sherrill and Prevost farms. Mr. Vanderbilt is one of Greenville's most public-spirited citizens, and has shown this in many ways. He built in the village a beautiful opera house, and gave a great stimulus to the introduction of water in the town by placing it in all of his buildings.

Mr. Vanderbilt married in 1876 Miss Mary J. Hickok, of this town, a descendant of one of the old and leading families. She died at the age of thirty-three, leaving one daughter, Lizzie H. Vanderbilt. On November 14, 1888, Mr. Vanderbilt married Mary Reed, daughter of John K. and Ann (Sherrill) Chapman. Her father was born at Salisbury, Conn. While yet a mere lad his father, Robert L., moved to the vicinity of Greenville, where he died in 1857, eighty-two years old. Mrs. Vanderbilt's father was an early gold hunter on the Pacific Coast, going to California by the way of the Isthmus of Panama in 1849. After acquiring considerable money for those days, he returned to Greenville, was married, and shortly after went to Janesville, Wis., where with a brother, he engaged in the dry-goods business. Here his daughter Mary was born. He returned to Greenville in 1865, residing there until his death in 1888, at the age of seventy years. His wife, Mrs. Vanderbilt's mother, was the daughter of Lewis Sherrill, a descendant of one of the pioneer families of the town. Her grandfather, Jonathan Sherrill, had extensive tanneries. One of them was located on the corner where Coonleys Hotel now stands. Jonathan Sherrill built and occupied the house that is now the residence of Dr. B. S. McCabe. His home at the time of his death was the house on North Street owned by Charles R. Knowles, of Albany (a grandson), and used as a summer residence. He died in 1851, in his eighty-second year.

Lewis Sherrill, for many years president of the old Greenville Academy, was a broad-gauge public-spirited man. He was a successful farmer and stock-raiser, a life-member of the New York State Agricultural Society, and the first president of the Greene County Agricultural Society. The stone walks about the village, among other things, are largely the result of his energy and push. He died in March, 1889, at the age of eighty-eight. His wife, Esther Ford, died in 1872, at the age of sixty years. Mr. and Mrs. Vanderbilt have two children living, the elder being William Stephen, and the younger George Vanderhoef Vanderbilt.

In politics Mr. Vanderbilt is a Republican, and some years ago he was very active in all political matters. He is a member of James M. Austin Lodge, F. & A. M., of which he has been treasurer for a number of years, and he holds membership in the Royal Arch Chapter, of Greenville. He is also a charter member of the Knights of Pythias organization here. He is warden and treasurer of the Episcopal church, and treasurer of Greenville Fire District.

PAGE T. HOAGLAND, editor and proprietor of the *Record*, Oak Hill, was born in Malugin's Grove, near Dixon, Lee County, Ill., March 23, 1856, son of Abram Allen and Eunice E. (Bloodgood) Hoagland. He is of the eighth generation in descent from Christophal Hoagland, who was born in Holland in 1634, emigrated to America about the year 1654, and settled in New Amsterdam.

From Christophal the ancestral line is traced through his eldest son, Christopher,[2] who was born in the vicinity of Brooklyn, N.Y.; John,[3] who was born in Flatlands, N.J., in 1701, and died in 1767; Jacob Hoageland,[4] born in Harbinger, N.J., in 1735; Abraham Hoogland,[5] who was born in Sowerland, New Harbinger, Somerset County, N.J., about the year 1773; Benoni Hoogland,[6] who was born in Gilboa, N.Y., February 25, 1796; and Abram Allen Hoagland,[7] who was born in Gilboa in 1831; to Page T. Hoagland,[8] the subject of this sketch.

Jacob Hoageland resided in New Jersey until after the settlement of his father's estate, when he came to New York, and, after sojourning for a time in Schoharie County, went from there to Albany County, where he passed the rest of his life. Abraham Hoogland, of the fifth generation, accompanied his parents to Gilboa in 1785. He married Polly M. Fraser, daughter of Benoni Fraser, who was one of the earliest settlers in Schoharie County and a Revolutionary soldier. On September 11, 1817, Benoni Hoogland, the grandfather, married Katy Shoemaker, who was born August 29, 1791, daughter of Jacob Shoemaker. Grandfather Hoogland died May 25, 1867, and the grandmother died May 27, 1868. They were the parents of nine children, two sons and seven daughters, and five of their family are now living.

About the year 1854 Abram Allen Hoagland, Mr. Page T. Hoagland's father, removed from New York to Illinois, where he followed his occupation of carpenter and joiner for a short time. Then going from there to Eau Claire, Wis., he purchased a farm of one hundred and sixty acres adjoining the town site. Two years later he returned to New York, and from 1859 to 1866 resided in Ashland and Jewett, Greene County. After the close of the Civil War he again went to Illinois. He located in Rockford, and resuming his trade remained there until shortly after the death of his father, in 1868, when he came to Gilboa to care for his mother, who died suddenly within the following year. The next two years he spent upon a farm in Johnson Hollow, town of Roxbury, N.Y., and in 1870 removed to Oneonta, this State, where he was employed in the car-shops of the Albany & Susquehanna Railroad Company. He next settled in Binghamton on a leased farm, which he carried on until 1876; and the year after he cultivated the G. H. Bloodgood farm in Conesville. He then came to Oak Hill, followed his trade here for two years; and in 1879 he returned to Conesville, occupying the Hawver farm for about one year. Removing to Superior, Neb., in 1880, he resided there some years. He is now living upon a large farm in Oak Hill. His first wife, Eunice E., whom he married in 1854, was a daughter of Abraham Bloodgood. Her father, who was a tanner, spent most of his life in Jewett, and her mother was a representative of the Tower family of New England. It is said that some of her ancestors came over in the "Mayflower." Abram Allen Hoagland's first wife died in 1894, at fifty-nine years of age. The maiden name of his second wife was Eugenia Brand Lynam. He is the father of two children, both by his first wife: Page T., the subject of this sketch; and Edith G., who married William J. Winn, of Bridgeport, Conn.

Page T. Hoagland came from Wisconsin to Greene County with his parents when about three years old. His educational opportunities were confined to the schools of the various localities in which he lived up to 1870, when he became a pupil in the Oneonta graded school, under the supervision of Professor N. N. Bull. He was graduated in 1872, and immediately entered the store of L. Goldsmith as a clerk. Afterward he worked for Joseph and Morris Price in the same capacity, and later for Miller & Pope, dealers in flour and provisions. He taught school in Sullivan County during the ensuing winter, and then, joining his father on the farm at Binghamton, he remained there the following season. In the fall of 1879, having previously taught schools in Conesville and Rensselaerville, he entered the store of Hagadorn Brothers, Gilboa. A year later he went to Superior, Neb., and, after being employed as a clerk during the fall and winter of 1880 and 1881, he in the spring became a cow-boy, and remained on the ranch until July of that year, when he went to Plattsmouth, Neb., twenty miles below Omaha. Failing to find employment in the city stores, he worked in a brick-yard until, through the influence of a friend, he obtained a subordinate position upon the clerical force of the Burlington & Missouri River Railroad. In 1883 he was appointed assistant station agent on the Chicago, Burlington & Quincy Railroad at Pacific Junction, Ia., resigning in January, 1884, in order to take the position of manager of the loss and damage department of the Burlington & Missouri Railroad at their headquarters in Omaha. He continued to serve in that capacity until the ensuing fall, when he was forced by ill health to return to Gilboa.

In March, 1885, he purchased of H. V. Jones the Jefferson (N.Y.) *Courier*, which he conducted for over three years, selling in August, 1888, to George M. Proper, of Eminence, N.Y. He next purchased the *Monitor*, a paper published in Gilboa, which he carried on until 1893, when he disposed of it to Berton G. Griffin, and coming to Oak Hill in the spring of 1894 established the *Record*, which he has conducted successfully ever since. He has a well-equipped plant with ample facilities for handling the constantly increasing circulation of his paper, and his advertising department is both popular and profitable.

In June, 1882, Mr. Hoagland was united in marriage with Frances Stryker, daughter of Abraham Stryker, of Gilboa. She died in 1894, at the age of thirty-seven, having been the mother of seven children. Of these, five are living — Scott R., Hazel C., Guy W., Cecil A., and Ellen F. On September 4, 1895, he married for his second wife Ella Cherritree, daughter of Walter S. Cherritree, a native of Durham and prominently identified with the foundry interests of Oak Hill.

In politics Mr. Hoagland is a Republican, and during his residence in Jefferson he served as Town Clerk and as School Trustee. He served in the same capacity in Gilboa, where he was candidate for Supervisor in 1893, and was again his party's candidate for Town Clerk in 1898. He has been a member of the Republican County Committee since 1896. He was made a Mason at Jefferson in Working Lodge, No. 554, F. & A. M., of which he was Junior Warden for two years. In 1889 he was demitted to Gilboa Lodge, No. 630, of which he served as secretary four years. He is now a member of Cascade Lodge, No. 427, Oak Hill. In 1892 he joined Blenheim Lodge, No. 651, I. O. O. F., from which he withdrew to become a charter member of Lyman Tremaine Lodge, No. 265, Oak Hill, of which he was treasurer for the years 1896 and 1897, and was chosen Vice-Grand in 1898. He was made Noble Grand January 1, 1899, serving until July 1 of the same year. During this year he was recommended to the Grand Lodge as secretary to the Grand Committee, District of Greene. He is also a member of Middleburg Encampment, No. 129, and Valley Chapter, No. 38, Order of the Eastern Star. At the age of fourteen he was confirmed by Bishop Doane, of Albany, and has served as vestryman of the Episcopal church. Educational and literary matters have absorbed his leisure time, and he has a well-selected library of standard works.

ELDA B. CHAPMAN, wife of J. P. Chapman, of East Cobleskill, Schoharie County, N.Y., and a prominent worker in the Woman's Christian Temperance Union, was born at Bramanville, in the town of Cobleskill, on April 9, 1852, her parents being Nelson and Catherine M. (Braman) Bice. Her family is of Dutch origin, a representative of it coming from Holland in 1657, and settling in New York when it was called New Amsterdam. The name was originally spelled Buys, as it still is in Holland.

Mrs. Chapman's paternal grandfather, Joshua Bice, who was a farmer and later a merchant, settled on land in East Cobleskill. He was a man of strong Christian character, and for sixty-two years was an earnest and devoted member of the Methodist church. He was the first member of the church here. At the age of seventy-four years he handed in the class-book that he had used in the many years when he had held the position of class leader, saying he was too old to attend to it any longer.

Mrs. Chapman's father, Nelson Bice, was born at East Cobleskill, where his daughter now resides. He lived in this county nearly all his life, and for the nine years preceding his death he lived on this place. He was a farmer by occupation. For six years, while residing in Middleburg, he served as Assessor of the town, being nominated to the office by acclamation. In politics he was a Democrat. At the age of twenty-three he joined the Methodist Episcopal church, and from that time until his death, in 1880, he was one of its faithful members. For many years he held the office of superintendent of the Sunday-school, for eight years that of class leader, and for many years he was one of the church trustees. He served his townspeople as school trustee for a number of years. His wife,

Catherine, was born in Bramanville, daughter of John W. Braman. Her grandfather, William Braman, was an Englishman; and his wife, whose maiden name was De Lamater, was half French and part Dutch, being a descendant of the Rev. Everardus Bogardus and his wife, Anneke Jans. John W. Braman built a woollen-mill in Bramanville. The place was named in his honor, and he was one of its most highly valued citizens. He was a strong advocate of temperance. When at the advanced age of seventy he taught the village school in Bramanville. For twelve years he was a Justice of the Peace. He married Elizabeth Wetsell, daughter of Christopher Wetsell, a German who owned about a thousand acres of land and a number of slaves. When the State gave them freedom, some of Mr. Wetsell's negroes remained with him, and some of them accompanied Elizabeth Wetsell when she married and left home.

Mrs. Chapman's father was an owner in the woollen-mill built by her grandfather Braman, but when she was three years of age he removed to East Worcester. There the family lived for the next five years, at the end of which time they went to East Cobleskill. Six years later they removed to Fultonham, and after staying in that place four years they returned to East Cobleskill, where Mrs. Chapman has since made her home. She attended the district schools until she was sixteen years old, and was then sent to Schoharie Academy, where she remained for some time, studying academic branches and music. She subsequently studied music with Miss Rankin, of Middleburg. Her marriage occurred on October 25, 1871, and since that time she has shown her ability not only in the administration of her domestic duties, but in various responsible public positions. In connection with her efforts in behalf of the cause of temperance she has been county superintendent of the Sunday-school work of the Woman's Christian Temperance Union. For twenty-one years she was a teacher in the Sunday-school of the Methodist church, of which she is a member.

Mr. Chapman was born in Fulton, his parents being Jacob and Huldah (Winans) Chapman. His mother was the daughter of the Rev. Mr. Winans, a Baptist minister. Mr. Chapman is an enterprising farmer and a man who commands universal esteem. He has been twice elected Supervisor of the town of Middleburg.

Mrs. Chapman takes an active interest in the advancement of agriculture, and has written several valuable essays, which were read before the State Agricultural Society and before the State Dairymen's Association. She has also read papers before the county Sunday-school conventions, and has been one of the judges of award at two silver medal contests. Mrs. Chapman is the mother of three daughters — Lena May, Mildred H., and Agnes E. The first named is a graduate of the Cobleskill High School and of Syracuse University. Mildred H. is a graduate of the Cobleskill High School, and is now preparing to take a course of study in Syracuse University. Agnes E. is ten years of age.

J. AUGUSTUS SNYDER, superintendent of the Foltz summer home at Cobleskill, N.Y., near Warnersville, was born in this town, October 6, 1844, son of William and Rebecca (Bouck) Snyder. He is of thrifty German ancestry, and a lineal descendant of one of the original settlers of this section of Schoharie County.

William Snyder, first, his great-great-grandfather, emigrated from Germany in Colonial times, and located on Helderberg Mountain, near Albany, N.Y., but prior to the Revolution he came to Cobleskill, where he took up a tract of wild land and began the improvement of a homestead. In the ensuing struggle for independence William Snyder took an active part, serving as a soldier in the army until the close of the war. The Lutheran church, which was built by him, contained a tablet bearing his name.

Peter W. Snyder, the grandfather of J. Augustus, was born on the old Snyder homestead, which later passed into his possession. He was an industrious, energetic worker, and added materially to the improvements on the estate, erecting the present comfortable set of buildings. He married Catherine Warner, a daughter of Nicholas Warner, who also was one of the earliest settlers of this part of Schoharie County, and formerly the owner of almost the whole of the present site of the village of Warnersville. A man of good understanding, interested in the cause of education, Peter W. Snyder had the distinction of being the first English school-teacher in this valley. For many years he served as Justice of the Peace; in 1826 and 1827 he was a member of the Assembly; and was also one of the first railway commissioners in this locality. He died at a ripe old age in 1850. Peter W. Snyder and his wife were members of the Lutheran church. Of their union seven children were born. Mrs. Catherine W. Snyder survived her husband a score or more of years, attaining the venerable age of ninety-three.

Their son, William Snyder, second, was born and reared on the old home farm, and eventually succeeded to its ownership. He carried it on successfully for many years, but later sold it, and, buying a farm near by, there spent his remaining days, dying at the age of seventy-six years. In addition to general farming he was extensively engaged in milling, and built the plant now known as Snyder's mills, a large mill having four runs of stone, which is now operated by one of his sons. He manufactured large quantities of flour and made a specialty of custom grinding, for years carrying on a lucrative business. He was an uncompromising Democrat, influential in local affairs, and held many public offices, being Supervisor five years, Excise Commissioner eighteen years, and Justice of the Peace a number of terms. He attended the Lutheran church, and gave generously toward its support. He was three times married. His first wife, whose maiden name was Diana Bouck, died at an early age, leaving two children — George W. and Margaret. George W. attended Franklin and Schoharie Academies and Union College, after which he entered West Point, where he was graduated at the head of his class in the engineer's department. In 1858 he was appointed Second Lieutenant, and he was afterward stationed at different points along the coast, including Boston, Pensacola, Key West, Charleston (S. C.), and Fort Moultrie. In 1861 he was ordered to Fort Sumter, and while there was twice promoted, first to the rank of First Lieutenant and then Captain. He was subsequently paroled for a time, and on returning to Washington was appointed as Aide-de-camp to General Heintzelman, and was with him at the battle of Bull Run. Taken sick with typhoid fever just after the battle, he died November 17, 1861. He had been brevetted Lieutenant Colonel. As a soldier he was brave and courageous, faithful in the performance of every duty. The father's second wife, Lavina Bouck, lived but a few years. He subsequently married for his third wife Rebecca Bouck, who was born in Cobleskill, a daughter of David Bouck, and a lineal descendant of Governor Bouck. She bore him seven children, of whom three are now living; namely, J. Augustus, David B., and William. The mother died at the age of fifty-eight years.

J. Augustus Snyder lived with his parents until sixteen years old, when he began life for himself. While working with his father he had learned the miller's trade, and he subsequently operated for five years a grist-mill that his father bought in Hyndsville. He then went West, and at Saginaw, Mich., he engaged in railroad construction and lumbering six years. Returning home in 1875, he entered the mill now owned by his brother, David B., and this he operated a few years. After that he carried on a farm seven years, selling out at the end of this period and removing to Richmondville, where he was engaged as a retail grocer and marketman for five years. During the next six years Mr. Snyder kept a hotel, and shortly after selling that property he assumed his present responsible position as superintendent of the Foltz place. Under his efficient management marked improvements have been made on the estate. The grounds have been finely laid out and beautified, and the new house has been built, the homestead being now one of the most attractive in the vicinity.

On June 26, 1882, Mr. Snyder married Miss Mary O. Baker, who was born in Worcester, Otsego County, N.Y., one of the six children of Sherman S. Baker, a well-known cattle dealer of that town. Politically, Mr. Snyder is a straightforward Republican, interested in public matters, and while in Michigan served as Justice of the Peace. Fraternally, he is a thirty-second degree Mason, prominent in the order, and a member of Cobleskill Lodge, F. & A. M.; the John L. Lewis Chapter, Cobleskill; St. George's Commandery, K. T., of Schenectady; and Temple Consistory, No. 2, of Albany. He also belongs to Cobleskill Lodge, No. 500, I. O. O. F. In religious matters he is broad and liberal.

HON. EMORY ALBERT CHASE, of Catskill, Justice of the Supreme Court for the Third Judicial District of New York, was born on August 31,

1854, at Hensonville, Greene County, N.Y., where his parents, Albert and Laura (Woodworth) Chase, are still living. On the paternal side he is of English descent, and on the maternal of Scotch.

The ancestral home of the Chase family was at Chesham, England. Thomas Chase, a prominent resident of Chesham, had a son Richard, who married Joan Bishop at Chesham, April 16, 1564. This couple had a son Thomas, born at Chesham, who emigrated to America about the year 1639, and settled at Hampton, N.H. He married Elizabeth, a daughter of Thomas Philbrick, and remained in Hampton until his death in 1652. He had a son Isaac, born April 1, 1647, who is commonly referred to as Lieutenant Isaac. This son married for his second wife Mary Tilton, and lived at Vineyard Haven, Martha's Vineyard. He died there, May 19, 1727, and is buried on the hill overlooking the head of Vineyard Haven.

Isaac Chase and his wife had a son Joseph, born February 26, 1689, who married Lydia Coffin. Their first child, Abel, was born October 9, 1719. He married February 14, 1744, on Martha's Vineyard Island, Mercy Mayhew. They had a son Zephaniah, born March 14, 1748. He married for his first wife Abigail Skiff. Zephaniah Chase was a member of Captain Smith's seaport company during the Revolutionary War. After the close of the war and in the year 1787 he sold his property in Vineyard Haven and migrated to the present town of Lexington, Greene County, N.Y., then County of Albany. His son Benjamin, born January 21, 1774, married Lydia Skiff, and had a son Albert, born January 4, 1819.

Albert Chase and Laura O. Woodworth were married on September 1, 1844. They have two sons, namely: Demont L., of Hensonville, N.Y.; and Emory A., of Catskill, the special subject of this biography. Albert Chase was engaged for many years in contracting, building, and lumbering. Since retiring he has lived on a farm.

Most of the early life of Judge Chase was spent on his father's farm. He attended the public school at Hensonville, and continued his studies at the Fort Edward Collegiate Institute, but did not graduate. He was fitted for the legal profession in the office of King & Hallock (Rufus H. King and Joseph Hallock) at Catskill. In April, 1880, he became interested in the firm of Hallock & Jennings; and in 1882 he became one of its members, the firm name being changed to Hallock, Jennings & Chase. After Mr. Hallock's retirement, September 22, 1890, the business was continued under the style of Jennings & Chase until December, 1896, when it was dissolved in consequence of Mr. Chase's election as Justice of the Supreme Court for the Third Judicial District. In a district usually Democratic he was elected on the Republican ticket by a majority of about thirteen thousand. Since the 1st of January, 1897, he has devoted himself to the duties of that office.

The jurisdiction of a Supreme Court Judge extends throughout the State, but the judges are elected by districts. The Third District is composed of seven counties — Rensselaer,

Albany, Schoharie, Columbia, Greene, Ulster, and Sullivan. Judge Chase has always been a Republican in politics, and up to the time of his election as a Supreme Court Judge he attended as a delegate nearly every town, county, district, and State convention of the Republican party. During his career at the bar he was constantly connected with important litigations in the Third Judicial District and other parts of the State. He has been admitted to practice in the United States District and Circuit Courts and in the United States Supreme Court.

Judge Chase has long been prominent in the local affairs of Catskill. He was a member of the Board of Education for fourteen years previous to December, 1896, and for five years was its president. He served for a long period as corporation counsel of the village of Catskill, retiring from that office in 1895, and was Supervisor of the town of Catskill in 1890. He has also been conspicuously identified with several of the most representative local interests. He is now first vice-president of the Catskill Savings Bank, a director in the Tanners' National Bank and in many other local enterprises. He is a member of the Presbyterian church.

Emory A. Chase married Mary E. Churchill on the thirtieth day of June, 1885. They have two children — Jessie Churchill Chase and Albert Woodworth Chase — and have a pleasant home at 25 Prospect Avenue.

Although Judge Chase is one of the youngest men elected to the Supreme Court in this State, he has met with a very favorable reception, as shown by the following resolutions and newspaper comments.

At a meeting of the Schoharie County bar, held at the Surrogate's office in the village of Schoharie, the twenty-fifth day of January, 1897, the following resolutions were unanimously adopted: —

"*Resolved*, that the bar of Schoharie County have watched with pleasure and approbation the holding of Judge Emory A. Chase's first trial term following his recent election, and they congratulate themselves that Schoharie County has had the privilege and honor, as well, of seeing him start out in their midst of what we trust and expect will be a long and distinguished judicial career.

"*Resolved*, that, while hitherto he has been a stranger to many of us, yet we desire to testify to his patience and kindness; to his fairness, skill, and judicial ability, as manifested in conducting the trial of causes; to the ease and facility with which he has put off the lawyer and assumed the dignity of the judge; to his evident desire to be right and impartial in his rulings; and we congratulate the bar and the people of this State, and assure them that they have made no mistake in elevating to the bench Judge Emory A. Chase. We extend to him the pledge of our loyalty and friendship, and express the desire that he shall long continue to wear the judicial ermine."

From the Albany *Daily Press Knickerbocker:* —

"Judge Chase has won a very enviable reputation during his sitting for ability and in expediting the administration of justice."

From the Albany *Times Union:* —

"It was the first term of Justice Chase in this city, and he has made a favorable impression on the members of the bar in this county, not only as an honorable gentleman, but a fair and impartial lawyer, possessing extensive legal knowledge."

From the Albany *Morning Express:* —

"Justice Chase convened the March trial term of the Supreme Court on the first day of March. He came to Albany for the first time as a presiding justice, and was unknown to many members of the bar. He adjourned the term yesterday, and left the city, having won a reputation for judicial ability, fairness, and courtesy that is well deserved.

"Justice Chase has been a model presiding justice. He was confronted with a calendar of three hundred and forty-four cases, and during the three weeks of the term he disposed of sixty-six cases. Of this number twenty-six were settled, twenty-eight tried, eleven referred, and a change of venue was made in one. This is a somewhat remarkable record; and, if other justices were as anxious to expedite business as is Justice Chase, many cases would not drag along in the courts for an extended period of time."

From the Albany *Evening Journal:* —

"The Judge has proved himself to be one of the most popular men who ever have sat upon the bench in the court room in the City Hall."

From the Albany *Evening Journal:* —

"During the term just concluded Justice Chase has shown himself to be a model presiding officer. His first circuit has demonstrated him to be practically all that a judge should be."

From the Troy *Times:*

"The Hon. Emory A. Chase, of Catskill, Justice of the Supreme Court, has just finished his first trial term in Schoharie County. The term was highly successful, and Justice Chase was congratulated by the bar on the impartiality of the rulings and the fairness of his charges. Justice Chase has a fine command of language and a thorough knowledge of the rules of evidence. The opening of his judicial career fulfils the prophecy of his nomination."

From the Hudson *Republican:* —

"The Hon. Emory A. Chase, of Catskill, Justice of the Supreme Court, Third Judicial Department, has accepted the invitation of the Appellate Division of the Supreme Court in the First Department to hold a special term in New York City beginning May 17 and continuing until June 5. Justice Chase was chosen to the bench at the last election of a Supreme Court Justice in this judicial district, and he has already so thoroughly proved his efficiency as to warrant the high compliment which is contained in this invitation from the judiciary of New York City. Justice Chase has just finished holding a term of court at Hudson, where, as usual, his impartiality and judicial ability were praised by everybody. He is remarkably well fitted for the office which he fills, and it has not taken the courts, the bar, and the people long to find it out."

From the Troy *Times:* —

"The term of the Supreme Court just closing in this city has given the lawyers and the people an opportunity to become acquainted with the judicial qualities of the presiding justice, the Hon. Emory A. Chase, of Catskill. Acquaintance has meant admiration. In sitting as judge at civil and criminal trials of unusual magnitude Justice Chase has shown promptness, fairness, and mastery of the law and its principles that have assured to him the place of a favorite in the esteem of the people hereabout. His future visits to this city in either a judicial or a social capacity will be cordially welcomed."

The Albany *Express*, speaking of the October trial term of the Supreme Court, presided over by Judge Chase, says, "The term has been one of the longest and most satisfactory ever held in this county."

PETER I. STANLEY, M.D., an able physician and a highly esteemed citizen of Windham, Greene County, N.Y., was born in Harpersfield, Delaware County, this State, on August 11, 1825, son of Nathan and Pamelia (Hogaboom) Stanley. His grandfather, Richard Stanley, came to New York State from New Jersey during the Revolutionary War, being among the farming population of that colony who were so harassed by the Hessian troops brought over to re-enforce the British army that they abandoned their homes.

Richard Stanley, settling in the wilderness, cleared a farm in what is now the town of Gilboa, Schoharie County, where he resided for a number of years. His last days were spent in Harpersfield. He was the father of three children. Information at hand does not locate for a certainty the birthplace of his son Nathan, the Doctor's father, but he was probably reared in Schoharie County. He served as a soldier in the War of 1812.

Nathan Stanley accompanied his father to Harpersfield, and, succeeding to the ownership of the homestead, he resided there for the rest of his life. His wife, Pamelia Hogaboom, was a native of Prattsville, Greene County. She became the mother of fourteen children, only three of whom are living, namely: John L., who is residing in Kansas; Peter I., the subject of this sketch; and Jane, who married William Sampson. The parents both lived to be seventy-eight years old. They were originally Presbyterians, but in their later years attended the Methodist Episcopal church.

Peter I. Stanley acquired his early education in the district schools and at the Stamford Academy. He remained upon the home farm until he was twenty-one, when he went to work in a woollen factory, and continued in that employment one year. Deciding to enter professional life, he began the study of medicine at the age of twenty-two with Dr. Covel, of Stamford, and completed his preparations at the Albany Medical College, from which he was graduated in 1853. Locating in Ashland, he resided there for sixteen years; and, as he was the only physician in the town, he was kept constantly busy in attending to a large and lucrative practice, which extended over a wide circuit. At the earnest solicitation of the people of Windham he in 1869 removed

PETER I. STANLEY.

to this town, where he has ever since found an ample field in which to demonstrate his ability and usefulness; and it may be truthfully said that the entire community has profited by his fidelity, promptitude, and skill. He has reported many interesting cases to the County Medical Society, of which he has been a member ever since its organization, some forty years ago; and he has several times been called upon to serve as its president. As his physical powers remain unimpaired, he still continues to take long rides; and the inhabitants of all this locality consider themselves fortunate in being able to reap the benefits arising from his long experience as a practitioner.

In 1853 Dr. Stanley was united in marriage with Sarah Bassett, a native of Harpersfield and a daughter of Joshua Bassett, a prosperous farmer of that town. Dr. and Mrs. Stanley have had ten children, five of whom are living; namely, Ella M., Ada E., Josephine A., Nathan Wilmot, and Sarah Kathleen. Ella M. married J. C. Talmadge, a lawyer of Catskill, and has two children — Leone S. and N. Edna. Ada E. married Edgar C. Moon, a printer in New York City, and has two children — Vernon S. and Lena A. Josephine A. is the wife of Lawyer Mellen, a boot and shoe dealer in Windham, and has three children — Stanley H., Edith A., and Sheridan Wilmot. Nathan Wilmot Stanley is a civil engineer employed in the department of public works in New York City. Sarah Kathleen Stanley is an artist of local repute, her talent, which is of a high order, having been cultivated under competent instructors in New York. Of the other children one died in infancy; Belle and Charles died while young; Vernon C. died at the age of twenty-two years, while pursuing his medical studies; and William Sheridan, who was a hardware merchant in Cairo, N. Y., died at the age of thirty-one years. The latter was also an artist of ability both with the brush and needle. Among the dearly-prized products of this genius is a piece of work five feet long and three feet wide, executed from an original design, and representing a deer in the forest on its way to drink. Another, which is a painting representing two admirably drawn dogs of different sizes, called "David and Goliah," has received favorable comment from artists of note.

Politically, Dr. Stanley is a Republican. He was a member of the Ashland Board of Supervisors in 1860, has served as Town Clerk in Ashland for two years and as Coroner for the same length of time. He is a Chapter Mason, and formerly belonged to the Independent Order of Odd Fellows. For the past twenty-five years he has been a Pension Examiner.

JACOB M. SNYDER, the genial, accommodating, and popular proprietor of the Snyder House at Gallupville, in the town of Wright, Schoharie County, was born in Berne, N. Y., May 6, 1837, a son of Peter I. Snyder. He is the worthy representative of one of the early settled Dutch families of this section of the State. His grandfather, John Snyder, and his great-grandfather,

Ludwig Snyder, natives of Holland, emigrated to America in Colonial days, and both served as soldiers in the Revolutionary army.

John Snyder came with his parents to Schoharie when a young man, and with them settled in the unbroken woods. At the beginning of the Revolution he entered the Continental army, and on July 26, 1782, was carried as a prisoner to Canada. He there enlisted in the British army, from which he very soon after made his escape, and returned to Schoharie. Here he was afterward engaged in agricultural pursuits until his decease, in 1850. He married a Miss Dorstein. She died at an advanced age, after bringing up a large family of children.

Peter I. Snyder was born on the homestead in Schoharie in 1802. Learning the trade of a shoemaker in his youth, he followed it for a time in Berne, Albany County. Returning to Schoharie, he lived there a while, and after that he was located in Gallupville as a shoemaker a few years, and then he removed to Knox, Albany County, where he died at the age of sixty-seven years. He was a Democrat in his political affiliations, and served as an Overseer of the Poor. While a resident of Berne he united with the local lodge of Odd Fellows, an organization in which he took great interest all his life. Both he and his wife were active members of the Lutheran church. Her maiden name was Eva Dietz. She was born in the town of Berne of German parentage, being one of the fourteen children of John B. Dietz. Eleven of these children grew to mature life, and the average age of nine of them was seventy-nine years, a record for longevity seldom equalled. Of the seven children born to Peter I. and Eva (Dietz) Snyder four grew to years of maturity and two are now living, namely: Jacob M.; and Elizabeth, wife of Sidney Shufildt. The mother died December 12, 1885, aged eighty-two years.

Jacob M. Snyder received his early education in the district schools of Berne, and after finishing his studies learned the shoemaker's trade, which he followed in Knox until 1863. Coming then to Gallupville, he opened a custom shop, in which for twenty-two years he made shoes to order, being the pioneer of that line of industry in this region. In 1885 he purchased from the former owners, Twitchell & Collins, the old Collins House, to which he has since built an addition. It is now known as the Snyder House, has been entirely refurnished, and is one of the best country hotels in this section of the State. Mr. Snyder also owns a livery stable, which he carries on successfully in connection with his hotel.

He is prominently identified with the Democratic party of this locality, which he has represented at various county conventions as a delegate. In 1891 and 1892 he was one of the Board of Supervisors, and for six years he has served as Town Clerk.

On November 27, 1862, Mr. Snyder married Julia Allen. She is a daughter of Sylvester Allen, who was formerly a carpenter of Knox, Albany County, but is now successfully engaged in farming in that town. Seven children have been born of this union, and four of them are now living; namely, Jefferson, Edna, J. Miner, and Ursula. Jefferson, who married Nellie Becker, was for seven years connected with the Albany day line of steamboats, and for four years was connected with the management of Stanwix Hall in Albany, but is now proprietor of Hotel Berne in Berne, N.Y.

Edna is the wife of Sanford D. Schell, a farmer in Gallupville, and has six children — Eva, Libbie, Hazel, Martin, Jefferson, and Howard. J. Miner, for four years connected with the Albany day line of steamers and now manager of the Snyder House, married Carrie Zimmer. Ursula is the wife of Charles E. Spatcholts, a farmer of Wright. Mrs. Snyder is a Methodist in her religious belief and a regular attendant of the church of that denomination.

JOSEPH W. VAN SCHAICK, for many years a prominent farmer of Sharon, Schoharie County, was born in this town, June 5, 1804, son of Koert and Margaret (Wilson) Van Schaick. He was a descendant in the fourth generation of Francis Van Schaick, one of three brothers who emigrated from Holland and settled in New Jersey. Francis Van Schaick died in New Jersey; and his son William, grandfather of the subject of this sketch, settled in Glen, N.Y., where he probably spent his last days. William Van Schaick married Patience Schenck, who also was of Dutch descent.

Koert Van Schaick, father of Joseph W., served in the Continental army during the Revolutionary War, several others of that name, who were relatives, being enrolled among the patriots. He came from Glen to Sharon some time between the years 1790 and 1796; and the title to the homestead, upon which his grand-daughter now resides, was issued in the latter year. He cleared a large farm, built the present residence, which is now about one hundred years old, and was favorably known throughout this locality. He lived to be over seventy years old. His wife, Margaret, who came from New Jersey, was of English and Scotch descent. She became the mother of nine children; namely, Mary, Patience, Margaret, Joseph W., the subject of this sketch, Leffert G., Rachel, Sarah, James, and another son who died in infancy. James, who served as an officer in an artillery company connected with the State militia, was accidentally killed by the premature discharge of a cannon at an election celebration in 1844. He was unmarried. The other seven married, and had families.

Joseph W. Van Schaick succeeded to the homestead, which he occupied his entire life, and was one of the stirring farmers of his day. Though not an aspirant for public office, he was honored with election to various local positions of trust, serving acceptably as Supervisor of the town in 1849, and was highly esteemed for his many excellent qualities. He was a firm, stanch, and lifelong Democrat. He was a prominent member of the True Reformed church of Sharon, and by his liberality and labor was instrumental in a great measure in the building of the church edifice. He died on April 23, 1880, honored and esteemed by all who knew him.

Joseph W. Van Schaick married Elizabeth Slingerland, daughter of Captain Jacob Slingerland, of Bethlehem, Albany County, who died in 1890. Her father died when she was young, and she was reared in Sharon by an aunt. Mr. and Mrs. Van Schaick were the parents of eight children; namely, Koert, Elizabeth, Mary, Catharine, John, Slingerland, Sarah, and Emily. The eldest, who was a well-known singer and teacher, died at the age of thirty-three years, leaving one son, William, who is now residing in Rochester, N.Y. Slingerland died in California. Elizabeth, Mary, and Sarah are no longer living. Emily is the wife of Mr. Van Schaick, of Montgomery County. John is an attorney in Cobleskill, and an ex-State Senator.

Miss Catharine Van Schaick is a graduate of the State Normal School at Albany. She was for several years a successful teacher, but gave up educational work in 1883 in order to care for her mother. After the death of her mother in 1890, Miss Van Schaick took charge of the homestead; and, being a woman of good executive ability, she has managed the property energetically ever since. She possesses literary tastes and attainments of a high order; and these, together with her excellent social qualities, endear her to a large number of friends and acquaintances. She is a strict adherent of the Dutch Reformed church. The house she occupies has long been conspicuous as a landmark. It contains many relics in shape of family utensils used by her grandparents; also the Revolutionary musket, with its highly prized date of 1776 engraved thereon, and the old sword hanging idly in its scabbard high up on the wall.

The Van Schaick family are sturdy-going Americans, and in every generation men of this name have gone forth to serve their country upon the battlefield and in the council chambers of the government. The family cherish the traditions of Alkmaar, Leyden, Brill, and the Beggars of the Sea. They reverence the memory of William of Orange and Prince Maurice, under whom their ancestors fought the Spanish tyrant. But they have transplanted these memories and traditions to American soil, and are thorough patriots. Down to the latest generation the strong qualities of the race have descended. The recent appointment of Louis J. Van Schaick, son of ex-Senator Van Schaick, to a Second Lieutenancy in the United States regular army, marks the beginning of another career which bids fair to be an honored and a useful one.

STEPHEN P. HALLOCK, of Coxsackie, N.Y., dealer in provisions, grain, hay, and straw, was born in New Baltimore, N.Y., on March 5, 1838, his parents being Joseph Z. and Phœbe (Herrick) Hallock. His paternal grandfather, Zebulon Hallock, was either born in New Baltimore or came there as a child in the early days of its settlement. He was a tanner and shoemaker, and worked at those trades all his life.

He died at the age of seventy-two. His wife was before her marriage Sally S. Kidmore. They had a large family of children.

Joseph Z. Hallock was a farmer. He spent all his life in New Baltimore, and died there on January 28, 1899, at the age of eighty-four years. He was a prominent citizen in his town and a farmer on a large scale. He was a member for sixty-four years of the Christian church, and held leading offices in the church. His wife, Phœbe, was born in New Baltimore, daughter of John Herrick, a well-known farmer of that town. She is still living at the age of eighty-two. Of the five children that have been born to her, four are living, namely: Stephen P.; Andrew, who resides at the Upper Village; Leander; and Charles.

Stephen P. Hallock received a practical education in the public schools of his native town. The first twenty-four years of his life were spent on his father's farm, and at the end of that time he came to Coxsackie, and entered the dry-goods store of Collier & Van Vliet as clerk. Three years later he purchased Mr. Van Vliet's interest in the business, and the firm became Collier & Hallock. This partnership continued until 1880, when Mr. Hallock sold out to Mr. Wolf, and bought out the grocery business of David Hallock. He was then located on the opposite side of the street, but a few years after he bought out Platt Coonley's business, with his entire stock of groceries and provisions, and then removed to his present stand. In 1896 his son Roscoe was admitted to partnership in the business. This is the largest grocery in Greene County, carrying on besides its immense retail trade a large wholesale department. Mr. Hallock is the oldest grocer in the town, and in course of his long business career he has seen many changes in the village and a great increase in population.

Mr. Hallock was married in 1864 to Carrie Webber, who was born in this town, daughter of William Webber. She is of Holland descent on her grandfather's side, her grandmother having been a native of Connecticut. Her father spent his life on a farm in this town, and was not only a farmer but the leading auctioneer of Coxsackie. He was a prominent Democrat, and held a number of town and county offices, among them being that of county superintendent of the almshouse at Cairo. His death occurred at the age of seventy. He and his family attended the Dutch Reformed church. His wife, whose maiden name was Elizabeth Vermillia, was born in Coxsackie. She died at the age of seventy-five, having been the mother of seven children — Christina, Millisson, Robert, Carrie, John W., Addie, and Sallie. Of these two are deceased, namely: Millisson, who married J. H. Brandow; and Robert. Christina, who is a widow, married for her first husband Richard Halstead and for her second husband Richard Cornwall. Addie is the wife of O. T. Schermerhorn, of Cairo, and Sallie married J. O. Cornwall. Mrs. Hallock's paternal grandmother lived to be ninety-two years of age, dying on the farm where her son William was born and where he lived and died. Mr. and Mrs. Hallock have an only child, Roscoe, who has always been in his father's store except during the four years when he was Assistant Postmaster. He bought an interest in the business in the spring of 1896.

Mr. Hallock is a Republican and a strong advocate of the principle of protection. He has served many years on the Board of Education, for several terms as Trustee and Treasurer of the village, and has always taken an active part in all public matters. He was one of the most earnest promoters of the beautiful new school-house, which was erected at a cost of thirty thousand dollars. For more than thirty years he has been a member of the Second Reformed Church, of which also his wife and son are members. Mr. Roscoe Hallock is a member of Ark Lodge, F. & A. M., of Coxsackie. Although Mr. Hallock's best energies have been given to his store, he has found time to devote to other business interests. For a number of years he operated the Hallock steam-mill and the foundry connected with it. This was started by his brother David, who erected the buildings, but the plant was burned in 1892. It was an important industry in Coxsackie for many years. At one time Mr. Hallock carried on a feed, grain, and salt business at West Coxsackie. During early life, for a number of years, he taught school in the winter time.

EUGENE E. HOWE, a rising young lawyer of Gilboa, was born in South Londonderry, Vt., May 22, 1867, son of Elwin A. and Jennie (Walker) Howe. He is a descendant on both sides of early arrivals at Plymouth, Mass., and his paternal grandfather was prominently identified with the public affairs of Vermont in his day. Elwin A. Howe enlisted as a private at the breaking out of the Civil War, and was later commissioned Captain of a company belonging to the One Hundred and Eighth United States Infantry, a colored regiment. After the war he engaged in the wooden-ware business in Ludlow, Vt., becoming one of the principal stockholders in a large enterprise known as the Ludlow Toy Manufacturing Company, of which he was superintendent. He is widely and favorably known throughout the Green Mountain State as a leading Republican, having served four years in the lower house and two years in the State Senate. He was formerly Postmaster of Ludlow and superintendent of the water-works. He married Jennie Walker, a representative of a highly reputable Vermont family and a sister of the Hon. William H. Walker, a prominent lawyer, who served in both branches of the legislature and as a Justice of the Supreme Court. Mr. and Mrs. Elwin A. Howe have had six sons and three daughters, all of whom are studiously inclined, and are making good use of the liberal education which it has been their good fortune to receive.

Eugene E. Howe pursued his preparatory course at the Black River Academy, Ludlow, and was graduated at Middlebury College with the degree of Bachelor of Arts in 1888. He was one of the honor men of his class, and

D. B. HITCHCOCK

belongs to the various college fraternities. In 1887 he was appointed official reporter for the Vermont legislature, holding that office for four years in the House and two years in the Senate. His law studies were begun in the office of Batchelder & Barber, of Vermont; and, while pursuing the regular course at the Albany Law School, his spare time was spent in the office of the Hon. Alden Chester, of that city. He was admitted to the bar in 1891, and, beginning the practice of his profession in company with J. S. Frost, he remained in Albany some four years, during which time he figured in several important cases. In 1895, at the advice of friends, he came to Gilboa, where he has already established a large general law business, and has become a familiar figure in the courts of Schoharie, Greene, and Delaware Counties. He is a forcible advocate and a fluent speaker, is familiar with court procedure; and these essential qualities, together with the ability he displays in preparing his cases, give ample evidence of the brilliant future which has been predicted for him. In politics he is a Republican.

Mr. Howe married Florence Eaton, daughter of William Eaton, a successful business man and highly respected citizen of West Arlington, Vt. Her father's people were natives of Vermont, and her mother's family were from the South. She is a graduate of the State Normal School at Albany, attended the Emerson School of Oratory, Boston, and was a successful teacher previous to her marriage. Of this union there are sons, Eugene S. and Carroll E., and a daughter Marion. Mr. and Mrs. Howe are members of the Dutch Reformed church.

DWIGHT B. HITCHCOCK, a retired business man of Windham, was born in this town on February 3, 1830, being the son of Lucius and Eveline (Hayes) Hitchcock. He is a grandson of Lemuel Hitchcock, a native of Connecticut, who was one of the pioneer settlers of Greene County, coming first to Durham.

Later Lemuel Hitchcock removed to that part of Windham known as Big Hollow, where he settled, and subsequently remained until his death, at the age of seventy-five. He had ten children. His first home here was a log cabin; but later, as increasing prosperity attended him, he erected a large frame house. He was one of the prominent men in this part of Greene County, and during the Revolution served the country as a military officer, holding the rank of Lieutenant.

Lucius Hitchcock was born in Durham. He was brought up on a farm, and all his life was devoted to agricultural pursuits. He built a house in Big Hollow near that of his father, and there made his home to the end of his days. In politics he was a Republican, and in religious faith he followed the teachings of his father and was a member of the Presbyterian church. His wife, Eveline, who died at the age of forty-six, was born in Granby, Mass., and was one of a family of ten children. Her father, Luther Hayes, who was a saddler of that town, settled eventually in Durham, where he died at the age of eighty years. Mr. and Mrs. Lucius Hitchcock were the parents of five children. Four of these are living, namely: Dwight B.; Platt O.; Harriet, who married the late George P. Townsend, of Windham; and William.

Dwight B. Hitchcock lived with his parents in Big Hollow, and helped on the home farm until he was twenty-one years of age, when he began working out by the month. His habits were frugal. He saved his wages, and eventually bought a farm near his father's. There he remained ten years. He then removed to Ashland, and, in company with Mr. R. L. Parsons, bought out a store, where he carried on business for five years. Selling out at the end of that time, he came to Windham and went into partnership with John Patterson. After twelve years of successful enterprise he retired from business. Mr. Hitchcock's place is one of the finest in Windham. It is known as the Colonel Robertson homestead.

Mr. Hitchcock has been twice married. His first wife, whose maiden name was Julia Atwater, died in her thirtieth year. She was born in Big Hollow. Her father, Alfred Atwater, farmed for some time in Big Hollow, later for twenty years in Windham, and finally removed to Colorado, where he died. Mrs. Julia A. Hitchcock was the mother of two children, neither of whom is living. She was a devoted member of the Presbyterian church.

Mr. Hitchcock's second wife, also a native of Windham, was before her marriage Sarah R. Barney. Her parents were Ahira and Lydia (Robertson) Barney, and her grandparents were Aaron and Rebecca (Saxton) Barney. Her grandfather, Aaron, was a native of New Hampshire, but came to Windham in early manhood and began work as a journeyman carpenter, settling near the village. He lived to a good old age. He is well remembered as the builder of the tanneries in this section. Rebecca, his wife, died at the age of thirty-four years, having been the mother of three children. She was a native of Rensselaerville, of which place her parents were early settlers.

Ahira Barney, who died in his seventieth year, carried on a farm where the cemetery now lies. He was a lifelong resident of this locality, having been born in the town and reared in the village. His wife, Lydia, was a daughter of Colonel James Robertson, who was one of the first to take up and clear land in the town of Windham. He was a prominent man in these parts, very active in all public affairs. He died at the age of seventy-eight. Of his eight children two are living: James, of Oswego County, New York; and Elbert, who resides in Washington, D.C. Mrs. Lydia R. Barney died at the age of eighty-one. Of her four children one son, Elbert, died in 1896, and the other, Samuel, died at the age of twelve years. The living are: Mrs. Hitchcock and Mrs. L. V. Brisack. Mrs. Hitchcock's parents and grandparents were members of the Presbyterian church.

Politically, Mr. Hitchcock is a Republican. He has always taken an active share in local matters and in all questions of public interest.

He and Mrs. Hitchcock are members of the Presbyterian church and active workers in that body. Mr. Hitchcock is an Elder of the church.

STANTON COURTER, a well-known manufacturer and builder of Cobleskill, N.Y., was born in this town, February 23, 1839. His father, the late Charles Courter, was for many years an influential resident of Cobleskill. His paternal grandfather, Ralph Courter, who was born and bred in Germany, came to America, and, after living a short time in New Jersey, removed to Schoharie, where he engaged in the manufacture of shoes.

Charles Courter, one of a family of seven children, spent his early life in Schoharie, but when a young man began work on his own account in Middleburg as clerk in a store. Going thence to Lawyersville, he there engaged in business until his removal to Cobleskill, in 1837. He subsequently assisted in building the Albany & Susquehanna railway, of which he was for many years a director. He also built many fine brick blocks in Cobleskill; but after the disastrous fire of 1873, in which he lost heavily, he practically retired from active pursuits, although he retained real estate interests until his death, which occurred in 1879, at the age of threescore and ten years. He was a stanch Democrat in politics, and served as one of the village trustees a number of years. His wife, whose maiden name was Helen Lawyer, was born in Lawyersville, and was a daughter of Thomas Lawyer, a lifelong resident of that town. She died at the age of sixty-eight years. Both parents were attendants of the Lutheran church. Five of their children survive; namely, Josephine, Stanton, Henrietta, Cordelia, and Helen C.

Stanton Courter in his youth attended academies at Schoharie and Fort Plain, and was afterward graduated from the Buffalo Commercial College. Before attaining his majority he went to Chicago, where his father had been instrumental in establishing the extensive lumber firm of C. Courter & Co., which dealt in lumber manufactured in its own mills in the timber districts of Michigan. He was there for a time in the employ of that company, and going thence to Milwaukee, Wis., he was connected with the extensive railway operators, Rogers, Courter & Co., until they sold the Milwaukee & Western Railroad to the St. Paul Railway Company, when he became confidential secretary of Sherburne S. Merrill, manager of the road under the new officials. In 1864 Mr. Courter returned to Cobleskill, and for eleven years was first cashier of the First National Bank, which he and his father had established. The following three years he spent in Pensacola, Fla., looking after the lumber interests of his father in that State. The Florida property being then sold to an English syndicate, Mr. Courter again returned to his native town, and on the death of his father succeeded him in business, becoming owner of the manufacturing plant of Courter & Overpaugh. With characteristic enterprise he has almost entirely rebuilt the original works, and now has a large factory finely equipped with modern machinery and appliances. In addition to turning out vast amounts of dressed lumber and building materials of all kinds each year, he manufactures furniture of all descriptions, and as a contractor for buildings has erected some of the finest residences in this part of the county. His own dwelling, on the corner of Main and Grand Streets, is a spacious Colonial mansion, with large rooms and halls and high ceilings.

Mr. Courter also built the Cobleskill electric light plant, which has proved of inestimable value as a means of lighting the village, the corporation, and the residences of the town. Fraternally, he is a Mason, belonging to Cobleskill Lodge, F. & A. M.; and to John L. Lewis Chapter, R. A. M.

LUCIUS A. WOODWORTH, proprietor of the Ripley House in Hunter, was born in Jewett on January 18, 1833, his parents being Abner and Sophronia (Judson) Woodworth. The family, which is of Scotch descent, was a pioneer one of Jewett, living there first in a log cabin and clearing the wild forest land. Mr. Woodworth's grandfather, Lemuel Woodworth, was born in Jewett, and lived there to a good old age. His wife, whose maiden name was Lydia Winters, lived to be seventy-five years old. Their children were as follows: David; Alanson; Hiram; Lemuel; Reuben, who died young; Lydia, who married a Fuller; Nancy, who married a Fairchild; and Sally, who married a Slater.

Abner Woodworth was born in Jewett. He was reared on a farm, and was interested in agricultural labors as long as he lived. When about eighteen years of age he became the owner of a farm, and this he carried on until his death, a period of nearly sixty years. He was a very earnest Christian man and an active worker in the Methodist church, of which he and his wife were members. Mrs. Sophronia Woodworth, who died at the age of forty-seven, was born in Jewett. She was the daughter of Dr. Judson, an old-time physician of Windham, who is believed to have come from Hartford, Conn. Abner and Sophronia Woodworth were the parents of six children.

Lucius Woodworth lived with his parents until he was twenty-one years old. He was educated in the common schools and at Fergusonville Collegiate Institute. He taught school one winter in Hunter, and worked in this vicinity at carpentering with his brother-in-law during the summer. At twenty-one years of age he went out to Wisconsin, where he stayed for three years, working at his trade in the summers. One winter he taught school at Elkhorn, in that State; one winter he attended school; and the third he worked in a shop. In 1861, in company with two other men, he started for Colorado, journeying in his own conveyance, which was a large covered emigrant wagon. The distance was eleven hundred miles. Indians were often seen, but they were not hostile, and the trip was made in safety. Arriving in Denver, Mr. Woodworth remained there a short time, and then went up to Black Hawk, forty miles farther, into the mining region. There for a year he was engaged in building quartz-mills, and at the end of that time he became himself proprietor of a mill, which he operated for the next three years. The country was then almost a wilderness, and this mill was one of the first started in that locality. At the end of three years he sold out his mill and returned East, but only to remain for a short time. The Western fever was on him strong, and he returned to Wisconsin and purchased a farm. Not long after he had an opportunity to go to Nashville, Tenn., to do carpentering for the Northern army; and, when some time later he returned to Wisconsin, he sold out his farm and decided to push on farther west to Montana. Going down to Chicago, he bought twenty mules, loaded a wagon train with freight, and started westward. The freight was to be delivered in Denver. This was in the dead of winter, and the undertaking was most perilous. For two months Mr. Woodworth travelled without seeing a spark of fire, except for cooking purposes. But he reached Denver safely, delivered his load, and then returned to Council Bluffs, where he hired his mules kept until spring opened. Then securing a load in Omaha for Denver, he carried it out there, a distance of six hundred miles, and upon delivering it reloaded in Denver for Salt Lake City. After covering the eleven hundred miles, he camped for about ten days, and then sold out his mule train, and went to work for another man to drive a freight team to Helena, Mont. With a wagon drawn by four mules he traversed the five hundred miles in twenty-five days. Artisans were scarce in Montana, and Mr. Woodworth went to work at his old trade, building a mill, and receiving in payment his board and ten dollars a day in gold. After a time he formed a partnership with a Mr. Hendricks, bought a quartz mine and put up a quartz-mill, which he operated for three years. Upon selling out his own business he took charge of a quartz-mill for Daler & Larkey at Iron Rod, on Jefferson River, and was superintendent there for six years. In 1882, after a varied and hazardous experience in journeying through the Far West, he returned East, and the following year began business at his present occupation. The hotel of which he is now proprietor was built in 1886. It has accommodations for fifty guests, and during the summer months he has a large number of boarders. Since 1883 he has conducted a livery stable, having been the first man in town to open one.

Mr. Woodworth has been twice married. The first Mrs. Woodworth was born in Big Hollow, and her maiden name was Adele Hitchcock. She was the daughter of Anson Hitchcock, a leading farmer of Big Hollow. Her death occurred at the age of thirty. The second Mrs. Woodworth was born in New York City, her maiden name being Mary Ranson. She was one of a family of four children, the others being: Gussie, who married John Coreja; Addie, who lives in Brooklyn; and Georgiana, who married Bert Allen,

Mrs. Mary Woodworth died at the age of thirty-five. She was a member of the Methodist church. Mr. Woodworth has one daughter, Ada C.

Politically, Mr. Woodworth is a Republican. For two years he was a member of the Board of Education, and in 1894 he was Assessor. He is one of the most popular men in Hunter and one of the most popular landlords in this section of the State. He is a man of remarkable intrepidity, as shown by his daring journeyings in the West.

FRANK A. CHAPMAN, proprietor of Hotel Chapman at Blenheim, Schoharie County, N.Y., may be spoken of as an ideal landlord, being active, enterprising, and at all times obliging and pleasant. He was born in the nearby town of Fulton, June 25, 1871, a son of Moses L. Chapman, a lifelong resident of that place.

His paternal grandfather, Jacob Chapman, was born in Rensselaerville, Albany County, and lived there after marriage. Removing then to Fulton, he bought a large tract of timbered land at Bouck's Falls, where he cleared and improved a homestead, and passed his remaining days, dying at the advanced age of eighty-eight years. He was prominently connected with the Methodist church of that place, in which he served in various official positions. His wife, Huldah Wynans, a native of Cooksburg, N.Y., bore him eleven children, of whom seven are living, being, with one exception, residents of Schoharie County. They are: Spencer, a farmer at Bouck's Falls; Nancy C., wife of Chauncey Shattuck, of Michigan; Maria Mann, of Breakabeen; Moses L.; James P., ex-Supervisor of Middleburg; Elizabeth L., wife of Dr. Holmes; and William W., of Bouck's Falls, ex-Supervisor of Fulton. The deceased are: Adam, late of Bouck's Falls; Harriett E.; Isabella, deceased, who married Hiram Ackerson; and Dr. Peter L.

Moses L. Chapman remained at the parental homestead until he was of age, and then engaged in agricultural pursuits on his own account. He bought a large farm in Fulton, on which he made substantial improvements, including the erection of a new set of buildings, and was there successfully employed as a general farmer until his death, at the comparatively early age of forty-two years. He was a Democrat in politics and an active member of the Methodist Episcopal church, to which his wife also belonged; and both were interested in its Sunday-school. He married Huldah A. Beard, daughter of Jacob and Adeline (Phillips) Beard. Her parents were wealthy members of the farming community of Richmondville. They reared three children, namely: Sarah, who married Judge Holmes, for twelve years Judge of Schoharie County; Huldah A.; and John. Mrs. Beard died at the age of forty-five years, and Mr. Beard afterward removed to Genesee County, where he attained the venerable age of ninety years. Of the nine children born to the parents, six are still living, as follows: William

H.; the Hon. Charles Chapman, a member of the Assembly; Ida, wife of J. S. Hunt, of Boston; Frank A.; Flora, of Boston; and Dora. Hattie is deceased. The mother passed to the life beyond when fifty-five years of age.

Frank A. Chapman was but eight years old when his father died. He remained at home until after completing his education in the schools of West Fulton and Blenheim, and then came to his present hotel as a clerk for his brother, a capacity in which he remained two years. Going then to Worcester, Mass., he was an attendant at the asylum for the insane three years. In 1893 Mr. Chapman returned to Blenheim and purchased the hotel, which he has since conducted with eminent success. He has enlarged the building, partly refurnished it, made substantial improvements in and around it, and has now a model public house, the leading one in this section of the State. It is well adapted for the entertainment of guests from the city. Connected with it is a first-class livery, with a number of horses of good qualities, one pair especially being the finest of any in the vicinity. Mr. Chapman has had charge for some time of the stage line between Middleburg and Gilboa, and also of the line from the latter place to Grand Gorge, six miles beyond, and has the contract for carrying the mails between these places.

On December 28, 1893, Mr. Chapman married Elizabeth M. Ross, who was born in Littleton, Me., a daughter of Joseph and Hester (Weeks) Ross. Her mother was born in St. John, N.B. Mrs. Chapman was educated at the Ricker Classical Institute in Houlton, Aroostook County, Me., and previous to her marriage she taught school in that town. Mr. Chapman is a Democrat in politics, and a member of the Middleburg Tribe of Red Men and of Gilboa Lodge, F. & A. M. Mr. and Mrs. Chapman are both members of the Eastern Star Lodge, F. & A. M., of Gilboa.

DANIEL D. FRISBIE, editor and proprietor of the Schoharie *Republican*, was born in Middleburg, his present home, on November 30, 1859. Son of Grandison Norton and Kate (Dodge) Frisbie, he is the representative of a family that has done much to promote the industrial, educational, and political advancement of this county. The family traces its line back to New England ancestry, and two of its early members in this country bore officers' commissions and served with distinction in the Continental army during the Revolution. A biographical sketch of Grandison Norton Frisbie appears on another page of this volume.

The Dodge family were among the early settlers of the county, coming from New England and becoming allied by marriage with the good old Dutch stock, of which Colonel Zelie, of Revolutionary fame, was the best early representative, and the Hon. Daniel Danforth Dodge, grandfather of the subject of this sketch, was later the most prominent, having represented this county in the State legislature and attained the greatest success as a merchant and financier.

Daniel D. Frisbie was educated in the schools of his native town and at Hartwick Seminary, one of the oldest seats of learning in the State. At the latter institution he laid the foundation of a thorough, broad, and liberal education, developing marked literary tastes, which in after years found opportunity in journalism for employment. In the Philophronean Society, of which he became president, were brought out an aptitude for debate and the qualities which have since made him an easy, graceful, and forceful public speaker.

On the completion of his course at the seminary, he entered actively upon a business career which has proved singularly successful. He accepted a clerkship in the store of his father in the spring of 1876, and continued in that capacity until 1881, when he was admitted to partnership. Later the firm became G. N. Frisbie & Sons by the admission of his brother. In 1892 the senior retired, and the firm became D. D. & G. D. Frisbie, continuing thus until April 1, 1899, when a multiplicity of business cares lead the subject of this sketch to retire in favor of his brother-in-law, Nathaniel Manning, Jr. During the twenty-three years of his connection with the business he had the satisfaction of seeing the modest country store develop into a modern department store, the largest, perhaps, in the county in point of sales and stock carried, and widely known for its exact and honorable methods.

Believing that it is the duty of every citizen to take an intelligent interest in public affairs, Mr. Frisbie, within a year after attaining his majority, was made president of the local Democratic Club in the fall of 1882, and again in 1884, when Mr. Cleveland carried New York and won the Presidency for his party. It is worthy of remark that the town of Middleburg in those years rolled up the largest Democratic majorities in a decade. In 1886-87 he was a member and treasurer of the Democratic County Committee, rendering valuable service. For several years he has served as chairman of the Town Committee of his party. Mr. Frisbie has never held a political office, but his services in behalf of the Democratic party have been so conspicuous for so many years that he has been prominently mentioned for member of Assembly; and, if merit meets with due reward in old Schoharie, he will soon be thus honored.

Seeking a wider opportunity for the advocacy of his political principles and for the exercise of literary tastes, he purchased, August, 1887, the Schoharie *Republican*, of the estate of A. A. Hunt. The paper was established in 1819 by Derrick Van Vechten, and is probably the second oldest in the State. In January, 1896, its size was enlarged, and its circulation has increased threefold under the present management. Its columns are rich with the best reading of the day, and its hop reports are regarded as thoroughly reliable and comprehensive. As an advertising medium it unquestionably takes the lead, as its circulation is principally among the large purchasing classes of the Schoharie valley.

Politically, the *Republican* is soundly and unequivocally Democratic. It was established as a Democratic organ, and has always been true to its first principles. Its editorials are often quoted in the leading papers of the State, and it is regarded as in every way the equal of the best county-seat papers to be found in the Commonwealth. In 1894 the seventy-fifth anniversary of its founding was celebrated; and upon that occasion Mr. Frisbie purchased the three-story block in the central part of Schoharie, and made it the permanent home of the paper. The editorial offices are on the first floor, as are also the mechanical and job printing departments. The composing-rooms are on the second floor.

The esteem in which Mr. Frisbie is held by his brethren of the press is shown by his election in 1898 as second vice-president of the Democratic State Editorial Association. He is also a member of the State Editorial Association, a non-partisan organization.

In recognition of his interest in the cause of education, Mr. Frisbie was in 1893 appointed treasurer of Middleburg High School, and was reappointed for a second term. In 1895 he was elected a member of the Board of Education, and re-elected in 1898. Since September, 1897, he has been president of the board. In concert with his associates, the school has been advanced to a proud position among the educational institutions of the State, its finances strengthened, and the number of its students increased.

In 1894, when the business men and farmers of the interior counties felt severely the exactions of the stock fire insurance companies, Mr. Frisbie assisted, with others interested, in the formation of the Mutual Fire Insurance Company, became one of its directors and a member of its Executive Committee. In 1897 the necessity arose for another company in this county, and the Merchants' and Farmers' Mutual Fire Insurance Company was organized, with Daniel D. Frisbie as president. The company during its two years' existence has saved thousands of dollars to its policy holders, and has accumulated a substantial surplus. In time it promises to become one of the strongest institutions of the county.

Mr. Frisbie is a director of the Middleburg & Schoharie Railroad Company, and since 1894 has been its secretary and a member of its Finance Committee. He is identified with St. Mark's Lutheran Church, was for five years superintendent of its Sunday-school, and is at present its financial secretary. Of fraternal orders he is a member of Middleburg Lodge, No. 663, F. & A. M.; and is also a Past Sachem of Oucongena Tribe, I. O. R. M., No. 242. He is also president of the Columbian Literary Union Association, which was an inspiration to young men in Middleburg for many years, and holds its reunion, January 1, 1900. He is a hop-grower, and has done much, through his paper and otherwise, to advance the interests of the growers of the county.

The latest enterprise to engage the attention of the subject of this sketch, and one that he hopes to utilize largely for the public good, is the mills and water privilege located midway between Middleburg and Schoharie, which he acquired April 1, 1899. The mills are being improved by the addition of modern machinery, and their capacity greatly increased. Under the Frisbie Milling Company the business will be extended, and a good market afforded farmers for their grain. Mr. Frisbie also has in mind the establishment of an electric plant, to be operated by water power, whereby the people of Middleburg and Schoharie may have the benefit in their business places, streets, and homes of that great modern convenience, electric lights. Should this be accomplished, a great public service will be placed to the credit of the subject of this sketch.

Mr. Frisbie was married in 1882 to Eleanor Manning, third daughter of Nathaniel Manning, Esq., a leading citizen of Middleburg, who traces his ancestry back to Governor Bradford, first Plymouth colony, who came over in the "Mayflower." The family was among the earliest in the county, and has held an honorable place in its annals. Mr. and Mrs. Frisbie are the parents of three children — G. Norton, Cornelia M., and Daniel Manning.

DAVID CHAMBERS, a thriving agriculturist of Cobleskill, N.Y., owning and occupying a well-improved farm of one hundred and sixteen acres on the Carlisle road, about three miles from the village of Cobleskill, is one of the town's most respected citizens. He was born January 11, 1837, in Carlisle, being a son of William Chambers, who was born in the same town, June 2, 1810. His paternal grandfather, David Chambers, first, was born and reared in Charlton, Saratoga County, whence he removed in 1800 to Carlisle, Schoharie County. Purchasing three hundred acres of heavily timbered land, Grandfather Chambers began the improvement of a homestead, on which he subsequently resided until his death.

William Chambers was one of a family of ten children born in the old log house which his father reared in the forest, and in common with his brothers and sisters was educated in the pioneer school of the district. Soon after attaining his majority he purchased land near the old homestead in Carlisle, and was there successfully engaged in tilling the soil until 1848. In that year he sold his property in Carlisle, and, going to Cherry Valley in Otsego County, bought a farm that he owned till his death, which occurred on April 22, 1899. He carried on general farming until 1890. From that time on he lived retired from active pursuits, at the home of one of his sons in Decatur, not far from Cherry Valley. He was a strong Republican in politics and a member of the Christian church, to which his good wife also belonged. Her maiden name was Betsey Salisbury. She was born in Carlisle, and was a daughter of James Salisbury, formerly of Albany County. She died at the age of seventy-five years. Of her eight children these six are still living: Mary, David, James, Norman, Stewart, and Elizabeth.

WILLIAM H. BALDWIN.

David Chambers completed his education at the Cherry Valley High School, and afterward, until he was twenty-three years old, assisted his father in the labors of the home farm. He then married, February 15, 1860, Catherine M. Richtmyer, daughter of Christian Richtmyer, a farmer of Cobleskill. Mr. Richtmyer was born, and he lived and died, on the farm which Mr. Chambers now occupies, and which he has managed to good purpose ever since his marriage, now thirty-nine years ago. He carries on general farming, raising principally hops and hay, although he has other crops, and pays some attention to raising sheep of the Shropshire breed. He has on his place a fine grove of maple-trees, from which he makes considerable sugar each season. The original owner of this homestead was Conrad Richtmyer, Mrs. Chambers's grandfather, who was one of the first settlers of the town, coming here with his family when his son Christian was about three years old. This son succeeded to the ownership of the paternal acres, and here reared his two children — one son, Elias, and one daughter — Mrs. Chambers being the only survivor. Mr. and Mrs. Chambers have one child, Florence. She is the wife of Adam J. Karker, and has four children — Orrin C., Blanche M., Lloyd D., and Myra A. Mr. Karker and his family reside with Mr. and Mrs. Chambers, and he assists in the management of the homestead property, although he has a fine farm of his own near by.

In politics Mr. Chambers has always affiliated with the Republican party, which is in the minority in this section of the State, and he has the distinction of being the only Supervisor elected on that ticket in Schoharie County for thirty years. He held the office in the years 1894 and 1895, being elected by a majority of forty-three votes in a town whose Democratic majority was usually three hundred. He attends and liberally supports the Dutch Reformed church, of which Mrs. Chambers is a member.

WILLIAM H. BALDWIN, New Baltimore, N.Y.—The Baldwins are of English descent. Their ancestors held the manor of Osterarsfee in Aylesbury, Buckinghamshire, in the time of Henry II. The owner of the manor in 1190 was Sylvester Baldwin, known as Aylesbury. In 1546 the manor of Dundridge, Aston-Clinton, four miles from Aylesbury, was added to the estate. In 1638 Sylvester Baldwin embarked for America in the ship "Martin," accompanied by his wife, two sons, Richard and John, and four daughters. He died during the passage, and his will was admitted to probate in Boston the same year. He left a large estate. His family settled in New Haven, Conn. His son John, after losing his wife and child, settled in New London in 1664. In 1672 John married again, and removed to Stonington. His son Theophilus married Priscilla Mason, grand-daughter of the famous Captain John Mason, who led the settlers against the Pequod Indians in 1637, and destroyed the tribe.

John Baldwin, son of Theophilus and Priscilla (Mason) Baldwin, married Eunice Spalding. Their son Ziba, born in 1752, was the great-grandfather of William H. Baldwin.

William H. Baldwin was married in 1874 to Kittie Van Bergen, daughter of John Van Bergen, of Coxsackie, N.Y. She died in 1876, the infant daughter Lizzie surviving her a few months.

In 1880 William H. Baldwin married Lillie Summers Jones, of Philadelphia. Mrs. Baldwin is a member of the Chester County Chapter of the D. A. R. Her ancestors were among the earliest settlers of Pennsylvania. Her great-grandfather, Colonel Jonathan Jones, served his country in the capacity of Captain, Major, Lieutenant-Colonel, and Colonel of the Continental army, being promoted after active service in the campaign in Canada in 1776.

MARSHALL D. BICE, of Schoharie, dealer in gentlemen's furnishing goods, hats, caps, boots and shoes, in business on Main Street, was born in this town on June 1, 1837, son of Joshua and Jemima (Beadle) Bice. His grandfather, Aaron Bice, was a native of Holland. He came to New York in early manhood, lived for a time in Dutchess County, and subsequently removed to Schoharie, where he spent the last years of his life.

Joshua Bice, above named, who was born in Dutchess County, was brought up on a farm, and was early accustomed to farm work. He also learned the shoemaker's trade. He came to this town shortly after his marriage, and settled on a small farm which he carried on, engaging in shoemaking during his spare time. A man of great industry and very frugal, by degrees he added to his property till he was the owner of one hundred and twenty acres. He resided here sixty-two years in all, and died at the age of eighty-one. He was an old-fashioned, zealous Methodist, always active in church work, and was one of those who took a leading part in building the Methodist church edifice at East Cobleskill. He also took a warm interest in the Sunday-school. It is said that in every-day life he applied the principles he professed to believe. His wife, Jemima, who also was an active church worker, was born in Dutchess County. They reared a family of thirteen children, only three of whom are living. These are: Levi M., Marshall D., and Asher.

Marshall D. Bice received a practical education in the public schools of Schoharie, and subsequently, at the age of sixteen, began his working life as clerk in the store of O. B. Throop in this village. Three years later he went to East Cobleskill, where for three years he was in partnership with his father. At the end of that time he removed to Cobleskill and started in business for himself, which he continued for two years. Going then to New York City, he was employed for two years in a wholesale hat store. This brought him up to the close of 1863, and in December of that year he enlisted in Company H of the Third New York Regiment of Cavalry. For a year he remained in New York Harbor at draft rendezvous; but at the end of that time he was appointed Lieutenant of a company of cavalry, and went to the front, joining his regiment at Petersburg. Later his company went to Norfolk to do general duty, and thence to North Carolina, where Mr. Bice was appointed a provost-marshal. Subsequently he was assistant provost-marshal at Norfolk, Va., and then Aide-de-camp on General Mann's staff. After being mustered out of the service in 1865, he remained at Norfolk, Va., for a year and a half, and was engaged in buying up government horses and mules at auction and selling them at private sale. In addition to this he carried on some mercantile business. He then received an appointment as United States Inspector of Spirits at Chicago, and went to that city. Returning to his native town at the end of nine months, he engaged in the general grocery and house furnishing business, which he continued for ten years, or up to 1894, when he purchased the block where he is now carrying on business. He put in a large stock of goods, and has met with all the success he could have hoped for.

Mr. Bice was married in 1879 to Melissa M. Jones, who was born in Duanesburg, N.Y. In politics he is a Democrat. He has been Constable for some years, also Overseer of the Poor, but has refused all other public offices. Forty years ago he joined Schoharie Valley Lodge, No. 491, F. & A. M., and he is at the present time the oldest member of this lodge. He has been Master for several years, and has filled all the other offices. In 1861 he joined the Chapter of Canajoharie, and in 1863 he joined the Masonic chapter at Cobleskill, being one of its charter members. He is a member of the Schoharie Lodge of Odd Fellows, and has for many years been connected with the fire department. Mr. Bice attends the Methodist church, and is a trustee of the society.

DAVID M. HINMAN, the popular merchant of New Baltimore, Greene County, N.Y., was born in this town on the last day of January, 1863. He is the only surviving son of the late William C. Hinman, who established the Hinman store, and who for many years was one of the leading citizens of New Baltimore. Mr. David M. Hinman's grandfather was a native of Connecticut, and came from that State to Albany County, New York, when it was being cleared and settled. He was a school teacher by profession, and followed that calling through a long life. He taught music as well as the common branches of learning. He died at the age of eighty.

William C. Hinman was born in Albany County, and reared on a farm near Ravena. He pursued his studies in the district school, and in addition was privately instructed by his father. In early life he learned the carpenter's trade. Later he became a tradesman on a small scale near Utica, and subsequent to that he came to New Baltimore. Here he was clerk for John G. Raymond for a time, and he subsequently established the business, which has since become the largest of its kind in the town. The buildings now in use were built by him some time after the business was started. At first he was in partnership with his brother, Herman H. Hinman, later with William Fuller down to 1876. Then for eleven years, or up to the time of his death in 1887, he carried on the business alone. He died aged sixty-nine years. His wife, whose maiden name was Jane Terry, was born in Coeymans, N. Y. She was one of the ten children of John Terry, a lifelong farmer of that place. She is now seventy-five years of age. Of her seven children three are living — Elizabeth, Annie, and David M. Both Mr. and Mrs. William C. Hinman were active in the affairs of the Methodist church, and both worked earnestly to secure the building of the church edifice, Mr. Hinman being on the committee having the matter in charge. He was for years the strong man in the church, and to him all looked for counsel. He was a Republican in politics. At the time of his death he was the oldest merchant in the town.

David M. Hinman attended the public schools of New Baltimore, and subsequently received private instruction for some time. He went to work in the store at an early age, and soon became his father's most trusted and efficient clerk. Upon the death of his father he succeeded to the business, which he has since successfully managed. He carries a large stock of general merchandise, including groceries and provisions, dry goods, hardware, paints, oils, glass, oil-cloths, and ladies' and gentlemen's furnishing goods. The store has been the largest in the town since it was started fifty years ago. Mr. Hinman's sister now acts as book-keeper, and she is also the operator on the Western Union Telegraph line here. There is a long distance telephone in the store. Mr. Hinman has in a measure stepped into the place his father formerly occupied in the church. He is a member of the Board of Stewards, for six years has been superintendent of the Sunday-school, and he is vice-president of the Epworth League, of which he has been a member ever since the branch here was organized. His politics are Republican. He has held the office of Town Clerk for a year.

JUDSON BURHANS, junior member of the enterprising firm of Borst & Burhans, Cobleskill, N. Y., millers, manufacturers of buckwheat, wheat, rye, and graham flours, and custom grinders of general feed, is a well-known business man of this town. He was born the first day of January, 1849, in Carlisle, Schoharie County, which was also the birthplace of his father, John Burhans.

The emigrant ancestor of the Burhans family emigrated from Holland to the State of New York in the seventeenth century. Mr. Judson Burhans's grandfather, Peter Burhans, spent the early part of his life in Greene County, New York, whence he removed to Carlisle with his parents. He married Annie Hummel, the descendant of a Dutch family of Greene County, and was the father of eight children, of whom two are yet living. His wife died in Carlisle at the age of threescore and ten years.

John Burhans, son of Peter and father of Judson, received his education in the district schools of Carlisle, and on the parental farm was well drilled in the various branches of agriculture. Deciding to make farming his life occupation, he purchased the old homestead when he became of age, and from that time until his death, at the age of seventy-six years, carried on general farming most successfully. He married Lavinia Loucks, who was born in Carlisle, the daughter of Peter Loucks, a well-to-do farmer, and descendant of an early settler of the town. Six children were the fruit of their union, namely: Judson, the subject of this brief sketch; Andrew; Melvin; Peter; Romeyn; and Walton. Mrs. Burhans is still living, an active woman of seventy years. She is a member of the Lutheran church, to which her husband also belonged.

Judson Burhans attended the district school until fifteen years old, when he began working out as a farm laborer and carpenter's apprentice. After learning the trade he worked at carpentering in the summer season and taught school winters for ten years, finding time also to fit himself for a book-keeper at the Poughkeepsie Business College. After that he was employed as a book-keeper at Cobleskill for a while, and then went to Albany, where he was engaged as a commission merchant from 1882 until 1886, when he disposed of his business in that city and returned to Cobleskill. Buying an interest in the Cobleskill mills, he has since, with the co-operation of his partner, Mr. Borst, materially increased the capacity of the plant, which now produces on an average one hundred barrels of buckwheat flour, fifty barrels of rye flour, and forty tons of feed every twenty-four hours. These gentlemen make a specialty of buckwheat flour, which they manufacture from a number one grain, bought directly from the producer; and for the past few years they have sold to wholesale and retail dealers in all parts of the Union large amounts of their "Sure Rising Buckwheat," which is pronounced by the trade to be one of the most popular on the market, rivalling Hecker's, the Martha Washington, and the I. X. L. brands.

On July 24, 1878, Mr. Burhans married Miss Mary E. Becker, one of the six children of Francis Becker, formerly a miller in this part of Schoharie County, but later a resident of Berne, Albany County. She was born and educated in Gallupville, a village not far from Colbeskill. Mr. and Mrs. Burhans have two children — Frank J. and Ella Floy, both of whom are in school.

Fraternally, Mr. Burhans belongs to the Albany Lodge of Odd Fellows. He also joined the Improved Order of Red Men while living in that city. He was one of the incorporators of the Farmers' and Mechanics' Bank of Cobleskill, and is one of its directorate. In politics he is independent, voting with the courage of his convictions for the best men and best measures, regardless of party ties. He attends the Methodist Episcopal church, of which Mrs. Burhans is an active member.

PETER MAGEE, a well-known shipbuilder of Athens, N.Y., was born on November 23, 1838, in Baltimore, Md., where his parents, John and Anna (Cahill) Magee, settled when they emigrated to this country from Ireland. He is the only one now living of a family of eight children. Both father and mother were members of the Catholic church. The mother died at the age of seventy-one.

Mr. Magee was reared in Baltimore, and in his childhood attended a parochial school in that city. When he was only thirteen years old, his father died and he had to begin to assist his widowed mother. He learned the ship-builder's trade, serving a four years' apprenticeship with John J. Abraham, who was reckoned one of the best ship-builders in that region. When he had completed his period of apprenticeship, he began working for Mr. Abraham as a journeyman, and in a short time was receiving higher wages than any other man in the yard. After this he spent one year in Mound City, Ill.; and, when he returned, he again engaged with Mr. Abraham. Leaving Baltimore a second time and going to New York City, he worked a while for Theodore Roosevelt, now Governor of the State, several months for William H. Webb, and then put up a vessel for Van Duzen Brothers. He next entered the service of the United States as a mechanic at Port Royal, and there remained two years and one month. Upon leaving Port Royal he came to New York and took a contract for work at the foot of Sixteenth Street, being then only twenty-three years of age. After executing this to the satisfaction of all concerned, he went to work for Simonson, the ship-builder, this being during the eight-hour strike.

Subsequently he was employed in Mr. J. R. Baldwin's yard at New Baltimore, and from that place he came to Athens and started business for himself. He was first in company with Mr. Matthias Van Loan in 1871, and this partnership continued for twenty years, the firm being known as Van Loan & Magee. Since 1888 Mr. Magee has been without a partner. During the time he has been in the yard here he has built over two hundred vessels, and has rebuilt many more. He is one of the best known and most reputable ship-builders in this region. His son Joseph acts as his foreman.

Mr. Magee was married in 1871 to Mary J. McCabe, who was born in Greene County. She has borne him three children: Joseph, above mentioned; Mary; and Hannah. All the children have received a public-school education. The daughters reside with their parents. Joseph married Mary Brennan.

Mr. Magee is a Democrat in politics, and for many years has been member of town and county committees. He has attended many conventions as delegate. In 1885 he was elected Sheriff of the county, and for the three succeeding years he efficiently filled that office. He has been a member of the School Board for thirty years, and for the same length of time a Trustee of the village.

Mr. Magee's house is one of the finest in Athens. He puts a large amount of money in circulation in the town every week when he pays off his force of workmen. He and his family attend the Catholic church. They are actively interested in all efforts to promote the welfare of the community.

LUTHER ZELIE, a wide-awake, enterprising business man of Fulton, Schoharie County, prosperously engaged as a general merchant in the village of Breakabeen, was born in this town on July 7, 1874. The son of Ephraim and Helen (Becker) Zelie, he is the representative of one of the earlier families of this part of the county, and comes of patriotic stock, his great-grandfather, Colonel Zelie, of the Revolutionary army, having had command of the Upper Fort in Fulton during the Colonial struggle for independence.

Peter Zelie, son of Colonel Zelie and grandfather of Luther, spent his entire life of seventy-five years in Fulton, and here married Eliza Vroman. He was a carpenter, and followed his trade until well advanced in years, when he retired from work, and spent his remaining days with his son Ephraim. His wife survived him, attaining the age of fourscore years. Both were devout members of the Reformed church. They had eleven children.

Ephraim Zelie, the father above named, was born in 1839 in Fulton, and obtained his education in the district schools. At the age of ten years he began working out, and from that time fought the battle of life for himself. When old enough to labor at the anvil, he learned the blacksmith's trade, at which he subsequently worked as a journeyman in different parts of Schoharie County. Going then to Cleveland, Ohio, he remained there three years, but preferring to establish himself permanently in New York he returned home, and in 1861 located in Breakabeen, where he continued at his trade for twenty years. From that time until his death, May 20, 1897, he lived on a farm in Fulton. He was a firm supporter of the principles of the Democratic party, and served for a while as Collector of Taxes. He married Helen Becker, one of the two children of Henry and Rebecca (Berg) Becker. Her father, who was a farmer, died at the age of fifty years, and her mother died at the age of forty-eight. Five children were born to Mr. and Mrs. Ephraim Zelie, and of these two are living; namely, Luther and Laura, twins. Laura is the wife of Floyd Mattice, of North Blenheim. Both parents were active members of the Lutheran church, in which the father served as an Elder, besides holding other offices, being for a number of years a teacher in the Sunday-school.

Luther Zelie in boyhood and youth attended successively the village schools of Fulton and the Middleburg High School, and afterward completed the course of study at the Albany Business College. Returning to Fulton, he taught school a year in this town, and then began his mercantile career as a clerk in the store of Cottrell & Leonard, hatters and furriers in Albany, where he remained three years. Coming to Breakabeen in 1895, Mr. Zelie bought out the long-established business of Mr. E. Patterson, a well-known merchant, and has since conducted the store with eminent success. He has considerably increased the original stock, carrying now a complete assortment of groceries, provisions, boots, shoes, hats, gentlemen's clothing and furnishing goods, and also a full line of hardware, in all of which he has built up a substantial trade.

On January 26, 1898, Mr. Luther Zelie was united in marriage with Miss Keziah Shafer, daughter of Joseph A. Shafer, of Breakabeen.

Mr. Zelie is an Odd Fellow, being a member of Blenheim Lodge, I. O. O. F. In politics he affiliates with the Democratic party, and is now serving as Town Clerk. He and his wife are faithful members of the Lutheran church and of the Sunday-school connected with it, Mr. Zelie being the superintendent of the school.

EGBERT B. DODGE, of Ashland, was born in Greenville, Greene County, N.Y., October 24, 1822, son of Andrew and Ruth (Blackmar) Dodge. He is a grandson of Moses Dodge, who moved his family from Massachusetts to Freehold, Greene County, in 1804, and followed the blacksmith's trade in connection with other mechanical occupations for the rest of his life. Moses Dodge is said to have been a descendant of William Dodge, one of the early settlers of Salem, Mass.

Andrew Dodge, father of Egbert B., was born in Massachusetts. When a young man he engaged in farming in Freehold. From 1815 to 1847 he carried on a general store, and he also manufactured potash. His last days were spent in retirement upon his farm, and he died at the age of eighty-one years. He served as Postmaster for thirty years. In politics he was originally a Whig and later a Republican. During the somewhat violent agitation against the Masonic fraternity which took place in his day, he sided with the opponents, and was known as an anti-Mason. Andrew Dodge married Ruth Blackmar, a native of Great Barrington, Mass., daughter of Abel Blackmar, a prosperous farmer and cattle dealer. She became the mother of ten children, three of whom are living; namely, Egbert B., Augusta, and Louisa. Augusta is the widow of the Rev. John N. Spoor; and Louisa married Daniel G. Searles, of Greenville. Mrs. Ruth Dodge died at the age of fifty-five years. The parents of Ruth Dodge were members of the Christian church, of which she was also a member.

Egbert B. Dodge obtained his knowledge of the primary branches of learning in the common schools of Freehold, and completed his studies at the academy in Greenville. He taught several terms of school in Greene and Dutchess Counties previous to 1847. In that year he engaged in trade at Freehold, where he continued in business some thirteen years, and in 1860 he removed to Ashland. Securing a site adjoining the hotel, he opened a general store, which for the succeeding two years was the only source of supply in this vicinity. He was therefore called upon to carry a varied stock, which was transported from New York City by river boats to Catskill. After being out of business two years he (in 1869) built a new store; and, putting in a large stock of general merchandise, he continued in trade until 1880, when he was succeeded by his son. After being relieved of the cares of business he could not remain idle, preferring instead to continue in the store; and as Assistant Post-

EGBERT B. DODGE.

master he has handled the mails here for the past thirty years. He was Postmaster under President Fillmore and during a part of the Pierce administration. He has witnessed many changes and improvements in the postal service, and has a distinct remembrance of the days when stages were the only means of conveyance. He has voted at every Presidential election since 1844, when he supported the candidacy of Henry Clay, and is now a Republican. He served as a Supervisor in 1868, as Town Clerk in 1870, was a Justice of the Peace for fourteen years, and has settled many estates.

In 1853 Mr. Dodge was united in marriage with Eliza C. Sax, who was born in Cairo, Greene County, daughter of Jacob Sax, the descendant of an early Dutch settler and a prosperous farmer of that town. Mr. and Mrs. Dodge reared three children; namely, Francis, Edgar S., and Ella M. Dodge. Francis succeeded his father in business, and is now the leading merchant in this section, also Postmaster at the present time. He married Mary Clark, and has two children — Frederick C. and Florence. Edgar S., who is a horse dealer, married Sarah Frances Martin. Ella M. married Edward Snow, a carpenter of Kingston, and has three children — Herbert, Harold, and Laura. Mrs. Eliza C. Dodge died August 28, 1897, aged sixty-six years.

As an intelligent, progressive, and public-spirited citizen, who can be depended upon for assistance in forwarding any movement calculated to be of benefit to the community, Mr. Dodge is highly esteemed by his fellow-townsmen, among whom he has for years been a prominent and influential figure. He possesses an extensive knowledge of the town's history for the past thirty-eight years, has been a careful reader of instructive books, and his judgment in matters of public importance is still sought for and relied upon. He was formerly a member of the Independent Order of Odd Fellows. In his religious belief he is a Presbyterian, and his son Francis is prominently identified with the Presbyterian church.

CHARLES P. McCABE, M.D., of Greenville, one of the foremost practising physicians of Greene County, was born on August 11, 1856, in the house where his father, Bradley Selleck McCabe, M.D., now resides. His family is an old one in the county, having been prominent here since 1783, when Stephen McCabe, his great-grandfather, settled in New Baltimore.

Stephen McCabe was born in New Jersey in 1755. During the Revolution he enlisted and served for a time in the Continental army. At the close of the war he came to New Baltimore with his wife, Mary Farrar, and their family, his son Benjamin being then three years of age. There he settled on the estate now owned by Hiram Miller.

Benjamin McCabe, the third son, was married in 1812 to Sarah Gedney, of New Baltimore, and continued to reside on his father's place till 1825, when he purchased and removed to the farm now occupied by Mrs. Cathcart. In 1834 he bought and removed to the farm now owned by Adam Lorenz. Benjamin's wife, Sarah, was the daughter of Joshua Gedney, who was one of the pioneer settlers of New Baltimore, where he became the owner of a fine farm. He was born in Westchester County, of which his father was an early settler, and it was on his father's land in that county that the battle of White Plains took place. Joshua Gedney and his wife, whose maiden name was Bennett, were zealous Methodists, and their descendants to the present generation have continued in the faith of that church. Mrs. Gedney died at seventy. She was born in Westchester County. Her children were: Peter, Bartholomew, Joshua, Samuel, Absalom, Sarah, Hannah, and Patience. Of Benjamin McCabe it has been written, "He was possessed of a discriminating mind and a sound judgment, and was never known to shed a tear nor to laugh audibly, so perfectly were his passions under his control." He died on November 6, 1855, surviving his wife only nine days. He was the father of the following-named children: Caroline, Jane, Hamilton, Bartholomew G., Bradley S., Philip E., and Mary. Of these, Hamilton J., the eldest son, has for many years been engaged in the tin and hardware business in Greenville village; and Bartholomew G., the second son, who was graduated in medicine, died at Deposit, Delaware County, N.Y.

Bradley Selleck McCabe, M.D., father of the subject of this sketch, received his medical diploma from the Albany Medical College in 1850, and shortly entered on the duties of his profession in partnership with Dr. Gideon Botsford, with whom he had begun the study of medicine some years before, after attending Greenville Academy. The late Dr. Botsford was a notable man of his time in Greenville, and had a very large practice. Dr. McCabe, who has been his worthy successor, is known throughout the county for his skill both in medicine and in surgery. He has been for a number of years a member of the Board of Trustees of Greenville Academy. He represented his town in the Board of Supervisors six years, was twice chairman of the Board. He has also represented the county in the State legislature.

He was married on June 26, 1850, to Mary L., youngest daughter of the late Dr. Amos Botsford. Three children have been born to him — Amos B., Charles P., and George G. Amos B. McCabe, who has been in the sub-treasury in New York City since 1890, was born on September 17, 1852, and during early manhood engaged in agricultural pursuits. He married Helen Kyle, of Albany, and has two children -- John C. and Mary B., the son being now in the employ of the New York Life Insurance Company. George G. McCabe was born on June 26, 1860. He was formerly in the employ of P. Winne & Co., of this place, but is now carrying on a drug business for himself. He was Postmaster for eight years under Cleveland, and he is the present Supervisor of the town. He married Emmeline Stevens, the ceremony taking place on January 8, 1895. Dr. Bradley S. McCabe was Postmaster for four years under Franklin

Pierce, and also under James Buchanan. He was formerly connected with the Odd Fellows, and was for some years an active worker in that organization.

Charles P. McCabe after attending the Greenville Academy went to Boston, Mass., and entered the Conservatory under the famous teacher, Petersilea, where he remained for two years. Returning to his native place, he taught music for some years, but in 1880 began the study of medicine with his father. Subsequently he entered the Medical College at Albany, and in March, 1883, took his degree from that institution. After some time spent in the Boston hospitals and attendance on the clinics there, he came back to Greenville and settled to practise with his father, continuing in partnership with him till 1890. He has since practised alone. He has patients in all the surrounding towns over a radius of fifteen miles, and besides his extensive medical practice has many difficult surgical cases. He built his present residence in 1889.

Dr. Charles P. McCabe was married on September 10, 1884, to Helena F., eldest daughter of the late Robert Elliott, of Hunter, a sketch of whom appears elsewhere in this work. Of this union three children have been born, of whom Clara, the eldest, died at the age of fourteen months, and Millicent at the age of five and a half years. One daughter is living, Dorothy K. In religious faith Dr. Charles P. McCabe is a Methodist. Both he and his wife are prominent workers in the church, and he has been superintendent of the Sunday-school and for many years one of the stewards. For many years he sang in the choir, and formerly he held the position of organist. He organized the Greenville Musical Union, a chorus of seventy voices, and so great was its reputation that at one time the largest hall in the town was filled on six successive evenings to listen to it. Mrs. McCabe was a teacher in the Sunday-school for many years, and also sang and acted as organist. She is a graduate of Kingston Academy and of Chamberlaine College in Randolph, N.Y. She was born in Hunter.

Dr. Charles P. McCabe is a member of the New York State Medical Society, and is now president of the Greene County Medical Society. In politics he is a Democrat. In 1893 he was elected and served as Supervisor, but he refused to accept the nomination a second time, and has uniformly declined to run for other offices, feeling that his practice needs his undivided attention. He is, however, connected with various fraternal societies, namely: with James M. Austin Lodge of Masons, of which he was Master for three terms; with Zeus Lodge of the Knights of Pythias, of which he was Chancellor for two years, and of which he is a charter member and was the first commanding officer. He has unusual business aptitude. He is president of the Greene County Mutual Fire Insurance Company, and was formerly president of the Village Fire Association, which operates in Greene, Albany, Delaware, and Schoharie Counties, and he is a director in both companies. Ever since the Greenville Board of Education was organized he has been one of its most active members.

CHRISTIAN RECTOR, who owns a good farm in Glenville, N.Y., on the banks of the Mohawk River, was born where he now resides on October 16, 1836, son of William and Susan (Haverley) Rector.

William Rector was a native of this State. Settling when a young man upon the farm his son now owns, he successfully followed agricultural pursuits for the rest of his active period. He took a leading part in public affairs, holding various town offices, and in politics he was a Democrat. He was a Deacon and Elder of the Reformed church. His wife, Susan, was born in the house which her son Christian now occupies. She was the daughter of Christian Haverley, who built the house with brick made upon the farm. She became the mother of three children, namely: Anna M., wife of James T. Wyatt, of Glenville; Christian, the subject of this sketch; and Susan Rosa, who is no longer living. William Rector lived to be nearly eighty-five years old, and his wife died at eighty-three.

Christian Rector was reared and educated in Glenville. From his youth upward he has been engaged in tilling the soil, and, succeeding to the ownership of the homestead property of two hundred and seventy acres, he has realized excellent returns as a general farmer. His success is the result of practical knowledge, diligent effort, and sound judgment.

On October 10, 1866, Mr. Rector married Emma Vedder, who was born in Schenectady, June 4, 1845, daughter of Peter and Prudence (Gates) Vedder. Her father was born in Niskayuna, N.Y., and her mother was a native of Schenectady. Peter Vedder was a carpenter and lumber dealer in Schenectady for many years, and the business is now carried on by his sons. He served as Supervisor and Alderman, to which offices he was elected by the Republican party; and as a generous, public-spirited citizen he was accorded the esteem and good will of his fellow-townsmen. In his religious belief he was a Baptist. Peter Vedder lived to be seventy-six years old. His wife died at thirty-nine. He was the father of eight children, namely: Mary C., who is now Mrs. Van Dyke; Emma, who is now Mrs. Rector; Theresa, who is now Mrs. Gilbert; Daniel G., Sharratt G., Albert, William, of Pasadena, Cal.; and Prudence G., who is now Mrs. Betts. Mr. and Mrs. Rector have three children, namely: William, a druggist in Schenectady; Susan R., who married George Koonz, of Glenville, and has two daughters — Mabel and Berdena; and Prudence, who resides at home.

Mr. and Mrs. Rector are members of the Reformed church. Politically, Mr. Rector acts with the Democratic party.

CLARENCE M. BOORN, station agent, telegraph operator, freight agent, and passenger agent at Seward station, Schoharie County, is a capable, pleasant, accommodating official, well adapted for the responsible position that he holds. He was born September 6, 1863, in Decatur, Otsego County, N.Y., the town in which both his

CHRISTIAN RECTOR.

father, Nathan Boorn, and his grandfather, whose name was Amos, first drew the breath of life. Amos Boorn was the son of one of the earliest settlers of Decatur, and was born and reared in a log cabin. A man of industrious habits, energetic and ambitious, he cleared the timber from a large tract of land, and thus reclaimed from the wilderness a fine farm. He lived to the age of seventy years.

Nathan Boorn was born in the log house in which his parents began housekeeping. In the days of his boyhood and youth he greatly assisted his father in felling the giant trees of the forest and in tilling the soil. He afterward learned the blacksmith's trade, and for many years followed it in his native town. Subsequently removing to the near-by town of East Worcester, he there set up his smithy, and now, though he is seventy years of age, he is still active.

> "Week in, week out, from morn till night,
> You can hear his bellows blow."

He married Catherine Brazie, one of the thirteen children of Francis Brazie, of Cooperstown, N.Y. Four children were born of their union, and three are living, as follows: Clarence M.; Ortentia, wife of Alfred R. Robbins; and Friend. Both parents are consistent members of the Methodist Episcopal church. In politics the father is an uncompromising Republican, and, though never an office-seeker, has served two terms as Town Clerk.

Clarence M. Boorn was educated in the public schools, and at the age of seventeen he left home in order to study telegraphy. As soon as he had acquired a sufficient knowledge of the art, he was appointed night operator at one of the stations on the Delaware & Hudson River Railroad, and he has since, for a period of seventeen years, been in the employ of the same company. For some time he had charge of the telegraph office at Unadilla, whence he was transferred as agent to Schenevus, also in Otsego County, and in 1896 came to Seward. Here he has faithfully and satisfactorily performed the duties pertaining to his office, and in every way has proved himself worthy of the confidence reposed in him. Politically, he is a supporter of the principles of the Republican party.

On March 19, 1890, Mr. Boorn married Miss Edna M. Winegard, who was born in Seward, one of the two children of Mr. and Mrs. Abram Winegard, well-to-do and prominent members of the farming community of this town, and pillars of the Methodist Episcopal church. Mr. and Mrs. Boorn have one child, Carl W. Mr. Boorn attends the Methodist Episcopal church, of which Mrs. Boorn is an active member.

WILLIAM B. KNISKERN, an energetic farmer and one of the most popular young men of Blenheim, N.Y., was born in Fulton, this State, September 6, 1868. He is the son of Rufus and Helen M. (Best) Kniskern, and is of the fifth generation in descent from Johannis Kniskern, his pioneer ancestor, who was the original owner (as early as 1775) of the farm on which he resides with his father and mother. This is the line: Johannis,¹ Joseph,² Christopher,³ Rufus,⁴ William B.⁵

The grandfather, Christopher Kniskern, son of Joseph, succeeded to the ownership of the homestead, and was an industrious farmer. He married Olive Dornburgh. Their children were: Hamilton, who resides in Blenheim, and is a cooper by trade; Angeline, wife of Joseph Fink; Adeline, who married S. L. Perry; Mary, who married William S. Hager; Elizabeth, who is unmarried; Rufus, the father of William B.; Caroline, who married Jeremiah Zeh; and Martha, who married a Mr. Shaffer.

Rufus Kniskern was reared on the ancestral farm, which he inherited in turn, and here he continues to make his home. Devoting himself to its cultivation during the active period of his life, he gave particular attention to carrying on a dairy and raising hops, making the most of his opportunities for success. He married Helen M. Best, daughter of William and Nancy (Hagadorn) Best, of Fulton. Rufus Kniskern is a member of the Methodist Episcopal church, and his wife is a Lutheran.

William B. Kniskern acquired a public-school education. From his youth he has worked upon the homestead farm, which for some time he cultivated jointly with his father. He now crops about twenty-five acres, has fifty acres of excellent pasture land, and keeps from twelve to fifteen cows. He has relinquished the growing of hops, preferring to devote his energy to general farming and dairying.

Mr. Kniskern married Mary C. Hanes, daughter of John Hanes, of Fulton. They have one son, Harold. Politically, he is a Democrat. Although frequently solicited to accept nominations to town offices, he has generally declined, but has rendered valuable service to the party as a member of the town and county committees, and was a candidate for Supervisor in 1898. He attends the Methodist Episcopal church.

LOREN P. COLE, attorney-at-law and farmer of Conesville, N.Y., was born in this town, May 31, 1852, son of Elder Loren P. and Charlotte (Weed) Cole. He is a grandson of Avery Cole, who moved with his family from Vermont to that part of Blenheim which is now Gilboa, Schoharie County, and was engaged in farming for the rest of his life, his death occurring at the age of seventy years.

Avery Cole was an active member of the Baptist church. He was a Whig in politics, and held some of the town offices. The maiden name of his wife was Polly Blair, and their children were: Suel, Ambrose, Loren P., Anson, Barnard, Ahaz, Rosetta, Mary, and Esther. Of these Ambrose, who resided in Indiana, and Rosetta, who married Patrick Van Dyke, are the only survivors. Mary married Warren W. Parsons; Esther married Daniel C. Leonard; Suel and Barnard died in Gilboa; Anson died in Western New York; and Ahaz died in Windham, this State. All except Suel lived to be sixty-three years old.

Elder Loren P. Cole, father of the subject of this sketch, was born in Vermont in 1808, and came to Schoharie County when he was four years old. He resided in Gilboa until 1845, when he came to Conesville and became an extensive farmer, owning some three hundred acres of land. He was an ordained minister of the Baptist denomination. He supplied pulpits in this section for many years, and also taught school. He served as Supervisor for the years 1853-59, 1864, and 1879, being in the latter year the oldest man on the board. He also served as Highway Commissioner, Superintendent of Schools, and General Inspector. Elder Cole died in 1886. He was twice married. His first wife, Phœbe M. Pierce, died two years after marriage, leaving one daughter, Phœbe Ann, who married E. G. Case. For his second wife he married Charlotte Weed, whose ancestors came from Connecticut. Seven children were born of this union, namely: Alzina, who married W. H. Braman; Pluma, who married Bartholomew Becker; Julia E., wife of James A. Bouck; Ianthe, wife of George W. Gurnsey; Charlotte, who married Giles P. Guernsey; Leander, a farmer of Conesville; and Loren P., the subject of this sketch. The mother's death occurred a few weeks prior to that of her husband.

Loren P. Cole was given the advantages of a good education, and after the completion of his studies he taught seven terms of school in winter, and worked summers on a farm of his father's. Purchasing the home farm in 1876, he carried it on until 1889, when he sold the property to his brother Leander, and bought a residence in the village. His law studies were pursued in the office of Le Grand Van Tyle, now District Attorney; and since establishing himself in practice he has built up a large business both in Conesville and Gilboa. In public affairs he has rendered able services to the town and county as Supervisor for eight years, acting as chairman of some of the most important committees. In politics he is a Democrat.

Mr. Cole married in 1873 Martha Leonard, daughter of Peter H. Leonard, formerly of Prattsville, and now of Bainbridge, N.Y. Mr. and Mrs. Cole have no children. They attend the Methodist Episcopal church.

DAVID T. SLATER, general merchant of Hensonville, in the town of Windham, Greene County, N.Y., was born in Jewett, July 24, 1839, son of Hugh and Sally (Woodworth) Slater. His parents were natives of Greene County, his father having been born in Cairo, and his mother in Hunter.

His paternal grandfather, Elihu Slater, who was born in Connecticut, came to Cairo as a pioneer, built a log cabin, cleared a farm, and tilled the soil during his active period. Grandfather Slater died at the age of seventy-three; and his wife, Sally Beach Slater, who was the mother of a large family, died at seventy-two years of age. They were members of the Methodist Episcopal church.

Hugh Slater, father of David T., was reared on a farm in Cairo, and resided there until twenty-one years old. He then went to Jewett, where he followed the occupation of a farmer until his death, which occurred at seventy-two years of age. In politics he was a Democrat until 1856, when he became a Republican, his views having changed on the slavery question. He held several town offices. His wife, Sally, was a daughter of Lemuel Woodworth, a prosperous farmer of this section. Four of the five children born to them are living, namely: David T., the subject of this sketch; Mary, who married Henry Whitcomb; Lydia, who became the wife of Anson R. Mott; and Dayton, who is a druggist in Hunter. The mother, Mrs. Sally Woodworth Slater, died at seventy-one.

David T. Slater began his education in Jewett, and completed his studies at Ashland Seminary. At the age of twenty-six he went to Cairo, where he followed farming and ran a saw-mill for six years, at the end of which time he sold his property and came to Hensonville. Purchasing an interest in a general store, he was a partner in the concern for twenty-two years, then becoming sole proprietor of the establishment. He conducts a thriving business here, carrying a large stock of dry goods, groceries, clothing, boots and shoes, patent medicine, hats, caps, and other wares.

In 1864 Mr. Slater was united in marriage with Miss Elizabeth Winter, daughter of Harrison Winter, of Jewett. They have had eight children, four of whom survive — Jonathan, Lilian, Dayton, and Eva. Jonathan married Laura Sherer. He is a minister of the gospel in Brooklyn, N.Y. Lilian is a pupil at a seminary in New York City, and the others are also attending school.

Since 1884 Mr. Slater has acted with the Prohibition party, and has been Inspector of Elections. He is a member of the Methodist Episcopal church, has been class leader, and also superintendent of the Sunday-school.

DUNCAN M. LEONARD, M.D., of Broome Centre, Schoharie County, was born in Roxbury, Delaware County, N.Y., August 27, 1837, son of Henry and Huldah (Hull) Leonard. His grandfather, John Leonard, was a native of Germany, being the son of an Englishman who settled in that country and married there. John Leonard, on coming to America, first settled at Black River, Vt., but later removed to Delaware County, New York, and was one of the first to make a clearing in Roxbury. He died in that town, August 23, 1826. He was an active member of the Baptist church. His wife, whose maiden name was Ruth Olmstead, died March 19, 1842. They had but one son, Henry, Dr. Leonard's father.

Henry Leonard was born in Roxbury, July 4, 1789. Succeeding to the ownership of the homestead, he gave his principal attention to dairy farming and stock raising, and through energy and thrift he realized good financial results. In politics he was a Whig. Henry Leonard died December 20, 1871. His wife, Huldah, who was born June 20, 1799, was a daughter of Seth Hull, of Hartford, Conn. She died September 10, 1864. They were the parents of twelve children, namely: Salina J., born October 5, 1820; John, born June 6, 1822; Peter H., born May 21, 1824; George H., born January 11, 1826; Daniel C., born September 16, 1827, died in July, 1897; Asa D., born September 4, 1829; Lucy, born March 13, 1832, who married John Weckle; Samuel W., born December 8, 1833; William H., born June 27, 1835; Duncan M., the subject of this sketch; Mary E., born April 25, 1839; and Charles K., born May 20, 1842. George H., who practised medicine, served in the Civil War, and died in Brooklyn, N.Y.; John, who became a surgeon of repute, served three years in the army, and owing to ill-health he subsequently engaged in farming; Peter H., Daniel C., and Asa D. were farmers; Samuel W. remained upon the homestead; and Mary E. married Christian Enderlin, of Roxbury. Charles K., while pursuing his medical studies, received injuries which later resulted in his death. Several of the sons taught school in their younger days. The father was a Baptist and a prominent church member.

Duncan M. Leonard completed his early education at the Roxbury Academy, and having begun his medical studies under the direction of his brother George, he attended the University Medical College, Castleton, Vt., from which he was graduated in 1857. Locating at Broome Centre on January 1 of the following year, he has resided here ever since, and although he has practised his profession steadily for a period of over forty years he still retains much of the vigor and activity which characterized his youth, and attends regularly to his every-day duties. As a physician he stands high in the community, his professional skill and reputation for promptitude enabling him to maintain among the well-to-do residents of this vicinity a practice sufficient to keep him constantly busy; yet he has never been known to refuse when called to attend the poor, from whom he could expect little or no compensation, and he has never instigated a law suit for the collection of fees. Prompted by the belief that good physicians are an urgent necessity to the welfare of mankind, he has not only directed the preparation of several students and provided for their personal wants during their preliminary studies, but has also assisted them in securing an adequate college training.

On January 1, 1860, Dr. Leonard married for his first wife Vashtie McHench, who died June 4, 1877; and on January 1, 1879, he wedded her sister, Emma J. Their father was William McHench, the son of John, who came from the north of Ireland, and was a pioneer farmer in this section. The family is of Scotch origin.

John McHench had a family of four children; namely, Submit, William, Catherine, and John. Submit married Benjamin Thornington. Catherine married John Goodfellow. William remained on the homestead, and John settled in another part of the town. William McHench, who was a prosperous farmer, took an active part in public affairs, and held some of the important offices in this town. In early life he was interested in military affairs, and acquired the title of

Captain. He was one of the leading members of the Christian church. He died at the age of seventy-seven years. William McIlench married Ann Ferguson, and was the father of nine children, namely: Willard, deceased; James R., deceased, who settled in Minnesota, and became wealthy; Nancy, deceased, who married Elder Brown, and had four children; Vashtie, Dr. Leonard's first wife; William and Wilson, twins; Andrew and Francis, also twins; and Emma J., Dr. Leonard's second wife. Of these, William, Andrew, and Emma J. are still living. William McIlench, second, was graduated from the medical department of the University of Michigan, and is now practising his profession in Brighton, that State.

Dr. Leonard is the father of four children, all by his first marriage, namely: Emma R., born October 19, 1860; Frances A., born September 12, 1863; Ursula J., born April 16, 1866; and Rutson R., born June 3, 1868. Emma R., who is a graduate of the State Normal School, Albany, is a successful school teacher. Frances is the wife of F. B. Mackey. Ursula J. married C. S. Best, M.D., who is practising in Middleburg, N.Y. Rutson R. Leonard, M.D., who is now located in Bloomville, Delaware County, New York, began his preparation under his father's direction, and pursued his advanced studies in the universities of Vermont, New York City, and Michigan.

Dr. Duncan M. Leonard cultivates a good farm, and is quite an extensive real estate holder, owning about seven hundred acres in all. He formerly acted with the Republican party in politics, but now votes independently. He belongs to the County Medical Society, and was at one time its president. For years he has devoted his leisure to reading, and has studied the natural sciences, including astronomy. In his religious belief he is a Baptist, and for many years has been prominently identified with that church.

ELI ROSE, former superintendent of the Howe's Cave Lime and Cement Company and proprietor of a general merchandise store, is now retired from business and residing at Central Bridge, N.Y. He was born in Maryland, Otsego County, N.Y., on February 20, 1840, son of Nathan and Deborah (Morehouse) Rose. He comes of English stock.

His paternal grandfather, Nathaniel Rose, probably a native of Massachusetts, said to have been the descendant of one of the early settlers of that State (whether of Thomas Rose, who was an inhabitant of Scituate, Plymouth County, before 1660, or of another emigrant, the present writer is unable to say), came to Columbia County, New York, in young manhood. From Columbia County Nathaniel Rose removed to Warren, Herkimer County, N.Y., and finally to Maryland, N.Y., where he spent the last years of his life. He started as a poor boy, but before he died he accumulated a large property, chiefly comprised in land. He was able to give to each of his six sons a fine farm, and then had some three hundred acres left for himself. Each son also re-

ELI ROSE.

MRS. ELI ROSE.

ceived a pair of horses, farm stock, and grain for planting. Nathaniel Rose was a Captain in the State militia. He died at the age of seventy-six years. His wife, who died at the age of seventy-five, was before her marriage Loviua Spencer. Her family were people of importance in Columbia County. She was the mother of eight children, all of whom married and had families. Both she and her husband were members of the Baptist church, and were active and liberal in their support of all church matters. So interested were they that they were instrumental in building a house of worship almost without assistance from others.

Nathan Rose, son of Nathaniel and father of Eli Rose, was born in Columbia County, New York, and was educated in the common schools there. Shortly after his marriage he settled upon the farm given him by his father, and there engaged in farming with great success. In time he developed dairying to some extent and also lumbering, carrying on in the last-named industry a very large business. He was active in town affairs and a liberal supporter of the Baptist church. He died at the age of sixty-nine. His wife, Deborah, who died at the age of eighty-one, was a daughter of James Morehouse, a farmer on an extensive scale, residing at Maryland, N.Y. Her grandfather, who lived to be eighty-five years of age, was one of the early pioneers of that place. Her father was killed when only thirty-four years old by being thrown from a horse. Her mother, whose maiden name was Jane Burnside, was born in Maryland and died at the age of sixty. She was twice married, and had five children by her first marriage and three by the second. All of them grew to maturity, but all are now deceased save one. Nathan and Deborah Rose were the parents of five children, namely: John J., of Maryland, N.Y.; Betsey, who is the wife of Harvey Baker, of Oneonta; Mary, who married Amos Graves, of Glens Falls, now deceased; Lovina, who is the widow of Nelson Goodrich, of Oneonta; and Eli, the special subject of this sketch.

Eli Rose received a public-school education, and subsequently assisted his father on the farm until about twenty-seven years of age. He also taught school for two terms. In 1867 he entered the employ of the Howe's Cave Lime and Cement Company, which had just been formed, as book-keeper. The following year he purchased an interest in the business, and he was afterward promoted through the position of foreman to general manager and treasurer. He had sometimes as many as eighty men under his charge; and, besides managing the lime and cement business, he operated a general merchandise store, which he started in 1868 and which is now one of the oldest in the county. In February, 1898, Mr. Rose sold all his interests at Howe's Cave to a wealthy syndicate, and removed to Central Bridge, N.Y., where he is now living.

A word in regard to the cement company with which he was so long connected may be interesting to the reader. This company was incorporated under the laws of the State of New York in 1867 by Hon. John Westover, of Richmondville, N.Y., Jared Goodyear, of Colliers, N.Y., and E. R. Ford and Harvey

Barker, of Oneonta, N.Y., as charter members and owners. The seventy or more acres of land owned by the company were rude and rugged in the extreme, and no appliances were at hand. But generous ledges of limestone gave promise of rich reward to those who should quarry it. Houses for the employees, barns for the work horses, shops, kilns, and mills were erected; and derricks, engines, and other appliances were brought here. Fortunately for the company, the line of the Albany & Susquehanna, now a part of the D. & H. C. Company, ran near — so near, in fact, that often in blasting large pieces of rock were thrown on the track. The ledge nearest the railroad, which is of dark blue limestone, is forty-four feet thick, and is composed, of course, of comparatively thin and light rock. Next above this is a ridge of gray limestone in massive blocks and of excellent quality and soundness, such as are eminently suitable for the construction of piers, abutments, canal locks, retaining walls, and all kinds of massive masonry. The lime produced in the kilns is very strong, adhesive, and of great durability. Its lasting virtue is well shown in the stone fort at Schoharie Court House, which was built more than a hundred years ago, and as yet presents no imperfection of either stone or mortar. Among the important structures in which this cement has been employed are the following: the new capitol at Albany; Holland House, New York City; the Scranton Steel Works; Troy Steel and Iron Works; and the reservoir at Fair Haven, Vt. As all the process of manufacture and the disposal of the output was under Mr. Rose's supervision until his recent retirement, no further commentary upon his ability both as an executive officer and as a financier is needed.

Mr. Rose was married in 1870 to Mary C. Warner, who was born in Richmondville, daughter of Henry Warner. Her father, a farmer, who was a descendant of an old and honored family, died at the age of seventy years. Her grandfather and great-grandfather Warner were both carried captives to Canada by the Indians and held there as prisoners for a year. Mr. and Mrs. Rose have one daughter, Sophina, who assists her father in the store. In politics Mr. Rose is a Republican. He is a member of the Lutheran church, and is a trustee of the society. His wife and daughter are also members of the church.

EDGAR HARTT, Greenville's veteran merchant, member of the firm of J. G. & E. Hartt, was born on Norton Hill in this town on January 2, 1828, his parents being John and Salome (Miller) Hartt. His paternal grandfather, Joseph Hartt, was a native of Dutchess County, New York. The maiden name of his grandmother was Polly Green.

John Hartt, the father, was born in Hartsville, Dutchess County, and was a shoemaker by trade. He came to Norton Hill in 1820, previous to his marriage, and carried on a successful business here during the remainder of his working life. He hired a number of hands, and did considerable custom work. His death occurred at the age of seventy-four.

He and his wife were members of the Christian church; and he was a Deacon and active worker in the church. The house of worship was four miles from their home. In politics he was a Republican. Mrs. Salome Miller Hartt was born in Dutchess County. She lived to be eighty-seven years old. Of her seven children, five are living, namely: Mary Ann, who resides in Greenville; Edgar, the direct subject of this biography; John G., a sketch of whose life appears below; William B.; and George A., who is in the employ of John G. Myers, of Albany.

Mr. Edgar Hartt received a practical education in the public schools of Norton Hill. His first business experience was in shoemaking, which he learned by working with his father. He followed his trade about nine years. The partnership with his brother was formed in 1856, at the old stand; and three years later the store where they are now doing business was built. It is doubtful if there is a single partnership in the State that has existed longer than this. Messrs. Hartt still buy goods in some instances of the firms from whom they bought when they began business. They carry a very complete stock of general merchandise, including dry goods, groceries, boots and shoes, ready-made clothing, hats and caps, crockery and glassware, oil cloth, hardware, grain, drugs and patent medicines, wall paper and stationery. The business has grown from year to year with the growth of the village, which has nearly doubled in size since they began.

In 1860 Mr. Hartt married Augusta Chapman, a native of Westerlo and daughter of Robert and Eliza Chapman, her father a blacksmith. Both her parents died at the age of eighty. They had three children, two of whom are living. Mr. and Mrs. Hartt have three children — Gertrude, Clara, and Henry G. Gertrude is the wife of G. W. Palen, a tanner residing in Western Pennsylvania, near DuBois. Clara resides with her parents. Henry G. Hartt is a partner in the firm of Colier & Co., dry-goods merchants at Coxsackie, where they carry on a most successful business. He married Grace Vanderburg.

JOHN G. HARTT, brother of Edgar and his partner, was born at Norton Hill on October 3, 1829. Upon leaving home and starting life for himself, he entered the employ of Thomas Saxon in South Westerlo. From that place he came to Greenville and began working for Mr. Bentley, with whom he remained for the next nine years, during the first three of which he worked for fifty dollars a year and found his own clothes. His hours were from six o'clock in the morning to nine o'clock in the evening, and he often had to work until midnight. His motto always was that, no matter how small an amount he earned, he must save a little; and he always kept to it. He left Mr. Bentley to join his brother in business, starting, as has been said, in the old corner store.

Mr. Hartt married in 1859 Jane A. Tallmadge, a native of Greenville, N.Y. Her father, Henry Tallmadge, a native of Poultney, Vt., was a physician by profession; but he came to Coxsackie, and engaged in mercantile business there. He died at the age of sixty-three. His wife, whose name before marriage was Jane A. Reed, was born in Coxsackie, and died in Greenville at the age of seventy-five. She bore him eight children. Mr. and Mrs. Hartt have only one child, Arthur, who is a merchant at Ravena, Albany County, this State, and Postmaster in that place. He was in the Greenville *Local* printing-office for nine years, and has taken an active part in politics. He married Rose Wilsey, and has one son, Harold.

Both John and Edgar Hartt are prominent members of the Republican party in this section. The former has been Town Clerk and Assistant Postmaster. Neither has cared for public office. Both are attendants of the Presbyterian church, and their wives and the three children of Mr. Edgar Hartt are members of the church. The brothers are among the best-known men in the county, and command universal esteem.

ALBERT G. ROSEKRAUS, Esq., a general merchant in Fulton, Schoharie County, was born May 5, 1837, in Berne, Albany County, a son of Holmes Rosekraus, M.D. His paternal grandfather, Henry Rosekraus, removed from Westerlo, N.Y., to Wright, Schoharie County, when in the prime of a vigorous manhood, and from that time until his death, at the age of fourscore years, was engaged as a tiller of the soil. His wife, whose maiden name was Holmes, also lived to be eighty years old, and dying left five children; namely, Holmes, Frederick, Henry, Phebe Flansburgh, and Mrs. Hungerford.

Holmes Rosekraus received his elementary education in the common schools of Albany County, and after reading medicine for a time with competent instructors, entered the Albany Medical College, from which he was graduated with the degree of Doctor of Medicine. Locating at once in Berne, Albany County, he built up a very large practice in that town and vicinity, and became one of its most successful and favorably known physicians. After an active practice of thirty years, he passed to the higher life, at the age of fifty-four. He was deeply interested in local affairs, and served a number of years as Town Superintendent. He was a regular attendant of the Baptist church, of which his wife was a consistent member. He married Melinda Weidman, one of the three children of Jacob Weidman, a prominent farmer of Berne. Twelve children were born of this union, and six of them survive, namely: Jacob; Albert, the special subject of this sketch; James, a professor of music, and a minister; Thomas; Washington; and Elizabeth. All of the children are gifted with exceptional musical talent, and all but two are quite noted throughout Schoharie County. The mother died at the age of seventy-five years.

Albert Rosekraus attended the public schools of Berne until ten years old, and then came to Middleburg, in this county, where he contin-

A. J. KERR.

ued his studies at the high school and academy, and also worked for a while as a clerk. Going then to Albany, he served an apprenticeship of two years and a half at the printer's trade; but, not liking it well enough to continue it, he returned to Middleburg, where he was subsequently employed as a clerk ten years. Coming in 1864 to Fulton, he bought an interest in his present store, and in partnership with Charles Watson carried on an extensive business for three years. The partnership being then dissolved, he returned to Middleburg, where for the ensuing three years he was engaged in mercantile pursuits in the store occupying the present site of Wellington Bassler's establishment. Disposing of his property there, Mr. Rosekraus then bought his present store in Fulton, and has since carried on a very large and successful business as a general merchant.

In politics he is prominently identified with the Democratic party, which he has served three years as one of the Democratic County Committee. He has been Justice of the Peace sixteen years, an office which he still holds, his present term not expiring until 1900. He has been Town Clerk two terms, and on three occasions has received the nomination for County Clerk. He was one of the promoters of the Fulton Valley Telephone Company, of which he has been a stockholder and a director several years. Fraternally, he is a member of Middleburg Lodge, No. 663, F. & A. M., which he assisted in organizing, and he was for some years the chorister. He belongs to the Reformed church. He has served a number of years as a Deacon of the church, and he was for a long time the organist and chorister. He has also been actively identified with its Sunday-school as a teacher and superintendent and as the leader of singing.

In October, 1858, Mr. Rosekraus married Margaret Zeh, daughter of Joseph Zeh, a well-known farmer and an old and respected resident of Seward. She died at the age of threescore years, leaving three children, namely: Pauline, a teacher in Fulton; Dora, who was also a teacher for some years, and now is the wife of J. Brewster, a farmer in Seward; and Ida, who is the wife of Edwin Lawyer, and has one child, Albert. After the death of his first wife, Mr. Rosekraus married Mary Follett, daughter of John Follett, a cooper, of Fulton, their union being solemnized in October, 1897.

ALBERT L. KERR, general merchant and Postmaster at Haines Falls, N.Y., was born in this village, September 18, 1862. He is the son of Robert and Margaret A. (Haines) Kerr. His father was born at Tannersville, and his mother was born at Haines Falls. His paternal grandfather, George Kerr, who was a native of Ireland, came to America at the age of fourteen, and later settled in Tannersville, where he followed farming. George Kerr died at the age of sixty.

Robert Kerr, father of Albert L., engaged in agricultural pursuits in this section when a young man, and before the advent of railroads ran a stage-coach to Catskill. Since 1891 he has resided here summers, and spent his winters in New York City. He is now engaged in selling Christmas trees, cutting and shipping them to the metropolis, where they find a ready market. In politics he is a Republican. His wife, Margaret A., daughter of Peter B. Haines, formerly of this village, is a descendant of John Haines, who went from Staten Island to Putnam County, New York, where he died in 1771. Elijah Haines, son of John, moved from Putnam County to Greene County about the year 1779, as a pioneer, and spent the rest of his life here; and her grandfather, Edward, who was born in Greene County, New York, became a prosperous farmer in this county. Peter B. Haines, father of Mrs. Kerr, erected the first dwelling on the site of the Catskill Mountain House. He followed farming. He also carried on a saw-mill, and was a useful citizen. He had a family of ten children. Robert and Margaret A. Kerr have two children: Gertrude, who married Cornelius H. Legg, of Haines Corners; and Albert L., the subject of this sketch. The parents were members of the Methodist Episcopal church.

Albert L. Kerr attended the common schools. At the age of twenty he took a clerkship in the post-office in this place, and later went to Tannersville, where he occupied the same position in the post-office under Mr. Mulford for three months (the fall season). In 1888 he engaged in general mercantile business on his own account at Haines Falls; and, the post-office having been removed to his store, he acted as Postmaster thirteen months. He then purchased the building in which he is now located. In 1898 he was appointed Postmaster, and in order to more conveniently handle the business, which is largely increased during the summer, he erected a special post-office building adjoining his store. This office transacts a large money order business, has eight mails per day, averaging five sacks of first-class matter and three of papers; and there are two regular mails on Sunday.

In 1888 Mr. Kerr married Belle B. Brewer, daughter of Nathan and Mary (Williams) Brewer, of this town. Her grandfather, Samuel Brewer, was born in Connecticut. Her father was a prosperous farmer here, dying at the age of seventy; and her mother, who was born in Colchester, N.Y., daughter of Thomas Williams, died at the age of forty-three. Nathan and Mary Brewer had four children — Charlotte, Belle B., Scott, and Mott. Charlotte married Norman Kerr. Mr. and Mrs. Albert L. Kerr have had four children, two of whom are living: Louis A.; and Harold Maine, who was born February 15, 1898, a day made memorable by the blowing up of the battleship "Maine" in Havana Harbor.

Mr. Kerr is a Republican in politics. He attends the Methodist Episcopal church.

JACOB VAN VALKENBURGH, M.D., of Sharon, Schoharie County, N.Y., was born in this town, June 13, 1839, son of Henry and Olive L. (Roth) Van Valkenburgh. His ancestors were Germans from the Lower Palatinate of the Rhine, or Pfalz, Germany. They came in the great Palatinate exodus about 1709. The original surname was

Falkenburg. Some members of the family wrote it Valkenburg, and about the beginning of the present century it assumed its present form, Van Valkenburgh.

Dr. Van Valkenburgh is a lineal descendant in the sixth generation of Arnold Van Valkenburgh, who came to America accompanied by his wife and one son, the latter being then eight years old. Arnold Van Valkenburgh resided in Ulster County, New York, from 1709 to 1713, when he came to Schoharie County, and acquired from the Indians a tract of land. His son, John Joseph Van Valkenburgh, also resided in this county. The latter, who was the great-great-grandfather of the subject of this sketch, served in the French and Indian War as an Ensign. He was also a private in Colonel Kilian Van Rensselaer's regiment in the Revolutionary War, and acted as a scout. He had three sons — Adam, Joachim, and Joseph. The second son, Joachim, was shot by an Indian at Jefferson Lake in this county.

The third Joseph, who was Dr. Van Valkenburgh's great-grandfather, was born in 1744. He and his two brothers served in the Revolutionary War as privates in a regiment commanded by Colonel Peter Vrooman. Joseph Van Valkenburgh was the first of the family to locate in Sharon. The farm he cleared is now owned by John J. Van Valkenburgh, a distant relative of Dr. Jacob Van Valkenburgh. The log house of the pioneer stood about one mile from his great-grandson's residence. Joseph Van Valkenburgh married Magdaline Brown, who was born in 1742. Their children were: Lana, Merie, Eve, Adam, John Joseph, Elizabeth, Nancy, Peter, Merie (second), Margaret, Jacob, Joachim, and Henry. Joseph, the father, died March 28, 1815.

John Joseph Van Valkenburgh, second, the Doctor's grandfather, was born in Schoharie, July 23, 1771. The greater part of his life was spent in Sharon, where he owned a well-cultivated farm of one hundred and forty-four acres. He was one of the founders of the Bellinger sect, being a Calvinist in religious belief. Of reserved disposition, he held aloof from public affairs. During the War of 1812 he was drafted; but, being unable to go to the front, he furnished a substitute. He died on his birthday, July 23, 1855. His wife, whose maiden name was Mary Bender, was born in Bethlehem, Albany County, N.Y., October 13, 1776, and died June 4, 1860. Their children were: Henry, Lana, Christian, William, Maria, John, Joseph, Stephen, and Elizabeth. Joseph served in the Mexican War, was wounded at the battle of Chepultepec, and subsequently drew a pension.

Henry Van Valkenburgh, Dr. Van Valkenburgh's father, was born in Sharon, May 14, 1798. He belonged to the Bellinger church, of which he was Elder for many years. Studying theology, he became an evangelist, in which capacity he was widely known throughout New York and New Jersey. He left the homestead after his first marriage, but continued to make general farming his chief occupation. He died in this town, April 18, 1866. For his first wife he married Rachael Bloomingdale, who was born June 19, 1803, and who died April 26, 1835, leaving one son, Henry H. The latter, when fifteen years old, went to reside with a bachelor uncle in the town of North Greenbush, Rensselaer County, N.Y., whose property he afterward inherited; and he became a prosperous farmer and dairyman. He married, and at his death left five children. For his second wife Henry Van Valkenburgh married Olive L. Roth, who was born in Massachusetts, July 31, 1810, daughter of Joseph Roth. She was a descendant of John Roth, an Englishman, who was the progenitor of a long line of physicians and surgeons of Uxbridge, England. Some of her brothers were well known as bridge-builders and mechanics. She was given a good education, and was particularly proficient in vocal music. She was reared a Calvinist in religion. She died August 23, 1874, having been the mother of four children — Jacob, Albert A., Joseph, and Emily. Albert A., who was a farmer, enlisted in Company E, Forty-third Regiment, New York Volunteers, with which he served in the Civil War for two years, at the end of that time being assigned to the invalid corps. He died soon after his return from the army. Joseph, who is a merchant in Canby, Minn., is married, and has a family of five children. Emily became the wife of David Ottman, of Cobleskill.

Jacob Van Valkenburgh began his education in the district schools, and at a later date studied the classics and high mathematics under the direction of a private tutor. He afterward attended the Troy Academy, then presided over by Professor Wilson; and his classical studies were completed at the Hartwick Seminary. He taught school for a time, and also studied theology and medicine, with the view of becoming a missionary, but finally gave his whole attention to medicine. Beginning the study of that profession with Dr. William H. Parsons, an eclectic physician of Sharon, N.Y., he later received instruction from Dr. Robert Eldredge, and acquired a knowledge of botanic medicine under Dr. John Praymer. He also studied two years with Dr. J. S. Herrick, an allopathic physician of Argusville, N.Y.; and he received his degree from the Eclectic Medical College of Philadelphia, Pa., known as the Paine School, January 22, 1862. Locating in Charleston, N.Y., in April of that year, during the first five years of his practice he was obliged to contend against the animosity then existing between the eclectic and regular schools of medicine; but the skill he displayed in his profession at length gained for him the recognition of his opponents, and he has since received honorary degrees from two medical colleges. In 1867 he moved from Charleston to Sharon, where he has a lucrative practice.

Dr. Van Valkenburgh was one of the organizers of the Eclectic Medical Society of the State of New York, being one of the charter members named in the article of incorporation by the legislature of the State. He was corresponding secretary of the society, and served on various committees. He was also one of the organizers of the Twenty-third Senatorial District Medical Society, now known as the Susquehanna District Medical Society, and was one of its censors. He has been health officer many years, acts as a Notary Public, and was a trustee of Slate Hill Cemetery. He was a trustee of the public school in his village for many years. He delivers extemporaneous address on public occasions, on patriotic, educational, or religious subjects; frequently lectures to various societies, and writes for the medical and secular press. A book-lover and a close student from his boyhood, he has gathered a large library, to which he makes additions every year. Never idle, he employs each moment in some useful occupation. He owns a farm, and is out of debt. In politics he was formerly a Republican, but supported the candidacy of William J. Bryan in 1896. While now a Populist, he loyally supports President McKinley and Governor Roosevelt.

Dr. Van Valkenburgh married Harriet Moulton, daughter of Gurdon Moulton, of Lykers, Montgomery County, N.Y., and of English ancestry. Mrs. Van Valkenburgh, who was a teacher in the public schools, died May 31, 1892. She was the mother of four children, namely: Emma, widow of Irving A. Parsons; Minnie, who married Charles Van Horne; Moulton, who died at the age of twenty months; and Flora, who resides at home with her father. The daughters are all graduates of the Cobleskill High School, and the first and second were teachers prior to their marriage.

Dr. Van Valkenburgh assisted in building the Methodist Episcopal church, which stands on land given by him for that purpose. He has served as steward and trustee and as superintendent of the Sunday-school. He is also a class leader, and acts as janitor without fee or reward. He is a Master Mason, having been a member for thirty years, or since 1869, of Cobleskill Lodge, No. 394, F. & A. M.

EDWARD A. GIFFORD, the well-known lawyer of Athens, N.Y., for six years District Attorney, was born in this town on December 22, 1856. He is a son of Alfred and Christina (Hollenbeck) Gifford, and grandson of Joseph Gifford, late a farmer in Rensselaerville, N.Y. His grandfather died at the age of seventy-four, and his grandmother died at the age of eighty. Their children were: John, Rufus, Abraham, Warren, Alfred, Margaret, Sophia, James, and Jeremiah.

Alfred Gifford was born in Rensselaerville, Albany County, and was reared on a farm there. Coming to Greene County in 1868, he settled in New Baltimore, where he remained ten years. After that he was in Coxsackie for ten years, and he then went on the road as agent for the Capitol City Iron Works Company of Albany. He has travelled all over the country in the interests of their business. His political principles are Republican. He and his wife are members of the Christian church, and reside in Philadelphia, Pa. Mrs. Gifford's parents were Abraham and Jane (Van Horsen) Hollenbeck, both of Dutch ancestry; and her paternal grandparents were Casper and Christina Hollenbeck. Her father was for many years one of the prominent men of Athens. He had several children. Alfred and Christina Gifford are the parents of five sons — Lawrence F., Edward A., Frederick W., George B., and William L. George B. and Lawrence F. Gifford are in Philadelphia. William L. and Frederick W. Gifford reside in Boston, Mass.

Edward A. Gifford was reared on a farm, and received his elementary education in the common schools, subsequently continuing his studies at home. Early in life he formed the resolve to achieve a prosperous career. He obtained a legal clerkship in the office of J. Washington Hiseerd, of Coxsackie, and during his three years' stay there gained much valuable knowledge and experience. He then entered the Law Department of Union University at Albany, N.Y.; and on January 25, 1884, four months before his graduation therefrom, he was admitted to the bar in Albany, passing a brilliant examination. Three years later, after successful practice of his profession in New York City, he abandoned it in order to accept a position as superintendent and general passenger agent and excursion agent of the Seneca Falls & Cayuga Lake Railroad Company, and of the Cayuga Lake Park Company at Seneca Falls, this State. These offices he held until October, 1889; and the following month he again took up the practice of law, settling in Athens.

In November, 1892, he was elected District Attorney, being the second Republican to hold that office in Greene County. Re-elected in 1895, he served until 1898, a period of six years in all. As District Attorney, Mr. Gifford won a high reputation for ability and conscientious devotion to official duty. He conducted without assistance the prosecution of George W. Hess, indicted for murder in the second degree for the killing of Hezekiah Bedell (a colored man); also of Pasquale Caserta, who was tried for murder in the second degree for the killing of his cousin, Joseph Caserta. In the first case he had against him the Hon. Jacob H. Chute and the Hon. Eugene Burlingame, of Albany, but secured the conviction of Hess. In the second case the accused was defended by Egbert Palmer, Esq., of Catskill; but again Mr. Gifford won his case, and convicted Caserta of murder in the second degree, as charged in the indictment. Both cases excited great public interest, and rank among the most celebrated criminal cases ever tried in Greene County. Mr. Gifford is at the present time attorney for the Union Commercial Co-operative Bank of Albany, for the town of Athens.

Mr. Gifford was married on June 22, 1881, to Ella J. Porter, of Athens, eldest daughter of Clark and Charlotte C. (Mead) Porter. Her paternal grandfather was Israel R. Porter, who died in 1874; and her maternal grandfather was Daniel Mead. Clark Porter was born in Schoharie County, but in childhood moved with his parents to a farm in the town of Athens, where he still resides. He is a prominent townsman, having been Supervisor, Inspector of Elections, and for fifteen or twenty years Assessor. They had a family of seven children; namely, Ella J. (Mrs. Gifford), Clark I.,

ANDREW RAYMOND

Oliver G., Lottie C., Addison W., William, and J. Melvin. All are living except William.

Mr. Gifford is a member of the Knights of Pythias Lodge, No. 129, of Athens, and Grand Master of the Exchequer of the Grand Lodge of the Knights of Pythias of the State of New York. He is also a member of the Catskill Tribe of Red Men, and of the Board of Trade of Athens, and is vice-president of the Electric Light Company of his town.

REV. ANDREW VAN VRANKEN RAYMOND, D.D., LL.D, president of Union University, Schenectady, was born at Vischer's Ferry, Saratoga County, N.Y., August 8, 1854, son of the Rev. Henry Augustus and Catharine M. Raymond. On the paternal side he is descended from a long line of American ancestors of English origin, the first of whom crossed the Atlantic in 1629. The grandfather was Clapp Raymond, a native of Norwalk, Conn.

The Rev. Henry Augustus Raymond, the father, was born in Patterson, Putnam County, N.Y., May 30, 1804. He was graduated at Yale University with the class of 1825; and, entering the ministry, he labored in the Dutch Reformed churches in New York State during the greater part of his active period.

Andrew Van Vranken Raymond completed the regular course of study at the Troy High School in 1871, was graduated from Union College in 1775, and from the New Brunswick Theological Seminary in 1878. His initial call was to the First Reformed Church in Paterson, N.J., where he remained from 1878 to 1881. He occupied the pulpit of Trinity Reformed Church, Plainfield, N.J., for the succeeding six years; and, accepting a call to the pastorate of the Fourth Presbyterian Church, Albany, he labored in that city for seven years, or until 1894. He was the ninth pastor of that church, and the fifth occupant of its pulpit to be selected for college work, having been chosen president of Union University in 1894. He was honored by his Alma Mater with the degree of Doctor of Divinity in 1887 and by Williams College with that of Doctor of Laws in 1894. He was elected moderator of the Presbyterian Synod of New York in 1891; was a commissioner to the General Assembly of the Presbyterian church for the years 1888, 1891, and 1893. He belongs to the Phi Beta Kappa and the Alpha Delta Phi Societies.

ELMER E. PELHAM, proprietor of "The Kenwood," at Haines Falls, town of Hunter, Greene County, N.Y., was born near Palenville, this county, August 30, 1863, son of Snyder and Christina (Saxe) Pelham. His parents are natives of the same town, and his grandfather, Peter Pelham, was a lifelong resident of the vicinity of Palenville. His father learned the trade of a blacksmith, which he followed near Palenville many years, and he is still living at his former place of business. He is a Republican in politics. His wife, Christina, was a daughter of Jeremiah Saxe, a farmer near Palenville. She is the mother of four sons, all of whom are living; namely, Jeremiah P., Harvey C., Elmer E., and Adam A. The parents attend the Reformed church.

Elmer E. Pelham was educated in the common schools of his native town, and remained at home until sixteen years of age. He then came to the Haines Falls House, where he was employed for twelve years, and at the expiration of that time he erected the present house, known as "The Kenwood," situated near the Haines Corners railroad station. It is located on high ground, is equipped with all modern improvements, and has accommodations for fifty people. Mr. Pelham has been in the boarding business nearly ten years, has been successful, and is well known throughout the county.

In 1888 Mr. Pelham was united in marriage with Elida F. Fatum, daughter of Henry Fatum, of Saugerties, N.Y. Mr. and Mrs. Pelham have one son, Fred E.

EDWARD ADAMS, wholesale and retail dealer in meat at Haines Falls, N.Y., was born in Durham, Greene County, February 1, 1838, son of Seymour and Maria (Chidister) Adams. His grandfather, Joseph Adams, who was a native of Connecticut and of English descent, carried on a farm in the vicinity of Hartford when a young man, later moving to Durham, near Cornwallville, where he spent some years, and then settled on a farm in Cairo, where he died at the advanced age of ninety-seven years. Grandfather's wife, with whom he lived for over seventy years, died at the age of ninety-nine years and six months. She was the mother of five children.

Seymour Adams, father of Edward, was born in Hartford, Conn., and was educated in the common schools. He began to support himself by conducting a farm on shares, later coming to Cairo, where he purchased a piece of property and rented it to the agricultural society. He was engaged in business in the village of Cairo for a time, and on relinquishing that he gave his whole attention to his farm, which was devoted to dairy purposes. For forty-four years he supplied the Catskill Mountain House with poultry, butter, and eggs. In politics he usually voted the Republican ticket, and was well known throughout the county. He was a charter member of the Masonic lodge in Cairo. His wife, Maria, was a daughter of William Chidister, of Kiskatom. Her father was a farmer, and in early life owned the property which was later purchased by her husband. The last years of his life were spent in retirement at Cairo, where he died at the age of eighty-two. Seymour and Maria C. Adams were the parents of five children; namely, Edward, Emily, William, Elizabeth, and Eliza. Emily married William Lewis, of Cairo, N.Y.; William resides in Rensselaer County, New York; and Eliza died at the age of thirty-five.

Edward Adams was educated in the common schools. He worked on a farm in Acra until his marriage, when he purchased a farm in Cairo, on which he followed farming until

1870. In that year he came to his present location, three and one-half miles from Tannersville, on the Little Delaware Turnpike, and started in the meat business, having as a sole customer the Catskill Mountain House, which he has supplied for the past twenty-eight years. As the hotels increased in number, he added to his list of patrons the Laurel House, the Hotel Kaaterskill, and others, his business becoming extensive. He supplied in 1898 two hundred and thirty-two hotels and boarding-houses, selling in five Saturdays, from July 30 to August 27, forty-four thousand eight hundred and ninety-seven pounds of meat. He runs three two-horse and two one-horse wagons, and employs seventeen men. He buys the choicest cuts of beef, slaughtered for him in New York, and uses about two carloads per week. He kills all the lamb and veal on his own premises, employing a buyer of live stock on the road, and keeps from ten to twelve tons of beef on hand at all times during the summer, his two refrigerators holding five hundred tons of ice. By adhering to the principle of fair dealing he has built up this large trade unaided. His residence, barn, ice-house, slaughter-house, and refrigerators were built under his personal supervision. He keeps ten horses and five wagons for delivering his meat. He also owns a farm of one hundred acres.

In 1859 Mr. Adams married Adelia A. Crary, a native of Delaware County, adopted daughter of Jacob Craft. They have three children: Jennie and Jessie, twins; and Ida May. Jennie married George White, a hotel-keeper near East Durham, N.Y., son of William White; and she has one son, Edward. Jessie married Sherwood H. Camp, a carpenter in Catskill, N.Y., son of Harmon Camp, formerly of Windham, N.Y., and has one daughter, Edna. Ida May married Joseph Hand, of New York City, formerly manager of Marlboro Hotel and now clerk for a broker in Wall Street. They have three children — Eva, Florence, and Joseph.

Mr. Adams is a Democrat in politics, and takes an active interest in political matters. He was Supervisor one term in Cairo, but refused a renomination. He is a charter member of Kademak Lodge, No. 693, F. & A. M., was Junior Warden when the lodge was first established, and is one of the few now living who organized the lodge. He is also a member of the Royal Arch Masons. He is liberal in his religious belief and a strict observer of Sunday as a day of rest.

CHARLES H. RAMSEY, president of the Howe's Cave Association, was born in Lawyersville, N.Y., on January 3, 1853, son of the Hon. Joseph Henry and Sarah (Boyce) Ramsey. He comes from a line of able and honest men and stanch Republicans. His great-great-grandfather was one of the pioneer settlers of Schoharie County. Frederick Ramsey, his grandfather, was born in Guilderland, and worked there for a time at his trade, which was that of blacksmith. He subsequently settled on a farm in Cobleskill, where he spent the rest of his life, attaining the age of seventy-eight years. He died at the home of one of his daughters. His wife, whose maiden name was Sarah Van Schaick, lived to the advanced age of ninety-four. She was a native of this county, and a devoted member of the Methodist church. Of their ten children, seven daughters and one son are living, the latter being Robert Ramsey, of Argusville.

The Hon. Joseph Henry Ramsey, for many years a leading citizen of Schoharie County, was born in the town of Sharon on January 29, 1816, and died in May, 1894. He studied law with Jedediah Miller, and was admitted to practise in all the courts of the State in 1840. Subsequent to this, he continued for some time in Mr. Miller's office, and eventually succeeded to his practice; but he afterward removed his office to Lawyersville, where he remained until his removal to Albany in 1863. In 1855 he represented the Northern Assembly District, having as his colleague from the Southern District, Wilkinson Wilsey. This was the last time the county was represented by two members. In the fall of that year he was sent as a delegate to the Whig State Convention, and was made a member also of the Joint Convention, composed of the members of the Whig Convention and a State convention of Free Soil Democrats, which formed the Republican party in this State. This was followed by his election to the State Senate the same year, as a Republican from the Seventeenth Senatorial District, which comprised Schoharie and Delaware Counties. In 1866 he was nominated as a candidate for Congress, but failed of election. In 1871, 1872, and 1873 he was a delegate from Albany to the Republican State Convention, and also a member of the Republican State Committee. He took an active part against Judge Barnard, who made the order in favor of Gould and Fisk, and secured his impeachment by the Senate, and the passage of a decree forbidding the judge to hold further office under the civil government.

Joseph H. Ramsey was a well-known railroad man, having been officially connected with a number of important roads. Prior to 1858 he was active in securing subscription for the building of the Albany & Susquehanna Railroad, and showed himself so efficient that in 1858 he was chosen director and vice-president of the company. This company was organized in 1852; stock had been subscribed along the line and at Albany to the amount of a million dollars; and the city of Albany had been authorized to loan the company, on certain conditions, another million dollars of its bonds. Work had already begun at different points in Albany, Schoharie, Otsego, and Broome Counties, but an unexpected revulsion occurred in railroad affairs, which rendered it difficult to secure further funds. This created an uneasy feeling among the stockholders, and they were glad to accept a proposal made by the Delaware & Hudson Canal Company, by which the Canal Company assumed the payment of the principal and interest of the bonded debt of the road, and the original stockholders were to receive semi-annual dividends of seven per cent. per annum. As this was a virtual sale of the road and its franchises to the Canal Company, Mr. Ramsey and others of the directors were opposed to it. They would have preferred to keep it independent of any coal or other company, to have liberal rates for transportation in order to have contracted upon the line the largest amount of business possible, and to have the original stockholders reap the full benefits accruing. As few roads in the State have been better paying property, it is seen to-day that his judgment was correct. After the execution of the lease, Mr. Coe F. Young, the general manager of the Canal Company, was elected president of the road in place of Mr. Ramsey. The latter was also president of the New York & Albany Railroad Company, and, subsequent to the death of the Hon. Erastus Corning, president of the Albany Iron Manufacturing Company. The furnaces of the last-named company in Albany were built during his incumbency. Mr. Joseph H. Ramsey was also president of the Howe's Cave Cement Company. His wife, who was born in Sharon and died in 1892, at the age of seventy-six, was one of seven children born to Daniel Boyce, farmer and miller of Shirley, and the granddaughter on her mother's side of Colonel Rice of Revolutionary fame. Of Mrs. Ramsey's seven children, three are living, namely: Harriet, who is the wife of the Rev. Pascal Harrower, pastor of the Episcopal church at West New Brighton, Long Island; Frances, who married Dr. H. A. Crary; and Charles H. Ramsey.

Charles H. Ramsey fitted for college at Williamstown, Mass. He was graduated at Cornell University in 1874, and from the Albany Law School in 1875, and the following year was admitted to the bar. Shortly after he came to Howe's Cave as secretary of the company, which had then just started. Upon the death of his father he was made president. He has watched the growth of the plant, and has been closely identified with its development. It is now one of the leading industries of the county, and when running full time employs one hundred and fifty men. Large quantities of lime, cement, and plaster are manufactured; also building stone.

Mr. Ramsey was married in May, 1879, to Annie E. Stevens, who was born in Sloanesville, daughter of Mark W. and Lucy (Phelps) Stevens. Her father, who died at the age of sixty-eight, was the president of Schoharie County Bank, and a very prominent man in his section. Her mother died when Mrs. Ramsey was twelve years old. Mr. and Mrs. Ramsey have four children — Margaret, Joseph H., Mark W., and Charles H.

Mr. Ramsey is a man of very varied business interests. He is director in the Schoharie and Otsego Insurance Company, of Cobleskill; president of the New York & Canadian Pacific Railroad, which runs from Ogdensburg to New York; trustee of the Cobleskill Cemetery, and member of the Schoharie County Historical Society. He is an attendant of the Reformed church, while his wife is a member of the Presbyterian church. Fraternally, he is a member of the Masonic Lodge of Cobleskill, and of John L. Lewis Chapter; also of the Kappa Alpha, which is the oldest college society in existence. As might be expected, his political principles are Republican.

DR. A. W. CLARK, a skilful dental practitioner and graduate optician, of Jefferson, Schoharie County, the founder and for some years editor and publisher of the *Jeffersonian*, now known as the Jefferson *Courier*, was born in Blenheim, N.Y., August 20, 1843, son of John A. and Catherine (Van der Vort) Clark.

His paternal grandfather, Randall Clark, came to this country from Rhode Island and settled in Blenheim, where he became quite an extensive farmer and land-owner. Randall Clark married Phœbe Dorcas Tucker, and his children were: Benjamin, Eliza, Alfred, John A., Stephen, Lucinda, Charles, Mary J., William, and Hilmer. Of these the only survivor is Eliza, who is residing in Rhode Island. Hilmer died while still young, and the other sons all engaged in farming.

John A. Clark, Dr. Clark's father, came to this county when a boy, and was reared at the homestead which he occupied in part until his death. He was prosperous as a general farmer, and at one time owned about three hundred and fifty acres of land. Politically, he was in his later years a Republican. He attended the Methodist Episcopal church, and was an earnest advocate of temperance. He lived to be sixty-six years old, and his wife survived him ten years. They were the parents of nine children, namely: A. W. Clark, the subject of this sketch; Alzada, wife of C. B. Atwood, a lawyer of Watertown, Conn.; Lindon, a resident of Blenheim; Le Grand and La Grange, twins, both of whom live at the homestead; Fremont, who resides in Delhi, N.Y.; John J., also a resident of that town; Ida, who married W. L. Cranch, and resides at Thompson, Conn.; and Ida Ursula, who died when about six years old.

A. W. Clark pursued his elementary studies in the common schools of Blenheim, and advanced in learning by attending the Stamford Seminary. After leaving school he went to Auburn, N.Y., with a view of engaging in business, but at the solicitation of Dr. A. A. Wood, who was then practising in Jefferson, he began the study of medicine in that doctor's office, and continued it for eighteen months. Failing health caused him to relinquish his studies, and while resting he determined to abandon medicine for dentistry. He accordingly became a student in the office of Dr. H. S. Wood, of Stamford, with whom he made rapid progress, and in 1866 he began the practice of his profession in Jefferson, where he has since resided. An experience of over thirty years has given opportunities for acquiring a varied knowledge of dentistry, and his business is both large and profitable. He has availed himself of all modern improvements in the way of appliances. He is a graduate of the National College of Electro-therapeutics, Lima, Ohio, which college conferred upon him the degree of Master of Electro-therapeutics (M.E.). He deals in dentists' supplies, and has travelled considerably in the interests of this branch of his business.

In 1871 Dr. Clark purchased a small job printing-office for the purpose of devoting his leisure moments to some useful employment, and engaged in the printing of small handbills, letter-heads, etc. He was shortly afterward requested by his fellow-townsmen to establish a newspaper, which he agreed to do provided a sufficient sum was raised to purchase a press. Although but half the necessary amount was subscribed, he determined to see the scheme through; and, making up the deficiency from his own pocket, he bought the desired machinery. Without knowledge or experience, he entered upon his new enterprise, to which he gave every moment of time that could possibly be spared from his professional duties; and as a result of his indefatigable labors the initial number of the *Jeffersonian*, the first newspaper ever issued in Jefferson, was delivered to the people on March 6, 1872. The paper was a success from the start, and its subsequent enlargement was made necessary to meet the demands of local advertisers. For about nine years its founder continued to edit and publish the *Jeffersonian*, which, under his management, performed its mission in an able manner. He contributed much valuable matter in connection with the publication of the Roscoe History of Schoharie County, and has since written for publication in the Jefferson *Courier* considerable historic matter, collected as far back as 1730, pertaining to the history of Schoharie County and the border wars of New York, giving a detailed narrative of many tragic scenes enacted on the frontiers of New York. He is now engaged in collecting dates and writing the history of the Clark family.

Dr. Clark married Sarah A. Phincle, daughter of William and Anna (Toles) Phincle. They have had two children: Sarah, who died in infancy; and La Mancha, who was graduated at the Pennsylvania College of Dental Surgery at Philadelphia in 1898, that college conferring upon him the degree of Doctor of Dental Surgery. He stood high in his class of one hundred and eight, of which he was the youngest. He married Florence Lilian Lee, of Glen Castle, N.Y., on February 8, 1899. He is a fine operator, gold fillings and crown and bridge work being his specialty. The young Doctor is now associated with his father in a large and successful practice.

As a progressive, public-spirited citizen the Doctor takes an active interest in public improvements, and is a stockholder in the waterworks. He belongs to the Masonic order and other organizations, and frequently attends the meetings of the State Dental Society. The family are all members of the Methodist Episcopal church.

WILLARD LARKIN, a practical and progressive farmer of Schoharie, N.Y., was born at Central Bridge, Schoharie County, October 3, 1860, son of John W. and Nancy M. (Enders) Larkin. His paternal grandfather, Daniel Larkin, a native of Rhode Island, was one of the pioneer settlers of Central Bridge, where he settled in early life, and prior to his death, at the age of seventy years, had redeemed a good farm from the forest. He was a strong Republican in politics, very influential in public affairs, and served several years as County Sheriff, being the only Republican in the county ever elected to that office. His second wife, Nancy Boyd, bore him three children, one of whom was John W., the father above named. Both Daniel Larkin and his wife Nancy were members of the Reformed church, in which he held most of the offices.

John W. Larkin completed his education at the Charlotteville Academy, and subsequently assisted in the care of the old homestead, which came into his possession after the death of his parents. He was a very energetic and thrifty farmer, successful in his undertakings, and he added to the improvements of the estate the fine set of buildings now standing. He died in the prime of life, at the age of fifty-six years. An unswerving Republican in politics, he served as Supervisor during four terms of one year each, at one time being chairman of the board, the only Republican in the county to hold a similar office. For several years he was one of the trustees of the Lutheran church, to which he and his wife belonged, and he was also a valued worker in the Sunday-school. He married Nancy M. Enders, daughter of Peter I. Enders, an extensive farmer and land-owner of Central Bridge. Of the six children born of their union four are now living, as follows: Willard, the subject of this sketch; Daniel; Mary K., wife of Frederick R. Farquher; and Delia B., wife of Robert S. Arcularius, of Brooklyn, N.Y. The mother died at the age of forty-six years.

Willard Larkin received his education in the common schools and at the Schoharie and the Claverack Academies. Returning to the parental home, he assisted in the farm work for several years, and helped to erect the present farm buildings. When ready to establish a home of his own, he bought his present farm of one hundred and five or more acres, which by judicious toil and superior management he has made one of the most valuable and attractive estates in this section of the county. A few years ago he rebuilt the house, barn, and out-buildings, which are commodious and well equipped. Since the death of his mother Mr. Larkin has managed the homestead property in connection with his own farm, having now the charge of two hundred and twenty-five acres of land, which he devotes to general farming, stock-raising, and dairying. In politics he is a strong Republican, and in 1896 was elected Commissioner of Highways for a term of two years.

On November 29, 1881, Mr. Larkin married Ruth H. Hoag, who was born in Sloansville, Schoharie County, daughter of John I. and Mary (Carr) Hoag. Her grandfather, David Hoag, was one of the earliest pioneers of that village, where he was long engaged in clearing and cultivating the land. He attained the age of eighty-nine years. John I.

CLARENCE L. BLOODGOOD.

Hoag carried on farming on the old home farm until his death, March 20, 1898. His wife, Mary, was born in Carlisle, and was one of the fourteen children of John and Eliza (Sweetman) Carr, seven of whom are still living. Ten children were born to Mr. and Mrs. Hoag. The two now living are: Mrs. Larkin; and her brother, George W. Hoag, a merchant in Sloansville. Their mother died at the age of fifty-six years.

Mr. and Mrs. Larkin's only child, John H., died when eleven years old. Mr. Larkin and his wife are prominent members of the Lutheran church at Central Bridge, of which he is treasurer, and both are teachers in the Sunday-school, in which Mr. Larkin has been superintendent for six years. Mrs. Larkin is president of the Home and Foreign Missionary Society of Hartwick Synod; and Mr. Larkin has been president of the County Union of the Christian Endeavor Society for five years, attending four meetings each year in different parts of the county. In 1895 he went as a delegate to the convention in Cleveland. Mrs. Larkin is a member of the local W. C. T. U.

CLARENCE E. BLOODGOOD, of the firm of Bloodgood & Tallmadge, Catskill's well-known attorneys, was born in Jewett on February 3, 1849, son of Jason and Lucinda (Coe) Bloodgood. His father, who is now, at the age of eighty-four, living retired in the village of Hensonville, is the grandson of William Bloodgood, one of the pioneer settlers of Conesville, Schoharie County, coming to that place from New Jersey and originally from Long Island.

William Bloodgood fought for American independence in the Revolutionary War. His wife, whose maiden name was Mary Dingle, was from New England. She died in 1833, surviving her husband sixteen years, his death having occurred in 1817. Their son, Lewis, the next in line of descent, was born in Schoharie County, and spent his life there in the town of Conesville, engaged in farming. He married Catherine Califf. He died about 1821, when his son Jason was a lad of six years.

Jason Bloodgood began his working life when very young. He was engaged for a number of years at farming and lumbering in his native town, and then he removed to a farm in Jewett, where he remained until 1887. Since that time he has resided in Hensonville. He is a Democrat in politics. His wife, Mrs. Lucinda C. Bloodgood, died in 1893. She was born in Jewett on October 1, 1809, being the daughter of Justus and Ruth (Bailey) Coe and one of a family of six children. Her father was born in Goshen, Conn., and came to Jewett in the early days of its settlement, finding his way thither by means of marked trees. There he spent the remainder of his days, making his home at first in a tiny log cabin and having but the barest necessities of life. He was a Deacon in the Presbyterian church, which he helped to build, and one of its active supporters throughout his life. He died at the age of eighty-four, and his wife died at the age of sixty-five. None of their seven children are living.

Jason and Lucinda C. Bloodgood were the parents of seven children, of whom six are living. These are as follows: Levi; Cyrus E.; Clarence E.; Tremain S., of Jewett; Mary, who is the wife of Mr. Van Valkenberg, of Catskill; and Isaac L. All the men of this family are prominent citizens in the towns where they reside. Three of the brothers have been Town Supervisors. Levi and Isaac are in partnership, and conduct the large general merchandise business at Hensonville. Levi and his brother Cyrus E. bought the business in 1868 of Messrs. Brown & Loughran, and were in partnership for seventeen years, when Cyrus sold his interest to the youngest brother. Levi Bloodgood married Kate Bedford, of Delaware County, and has two daughters: Lena, who was educated at Stamford Seminary, and is now a teacher of vocal and instrumental music; and Lettie, who is in school. He is one of the leading Democrats of his county, was Town Supervisor in 1890 and 1891, has been chairman of the Town Committee and many times a delegate to both town and county conventions. He is a member of the Methodist church and prominent in Sunday-school work. Cyrus E. Bloodgood is at the present time Clerk of Greene County. He was chairman of the Board of Supervisors of the county in 1882. Tremain is a farmer. For two years he represented his town, Jewett, in the Greene County Board of Supervisors.

Clarence E. Bloodgood in his early years attended the common schools, and subsequently a school at Jewett Heights. He then taught two terms in Jewett, and in 1869 entered Stamford Seminary. There he continued his studies until July, 1871, with the exception of one winter, during which he was teaching. In July, 1871, he took the examinations for Yale, passing through New York on the twelfth of the month, while the Orangemen's riot was in progress. In the fall of that year he entered the Freshman class, and in 1875 was graduated in the classical department, receiving honors. Among his classmates were the following-named men, who have since been distinguished in national life: John Patton, United States Senator from Michigan; Albert S. Jenks, recently elected Judge of the Supreme Court of the Second District of New York State; John S. Seymour, formerly of Connecticut, now of New York City, who was Commissioner of Patents under Cleveland's last administration; Edward S. Jones, First Assistant Postmaster-General under the same administration; Edward S. Atwater, of Poughkeepsie, candidate for Comptroller on the Democratic ticket in 1898; and Edward C. Smith, at present Governor of Vermont.

In the fall of 1875 Mr. Bloodgood was elected School Commissioner of the First District of Greene County; and this position he held for nine years. In 1879 he began the study of law in the office of J. B. Olney, of Catskill, and in January, 1885, was admitted to the bar. He immediately began the practice of law, and twelve years later formed the partnership with Mr. Tallmadge. The firm has one of the largest law libraries in the county, and its practice is very extensive. Both partners have a wide circle of acquaintance throughout this section of the State, and command universal confidence.

In 1891 and 1892 Mr. Bloodgood served as State Senator from the Fourteenth District, which then included Greene, Ulster, and Schoharie Counties. He was a member of the Judiciary Committee, of the Committee on Finance, and of the Committee on Canals, Roads, Bridges, and Poor Laws, and was chairman of the last two. He introduced some bills of importance, among others one that had been many times before presented and as often failed to pass. Against the opposition of members from large cities he secured the passage of the law, enlarging the scope of investments for savings-banks. Mr. Bloodgood believes in "sound money." He has been continuously active in all duties of good citizenship since he graduated from college. In 1895 he was chairman of the Democratic County Committee. He is at the present time a member of the State Committee for the Twenty-fifth Senatorial District. He has been a member of the State Bar Association since 1892. In 1897 he was elected vice-president of the association for the Third Judicial District of the State of New York, and last January was re-elected to the same position for the current year. In 1896 also he was appointed by the Secretary of the Interior special commissioner to investigate certain matters connected with the Osage Indians; but, as the acceptance of the position would require him to spend an indefinite time in the Indian Territory, he felt obliged to decline the honor. Mr. Bloodgood was married in 1892 to Josephine L. Case, of Catskill, daughter of Hiram Case. Mrs. Bloodgood was born in what is known as Potter's Hollow, Albany County. Mr. Bloodgood during the two years, 1895 and 1896, was president of the Rip Van Winkle Club, which is the leading social club of Catskill. He is secretary and treasurer of the Commercial Mutual Fire Insurance Association of Catskill.

DOW FONDA VROMAN, a leading citizen of Middleburg and representative of one of the oldest families in the county, was born in this town on a farm adjoining his present dwelling-place on November 14, 1831, his parents being Henry and Catharine (Hagadorne) Vroman.

The first title to Schoharie lands known to have been recorded was obtained by his ancestor, Adam Vroman, from the Indians, and has since been known as Vroman's land. It is located two miles south-west of Middleburg. The conveyance is dated Schenectady, August 20, 1711. Adam Vroman obtained a royal patent to these lands from King George on August 26, 1714. On March 30, 1726, he obtained a new grant from the Indians. Twenty families of Hollanders settled here, and there was considerable friction between them and the Palatinates before friendly relations were established. Adam Vroman was born in Holland in 1649, and came to this country with his father, Hendrick Meese Vroman, in 1670, settling first in Schenectady.

The father was killed in the massacre there in 1690. Adam's two brothers were named Jan and Bartholomew. He lived in Schenectady during the greater part of his life, and is buried there; but his death occurred in Middleburg in 1730, at the home of his son. He was three times married, successively to Engeltie Ryckman, Grietje Van Slyck, and Grietje Takelse Hemstreet. His first wife and her infant child were killed in the massacre.

Adam's son Peter was born in Schenectady on May 4, 1684. He came from that place, and settled in Middleburg, in the part now called Fulton, on the banks of the Schoharie River, where he cleared a large tract of land. His relations with the Indians were most friendly. He died in 1777. His wife, Grietje Van Alstyne, who was born in Albany of Dutch parentage, was the mother of twelve children, seven sons and five daughters.

Adam Vroman, second, son of the above named Peter, and great-grandfather of Dow F. Vroman, was born at Fulton on September 21, 1707, and died of consumption in 1754. Despite his feeble health, he was a man of much energy, and one of the most progressive farmers of this region.

Jonas Vroman, grandfather of the subject of this sketch, was born in Middleburg, now Fulton, on April 1, 1735, and died on April 16, 1804. Upon reaching his majority, he moved to the farm which adjoins Dow F. Vroman's property, and there built in 1792-93 the house, the main part of which is still standing. He was a lifelong farmer. His wife, whose maiden name was Deliah Hager, died in 1830, at the age of ninety-one. They were the parents of two sons.

Of these Henry, above named, was born on the farm his father had settled, and there he continued to reside thoughout his life. Upon the death of his father he came into possession of the property. He was a man of considerable prominence hereabouts, and was at different times Lieutenant and Captain in the militia. Both he and his wife Catherine were members of the Dutch Reformed church. The latter was a native of Middleburg, now Fulton, and daughter of John Hagadorne. She died at the age of seventy-nine; and her husband died on March 2, 1859, at the age of eighty-two. Of their family of ten children, three are living; namely, Dow Fonda, Adam, and Susan, who is the wife of Isaac Borst.

Dow F. Vroman received good mental training in the public schools, and resided at home with his parents until he was twenty years of age, at the end of which time he left home and travelled for about four years. Returning then to Middleburg, he purchased the farm of forty acres adjoining his father's estate, which has since been his home. In 1854 he married Margaret Smith, one of a family of ten children born to Martin Smith, a farmer of Albany County, New York. Of this union nine children have been born, namely: Eugene, who resides in Middleburg; Charles, who married Mary Best, and is engaged in business here; Henry, who is a farmer in California; Kate, who resides with her parents; Dow, a lawyer of Tonawanda, Niagara County, a graduate of Union College and Albany Law School;

Smith, an engineer in California; Margaret, who resides with her parents; Guy, who is a civil engineer, a graduate of Union College, Schenectady, in the class of 1898; and Roy, who is attending the high school. Mr. Vroman is a man of superior intelligence, and possesses a wide and thorough knowledge of men and affairs. He has made a careful study of the family history, and is an authority on all points connected with it. In politics he is a Democrat; but, although he is one of the leading men in his party, he has never cared to hold public office. In 1890, 1891, and 1892 he served as Supervisor of Middleburg. His wife and two daughters are members of the Reformed church.

CHAUNCEY W. HINMAN, attorney-at-law and Justice of the Peace, residing at Schoharie, N.Y., was born in Middleburg on June 4, 1835, son of John S. and Margaret (Pausley) Hinman. His grandfather, Justus Hinman, by occupation a mechanic, was a native of the State of Connecticut. He removed to Kinderhook, Columbia County, in this State, among the early settlers, and he lived there during the remainder of his life. He died at the age of eighty-one. His wife, who was before her marriage Alice Spencer, was also born in Connecticut. She lived to be eighty years of age, and reared a family of eight children. Of these only one son, Franklin by name, is living. Both parents were members of the Baptist church.

John S. Hinman was born in Kinderhook, and was brought up in that town. When a mere boy he left home, and for some years subsequently he journeyed from one place to another, until at length he settled in Middleburg and carried on wagon-making, later engaging in the practice of law. He became an attorney of some note, and continued practice for a quarter of a century. He was also Justice of the Peace for many years. In politics he was a Democrat. His death occurred at the age of fifty-six. His first wife, Margaret, the mother of Chauncey W. Hinman, was the daughter of Frederick and Christiana Pausley, the father a lifelong farmer and during his last years a resident of Middleburg. She was born in Schoharie, and died at the age of thirty-three. Of the six children born to her, four are living, the record being as follows: Chauncey; Charles; Helen, who is the widow of William Bouck; and Mary Jane, who is the wife of Jacob L. Zimmer, of Wright. Mrs. Margaret Hinman was a devoted member of the Methodist church. The second wife was a sister of the first, and she was the mother of John, Justice, Albert, Alice, and Catharine, of whom John and Justice are living. She died at the age of fifty-eight.

Chauncey W. Hinman attended the public schools until sixteen years of age, when he left home and went to work in Franklinton and Livingstonville, where he remained for a short time. He subsequently worked in Utica and elsewhere in Oneida County, in Albany, and in Ohio, as a clerk, and then returned to Middleburg, where he learned the harness-maker's trade, and subsequently carried on business until 1862, when he enlisted in Company D of the One Hundred and Thirty-fourth Regiment as a private. He was in active service, and through successive promotions rose to the rank of Second Lieutenant and finally to that of First Lieutenant. He was at Chancellorsville and at Gettysburg, and at Tilton, in the fall of 1864, was taken prisoner by the rebel forces. He was carried to Andersonville, and there for six months endured horrors worse than those of open warfare. From being a solid, well-built man weighing one hundred and sixty-eight pounds, he became reduced to a mere skeleton, and escaped death only by the fortunate circumstance of his release. He saw thousands of men breathe their last in the prison, victims of starvation and disease. The daily rations, which were never varied, were one-half pint of corn meal, the same quantity of beans, and one spoonful of molasses or two ounces of meat. To this was added, once in three days, a small tablespoonful of salt. Thirty men of Mr. Hinman's company shared the horrors of prison life with him.

With peace came his release and subsequent discharge from the army. Returning then to Middleburg, Mr. Hinman began the business of harness-making, but in 1867 he came to Schoharie and began the study of law. Two years later he was admitted to the bar, and at once formed a partnership with his brother, which continued until 1871. Since that time Mr. Hinman has been alone. He is the second oldest lawyer in practice in the town. For eight years he has been a Justice of the Peace and for many years a trustee of the Union School.

Mr. Hinman was married in 1872 to Alice ver Plank, who was born in Wright, a daughter of Alanson ver Plank and one of a family group of five children. Of this union six children were born, as follows: Nellie M., Douglas A., Herbert W., Mabel, Alice, and C. Ford. Nellie M., who is a graduate of Vassar College, is the assistant principal of the Union School. Douglas is a graduate of the Albany Law School and a practising lawyer in Berne, Albany County. Herbert W. is in business with a florist in Saratoga Springs. Mabel, who was educated at the Young Ladies' Seminary at Binghamton, is now in Europe. Alice is a student in the Union School, Schoharie. C. Ford Hinman is studying law in his father's office.

Mr. Hinman is an Odd Fellow of To-wosscholer Lodge, No. 546. He is a member and trustee of the Stock Growers' Association. He has a general law practice, and also acts as pension attorney. In politics he is a Democrat. Mr. Hinman and his family are members of the Methodist Episcopal church, and he is a trustee of the society. Both he and his wife have been teachers in the Sunday-school.

LA GRAND I. TREADWELL, a progressive farmer and prominent citizen of Jefferson, Schoharie County, N.Y., was born in Harpersfield, Delaware

JAMES T. WYATT.

County, this State, October 7, 1845, son of James T. and Eliza A. (Buckingham) Treadwell.

His father, James T. Treadwell, was a native of Harpersfield, N.Y., born August 6, 1812. He was one of the leading men of his town, where he held the office of Supervisor. He was also a Colonel in the militia. A stanch Republican in politics, he was a great admirer of Lincoln, Grant, Seward, and other great men of his party who had proved their fitness for high place by the magnitude of their services to their country. In religion he was a Methodist and a prominent officer of that church. His wife, Eliza, who was born in Jefferson, Schoharie County, July 14, 1811, was a daughter of Isaac and Sally Buckingham, her father being a prosperous farmer. She died in her native town, February 27, 1896, having survived her husband nearly twenty-five years, he having passed away April 26, 1871. Their children were: Orrin, Sarah, Cassius, La Grand, and Addie.

La Grand I. Treadwell received a good district-school education. He began early to acquire a practical knowledge of agriculture, and since his youth has been engaged in farming. His present farm of one hundred and ten acres is well located, and, kept by him in a high state of cultivation, it produces satisfactory financial results. Mr. Treadwell is a man of good business capacity, progressive in his methods, an untiring worker, and thoroughly wide-awake to every opportunity for the improvement of his property. That he stands high among his fellow-townsmen may be inferred from the fact that he has been called upon to serve them as Commissioner of Highways and as Supervisor. He attends the Methodist church. He belongs to the Masonic order, being a member of Lodge No. 554, F. & A. M., of Jefferson.

He married September 22, 1885, Miss Jeanette C. Grant, a native of Stamford, Delaware County, N.Y., and a daughter of Alfred B. and Maria A. (Davenport) Grant. Mr. and Mrs. Treadwell are the parents of one child, J. Logan Treadwell, who was born August 12, 1887.

JAMES T. WYATT, ex-Supervisor of Glenville and a veteran of the Civil War, was born in Halifax, N.S., October 22, 1834, son of John F. and Charlotte (Stewart) Wyatt. His father was a native of New Jersey, and his mother of Nova Scotia.

John Wyatt, his grandfather, who was born in Charleston, S.C., served in the Revolutionary War, and for some years was a planter in his native State. Coming North, John Wyatt resided in New York State for a time, but his last days were spent in Nova Scotia. The family is of English origin. Probably its first representative in this country was Sir Francis Wyatt, one of the early Colonial governors of Virginia, the first term of his wise and pacific administration beginning in October, 1621.

John F. Wyatt, the father of the subject of this sketch, was a carpenter, and followed his trade during his active years. Moving from Nova Scotia to New York State, he resided in Albany until going to Cattaraugus County;

and he died in Jamestown, Chautauqua County, at the age of eighty-three years. In politics he was a Republican. His wife, Charlotte, was the mother of seven children, four of whom are living, namely: John A. and James T., both residents of Glenville; Eleanor, wife of M. G. Martyn, of Jamestown; and William H. Wyatt, of Akron, Ohio. The others were: Eliza C., Harriet, and Adelaide. Mrs. Charlotte S. Wyatt died in Akron, Ohio, at the age of seventy-six years. In religious faith the parents were Episcopalians.

James T. Wyatt was reared in Albany and educated in the schools of that city. When a young man he entered the grocery business as a clerk, and remained in that employment for four years. In October, 1861, he enlisted as a private in an independent organization known as the Havelock Battery, which was raised in Albany, and became attached to the Army of the Potomac. He participated in some of the most stubbornly contested engagements of the Civil War, including the battle of Chancellorsville, where he was wounded, and rose to the rank of First Lieutenant, being discharged as such, January 24, 1865. The State of New York gave him the rank of Brevet Major. Returning to Albany, he in 1866 became travelling salesman for Burton & Co., dealers in mouldings, picture frames, and similar wares, and remained with that concern for eight years. In 1877 he bought his present farm in Glenville, containing one hundred and forty-two acres of desirable land situated in the beautiful and fertile Mohawk valley, one of the finest agricultural regions in the State. He displays unusual practical ability and good judgment in managing his property, which yields a good income, the energy of its owner being visible on every hand.

In June, 1867, Mr. Wyatt was united in marriage with Anna M. Rector, who was born in Glenville, May 25, 1835, daughter of William Rector and a representative of an old family of this town.

Politically, Mr. Wyatt is a Republican. He served with ability as Supervisor during the years 1882, 1883, 1884, and 1886. He is a comrade of Horsfall Post, No. 90, G. A. R., of Schenectady. Mr. and Mrs. Wyatt have no children. They attend the Episcopal church.

ERNEST E. BILLINGS, M.D., the leading physician of Gilboa, Schoharie County, N.Y., is a native of Broome, this State. He was born on September 29, 1859, to Peter L. and Amelia (Brayman) Billings. His great-grandfather Billings came to this place from Connecticut. He was of English ancestry.

The Doctor's paternal grandfather, John Billings, lived and died in this county, and was a lifelong farmer. His children were as follows: Thaddeus; Peter; Charles; William; Emma, who is the wife of Lewis Brazee; Ellen, who is the widow of Emerson Campbell; and Luther, who died at the age of twenty-one years. Charles and William Billings both reside in this county.

Peter Billings during the greater part of his active life was engaged in farming at Broome, but he lived for a time in Greene County. Politically, he was a stanch Republican. For a number of years he was Poormaster. He was a member of the old school Baptist church and one of its most zealous upholders. His four children were: Ernest E. and Erwin B., twins; Anna, who married Albert Palmer; and Burton, who died at the age of twenty-three years.

Ernest E. Billings during his boyhood attended school at Broome and subsequently at Rensselaerville Academy. In his early years he had access to a well-selected library, which probably in a measure determined the course of his later life. This library consisted largely of works of science and history. It had been accumulated by his maternal grandfather, Benjamin Brayman, who resided in Broome. Mr. Brayman was a genuine lover of books. Not a volume on his shelves but was one of value and standing, and not one that he had not read and digested. His memory for facts was wonderful, and no one hereabouts could equal him in extent of knowledge. He was extremely logical, and could floor any one in an argument. Withal, he was a successful man of affairs. At that time, when good books, or indeed books of any sort, were difficult to get, his library unquestionably exerted a great influence in moulding the future of his grandson.

After leaving school Ernest E. Billings taught for four or five terms, as also his twin brother, who subsequently obtained a State certificate. From boyhood it had been his ambition to be a physician, and accordingly, as soon as the opportunity presented itself, he began the study of medicine with his uncle, Dr. E. Brayman, of Livingstonville. After a year spent there he entered the medical department of the University of the City of New York in 1881, and in 1884 he was graduated at that institution with the coveted degree of Doctor of Medicine. While there he showed especial proficiency in mathematics and in microscopy. He was one of two to receive a certificate in the latter study. He immediately began the practice of his profession in Conesville, where he remained until October 5, 1887. Since that time he has been settled in Gilboa. The Doctor still has more or less practice in Conesville, and, in fact, in the four counties of Delaware, Greene, Schoharie, and Albany. His calmness at all times and his sympathy in the sick-room fortify him for attendance on the most serious or critical cases, and his warm heart and generous expression of feeling win for him the lasting gratitude of his patients and their friends. He has made a special study of the diseases of women and children.

Politically, the Doctor is a Republican. He was Town Clerk in Broome in 1882, and is at the present time Health Officer of Gilboa. Since 1890 he has been a member of the Dutch Reformed church. For two years he was a Deacon in the church, and for the last three years has been Elder. He is a Mason of Gilboa Lodge, No. 630, and at the present time secretary of the lodge. Professionally, he is a member of the Schoharie County Medical Society. He is one of the stockholders in the weekly paper published at Gilboa.

Dr. Billings married Carrie Richtmyer, daughter of Peter Richtmyer and descendant of one of the old and honored families of this vicinity. They have one child, Ernestine.

WILLIAM W. CHAPMAN, a practical and prosperous agriculturist of Fulton, Schoharie County, was born on the farm where he now resides, known as the Chapman homestead, November 14, 1846, a son of Jacob Chapman. His great-grandfather Chapman was one of the very early settlers of Columbia County, New York, where he owned an extensive tract of land and about sixty slaves.

William Chapman, the grandfather of William W., was born and educated in Columbia County, but afterward became a pioneer of Albany County, whither he removed with his family at an early day. He also was a slaveholder, and before his death, which occurred when he was but forty-seven years old, he had cleared a large farm, and had come to hold an important position among the influential men of the town of Rensselaerville, in which he had settled. His wife, whose maiden name was Eva Solpaugh, died at the age of seventy-five years, after rearing a number of children. In religion they were both of the Baptist persuasion.

Jacob Chapman was born in Rensselaerville, Albany County, where he resided until twenty-seven years old. Coming then to Schoharie County, he purchased one hundred acres of woodland, on which almost the only improvement visible was a small log house that occupied the site of the present substantial dwelling on the Chapman homestead, the house subsequently erected by him. He cleared a large part of the land he first purchased, and, having bought another lot of forty acres, carried on general farming and stock-raising with great success until his death, at the venerable age of eighty-seven years. In politics he was a Jacksonian Democrat, and served one or more terms as Overseer of the Poor. His wife, Huldah Winans, was the daughter of Elder John Winans, for many years a Baptist minister at Preston Hollow, Albany County, where she was born and bred. They had eleven children, eight of whom are living, as follows: Spencer, a farmer residing near the old homestead; Nancy C., wife of Chauncey Shattuck; Adam M., a farmer at Bouck's Falls; Maria, widow of the late Almon Mann; Isabella, wife of Hiram Eckerson; Elizabeth, widow of the late Dr. George Holmes; James P., former Supervisor of Middleburg; and William W., the special subject of this sketch. The mother also attained a good old age, passing away at the age of fourscore and four years. Both parents were members of the Methodist Episcopal church, in which the father served long and faithfully as steward and class leader. Their son Peter, who was graduated from the Normal School, and afterward attended private lectures and the Philadelphia Medical College, went West when a young man, and, settling in Iowa, was

BARNARD O'HARA

there engaged first as a teacher and later as a physician. He subsequently lived in Nebraska, and for six years was School Commissioner in Lincoln. Returning to Schoharie County, he practised medicine in Richmondville for six years, going from there to New Mexico, where he had a lucrative position in a government land office until his death, at the age of forty-nine years.

William W. Chapman succeeded to the ownership of the home farm of one hundred and forty acres, on which he has spent his entire life, being known throughout the community as one of its most skilful and thrifty farmers. Energetic and industrious, and well versed in the science of agriculture, he is meeting with well-merited success in his chosen vocation. In addition to raising the crops common to this region, he carries on to some extent dairying and the raising of draught horses, in which he has been somewhat interested. A firm supporter of the principles of the Democratic party, he takes an active interest in local affairs. He has served on both the Town and the County Committee and in 1891, 1892, 1893, and 1894 he was Supervisor, having been elected and subsequently re-elected three consecutive years by a large majority.

On November 21, 1877, Mr. Chapman married Emma Zeh, who was born in Middleburg, a daughter of Philip Zeh, a farmer. She died at the age of thirty-one years. She was a devoted member of the Reformed church. On December 29, 1886, Mr. Chapman married for his second wife Miss Keziah Hilts, who was born in Fulton, a daughter of Gideon D. and Elizabeth (Zeh) Hilts. Her father, a native of Wright, removed to Fulton when but sixteen years of age, and from that time until his decease, at the age of sixty-three years, was engaged as a tiller of the soil. He affiliated with the Democrats, and was active in public life, serving as School Commissioner in his district and as Supervisor of the town a number of years. His wife, Elizabeth, who was born in Middleburg, died in Fulton in 1891. Both were active members of the Reformed church. Of their eleven children five are still living, namely: George, who was graduated from Claverack College, and now resides in New York City; Jennie, who married Marcus Zeh; Jay; Keziah, now Mrs. Chapman; and Elizabeth. Mrs. Chapman is a graduate of the Albany Normal School, and has had considerable experience as a teacher, having taught in her native place and for two years in the Ulster Academy. Mr. and Mrs. Chapman have two children — Leo H. and Alice Irene.

BARNARD O'HARA, proprietor of the O'Hara House, Lexington, Greene County, N.Y., was born in Fishkill, Dutchess County, this State, June 1, 1816, son of Peter and Lucretia (Darbee) O'Hara. His father emigrated from Ireland in 1801, first locating in New York City and later in Fishkill, where he worked by the month on a farm. Peter O'Hara was subsequently engaged in farming in Westfield Flats, Sullivan County, and in Greenville village.

His first purchase was a small piece of land, which he later sold. He finally bought a tract of forty acres situated on the Durham line, where he resided for the rest of his active period. By his industry and thrift he was enabled to increase his property by the purchase of adjoining land, owning at the time of his death, which occurred at the age of eighty years, a farm of two hundred acres. He was a capable farmer, possessing excellent judgment in all agricultural matters, which enabled him to make good use of his resources and opportunities. Besides the raising and selling of farm produce, he distilled apple brandy, an agreeable and somewhat seductive beverage, known to residents of the present day under the more familiar name of apple-jack. He was also a weaver of great renown. Peter O'Hara was a Democrat in politics, and took a lively interest in local public affairs, serving frequently as a grand juror at Catskill and holding minor town offices. In his religious belief he was a Roman Catholic and so true a follower of the precepts of the church that on one occasion he carried a child from Fishkill to Troy and thence to Lansingburg in order to have it baptized by a Catholic priest. His wife, whose maiden name was Lucretia Darbee, was a native of Goshen, Orange County, to which town her parents had removed from Goshen, Conn., settling as pioneers. Her father was a farmer and a cloth dresser for some years. Later he kept a tavern in Westfield Flats. He was killed by the overturning of a load of hay. Peter and Lucretia (Darbee) O'Hara had fifteen children, of whom six sons and seven daughters lived to have families; and six of the daughters were school teachers previous to their marriage. The only survivors are: Barnard, the subject of this sketch; and Levi, who still resides upon a portion of the old homestead, which, after the father's death, was divided into four farms. The mother died at the age of sixty-four. She attended the Methodist Episcopal church.

Barnard O'Hara in his boyhood and youth, from the time he was able to be of use, worked on the home farm during the farming seasons, and attended school winters.

Leaving home at the age of twenty-one, he went to Albany, N.Y., where he obtained employment in a dry and fancy goods store. His employer failed a short time later, and he made an arrangement with the assignee to peddle the stock upon the road. After driving through Central New York with a horse and wagon in the employ of others for some time, he invested what money he had saved in a team of his own; and, borrowing the sum of three hundred dollars of his father, he engaged in peddling for himself, soon establishing his credit in New York City by punctually meeting his obligations. After continuing upon the road some years, or until 1845, he settled in Lexington, where in the following year he completed the building of a store, which he stocked with general merchandise, and carried it on successfully for over thirty years. For a long period he was also engaged in the undertaking business.

After visiting some of the Western States he returned, feeling certain that his future prospects were just as promising in Lexington as elsewhere. The succeeding ten years were devoted to the management of his store and to the cultivation of his farm, which he purchased in 1865, and which he still owns.

In 1880, having admitted his son as a partner, he severed his active connection with the mercantile business. The son continued in charge of the establishment until 1888, since which time the store building has been leased to others.

The O'Hara House stands upon a site formerly occupied by a Baptist church. It was completed and opened in 1877, and is one of the largest hotels in Lexington, having accommodations for one hundred and twenty-five guests. Situated at an altitude of sixteen hundred feet above sea level, and provided with ample facilities for comfort and recreation, it offers special inducements as a health resort.

In 1845 Mr. O'Hara was united in marriage with Miss Charlotte Briggs, daughter of Darius Briggs, a well-known farmer of Lexington in his day. She became the mother of seven children; namely, Mary A., Edgar B., George P., Arthur, Arrietta, Ida, and Belle. Mary A. is the wife of James M. Van Valkenburgh, a hotel proprietor of Lexington, and has one son, George B. Van Valkenburgh, who is a college graduate. Edgar and George assist their father in carrying on the O'Hara House. Edgar also carries on a thriving business in the manufacture of cider. George O'Hara married Mary Smith, and has two children — Charlotte and Edgar L. Arthur O'Hara died at the age of two years. Arrietta died in 1876 at the age of twenty-one years. Ida married Peter J. Kelley, who is now a resident of New York City. Belle is residing at home. Edgar is a graduate of Manhattan College, New York, and of Eastman's Business College, Poughkeepsie; and George took a commercial course at Folsom's Business College. The daughters attended "Kenwood," a Catholic school in Albany. In politics Mr. O'Hara is a Democrat. He served as Supervisor in 1869 and 1870, receiving at his re-election the unanimous support of both the Republican and Democratic parties. He has been Clerk of the town and of the school district, and has frequently served as a grand and petit juror. Mrs. O'Hara died in December, 1880, aged fifty-four years. The family attend the Roman Catholic church.

JOEL H. MEAD, M.D., Hunter's veteran physician and surgeon, residing on Main Street in that town, was born in Jewett on June 15, 1838, his parents being Stephen and Caroline (Hosford) Mead. The family is of English descent, and early settled in Columbia County, New York, among the pioneers of that region.

Philip Mead, the Doctor's grandfather, was one of the first settlers in Jewett, coming to that town by a route marked with trees, and in company with two or three other young men settling in the heart of the forest to make a home for himself. His first dwelling was a rude log hut, but after he had made a clearing he erected a handsome frame house. The nearest town, Cairo, was ten miles distant, and all supplies had to be brought from that place. Bears and other wild animals were abundant, and fearlessly prowled near the little cabin. After eighteen years spent in Jewett, during which he had cleared a large tract of land, he removed to Cayuga County, then just being opened up. There he remained until his death, at the age of seventy-eight. His wife, Hannah, died at the age of eighty. Both were members of the Baptist church. Mrs. Hannah Mead was born in Columbia County, of parents who were pioneer settlers there. She had twelve children, all of whom are now deceased.

Stephen Mead was born in Columbia County, but the greater part of his life was spent in Jewett, where he purchased a farm in early manhood. In national politics he was a Republican. He took a warm interest in local public affairs, and held several minor offices in the town. His death occurred at the age of eighty-six. His wife was born in Jewett, being a daughter of Joel Hosford, who married a Miss Mann. Her father was one of three brothers who came from the town of Wallingford, Conn., to settle the town of Jewett. One of the brothers was named Reuben. They were pioneers of Jewett Heights. The Mann family was one of the first to settle on Manhattan Island, coming over from Holland. Mrs. Caroline Hosford Mead died at the age of sixty-seven. Both she and her husband were members of the Methodist church. One of their four children, a son, Alanson, is deceased. The living are: Dr. William H., who is practising in Windham (see sketch on another page); Dr. Joel H.; and Adeline, who is the wife of Alanson Woodworth.

After leaving the common schools Joel H. Mead studied medicine for a time with Dr. F. H. Holcomb, of Windham, and then took a course in medicine in the Albany Medical College, from which he was graduated in 1863. He at once began practice in Hunter, and in a short time had as many patients as he could care for. Besides his general medical practice Dr. Mead has given considerable attention to surgery, and has performed some remarkable operations. For twenty years he was the only physician in this and several of the adjoining towns. He is to-day one of the oldest practitioners in the county, there being only four physicians whose professional career antedates his. He is the Nestor of the medical fraternity hereabouts.

In 1866 Dr. Mead married Lucinda Woodworth, daughter of Abner and Sophronia (Judson) Woodworth. Her father, who was a farmer and one of the early settlers of Jewett, died at the age of seventy-eight. Her mother died at forty-six. Their six children were: Laura, who married Albert Chase, a son of Judge Chase of the Supreme Court; Buel; Lucius, a sketch of whom appears elsewhere in this book; Lemuel, who died at the age of twenty; Loren, who is deceased; and Mrs. Mead. The Doctor and his wife have been blessed with two children — Edith and Bertha, the last named of whom resides with her parents. Edith married R. A. Austin, a druggist of Cairo, and has one child, Joel by name. The daughters received their finishing educa tion in a private school. Both are fine performers on the organ and piano.

The Doctor takes a warm interest in all public matters, and gives the weight of his political influence to the Republican party. In 1887 he filled the office of Supervisor. He is a Master Mason and member of Mount Tabor Lodge of Hunter. He was a promoter, from the start, of the Maplewood Cemetery organization, and has always been one of its active supporters. In connection with Dr. Stanley he is pension examiner for Greene County, holding the position under government appointment. He is now president of the Board of Examiners. He has also been examiner for several years for various life insurance companies, among which may be named the Phœnix, the New York Life, the New York Mutual, the Equitable, and the Washington. The Doctor's family are members of the Methodist church.

WALLACE W. CRAPSER, a well-known business man of the town of Summit, Schoharie County, residing at Charlotteville, was born in Jefferson, this State, on April 12, 1842, his parents being Robert and Rosetta (Gardner) Crapser. His paternal grandfather, Albertus Crapser, who was of Dutch lineage, died in Claverack at the age of seventy. He was by occupation a farmer, and in politics at first a Whig and later a Republican. He had a family of five sons and four daughters.

Robert Crapser, son of Albertus and father of the subject of this biography, was born and reared in Greenville, N.Y., but moved to Claverack in early manhood. He was first a Whig in politics and later a Republican, and was very active and influential in public affairs. When about sixty years of age he was drowned while sailing on the Hudson as a passenger aboard the Berkshire boat. In early life he taught school for some time during the winters, and worked at boating during the summers. Later he gave all his time to farming. At the age of thirty he married Rosetta, daughter of Andrew Gardner. She is still living at the age of seventy-eight, and makes her home with her son Wallace. The father had at one time two hundred acres of land under cultivation. He was a Justice of the Peace for many years. His religious preferences were Lutheran. He had only one other child beside his son Wallace — namely, Jesse, who was taken prisoner by the rebels at the battle of Gettysburg, and who subsequently died from the hardships of his prison life, being still under his majority at the time of his death.

Wallace W. Crapser received a good common-school training in Summit. He early began farming, and engaged in that occupation until 1894, being located about a mile above the village of Charlotteville on a farm of a hundred acres, and giving special attention to dairying. On the 1st of April, 1897, he practically retired from business. Mr. Crapser is one of the valued workers of the Methodist church, with which he has been connected for the last twenty years. He is a trustee and steward of the church, also class leader; and for three years he was superintendent of the Sunday-school. In politics he is a Republican, but he has never sought office, though warmly interested in the success of his party.

Mr. Crapser was first married to Mary J. Whorton. She died in 1891, having been the mother of two children, namely: Albert, who died at two years of age; and Charles, who resides with his father. Mr. Crapser married for his second wife Mrs. Mary Multer Dorwin, the widow of Philip Dorwin. Her former husband was a lawyer and a leading citizen of South Worcester, also a prominent Democratic worker. She is a daughter of J. D. Multer, a very successful dairy farmer of this region and a strong Republican and active Methodist. Mrs. Crapser has four sisters, namely: Martha, who is the wife of James Fox; Alice, who is the wife of Thomas Spangler; Elizabeth, who is Mrs. Bulson; and Rose, who is Mrs. Calvin Butts. Mrs. Crapser taught school for some time before her marriage. She is a member of the W. C. T. U. and one of the active workers in the church. Mr. Crapser has always been opposed to the liquor traffic, and is exceedingly temperate in all his habits.

HOWARD EATON LOMAX, M.D., the leading physician of New Baltimore, Greene County, N.Y., is a native of the city of Albany, and was born on April 30, 1868, son of John and Martha (Eaton) Lomax. On the paternal side he is descended from French Protestants, or Huguenots, who, after the revocation of the Edict of Nantes in 1685, fled from persecution in their native country to England.

The Doctor's paternal grandfather emigrated from England some time after his marriage, and, settling in Boston, Mass., there engaged in the manufacture of soap and tallow candles. His son John was born in England, but was brought up in Boston, and learned the harness-maker's trade in that city. Nearly forty years ago John Lomax, the Doctor's father, took a position with Holland Terrell, the well-known harness manufacturer of Albany, and is now foreman of the establishment, which is said to be the largest of its kind in the world. He is an active Republican, and he takes a warm interest in all Masonic affairs. Among the Masonic offices he has held may be named the following: Master of Mount Vernon Lodge, F. & A. M., in 1870; secretary of the same for fourteen years; director in the Masonic Relief Association of Albany, and one of its trustees for fifteen years; and secretary of the Masonic Veteran Association for three years. His wife, Martha, was born in Chelsea, Mass. She is a member of the Episcopal church. Of their eight children five are living — Ella, Hattie, Fannie, Howard E., and Edith. Ella is the wife of Harry Knight, of Denver, Col.; Hattie is the wife of C. W. Forman, of Yorktown, N.Y.; Fannie is Mrs. Charles A. Pray, of Lebanon, Me.; and Edith is principal of the Albany Training School for Teachers.

Dr. Lomax was graduated from the Albany High School in 1888. He subsequently engaged as a draughtsman in New York City for a year with Gillam, the celebrated cartoonist of *Judge*. He then entered the Albany Medical College, from which he was graduated in 1892, and he has since been engaged in the practice of his profession in this town. During his first year in the high school he was awarded a gold medal for excellence in drawing, being the first boy and the first Freshman to receive a medal in the history of that school. He still retains much of his early skill with the pencil. The Doctor's course in the medical college was one of distinction. He won two prizes, and at graduation received honorable mention in three subjects. Since coming here he has built up the largest practice the town has ever known, and is as popular as he is successful. He has been three times vice-president of the Greene County Medical Society, and has written numerous papers and addresses on medical subjects, and some articles for publication in medical journals. He is a devoted student of natural history, and has a fine entomological collection, also an interesting collection of snakes and serpents.

Dr. Lomax is a fine singer and a skilful performer on the piano, organ, and flute. He began playing the flute in early boyhood, under the instruction of his father, who was a fine flutist and a member of Gilmore's celebrated band when first it was organized. When a boy of only sixteen the Doctor was in demand for orchestras. As he became older his musical ability was of great service to him, enabling him to pay his college expenses. For two seasons he performed on one of the day boats running from Albany, and in the evenings played in the orchestra at the Leland Opera House. For two seasons he was at Saratoga in the orchestra and for two seasons at the Prospect Park House in the Catskills. He has played under all the leading conductors of Albany, and is well known among the musicians of that city.

Like his father, Dr. Lomax is interested in masonry. He is now serving his second term as Master of Social Friendship Lodge, No. 741, of New Baltimore, and has held various other offices in the lodge, among them that of Senior Deacon. In politics he is a Republican. For the last four years he has been one of the health officers of the town. He is a Deacon in the Dutch Reformed church, of which both he and his wife are members, and Mrs. Lomax has played the organ for both church and Sunday-school.

The Doctor's marriage took place in September, 1897. Mrs Lomax is the daughter of Newton Sweet, a leading citizen of New Baltimore. Her grandfather, Joshua Sweet, who was born in Chesterville, Albany County, was a carpenter by trade. He worked on the old Catskill Mountain House, and later came to New Baltimore and engaged in contracting and building until his death, at the age of sixty-eight. His wife, Laura Baker, died at the age of seventy-four. She was one of the eight children of an Englishman who came with his family from England to Philadelphia, from there by stage to New York, thence up the Hudson to Albany, and thence by stage to Coeymans. He engaged in mercantile life in

New York City, and there fell a victim to small-pox. Joshua and Laura Sweet were the parents of three children: Frank; Newton; and Laura, who married Watson Ham.

Newton Sweet was born in this town on December 16, 1848. After attending Coeymans Academy for four years, he began teaching school winters and working at carpentering summers. This he continued till twenty-four years of age, when he left off his trade and thenceforward kept at his professional work all the year. He taught successively in the graded school at the Iron Works, Troy, where he remained five years; in the graded school in Coeymans; in New Baltimore for a year; and then, in the year 1893-94, in West Coxsackie. While at New Baltimore he was elected Supervisor for 1887 on the Republican ticket. The following year he was elected School Commissioner from the Second District of Greene County, which included the towns of New Baltimore, Coxsackie, Greenville, Durham, Ashland, Windham, and Prattsville. He had eighty schools to look after and a hundred teachers to examine, and must visit each school twice a year. After serving three years he was re-elected for a second term, at the close of which he began teaching in West Coxsackie. At the end of a year there he was secured for the New Baltimore school, but while attending a teachers' institute in Cairo, where the Republican convention was in session, he was nominated for the Assembly. He was triumphantly elected by a majority of four hundred, going ninety ballots ahead of the ticket in this town, and being the third Supervisor ever elected on the Republican ticket in this Democratic stronghold. He voted for the Raines Bill, and in 1897 was re-elected by a majority of five hundred and fifty. During his two terms he rendered his constituents valuable service. He introduced a bill to prohibit vivisection in the public schools, and served on various educational committees.

Mr. Sweet has resided in New Baltimore village for the last eighteen years. He is prominent in Masonic circles and in the Knights of Pythias. His wife, Adelaide, was born in Coeymans, the daughter of Philip and Jane (Van Allen) Winne. Mr. and Mrs. Sweet have five children — Frank, Jane (Mrs. Lamox), Laura, Isaac, and Arba. Frank is the foreman of Cushman's bakery in New York City. He married Marietta Vanderpool, daughter of Dr. A. V. S. Vanderpool, of this town. Isaac has been for the last three years quartermaster on the "Dean Richmond." Arba is preparing to be a locomotive engineer.

Mrs. Lomax taught school in New Baltimore with most flattering success for some time before her marriage. She is a fine musician. The Doctor and his wife have one son, Edmund W. Lomax.

WILLIAM E. THORPE, of Catskill, N.Y., member of the firm of Malcolm & Co., was born in Conesville, Schoharie County, on November 15, 1869, his parents being Douglass and Catherine H. (Ingraham) Thorpe. His paternal grandfather, Amos Thorpe, was born in the town of Broome,

WILLIAM E. THORPE.

Schoharie County. He was a blacksmith by trade, and worked at that occupation all his life. He also did some farming. The death of Amos Thorpe took place in Conesville.

Douglass Thorpe was born in Conesville on March 9, 1832. He worked somewhat in the smithy with his father, but when about nineteen years of age began learning the carpenter's trade. Subsequently he went to Dyberry Falls, Pa., to assist in putting up a tannery, and after it was completed he returned to Conesville and settled on a farm. While there he was twice Supervisor of the town. In 1881 he came to Catskill, and for the two succeeding years was in the grocery business in company with a Mr. Bassett, under the firm name of Bassett & Thorpe. Upon his retirement from business he was made Superintendent of Streets, which office he filled for two years. More recently he has been in poor health. He is a trustee of the Methodist church, and both he and his wife are members of it.

Mrs. Catherine H. Thorpe was born in Durham, and spent her life there until she was eighteen, when she removed to Conesville. She taught school from the time she was fifteen years old until she was married, at twenty-two. She has been the mother of two children — William E. and George N., the last-named of whom resides on a farm in Conesville. Mrs. Thorpe's father was Ezra Ingraham, son of William and Hester (Doty) Ingraham. Her mother was Charlotte Newell, daughter of Seth Newell, a soldier of the War of 1812, who contracted disease while in the service and died from its effects. William Ingraham, her grandfather, was born in Saybrook, Conn. He came to Durham among the early settlers, and had a grant of a small farm, but worked most of the time at his trade, which was that of a cooper. He died at the age of eighty. His wife, Hester, who was born in Saybrook, Conn., died at fifty-five. William and Hester (Doty) Ingraham had ten children, all of whom are now deceased. Their son Ezra was born in Durham. He was a shoemaker by trade, but much of his life was spent on a farm in Conesville, where he died at the age of fifty-six. His wife, who died at the age of eighty-two, bore him three children, of whom only Catherine (Mrs. Thorpe) is living.

William E. Thorpe attended school in Conesville until he was about twelve years old, when the family removed to Catskill. Here he entered the high school. At seventeen he had finished his studies, and entered the employ of Smith & Forshew, dry goods merchants, with whom he remained for a year. At the end of that time he took a position as book-keeper with Van Brocklin & Co. in the Catskill Knitting Mill. When, nine years later, Mr. Van Brocklin retired and the Malcolm Company was formed, Mr. Thorpe took an interest in the business, this being in January, 1897. The annual output of this mill is valued at between two hundred and fifty thousand and three hundred thousand dollars. Woollen underwear is manufactured, also men's dress shirts. This firm is one of the pioneer concerns in the making of fleece-lined goods. That its product bears a solid reputation in the market may be gathered from the fact that during all the recent business depression the mill has been running steadily and often over hours. Sales are made through the company's agents direct to the jobbing trade, and there is not a State in the Union that does not purchase goods of Malcolm & Co. One noticeable thing in the history of this business has been the cordial feeling between the employers and the workmen. Mr. Thorpe began work in the office at six dollars a week, and had his salary increased from time to time until it reached twenty-four dollars a week. He forms a striking example of what can be accomplished by faithfulness and application.

In March, 1898, Mr. Thorpe was chosen Trustee of Catskill and after one year President of the village. His politics are Republican. He is a member of Catskill Lodge of Masons, No. 468, and its organist; a charter member of the Catskill Royal Arch Chapter; member of the Order of Odd Fellows, Lodge No. 189, in which he has occupied the Noble Grand's chair; and also a member of the Rip Van Winkle Club. For two years he was a choir leader in the Methodist church, but he now holds membership in the Reformed church. For five years he was a member of the Sixteenth Separate Company, N. G. S. N. Y., and for two years, or until his discharge, a member of the First Ambulance Corps. He has always shown a warm interest in the fire department, and is at the present time president of Wiley Hose Company and vice-president of the Hudson River Volunteer Firemen's Association. He is a singer of unusual merit, and has sung on many public occasions. While in the employ of Mr. Van Brocklin, Mr. Thorpe was the recipient of many handsome presents, being remembered most generously on each recurring Christmas.

BENJAMIN F. AND WILLIAM C. PLATNER, of Prattsville, N.Y., are sons of Cornelius and Laura (Parmentier) Platner. Their paternal grandfather was a native and lifelong resident of Hudson, N.Y.

Cornelius Platner was born in Prattsville in February, 1821. He learned the trade of hatter, which he followed here for many years, first as a journeyman and later in company with Theodore Rudolph, as a member of the firm of Platner & Rudolph. Their shop was at one time destroyed by a flood, but they rebuilt it, and subsequently continued the business. Their partnership being finally dissolved, Mr. Platner opened a restaurant in the building now occupied by his sons, and carried it on for some time. He held quite a prominent position in the community, took an active interest in town affairs, and served several years as Deputy Sheriff. He was also active in military matters, and was connected with the militia in the early training days. In politics he was a Democrat.

His wife, Laura, was a native of Tannersville, N.Y., and a daughter of Winthrop Parmentier. Their family consisted of ten children, of whom six are now living, five being residents of Prattsville; namely, Charles H.,

Chester A., Joseph E., Benjamin F., and William C. Charles H. Platner is the proprietor of a general store in Prattsville. Chester A. is engaged in the feed business, and has also a large interest in the Stanley Hall farm of five hundred acres. He keeps one hundred cows, and deals largely in cattle, besides having other extensive business interests. Joseph E. is a druggist in Prattsville. Gustavus A. is a farmer residing near Ashland. Mrs. Laura Parmentier Platner died in 1895, at the age of seventy years.

Benjamin F. and William C. Platner were educated in the public schools of the village, and have always resided here. They formed their copartnership February 1, 1885, both having had some previous experience as clerks. They have since conducted a very thriving general mercantile business. Their store, of which they are the owners, stands on what was formerly the old Platner homestead, and measures fifty by fifty feet, exclusive of the house and store-rooms. They carry the largest stock of general goods in this section, their boot and shoe department being the largest between Kingston and Catskill. They have been very successful, and their business is continually on the increase. Quiet, unassuming gentlemen, they enjoy a wide popularity.

Mr. William C. Platner married on June 5, 1895, Miss Marion Becker, of Grand Gorge, an estimable lady, the daughter of Thomas and Elizabeth (Wyckoff) Becker, then of that place, but now of Stamford village. He is a Democrat politically, but hitherto has declined office, preferring to give his undivided attention to his business. He was formerly interested in the then proposed Kingston & Utica Railway, being secretary of the company. He is a member of Oasis Lodge, No. 119, F. & A. M., which he joined in 1888, and in which he has filled some of the chairs, being now Senior Warden. He and his wife belong to the Reformed church, which they attend and help support.

ARTHUR HENRY FARQUHER, late a well-known furniture manufacturer and dealer of Schoharie, N.Y., was born in the town of Berne, in Albany County, this State, on October 27, 1840, and died at his home in Schoharie, a few weeks since, August 9, 1899. He was a son of James and Margaret (Clark) Farquher. His paternal grandfather, John Farquher, was a butcher by trade, and was engaged for a time in the market business in Ireland. In 1830 Grandfather Farquher came to America and settled in Berne, N.Y., where his son James had preceded him.

James Farquher was born in Ireland, and remained in that country until after his marriage. He was educated in the public schools there, and subsequently engaged in the market business until he purchased a farm. Believing that the New World offered great opportunities to the industrious and enterprising, he came over to this country with his wife and one child, and eventually met with the success he had hoped for. At first, however, it was an uphill road to climb. When he arrived in Albany he found that his money had given out, and he was obliged to walk from that city to Rensselaerville. After prosperity came to him, he bought a farm, and there lived until his death, at the age of eighty-two. He made many friends in his adopted country, being highly respected by his fellows on account of his industry and honesty. He was at first a Whig and later a Republican; and he was warmly interested in the Presbyterian church, of which his wife was a member. Mrs. Margaret Farquher was born in Ireland, being the daughter of a farmer and one of a family of five children. She lived to be seventy-six years of age. She was the mother of thirteen children, of whom nine grew to maturity, namely: John; William; Joseph; Jane, who is the widow of Daniel Carey; Elizabeth; Arthur H.; Thomas; Mary, who is the wife of Rensselaer Taylor; and Francis.

Arthur H. Farquher spent his boyhood years in Berne, attending the public schools, and during vacation time assisting his father on the farm. In 1857, at the age of seventeen, he left home and went to Gilboa, where he served three years' apprenticeship at the cabinet-maker's trade, and subsequently remained a year as journeyman.

On September 25, 1861, Mr. Farquher enlisted in the military service of his country, and on the first day of the succeeding October was assigned to the United States Lancers. On November 2 of the same year he was transferred to Company B of the Fourth New York Heavy Artillery, and while a member of that company saw some of the hardest fighting that occurred in the whole course of the Civil War. The following are among the engagements in which he took part: battle of the Wilderness, on May 6, 1864; Todd's Tavern, on May 8; Hart's Farm, May 9; Spottsylvania Court House, May 12; North Anna River, on May 23; Sheldon Farm, on May 30; Cold Harbor, on June 3, 1864; Petersburg, on June 18 and July 30, 1864; Deep Bottom, on August 14; Ream's Station, on August 25; Mile Run, on December 9, 1864; Hatcher's Run, on February 5, 1865; assault on the lines, on March 25; opening the campaign, on March 28, 29, and 30; South Side Road, on April 2. He was at Appomattox at the time of the surrender of Lee, April 9, 1865. Mr. Farquher went into the service as a private, and came out of it as a Sergeant. The Colonel of his regiment was Colonel John C. Tiddball, and the Lieutenant Colonel, Thomas Alcott. D. F. Hamlin was the Major. The detachment of which Mr. Farquher's company formed a part left Washington for the front with twenty-two hundred men, and in five months' fighting, from March 23 to August 25, lost eighteen hundred. In one engagement of an hour's duration sixty men of his own company fell. Mr. Farquher was one of those who escaped unhurt. He seemed to bear a charmed life, and was not even wounded. The terrible slaughter at Petersburg he never forgot. It stood out among many other scenes of horror as the most direful of all.

Returning to Gilboa, after being discharged in October, 1865, Mr. Farquher worked for his old employer until the fall of 1866, when he came to Schoharie, and began working for a man who was located in the same building in which he, Mr. Farquher, subsequently carried on business. In 1874 he became a partner, and a year later the firm changed and became Farquher & Settle, which was in business for two years and a half. Mr. Farquher then took his first partner, who remained with him for some seven years. At the end of that time Mr. Farquher became full proprietor of the business, and henceforth he continued it alone. Occupying the four floors of his large building, he carried a very large stock of furniture, and had an extensive trade. After 1893 his manufacturing of furniture was confined mostly to custom work of the highest grade. The business has been established here for over fifty years, and has always merited the full confidence of the public. As a consequence its fair reputation has spread, and its patrons have come from long distances. The undertaking department has also been long established here, and is the only one in town.

Mr. Farquher was married to his first wife in 1865. She was Maria C. Benjamin, daughter of Ebenezer Benjamin, a farmer of Gilboa. In religious faith she was a Methodist. She died at the age of thirty-one, having been the mother of three children; namely, Fred R., Minnie E., and Benjamin J. Fred R., who married Mary R. Larkins, is a furniture dealer and undertaker at Central Bridge. Minnie married Robert A. Dewey, cashier in one of the Schoharie banks, and she is the mother of one son, Arthur. Benjamin J. was his father's assistant. He is an enterprising and able young man, and bids fair to equal his father in business ability. Mr. Arthur H. Farquher married for his second wife Ida M. Schoolcraft, who was born in the town of Wright, being one of a family of five children of Peter P. Schoolcraft, a farmer. She died at the age of thirty. She was a member of the Lutheran church. The present Mrs. Farquher was before her marriage Amanda Wright. She is a daughter of Ezra Wright and a native of Albany County.

In politics Mr. Farquher was a Republican. He was a trustee of the village for eight years, and at the time of his death was still serving as president, having held the office for four years. This is a strongly Democratic town. Mr. Farquher usually refused public office, but at one time, in order to gratify the wishes of the party leaders, he permitted his name to be used on the Republican ticket for Supervisor, and thereby reduced the Democratic majority from three hundred and sixteen to thirty-five. He was a member and for three years was treasurer of Schoharie Valley Lodge of Masons, No. 491, having held also numerous other offices in the lodge. For twenty-nine years he was a member of the fire department, and much of the time either foreman of the company or chief engineer of the department. He took an active part in all movements affecting the interests of the town and was one of those foremost in securing the incorporation of the village. He was a member and had been Commander of Hoosick Mix Post, No. 134, G. A. R.; also a member for many years of the Schoharie County Historical Society. He was an attendant of the Lutheran church of this place, and his son is Deacon of the church.

WILLIAM JAMES SMEALLIE, a thrifty farmer of Princetown, Schoharie County, N.Y., was born in this town, May 10, 1852, son of John and Jane (Milmine) Smeallie. His father was born here March 3, 1816, and his mother was born in Florida, N.Y., March 26, 1816. His paternal grandfather, James Smeallie, was born in Linlithgowshire, Scotland, April 18, 1786, and came to America in 1811. James Smeallie settled upon a farm in the northerly part of Princetown, where he resided the rest of his life. He was quite prominent in public affairs, serving as Supervisor and School Commissioner, and he was one of the founders of the United Presbyterian Church of Florida, N.Y. He married his cousin, Mary Smeallie. She was the daughter of his uncle, John Smeallie, first, a native of Scotland, who came to this country and served as a soldier in the Revolutionary War.

John Smeallie, second, son of James and Mary, was a prosperous farmer and lifelong resident of Princetown. Being a man of progressive tendencies, he made good use of his resources, and realized excellent results as a general farmer. In politics he was originally a Whig and later a Republican. He was a member of the Scotch church. Jane Milmine Smeallie, his wife, became the mother of three children, namely: Mary E., wife of John M. Conover; William J., the subject of this sketch; and Agnes Smeallie, of Princetown. John Smeallie, second, lived to be seventy-five years old, but Mrs. Smeallie died at thirty-eight.

William James Smeallie was educated in the district schools. He resided in Duanesburg for ten years, but with that exception has been engaged in general farming in Princetown ever since reaching manhood. He is now the owner of one hundred acres of fertile land, comprising one of the best farms in town. He makes a specialty of breeding Jersey cattle and fancy poultry, owning at the present time some fine specimens of each, and his buildings are well adapted for these purposes.

Mr. Smeallie has served with ability as Excise Commissioner twelve years, and is now holding the office of Overseer of the Poor. In politics he acts with the Republican party. The family has long enjoyed local distinction for thrift and prosperity, and the subject of this sketch has fully demonstrated his ability to maintain this reputation. Mr. Smeallie is unmarried. He attends the United Presbyterian church, of which he was elected Elder in 1883.

BENJAMIN H. AVERY,* an enterprising merchant of Jefferson, Schoharie County, and an ex-member of the New York State legislature, was born in Jefferson, December 29, 1852, son of Beriah and Lydia (Buckingham) Avery. His immigrant progenitor, Christopher Avery, came over from England early in the Colonial period, lived for some years at Gloucester, Mass., and was Selectman there in 1646, 1652, and 1654. In March, 1658-9, Christopher Avery bought land and one-half of a house in Boston, situated where the post-office now stands. This property he sold in 1663, and in 1665 he bought a house and lot in New London, Conn., his son James having moved to that colony some years before.

From Christopher the line is traced through James, Thomas, Abraham, William, Benjamin, John, and Beriah to Benjamin H., the subject of this sketch. The original dwelling-house, built by Captain James Avery in 1656 in what was formerly New London and afterward Groton, Conn., was burned in July, 1894. Some of the Avery ancestors fought in the Revolutionary War, and a monument to their memory has been erected by John D. Rockefeller, the Standard Oil magnate, who is related to the family.

John Avery, the grandfather, who was a tanner, served in the Assembly in 1850, and held other offices. Beriah Avery, Benjamin Avery's father, was engaged in mercantile business in Jefferson for a number of years, and was quite active in public affairs, serving as Supervisor with marked ability. He was a member of the Methodist Episcopal church. His wife, Lydia, who was a daughter of William Buckingham, of Harpersfield, became the mother of four children — William, Benjamin, Mary, and Edward. William, who succeeded to his father's business, died in 1876, aged about twenty-six years; and Mary and Edward died in early childhood. Beriah Avery died in 1891, at the age of sixty-seven years, his wife having died one week previous.

Benjamin Avery attended school in Charlotteville for a time, and completed his studies at the Stamford Seminary. Going to River Falls, Wis., he was employed there as a clerk until 1876, when he returned to Jefferson, and purchased the business left by his brother William. He has one of the largest and oldest established general stores in town, and ranks among the substantial merchants in this part of the county. As a member of the Board of Supervisors he was active in forwarding the interests of the town. In the legislature he introduced no less than twenty-four bills, fourteen of which became laws. He was assigned to the Committees on Internal Affairs, Villages, Fish and Game, and Agriculture, being chairman of the first-named body; and his work in the committee-room and upon the floor was heartily commended by the majority of voters, irrespective of party. Politically, he is a Democrat. He has been treasurer of the water company since its organization, having been instrumental in securing the construction of the works, and he was a director of the old railroad line.

Mr. Avery married Anna D. Fuller, daughter of J. Dean Fuller, of Jefferson. They have two children — William H. and Edna B. For twenty-two years Mr. Avery has been a member of the Methodist Episcopal church, in which he has served as steward and Sunday-school superintendent for a greater part of that time. Mr. Avery is an Odd Fellow, belonging to Richmondville Lodge, No. 525, and is also a member of the band, of which he has been leader for a number of years. Mrs. Avery is a member of the church and of the Woman's Christian Temperance Union.

JOHN MAGINNIS,* superintendent of the Athens Knitting Mill, was born in Gilboa, Schoharie County, on June 5, 1849, son of Patrick and Mary (Brady) Maginnis. His parents were both born in Ireland.

Patrick Maginnis was a tanner by trade, and followed that occupation after coming to this country and settling in Gilboa. He retired from business at about fifty years of age, and died about ten years later. His wife, who was also born in Ireland, died at sixty-six. Of their ten children four are living; namely, Bernard, Anna, John, and Mary. Anna is the wife of James Fitzpatrick. Mary married James Mitchell, since deceased. All the children were born in this country.

John Maginnis remained in his native place up to the age of nineteen. He received his early education in the public schools and at a seminary, and subsequently studied with private teachers and also in an evening school. His first industrial experience was in the cotton sheeting mill in Gilboa, and while there he worked in every department. His second was in the Harmony Mills at Cohoes, where he worked ten years as overseer in the weaving room. Following this he was for ten years in the Van Allen Cotton Mills at Stuyvesant Falls, five years in Valatie as superintendent of the Wild Manufacturing Company, and seven years superintendent of the Harder Knitting Company in Hudson. At the end of that time he settled here in his present business. He was one of the organizers of the company, and he superintended the building of the mill and the putting in of the machinery. The factory is two hundred and twenty feet long by fifty-five feet in width, and is two stories high. It has six sets of machinery, all of which are made after the most improved plans, and is devoted to the manufacture of fleece-lined knitted underwear. About one hundred and fifty hands are employed, all of whom are hired and superintended by Mr. Maginnis. He attends to the disposing of the output of the mill, sending goods to every State in the Union.

Mr. Maginnis has been twice married. His first wife, whose maiden name was Libbie Sparlin, was born in Hensonville. Her father was Philip Sparlin, a hatter. She died at the age of thirty-two, having been the mother of two sons — William and Byron. The former, who is a baker in North Adams, Mass., is married and has three children — Willie, Helen, and John. Byron is also married. He is an engineer in the fire department of Cohoes. Mr. Maginnis's second wife was before her marriage Emma Peck. She was born in Craigsville.

Mr. Maginnis is a Republican in politics. He served as Alderman from Ward Five in Hudson. He has always been a most success-

JOHN McGINNIS.

ful man, and since he began working has never been without a position. On account of his skill in his chosen line he has frequently been solicited to enter positions more profitable than the one he was holding when asked. In Cohoes he was one of thirteen to help put up the machinery, and was engaged as overseer. While in Stuyvesant Falls he introduced new machinery into the mill, and remodelled the old, so that the output of the mill there was largely increased.

Mr. Maginnis has been a member of the Methodist church for twenty years. Both his wives have also been members. In whatever town he has been living, he has taken an active part in all church matters and in the Sunday-school. While in Hudson he had charge of the prison work of the Young Men's Christian Association. He has been a trustee of every church with which he has been connected, and in Stuyvesant Falls and Valatie was superintendent of the Sunday-school.

CAPTAIN JAMES STEAD, superintendent and manager of the Catskill and New York Steamboat Evening Line at Catskill, N.Y., was born in Cairo, this State, on May 23, 1832, his parents being David and Hannah (Mackelwaite) Stead.

The father, David Stead, was born in Huddersfield, England, and in early life was employed there in a woollen manufactory. He came to America when forty years of age, and settled in Cairo, where he bought a farm. For a time he carried on a woollen manufactory in Woodstock, a part of Cairo, but he subsequently closed out the business and engaged in farming. He died at the age of eighty, after having lived retired for some time in the village of Cairo. He was an old-time Whig, but though warmly interested in all public affairs was never an aspirant for office. His wife, Hannah, who also was of English birth, died in Cairo at the age of seventy-nine. She bore him four children, of whom there are living -- James, John, and Levi. John, who resides in Cairo at the old homestead, carries on a boarding-house; Levi is in business in Chicago; and Charles is deceased. Both parents were members of the Episcopal church.

James Stead left home at eighteen years of age, and went to work as clerk in the office of Penfield, Day & Co., who managed a steamboat line between New York and Catskill. In time he rose to be a captain, and he was in their employ in that capacity for several years. Subsequently, for three years, he was captain of a steamer owned by Hamilton & Smith, and engaged in freighting between New Baltimore and New York, and at the end of that time he acted as salesman for the same firm on a line of boats plying between Coxsackie and New York. For a year during the Civil War he was in the employ of the government, acting as inspector of the bay for the army, it being his duty to load schooners at Jersey City and make reports to Quartermaster Brown. For the next three years after this he was captain of the "New Champion," a boat owned by Black & Donohue, running from Catskill to New York; and, following that, he was for two years in company with Mr. George H. Penfield, his first employer, running a line of barges. Then, for a second period of three years, he was master of the "New Champion," and at the end of that time he became one of the organizers of the Catskill and New York Steamboat Company.

Mr. Donohue was superintendent of the company at the start, and Captain Stead was in command of one of the boats; but, upon the death of Mr. Donohue, Captain Stead was made superintendent and general manager. At first there were two small boats, the "New Champion" and the "Water Brette." These were superseded after a time by the "Escort" and the "Charlotte Vanderbilt," which were much larger boats and which were in turn superseded by others of still greater capacity. In 1880 the company built the "City of Catskill," which has a keel two hundred and forty-seven feet in length, beam thirty-five feet in width, and sixty-one feet over all, and has a carrying capacity of five hundred tons and accommodations for two hundred and fifty passengers. In 1882 was built the "Katterskill," two hundred and eighty-five feet in length, thirty-eight feet beam, and sixty-six feet over all, and capable of accommodating five hundred passengers. This is one of the finest boats on the river, and one of the most popular. Both these boats were built under Captain Stead's constant supervision, and they met the needs of the business until 1893, when the "Escort" was rebuilt and her name changed to the "City of Hudson." In 1898 the "Onteora" was built, length two hundred and forty-seven feet, beam thirty-five feet, and sixty-three feet over all, and capable of carrying six hundred people. She was built for night service, and is the fastest night boat afloat, having a speed of twenty-three miles an hour. She has made the run from New York to Catskill, a distance of one hundred and twenty miles, and made one landing, in four hours and twenty minutes. Captain Stead takes much pride in this boat, as she was built by his plans and measurements. She is fitted with every convenience for the comfort of guests. This company is a stock concern, and does a large and constantly increasing business. Their boats connect with the Catskill Mountain Railroad, and in the summer they carry a large number of tourists and quantities of freight.

Captain Stead was married in 1865 to Rachel E. Pettit, who was born in Dutchess County, a daughter of Lewis Pettit. One child has blessed this union, Ida H., now the wife of Charles I. Fiero, superintendent of the Pratt branch of the Standard Oil Company in Greenpoint. Mr. and Mrs. Fiero have one daughter, Rachel S.

The Captain is a Republican in politics. In 1879 he was elected Sheriff, which office he held until 1882, when he declined to serve longer. In 1883 he was elected to the legislature, where he served one year. He is a prominent man in his party, was for a long time a member of the County Committee, and has many times been a delegate to Republican conventions. He helped nominate Governor Morton. For three years he was a trustee of the village, and for a year president of the

Board of Trustees. Captain Stead has the distinction of having been longer in the boating business than any other man on the Hudson. He built his present residence in 1897. He is a trustee of the Catskill Savings Bank, and president of the Catskill Ferry Company running between Catskill and Catskill Station, and an owner in the last-named corporation. He is also one of the directors of the Hudson Steamboat Company. He attends the Methodist Episcopal church, of which his wife and daughter are members.

LEVI M. DEFANDORF, a skilful farmer and dairyman of Seward, Schoharie County, owner and occupant of a fine farm lying about a mile and a half from Hyndsville village, is a representative of one of the oldest families in this part of the State of New York. He was born on this farm on April 26, 1831, son of John and Elizabeth (Petrie) Defandorf. His first progenitor in this country, his great-grandfather, came from Germany.

Jacob Defandorf, father of John, bought a large tract of heavily timbered land in Seward, N.Y., which included the larger part of the homestead of his grandson, Levi M., and the adjoining estate of one hundred and seventy acres. In common with his neighbors, who were few and were settled far apart, he suffered the hardships of pioneer life, but with true German habits of industry and perseverance worked steadily; and the end of each year saw more land cleared and larger crops harvested. He died, probably in the log cabin which he reared on coming to the wilderness, at the age of fifty years, leaving a widow, Mrs. Susan Defandorf, and six children. Mrs. Defandorf was born at Frey's Bush, Montgomery County, and died in Seward at the age of fourscore and four years.

John Defandorf remained beneath the parental roof until ready to establish a home of his own, when he purchased a portion of the parental estate. Here he was successfully employed in general agricultural pursuits until his death, at the age of sixty-four years. After he had made the last payment on his property, he began making needed improvements. The present dwelling-house was erected by him. A man of intelligence, he was greatly interested in all things pertaining to the welfare of the town, but was never an aspirant for official honors. He married Elizabeth Petrie, one of the seven children of John Handrake Petrie, a well-known farmer of Carlisle, Schoharie County. Four children were born of their union, and two of them are living, namely: Julia Ann, wife of Austin France, of Seward Valley; and Levi M. The parents were consistent members of the Methodist church.

Levi M. Defandorf attended the district school when it was in session during his boyhood and youth, and in the same period was so well trained at home that he became as familiar with the work of the farm as he was with his books. On attaining his majority, he bought one hundred and thirty-two acres of the old Defandorf homestead; and, having since added to it nineteen acres by purchase, he has a large farm, and one of the best in line of improvements and appointments of any in the vicinity. He devotes his time to general farming, raising grain and hops to a considerable extent, but making a specialty of stock-raising and dairying. From his herd of twenty or more grade Holstein and Jersey cows, he makes butter, the greater part of which he ships to his son, who is engaged in the grocery business in Troy, N.Y., and some to the markets in Ohio and in Washington, D.C. He has always taken a great interest in the establishment of permanent town, county, and State agricultural associations; and as an exhibitor at fairs, held under the auspices of these organizations, Mr. Defandorf has on several occasions taken the first premium on stock. The credit of establishing the products of his dairy as among the best in the market, he gladly gives to his deceased wife, who was an expert butter-maker.

Mr. Defandorf married, April 25, 1850, Miss Lucinda R. Sexton, daughter of Austin Sexton. Her father was formerly engaged in farming in this part of Schoharie County, but afterward removed to Oriskany Falls, N.Y., where he operated a grist-mill and where he spent his remaining days. Mr. and Mrs. Defandorf reared five children; namely, Mary E., Clark B., Jason F., John A., and Daniel A. Mary is the wife of Dr. Adam Myers, of Buskirk, Rensselaer County, and has two children — Victor and Ralph. Clark B., deceased, married Susan Ostrander, who bore him three children — Jessie, Arthur, and Lucinda. Jason F. Defandorf was graduated with high honors from the Cazenovia Academy, afterward spent three years at the Wesleyan University, Middletown, Conn., and still later attended the Law School in Washington, D.C., where he received the degree of Bachelor of Arts, and has since been employed by the government in the post-office and in the War and Treasury Departments in that city. He married Miss Hattie Holmes, and has four children — Elizabeth P., James, John Levi, and Marion. John A. Defandorf was for one year clerk in a store at Cobleskill, then was several years a clerk in Troy, and subsequently went into business for himself with his cousin, Charles H. Sexton, at Troy. He married Emma Smith, and they have one child, Clark. Daniel A., the youngest son, completed his education at the Cobleskill High School, and subsequently taught school several terms in Seward and Sharon. He assists his father in the care of the home farm, and is also a local preacher in the Methodist church. He married Carrie Vroman, daughter of Barney Vroman.

After forty-seven years of happy wedded life, Mrs. Lucinda R. Defandorf passed to the brighter world beyond, her death occurring June 6, 1897. She was a woman of exemplary character and great personal worth, in every way deserving the high respect universally accorded her. She was a faithful member of the Methodist church, of which Mr. Defandorf is one of the oldest members now living, and in which he has held all the offices, having been a trustee and steward for years, a class leader for a quarter of a century, and for fifteen years superintendent of the Sunday-school, in which his wife, Lucinda, was a teacher. Both assisted in every work indorsed by the church, and their hospitable home was ever open to receive the ministers of that denomination.

On January 25, 1898, Mr. Defandorf married Mrs. Catherine M. Somers, daughter of Joseph France, a farmer of Seward, N.Y. Three children were born to the present Mrs. Defandorf and her former husband, Peter N. Somers — Howard S., Ernest F., and Arthur L., deceased.

JAMES MADISON CASE, a prominent business man of Gilboa, N.Y., was born in this town, July 7, 1849, son of Daniel and Betsey (Chichester) Case. He is a descendant of John Case, who came over from England more than two hundred and fifty years ago.

A brief account of the life of John Case, the immigrant, by A. P. Case, of Vernon, N.Y., has recently appeared in print. In this book mention is made of records showing that John Case as early as 1640 was living in the vicinity of Hartford, Conn.; that in 1656 he was an inhabitant of Long Island, a year or two later removing to Windsor, Conn., and in 1669 one of the first settlers at Simsbury, Conn., so named in 1670. For four years he represented the town in the General Court, or Assembly. He married first Sarah, daughter of William Spencer, of Hartford. She died in 1691, and he afterward married Elizabeth Loomis, a widow. He had ten children, all by his first wife; namely, Elizabeth, Mary, John, William, Samuel, Richard, Bartholomew, Joseph, Sarah, and Abigail.

The Case family in England is said to have been numerously represented for a number of generations at Aylsham, Norfolk County. Calvin Case, who was born in Connecticut, April 10, 1763, came to Conesville, N.Y., and a few years later he moved to Gilboa, where he acquired two tracts of land, amounting in all to two hundred acres. The property he occupied, which is still known as the Case farm, now consists of one hundred and sixty acres, and the original title is in the possession of his grandson, the subject of this sketch. His first abiding-place was a log hut, the entrance to which was covered with a blanket; and from a struggling pioneer he rose to be a well-to-do farmer, stock-raiser, and grain dealer. Calvin Case, it is said, served as a minute-man in 1777, and was ordered to the front at the second battle of Stillwater, but arrived after the surrender of General Burgoyne. The Case family have an honorable record for patriotism, seventy or more of that name from Connecticut having served in the Revolution, upward of twenty in the War of 1812, and over fifty in the Civil War. Calvin Case was married in Connecticut, August 2, 1793, to Jerusha Griffin, and he brought three children with him to Schoharie County. He died January 4, 1854, aged ninety-one years, and his wife, who was born December 2, 1777, died May 7, 1849. They reared a family of thirteen children, namely: Calvin, who moved from Conesville to Blenheim; Luther, who died at Potter's Hollow; Elisha, Allen, and Erastus, who all died in Conesville; Ira, who now resides at Conesville; Daniel, James M. Case's father; Griffin, who died in Gilboa; Hiram, who resided in Catskill; Joel, who died while young; Jerusha, deceased, who married Orlean De Witt, of Oak Hill; Eliza, who married S. Mackey, of Gilboa; and Phœbe, who married William Ploss, of Gilboa. The sons were all farmers except Hiram, who was a cattle dealer, hotel-keeper, and general speculator. The grandparents were Presbyterians, and most of their children became members of that church.

Daniel Case remained at the homestead to care for his parents in their old age, and after their death he succeeded to the ownership of the property by purchasing the interests of the other heirs. He was an energetic, industrious, and successful farmer, and at his death, which occurred November 10, 1886, he left a good estate. His wife, Betsey, was a daughter of Joseph Chichester, and the maiden name of her mother was Welch. The Chichesters are of Scotch descent, and the Welches are said to be of Dutch origin. Joseph Chichester had a family of nine children. Daniel and Betsey Case reared but one child, James M., the subject of this sketch. The mother died February 19, 1875.

James Madison Case was educated in Gilboa, and taught several terms of school after the completion of his studies. He assisted his father in farming from the time he was able to be of use until the age of twenty-four, when he engaged in general mercantile business in company with Abraham Walker, a partnership that ended at the death of Mr. Walker some three years later. He continued in business alone some sixteen years, or until about 1893, when he sold out to George E. Hawver. He has since given his attention to the buying of country produce, including butter, which he handles quite extensively. He also buys large quantities of wool, which he ships to Boston; and during the past year his shipments amounted to over one hundred thousand pounds. He still owns the homestead, upon which he raises some fine horses, and he takes special pride in preserving the old dwelling which was built by his grandfather over eighty years ago. For the past ten years he has been actively interested in inland fisheries, in stocking the various streams in this locality, and is regarded as an authority on that subject.

Mr. Case married Hattie E. Hawver, daughter of William W. and Samantha (Hay) Hawver. She was the first-born of eight children, the others being: Emma D., who died at the age of six years; Ella, who married G. N. Thorp; George E., a merchant of Urlton, N.Y.; James B., a prosperous farmer, who occupies the old homestead in Conesville; Flora A., who died at the age of twenty-one years; Bertha, wife of James Carpenter; and Martha, who married D. T. Ferguson, of Alton, Ill. Mr. and Mrs. Case have had two daughters: Merta, who died aged four years; and Mina, who died aged one year.

In politics Mr. Case is a Democrat, and for a number of years was Postmaster. He has served upon the Town Committee several terms, has attended as a delegate many county conventions, but has never sought for or held local offices. He is a Master Mason, and belongs to Gilboa Lodge, No. 630.

FRANK RUFUS SEARLES, M.D., physician and surgeon, Catskill, N.Y., was born in Newton, N.J., April 29, 1868, son of Arthur and Alice (Martin) Searles. On the paternal side he comes of English ancestry, and through his maternal grandfather he is a descendant of French Protestants, or Huguenots. The first of the Searles family who came to America settled in Massachusetts, and was a farmer. Representatives of the family participated in the Revolutionary War, the War of 1812, and the French and Indian War. Dr. Searles's great-great-grandfather, John Finlay, was an aide on the staff of General Green and also on that of General Mifflin.

Arthur Searles, the Doctor's father, was reared in Massachusetts. He followed agriculture until of age, when he went to New Jersey. Later he entered commercial life in New York, and resided there until his death, which occurred at the age of thirty. Mr. Searles is survived by his wife, Alice, and their only child, Frank Rufus, the special subject of this sketch. The Doctor's mother, now Mrs. Lester Leggett, resides in Plainfield, N.J. She has one brother, Frederick Martin. Her parents were Lebbeus L. and Frances (Bench) Martin. Her father was a wholesale clothing merchant of Plainfield, N.J., moved from that town to Newton, N.J., and at one time resided in New York for a short period. His death occurred in Plainfield, N.J., in 1898, at the age of seventy-eight.

Frank Rufus Searles was educated in the common and high schools and at Leal's Academy, Plainfield, N.J. His medical studies were completed at the Long Island College Hospital, from which he was graduated March 22, 1892. He began the practice of his profession at Plainfield, N.J., where he remained one year, removing from there to Hunter, Greene County, and two years later settling in Catskill, N.Y. He has made rapid progress in his profession, and is highly esteemed both as a physician and citizen.

On November 8, 1893, Dr. Searles was joined in marriage with Miss Myra Rose Lowrie, daughter of Dr. H. H. and Myra G. (Burr) Lowrie, of Plainfield. Dr. and Mrs. Searles have one child, Frank Rufus Searles, second. There are twenty-two physicians in the Lowrie family, and Mrs. Searles's father has practised in Plainfield many years. Her mother, who is a native of Brooklyn, N.Y., and a descendant of a branch of the family to which Aaron Burr belonged, has reared four children, namely: Caroline, who is the wife of the Rev. C. G. Bristol, rector of Colts Memorial Church, Hartford, Conn.; Myra Rose, now Mrs. Searles; Maud Myra, now

Mrs. Julian Deane, who is residing at Springfield, Mass.; and H. H. Lowrie, Jr., who is manager of an insurance company in Philadelphia, Pa.

Dr. Searles has served as president of the Greene County Medical Society, and has frequently read papers before that body upon timely topics. He is now delegate to the Medical Society, State of New York. He is Assistant Surgeon of the Sixteenth Company, N. G. S., N.Y., now acting captain; is medical examiner for a number of life insurance companies; and is local health officer and secretary of the Board of U. S. Pension Examiners of Greene County. In politics he is a Republican. Dr. and Mrs. Searles are members of Christ's Presbyterian Church.

JOHN H. BURTIS, Jr.,* proprietor of the Hotel St. Charles, Hunter, N.Y., was born in Brooklyn, Long Island, October 24, 1869, son of John H. and Mary (Thompson) Burtis. His father is a native of Washington County, New York, and his mother was born in Nantucket, Mass. His immigrant ancestor came from Florence, Italy; and his great-grandfather Burtis and his grandfather, whose name was John, were natives of Washington County, this State.

John Burtis was a carpenter and builder and a manufacturer of sieves. In his latter years he removed to Hunter, where he carried on a large sieve factory until his death, which occurred in 1890. He was a Justice of the Peace many years, was familiarly known as Squire Burtis, and he enjoyed the esteem of all who knew him. In his religious belief he was a Presbyterian. He married for his first wife Eliza Lee, a native of Washington County, and had a large family of children, of whom the only one living is John H., Sr. The grandmother's death occurred many years prior to that of her husband.

John H. Burtis, Sr., was reared in Washington County. In 1845 he came to Hunter, and purchased a tract of land comprising three hundred and fifty acres, mostly covered with timber, which he at first used for sporting purposes, and later cleared for cultivation. For several years he conducted the stove and tinware business in New York City. After that he engaged in the dried fruit trade and still later in the wholesale drug and patent medicine business. At the present time he is a prosperous real estate dealer in Brooklyn, where he resides winters, his summers being spent in Hunter. His original residence here, which he built shortly after purchasing his property, he afterward enlarged for the accommodation of summer boarders; and it was conducted by his half-brother until 1882, when it was destroyed by fire. In 1883 the present large hotel was erected. For three years it was in charge of S. P. Van Loan, later in that of Mr. Scripture, and in 1893 John H. Burtis, Jr., became its manager.

John H. Burtis, Sr., is a Republican in politics. He was in the Assembly in 1875 and 1876, and is quite active in the public affairs of Brooklyn. In Masonry he has advanced to

the thirty-second degree. He has served as Deputy Grand Master, and belongs to the Mystic Shrine; is vice-president of the Union League Club, Brooklyn; and president of Aurora Grata Club.

His wife, Mary, is a daughter of James B. and Mary (Gardner) Thompson. Her father was a graduate of Yale and a well-known mathematician. He was the author of Thompson's Arithmetics, and has written over forty different volumes, known as Thompson's Mathematical Series, including arithmetic, algebra, geometry, and trigonometry. He was at one time principal of an academy in Nantucket, Mass. During the latter part of his life he made his home in New York, where he died at the age of eighty years. His wife, Mary Gardner Thompson, who is still living, is now seventy-five years old. Mrs. Mary Thompson Burtis was educated in Brooklyn and at a young ladies' seminary in New Haven, Conn. She is president of Memorial Hospital, Brooklyn, and is prominent in charitable work. She has had seven children, three of whom are living: Mary L., John H., Jr., and Grace L. Burtis. Charles Burtis, M.D., was graduated from the New York Homœopathic College, and at the time of his death was practising his profession in Atlanta, Ga. Grace L. is a student at Vassar College, Poughkeepsie. The parents are members of the Congregational church.

John H. Burtis, Jr., began his education in the common schools of Brooklyn, and fitted for college at the Latin school. He was graduated from Columbia College in 1894, with the degree of Bachelor of Arts, and subsequently studied law. During the summer of 1893 he managed the Hotel St. Charles in Hunter, and since 1894 he has resided here permanently. This hotel, which is situated upon the highest elevation in the Catskill region, occupies a desirable location on what is known as Breeze Lawn Farm. The building is seventy-five feet front, one hundred and sixty-three feet deep, and four stories high. It has broad piazzas on three sides, and is equipped with all modern improvements, including passenger elevator and telegraph office. With the annex it has accommodations for two hundred guests. The table is supplied with fresh cream, butter, eggs, and vegetables from the farm connected with the house; and the service is of the best. Aside from the hotel Mr. Burtis manages Breeze Lawn, consisting of three hundred and fifty acres. He carries on a dairy, and sends his surplus products to market.

On October 9, 1895, Mr. Burtis married Zaidee I. Scribner, a native of Hunter, daughter of Peter H. and Agnes (Merwin) Scribner. Her father, who at one time was engaged in mercantile business in Catskill, is at present residing in Palenville, where he accommodates summer boarders.

Mr. Scribner originally came from Connecticut. He has had four children: Zaidee I., now Mrs. Burtis; George H.; Bertha; and Merwin. Mr. and Mrs. Burtis are the parents of two children — Thompson H. and Grace Agnes.

Mr. Burtis is a Republican in politics, and

has been quite prominent in public affairs. He belongs to the Masonic Order, being a member of Mount Tabor Lodge and the chapter in Windham. He attends the Methodist Episcopal church.

EMORY STEVENS, of Conesville, an ex-member of the State legislature, was born in this town, September 24, 1839, son of Levi F. and Thirza (Sage) Stevens. His grandfather, Peter S., and his great-grandfather, Gershom Stevens, both came here from Fairfield, Conn., in 1805, Peter S. being then a young man.

Gershom Stevens became the second owner of the first grist-mill in this region, and he operated it for a number of years. His children were: Levi, Gershom, Peter S., Ozias, and two daughters. Some years after his death his son Peter S. remodelled the mill into a tannery. This was afterward destroyed by fire, and two other buildings erected upon the site were also burned.

Peter S. Stevens was the father of ten children; namely, Levi F., Walter, Alfred, Nelson, Tompkins, Thalia A., Sally, John F., Ozias D., and another son who died in infancy. The only one now living is Tompkins, who is a well-known dealer in hides in New York City. Thalia A. married Andrew Rickey, and Sally married Charles Sturgis. John F., who became a physician, was for five years president of a medical school in St. Louis, Mo., and afterward practised in Brooklyn, N.Y. Nelson died in Conesville, aged twenty-four years. Tompkins, Alfred, and Walter went to Sullivan County, and were instrumental in building up the town of Stevensville, where they operated tanneries for many years, being also engaged in lumbering and farming. The Stevens brothers built a hotel in Conesville, which was first opened by Gershom.

Levi F. Stevens, father of Emory, was in his younger days interested in the tannery at Conesville, and for a while he kept a store. He succeeded to the ownership of the homestead property, which was in his day a part of the original tract one mile square acquired by his grandfather. He was an able, energetic, and successful farmer, and favorably known through this section of the county. Politically he was a Democrat, and held some of the town offices. He was an active member and a prominent official of the Methodist Episcopal church, whose house of worship was built principally through the instrumentality of his father and David Sage. Levi F. Stevens died March 28, 1890, aged eighty years.

His wife, Thirza, was a daughter of David Sage, who removed with his family to Conesville from Connecticut. He was a descendant of David Sage, first, who was born in Wales in 1639, and coming to America was one of the earliest settlers in Middletown, Conn. The immigrant was also the ancestor of Russell Sage, the well-known financier. The Sage family, we are told, dates its origin from the time of the Norman conquest, its founder having fought on the winning side at the battle of Hastings. Mrs. Stevens's father, who was born in Connecticut, settled upon a tract of two hundred acres in that part of Broome which is now Conesville, and became a successful farmer. He was one of the founders of the Methodist Episcopal church at Strykersville. His children were: Daniel, Abiel, Simeon, Levi, Thirza (Mrs. Stevens), Polly, and Lucena. Abiel, twin brother to Thirza, died in Ashland, Greene County, N.Y.; Daniel died in Conesville; Levi died while young; and Simeon, who amassed a fortune in business in New York City, died in Windham.

Levi F. and Thirza (Sage) Stevens had seven children; namely, Diantha M., David S., Delphus T., Thalia A., Emory, Ozro, and Daniel T. Stevens. Diantha M. died at the age of fifteen years; David S., who resided in Gilboa, was for twenty years a Methodist preacher; Delphus T., who died at the age of twenty-eight, was a promising young lawyer in Oak Hill, N.Y.; Thalia A. died at sixteen; Ozro died at eighteen; and Daniel T. died at twenty-three years. The mother died in August, 1890, aged eighty-five years.

Emory Stevens completed his education at the Charlotteville Academy. He taught school for some time, and afterward he was employed as a clerk in mercantile business at Conesville and Gilboa. He then went to Iowa, where for the next few years he was engaged in various kinds of business, including mercantile. For some time he kept a sale stable in Des Moines, and while in that city he also speculated rather extensively in real estate. Since his return home he has devoted some of his time to educational work.

In politics he is a Democrat, and while residing in Iowa was chosen a delegate to represent Harrison County in the State Convention. He has served as a Supervisor in Conesville for three years. He also served as chairman of the County Canvassers' Committee, as foreman of the Grand Jury, and during his term in the Assembly he was a member of several important committees. Mr. Stevens is a member of the Methodist church, and was for a number of years superintendent of the Sunday-school.

Mr. Stevens married Emma Miller, daughter of William Miller, of Conesville. They have six children; namely, Ward E., Walter A., Linnie D., Ralph F., Levi F., and Susie E. Ward E. was graduated from the New York Dental College in 1897. Walter A. is a member of the police force.

JOHN WESLEY GAYLORD, a representative citizen of Conesville, N.Y., was born in this town on April 4, 1840, son of George and Fannie (Humphrey) Gaylord. On the paternal side he is of Huguenot descent. His emigrant ancestors on leaving France settled first in England, whence some of the family found their way to this country. His great-grandfather Gaylord served as an Ensign in the Continental army during the Revolutionary War. He was a man of considerable property.

John Gaylord, son of Ensign Gaylord, was but a young boy at the time his father died;

and he was bound out to a Captain Langdon, of Litchfield, Conn. He ran away, however, at about the age of eighteen, having received none of his inheritance, and with one Allen Griffin came to Conesville, journeying by way of Catskill, guided by marked trees. He settled on the Sotts patent, now known as the Van Dyke farm, and built a log house to live in. After remaining there a few years, he removed to a farm on the stage road between Gilboa and Cairo, in Manor Kill village. Subsequently he settled on the farm where his grandson, John Wesley Gaylord, now resides. He became the largest land-owner of his time, owning from four to five hundred acres. When he arrived here he had only fifty dollars in his pocket. He married Sabrina Atwood, returning to Connecticut for that purpose. She bore him three sons — Hiram, Henry, and George. To each of these he gave a handsome property upon his coming of age. He then himself started afresh, and in time accumulated as much as he had at first, so that during his life he owned between eight hundred and a thousand acres. Politically, he was a Democrat, and the leading member of his party hereabouts. In religious faith he was a Methodist. He helped to build the Methodist church here, and was always one of its most liberal supporters. He died at the age of seventy-eight, and his wife died later, at about the same age. His son Hiram became a wealthy merchant of New York City. Henry, who removed to Catskill in 1868, became a wealthy dealer in live stock and wool, and later in real estate. He died at Catskill in January, 1898, in the eighty-eighth year of his age. He had travelled extensively. The fine bell on the church at Manor Kill was presented by him some four years ago at a cost of four hundred dollars.

George Gaylord, father of John W., was born on April 28, 1815, in Conesville, and resided here all his life, dying in 1878. He kept a hostelry for drovers, the largest in the State, furnishing accommodations one night for fifteen hundred cattle. Drovers came here from different States, and it is said that one paid him ninety dollars for three tons of hay to feed his drove for a single night. He was famed far and wide for his hospitality and for his sunny and genial temper. Himself an expert judge of cattle, he bought and sold many head. He owned a farm of six hundred acres, upon which he raised annually from fifty to seventy-five tons of hay. During war time he kept three hundred sheep, and forty or fifty head of cattle. Like his father, he was a strong Democrat; but he was no office-seeker. He was married on December 31, 1838. Both he and his wife were active and devoted members of the Methodist church, and gave it generous financial support. The latter, who was born on August 21, 1818, died in 1868. She was the mother of four children, namely: John W.; Woodford, who was born on January 2, 1842; George E., who was born on June 9, 1846; and Ogden, who was born on June 13, 1849. George E., who was for many years engaged in the cattle business, is one of the largest land-owners here. He is an influential man, a political leader, and has twice been

Supervisor of the town. Ogden is in the meat business at Gilboa. Woodford is the well known ex-Sheriff.

John Wesley Gaylord was educated in the district schools, at Chartlotteville High School and Ashland Academy, being a student in the last-named institution in 1860, when it was burned. After his marriage he settled on a farm of his own, where he lived for ten years. He then came back to take charge of the homestead farm. Here he now owns some five hundred acres. He was formerly engaged to some extent in dairying and in growing hay. From youth also he has been interested in buying and selling cattle, being an expert judge of stock. In 1868 he went on the road in this business, but after some years gave it up, only to start again in 1880 in company with his brother George. The latter retired from the partnership in 1891, and Mr. J. W. Gaylord has since continued alone. In his early life he taught school for a time, but finally decided that business was much more congenial to him. As a cattle dealer, he has travelled into Canada and throughout this State, principally in Dutchess, Columbia, Green, Schoharie, Otsego, Montgomery, Jefferson, and Delaware Counties. He also went into Connecticut on some of his trips. He was usually absent from home three or four weeks at a time. Like his father, he is noted among all who know him for his genial hospitality. He is popular in his own town; and it is said that, if he takes a subscription paper among the people for any purpose whatever, he is sure to fill it with names. No family in the community has done more for the church of the town than the Gaylord family. Mr. John W. Gaylord in this respect has not been behind his father and grandfather in generosity and in the support of every good movement. In politics he is a Democrat.

At twenty-three Mr. Gaylord was united in marriage with Mary K. Porter, daughter of a Scotch family. Mrs. Gaylord died on December 17, 1897, having been the mother of three children. Of these, John H. died in infancy; and George Porter died on December 14, 1889, at the age of twenty-three. Fannie M., the only daughter, resides with her father. She attended the Albany Normal School, and subsequently taught school until her marriage with Coral E. Rietchmyer. She has one child, Mabel G. George Porter Gaylord was a young man of great promise. In his youth he attended a select school in Broome Centre, and then took a course in the Albany Business College. He was nearly qualified to take his degree of Doctor of Medicine at the University of the City of New York when he became ill. He was naturally a devoted student, and his close confinement to his books had undermined his health. He was a Mason of Gilboa Lodge, and remarkably well informed on Masonic history for one of his age.

P GARDINER COFFIN, cashier of the Catskill National Bank of Catskill and Supervisor of the town of Catskill, is a native of this village, and was born on August 10, 1859, his parents being Uriah H. and Elizabeth J. (Surfleet) Coffin.

The family of which he is a representative has existed for many generations in England. Tristram Coffin, the founder of the American branch, was the son of Peter and Joan (Thember or Thumber) Coffin, of Brixton, Devonshire, and a grandson of Nicholas Coffin of that place, who died in 1613. Tristram Coffin, born probably at Brixton, about 1605, married Dionis Stevens. He came to New England with his widowed mother and his family in 1642. After residing successively in Haverhill, Newbury, and Salisbury, he finally, about 1660, settled at Nantucket, where he died in 1681, and where some of his descendants live at this day. Mr. Coffin has in his possession a copy of the commission, dated June 29, 1671, granted by Francis Lovelace, Governor of New York, to Tristram Coffin to be chief magistrate over the islands of Nantucket and Tuckernuck.

Mr. Coffin's grandfather, Peter G. Coffin, was born in Hudson, N.Y., on July 30, 1794. For many years he owned and ran boats between Catskill and Albany. He died on December 5, 1858. He was three times married. His second wife, the grandmother of P. Gardiner Coffin, was before her marriage Lucy O. Green. She was born in Athens, N.Y., on November 1, 1793, and died there on February 7, 1834, having been the mother of only one child, Uriah H. Both she and her husband were Episcopalians.

Uriah H. Coffin was born on May 30, 1831. He was brought up in Athens, Greene County, N.Y., removed to Catskill, and engaged in grocery business there. He was captain for a time of the "P. G. Coffin" that ran between Albany and Catskill, and later he ran on the boats plying between New York and Catskill. After being engaged in the boating business for some years, he removed to Whitehall, N.Y. He enlisted during the Civil War, was commissioned as Captain of a company in the One Hundred and Twentieth Regiment, and remained in the service until the close of the war, being Quartermaster of the regiment, on the staff of Colonel George H. Sharp. Some time after being mustered out, he received an appointment in the post-office in New York City, and is now in charge of the record department of the registration office. In politics he is a Republican. His first wife, the mother of P. Gardiner Coffin, died at the age of thirty-five, having borne him three children. Of these the living are: Charles G., who is in the insurance business in this town; and P. Gardiner. The second wife was before her marriage Emma Johnson. She was born in Whitehall, N.Y. She is the mother of two sons now living — Arthur and Robert Coffin.

P. Gardiner Coffin lost his mother when he was an infant. He was born and brought up in Catskill, and has been a resident of this village all his life. In 1876 he was appointed Deputy Postmaster of the town; and, after filling that office in a most creditable manner for six years, he entered the Catskill National Bank as a general clerk. In a short time he was appointed teller, in 1889 he was made assistant cashier, and in 1896 was promoted to his present position of cashier, being also a member of the board of directors. This bank was organized in 1812, and is one of the oldest banks, not only in the State, but in the United States, and has a proud history. A sketch of Mr. Coffin appears on page 552, and his portrait on page 191, of the work recently issued, entitled "Prominent Bankers of America."

From 1885 to 1891 Mr. Coffin was interested with his brother in conducting a large general insurance business. In 1888 he helped to organize the Catskill Building and Loan Association, and he has since been its treasurer and one of its directors. For twelve years he was treasurer of Catskill village. In politics he is a Republican. He was elected Supervisor of the town in 1896, and again in 1898 to serve one year; but by a change in the law he will continue in office until 1900. In 1898 he served as chairman of the board. For many years he was a leading member of the Republican county committee, and he was its chairman for a year. His activity in promoting the best interests of the village has been unceasing, and his townsmen award him due credit for his disinterested efforts. He is well known in both town and county, and highly respected.

Mr. Coffin was married on November 9, 1887, to Ida Brown, who was born in Petaluma, Cal. Her father, Captain John Brown, formerly interested in the boating business on the Hudson and a resident of Catskill, now resides in California. He removed to that State in 1849, and was for many years with the Southern Pacific Railroad Company as master mariner in their steamboat service between San Francisco and Oakland. He has now retired from business. Mrs. Coffin frequently visits her family in California. She has made the overland journey eight times, Mr. Coffin accompanying her once. In 1883 she and her mother were in the railway disaster at Tehachepi, Southern California, where eleven out of twenty-three persons in one car were killed. In this accident Mrs. Coffin sustained injuries which kept her in the hospital for several months, and the injuries of her mother were of such a serious character that she never fully recovered from their effects. Mrs. Brown is now deceased. She was a woman of unusual literary attainments, and was the author of a work on botany. It was through her efforts that the library in Alameda, Cal., was established. Her maiden name was Helen Walter. She was born in Catskill, daughter of William Walter, for many years a leading merchant here. For a time she lived in the family of Captain Hugh Taylor. Mrs. Coffin is the only daughter in a family of four children. Her eldest brother Thomas is manager of the Western Union Telegraph at Reno, Nev. William Brown, second brother, is travelling freight and passenger agent of the Great Northern Railroad Company of California. George W. Brown, another brother, is in the Wells & Fargo Express Company

Mr. and Mrs. Coffin have three children— Charles G., Robert E., and Helen M. Mr.

Coffin is a member of Catskill Lodge of Masons, and chairman of Finance Committee. He has held membership in the Dutch Reformed church for many years.

FRANKLIN CLAPPER, the well-known merchant of Mackey's Corners, Gilboa, N.Y., is a native of this town. He was born on May 4, 1863, and is the only son of Philip and Betsy (Robinson) Clapper. The family is known to be of German descent, and it is believed that Mr. Clapper's great-great-grandfather was its first representative in America.

His great-grandfather, Henry P. Clapper, came to Gilboa from Coeymans, this State, about 1815, and settled in the north part of the town, then in Broome. He took up a tract of about a hundred and forty acres of wild land, and built first a log cabin and later a frame house. He felled the first trees, and did all the clearing. This farm is still owned by one of the family, a grandson of the pioneer. Henry P. Clapper died on the farm in 1849, at the age of eighty. His wife, whom he had married in Coeymans, died some years before he did. They had three sons — Sylvester, Silas, and George; and four daughters — Sarah, Peggy, Polly, and Harriet. George resided at the homestead. Silas settled in another part of the town.

Sylvester Clapper, grandfather of Franklin, was born in Coeymans in 1802, and died in September, 1884. He came to Gilboa with his parents when about thirteen years of age, and in time settled upon a portion of the homestead farm, where he spent the remainder of his life. He acquired some two hundred acres of land. In religion he was a Baptist of the old school. Politically, he was a strong Democrat, and a leader in his party in this vicinity, though he never sought office for himself. As a business man, he was shrewd and far-seeing. His judgment was much deferred to by his fellow-citizens. His wife, whose maiden name was Louisa Ryder, was born in 1807, and died in 1891. Her ancestors were of German descent, and came here from Columbia County. The children of Sylvester Clapper were: Philip, Henry, John, and George M. John, who remained on the homestead farm, died in 1885. George M went to Michigan in 1883. Henry B. is a very prosperous farmer in Albany County. He is married, and has four children. Sylvester Clapper was interested in the turnpike road between North Blenheim and Potter's Hollow, and together with Mr. Tibbits was instrumental in securing the legislation under which it was built.

Philip Clapper, above named, was educated in the public schools, and subsequently taught school for a number of terms. He has continued to be a student throughout his life, and has been much looked to by his neighbors and acquaintances for information on doubtful points under discussion. In politics he is a Democrat. His first farm consisted of one hundred acres, all tillable land. Later he became the owner of the homestead property, where he has resided since 1863, in his active years devoting his energies to general farming, giving special attention to dairying. His wife, whose maiden name was Betsy Robinson, is the daughter of John D. Robinson, whose ancestors were of Scotch-English descent, emigrants from Connecticut. Mr. and Mrs. Philip Clapper have one son, Franklin, whose personal history is given below, and a daughter Emmaline, who was married in December, 1894, to Edgar Hulbert, of North Blenheim.

Franklin Clapper was educated in the public schools and in a select school, receiving more than ordinarily good advantages. Then for some time he taught school during the winter terms in the towns of Gilboa, Blenheim, Breakabeen, and Fulton, and engaged in farming during the summers. As a teacher he met with great success, and in Breakabeen he had a school of seventy pupils. Deciding to go into mercantile business, he bought out his present stand in March, 1892, and since then has devoted himself exclusively to building up a trade. Although he had no previous experience as a tradesman to guide him, he has prospered even beyond his expectations. He carries at the present time thrice the stock that he carried at the outset, having enlarged his line of drugs, groceries, dry goods, hardware, and farm tools. He sends goods over a radius of four or five miles.

Since 1893 Mr. Clapper has been the village Postmaster. His management having proved satisfactory to both parties, no candidate has been put forth to oppose him. He is also serving on his third term as Notary Public. Mr. Clapper has often been delegate to both local and county conventions. Repeatedly importuned to accept the nomination for public office, he has declined, though he never loses an opportunity to work for the good of his party and of the community. He was instrumental in the construction of a telephone line to Mackey's Corners, thereby giving to the citizens of that little hamlet direct and rapid communication with the county seat and other parts of the county. He is a Mason of Gilboa Lodge, No. 630, of which he has been Junior Deacon, and is warmly interested in the ancient craft. When he joined in 1887, he was the youngest man in the lodge.

Mr. Clapper was married on April 21, 1897, to Harriet E. Wykoff, who is the eldest of the five children of George M. Wykoff. Mrs. Clapper was a successful student in the Oneonta Normal School, and previous to her marriage she taught school. Mr. Clapper has been a member of the Baptist choir for five or six years, and at the present time his wife is also a member. Both are popular in social circles, and have every outlook for a prosperous future.

CONVAS E. MARKHAM, of Fulton, teacher and farmer, well known in Schoharie County as Professor Markham, was born in this town, August 10, 1843, son of Alden, Jr., and Catherine (Cook) Markham. Through his father he traces his ancestry (by what line we have not been informed) to John Alden of the "Mayflower" company of Pilgrims who settled at Plymouth.

Professor Markham's paternal grandparents, Alden Markham, Sr., and Elizabeth Pease

Markham, were born, bred, and married in the State of Connecticut. Soon after their marriage they migrated westward to Otsego County, New York, where, in the town of Worcester, the grandfather took up a tract of forest-covered land, from which he cleared the timber and improved a homestead. He became actively identified with the interests of the town, and, while establishing a home for himself and family, also assisted in developing the resources of that section of the State. He was among the leading farmers of the community, and for many years served as Justice of the Peace. He lived there until well advanced in years, and then went to Massachusetts, where he died at the age of seventy-eight. His wife, who bore him seven children, also lived to a ripe old age. Both were Baptists in their religious beliefs.

Alden Markham, Jr., was born and educated in Otsego County; and, having been reared to agricultural pursuits, he followed farming for some years. He also taught during the winter terms in Otsego County for a while, and later on for a few terms in Richmondville, Schoharie County. In 1838, or soon after, he accepted a position in the public schools of Fulton; and, being pleased with this locality, he subsequently invested his money here in a farm, and resumed life as an agriculturist. A few years afterward he removed to Massachusetts, where he spent his remaining days, passing away at the age of forty-nine years. His wife, whose maiden name was Catherine D. Cook, was born in the western part of Fulton, being a daughter of Nathaniel Cook, an extensive farmer, who spent his life of threescore and ten years in this town. Mrs. Markham died at the early age of thirty-nine years, having borne her husband five children. Four of this family are now living, namely: Convas E.; Asher; Luther O., who for a quarter of a century has been Superintendent of Schools at Haverstraw, New York.; and Elizabeth, wife of E. W. Haverly. Both parents were persons of eminent piety, and active members of the Baptist church.

Convas E. Markham began teaching in the district schools when but sixteen years old. He afterward took a full course of study at the Schoharie Academy, and still further fitted himself for a teacher by attending the Albany Normal School, from which he was graduated in 1869. He has since taught in various towns, including Fulton, where he commenced his career, Gallupville, in whose schools he was employed twelve consecutive years, and Esperance. He also taught several years in Piermont and Haverstraw, Rockland County. Since his marriage he has resided on his farm of one hundred acres in Fulton, and, in addition to his professional labors in this vicinity, has been prosperously engaged in general farming and dairying. He is one of the oldest and best known teachers of the county.

Mr. Markham married Carrie Louden, of Fulton, a graduate of the Normal School, and for some years prior to her marriage a teacher in the public schools. She was born in Fulton, being a daughter of Stephen Louden, of whom a biographical sketch appears elsewhere in this volume.

FRANK H. FRANCE, a native of Seward, now residing in the village of Cobleskill, was born on March 31, 1859, son of Gilbert G. and Angeline (Ottman) France. He is a great-grandson of Sebastian Frantz, one of the pioneers of Schoharie County.

Sebastian Frantz came from Germany in 1752, shortly after his marriage with Anna Fritz. He was born in Würtemberg, in the year 1732, and his wife was born in the same place in the year following. They were Lutherans, and, with three others of that persuasion, left their native land in order to secure greater freedom of worship. The little party landed in New York in November, 1753. Sebastian was sent ahead to prospect for a place in which to settle, and he eventually chose a location in this county in what is now the town of Seward.

He was a man of deep piety and great religious zeal, and his unflinching boldness in defence of his faith has borne fruit in the lives of his descendants. He brought with him from the Fatherland his German family Bible, the first Bible ever brought into the town of Seward, and this is now in the possession of the heirs of his grandson, the late Gilbert G. France. Seven tedious years were spent in clearing the land and making it capable of producing harvests, and at the end of that time the desire of the immigrant's heart was fulfilled in the erection, at what was called New Rhinebeck, of a Lutheran church. The structure was a frame building, and was the second house of worship reared in the town. The society was presided over by the Rev. Peter Nicholas Sommer, a travelling Lutheran preacher, who preached also to the Methodist congregation in the other church, which was located at Seward Centre.

The children of Sebastian Frantz numbered twelve, and were named as follows: Anna, Ernest Christopher, Eva, Elizabeth, Jacob, Margaretta, John, Catherine, Henry, Lena, Lawrence, and David. At the outbreak of the Revolution, the two elder sons, Christopher and Jacob, enlisted as soldiers, and were quartered with their company in the Schoharie Valley. On October 18, while Sebastian was away from home doing government service, his home was entered by an Indian chief who was in the employ of the British; two of the sons, John and Henry, were taken captive; and the barns and out-buildings were burned. Thus in a moment were destroyed the results of years of earnest toil.

Mrs. Anna Frantz, with her ten remaining children fled to Gravel Mountain, where she secreted herself for three days, not daring to make a fire for fear that her hiding place might be revealed. John, one of the captured sons, was scalped and murdered, but Henry fortunately escaped. On the same day, the young woman who was to have been the bride of Christopher in two weeks, was murdered. A pair of silver shoe buckles, her wedding gift from her lover, is still in the possession of her family. After the war Sebastian Frantz repaired and re-established his home, and subsequently remained there until his death in 1805. His wife survived him eleven years. Both were buried on the home farm, but in

1891 the remains were disinterred by Gilbert G. France and were removed to the Zion Rural Cemetery at Seward Centre.

The descendants of this worthy pair now constitute a considerable portion of the population of Schoharie, and members of the fourth and fifth generations have become residents in other parts of the State. Henry Frantz, who escaped from the Indians, spent his early life on the homestead, and later bought a farm near by, where he lived until his death, at the age of eighty-eight. He was a most active Christian, and both he and his good wife were members of the Methodist church. Her maiden name was Maria Horn. She was born in Albany, the daughter of Joseph Horn, a prominent clothier of that place. She had one sister, Margaret, who married David Frantz.

Of the fifteen children of Henry Frantz, fourteen grew to maturity, and thirteen were married and had children. There were eleven sons, and of these seven became class leaders in the Methodist church, and of the seven two became preachers. Gilbert G. France was the latest survivor of this large family. He had at one time a hundred cousins, but all, with one exception, are now deceased.

Gilbert G. France was born on the homestead on December 25, 1816, the youngest child of his parents. He remained at home until the age of seventeen, attending school and assisting on the farm. Then he learned the trade of tanner and currier. Subsequently he went with his wife and children to Wisconsin, and in company with three others took up some government land, and founded and named the town of Sharon. His title deed to this, signed by President Polk, is still in the possession of his family. After remaining there for seven years, he returned East and traded his land for a farm in Richmondville, where he lived for five years. In 1856 he came to his farm in Seward, and from that time devoted himself to general farming, hop-raising, and dairying. He had at one period a hundred and forty acres, but later he cultivated about sixty acres, having also some outlying lands. He built the farm buildings, as well as another house and a store in the town, and several dwelling-houses. During the last forty years of his life he was a leader in every advanced movement. He was one of the early promoters of the railroad which runs to Cherry Valley, twenty-five miles from Cobleskill, beginning to agitate the subject in 1867 in company with Judge Campbell and Judge Bates. Upon being appointed one of the commissioners, along with Abraham Sternberg and Leonard Wiland, he was able to make arrangements for bonding the town for twenty-five thousand dollars. He was Railroad Commissioner for fifteen years.

Gilbert G. France was married in 1840, his wife being the daughter of Christian Ottman, and a native of this region. She died at the age of sixty-two, having been the mother of seven children. Of these, six are living; namely, Augusta, Anna, Helen, Millard Filmore, Ida, and Frank H. Augusta married Peter Haines, a farmer in the valley, and has one child, Vergil by name. Anna, who married Hannuil Strail, has two children — Grace and Gilbert. Helen married David Berger, who was killed by a stroke of lightning. She has two children — Ina and Arthur. Millard F., who always resided with his father, married Mary Brown, and has one child, Leland. Ida is the wife of David Emerick, a travelling salesman in Western New York, and is the mother of two children — Bertha and Grace.

Gilbert G. France was actively interested in politics prior to the Civil War, and served as Collector and as Overseer of the Poor. So far as possible he refused public offices. He was a charter member of the Grange, and was one of its lecturers. He was ardently in favor of prohibition, and was a delegate to the State convention at Syracuse for the Prohibition party. On the occasion of the centennial celebration of the anniversary of the town, he was the president of the day, and had full charge of affairs. For fifty-eight years he was a member of the Methodist Episcopal church, and fifty-six years a church officer. Thirty-three years he was a class leader, and twenty years superintendent of the Sunday-school. The beautiful grove fitted up by him is largely used for Sunday-school gatherings. At the time of his death, which occurred on April 5, 1898, he was the oldest member of the charge, which includes Hyndsville, Seward Valley, and Seward Centre, and was probably the oldest church official in the State.

Frank H. France is by trade a carpenter and cabinet-maker. Since the death of his father he has purchased village property in Cobleskill, where he now resides. He has charge of his father's farm, and is doing a prosperous business. He married Carrie M. Ireland, daughter of Daniel Ireland, of Albany, and she has borne him four children, as follows: Lulu A., Gilbert D., Daniel D., and Melville D.

EDGAR JACKSON,[*] attorney and counsellor at law, North Blenheim, Schoharie County, N. Y., was born in the town of Gilboa, this county, August 28, 1853, a son of John I. Jackson. His grandfather, David Jackson, was an early settler of Gilboa, where he bought a large tract of land, and for many years was one of its most successful farmers and the Justice of the Peace. To him and his wife, Peggy, three children were born.

John I. Jackson, who was brought up on a farm, and received his education in the common schools, followed agricultural pursuits in his early manhood, and after marriage purchased a farm not far from the site of the present post-office in Mackey. Taking up the study of law, he pursued it diligently, and, after his admission to the bar, in 1855, practised his profession in Gilboa for nearly forty years, and achieved considerable fame as a lawyer of sound judgment and superior knowledge. He was a Republican in politics, prominent in town matters, and served as Supervisor. He married Mary A. Moore, a native of Gilboa. She was a daughter of Samuel Moore, who came of pioneer stock. She died at the age of sixty-four years, March 31, 1879, leaving six children, namely: Rhoda, deceased; William M., a farmer in Iowa; Lucinda, deceased; Oscar D., a farmer; Edgar, the special subject of this biography; and Luther. Both parents were members of the Baptist church; and the father was for many years a member of Gilboa Lodge, F. & A. M. He died on October 23, 1893, at the age of fourscore years.

Edgar Jackson acquired the rudiments of his education in the public schools of Gilboa, and afterward continued his studies at the Delaware Literary Institute. He subsequently engaged in mechanical pursuits for a while, and then turned his attention to the study of law, which he pursued to such good purpose that in 1886 he was admitted to practice in the different courts by Judson S. Lawdon and Augustus Bakes, Judges of the Supreme Court at Albany. The following two years he practised with his father in Gilboa, whence, in 1888, he came to North Blenheim, where he has built up a large and lucrative general practice, being employed in the Justice, Surrogate, County, and Supreme Courts. In 1894 he built his present commodious office, which is centrally located. While living in Gilboa he served as Justice of the Peace some years and as Town Trustee. Since coming here he has been Commissioner of Highways. Politically, Mr. Jackson is a straightforward Republican; and, fraternally, he is a member of Gilboa Lodge, F. & A. M.

Mr. Jackson married in 1873. His wife's mother, whose maiden name was Sally E. James, is still living, and has two children: Mrs. Jackson; and Orville A., of Chenango County. Mr. and Mrs. Jackson have one child, H. Warren. Mr. Jackson is a member of the Baptist church, while Mrs. Jackson belongs to the Methodist Episcopal church.

JAMES K. ALVERSON,[*] who has been identified with the educational interests of Schoharie County, New York, as school teacher and School Commissioner for the past three decades, resides in Middleburg, where he built his present residence in 1883. He was born February 21, 1845, in Berne, Albany County, a son of Leonard Alverson. His grandfather, Isaac Alverson, formerly a blacksmith in the city of Albany, was killed in one of the battles of the War of 1812, while in the prime of manhood.

Leonard Alverson was reared on a farm in Duanesburg, N.Y. He learned the blacksmith's trade, which he subsequently followed in Berne, not far from Hunter's Land. In Berne he afterward settled on a farm, and also carried on a grocery store and conducted a hotel, being very popular as a landlord. In politics he was a sound Democrat. He served as Assessor of Berne and as Supervisor, and for a number of years he was a Deacon of the Christian church. He subsequently purchased a farm in Hunter's Land, on which he engaged in agricultural pursuits until his death, at the age of sixty-five years. He married Elizabeth Cutter, or, as she was familiarly known in her girlhood, Betsey Wilbur, who was born in Duanesburg, a daughter of Esquire Wilbur. Her father was a well-to-do farmer and an expert fox hunter. He reared four children, namely: Sarah, wife of Seth Owens;

William B.; Elizabeth, Mrs. Alverson, deceased; and Joseph W.

James K. Alverson attended the common schools of his district until he was fourteen years old, and then began earning his own living by working out by the month, being thus employed until the breaking out of the Civil War. At the age of eighteen he enlisted in Company M, Seventh New York Artillery, with which he served eighteen months. He participated in the battles of Spottsylvania, Anna River, and Cold Harbor, where he was twice wounded by minie-balls, once in the right forearm and once in the left thigh. He was taken to the hospital, from which he was discharged as a private at the end of eight months. Returning home, he commenced his career as a teacher, being employed in 1865 and 1866 in Berne. Afterward he was principal of schools in the village of Schoharie, in Middleburg, and Wright, and in other places in Schoharie and Albany Counties, for a continuous period of twenty years. In 1888 Mr. Alverson was elected School Commissioner of the First District of Schoharie County for a term of three years, and in 1894 was again elected to the same responsible position, and served until 1897. As School Commissioner he had to examine the one hundred and twelve teachers employed in the ninety-eight schools under his immediate supervision, and personally visit each school in the eight towns composing his district. Since the expiration of his last term in this capacity, he has resumed his former occupation as a teacher, and is now one of the oldest instructors in this part of the county and one of the most successful. He was formerly a member of the Schoharie County Teachers' Association, and while a Commissioner of the First District he built many new schoolhouses. He is a Democrat in politics, and was twice elected Collector of the town of Berne. Fraternally, he is a member of the Moses Tompkins Post, No. 149, G. A. R., in which he has served as Officer of the Day and been Commander, and belongs also to the Middleburg Lodge, Le Bastelle, I. O. O. F., in which he has passed all the chairs, and is now Past Noble Grand. He and his family attend the Lutheran church.

In 1876 Mr. Alverson married Miss Rhoda Shoemaker, a daughter of Abraham and Phebe (Layman) Shoemaker. Her parents spent their later years of life in Middleburg, where her mother is still living at the age of seventy-five years. Mr. and Mrs. Alverson have three children; namely, Leonard A., W. Layman, and Otis Ray.

CHARLES E. BARRUP,* Postmaster of Esperance, Schoharie County, N. Y., was born August 12, 1855, in Carlisle, this county. His paternal grandfather was a veteran of the War of 1812, and was attached to the staff of General Jackson.

Charles E. Barrup received his education in the district schools, which he attended until reaching the age of sixteen years, when he found employment and became self-supporting. In 1884 he opened a harness shop in Esperance, and he has since conducted the business very successfully up to the present time. Mr. Barrup has taken a prominent part in town affairs. He has twice been elected Town Clerk, and he has been a member of the County Committee. He is an active Democratic worker, and has done much to advance the cause of his party locally. He is a member of Schoharie Lodge, F. & A. M.

In 1879 Mr. Barrup was united in marriage with Miss Sarah Reed, daughter of Henry Reed, of Esperance. Mr. Barrup's mother is a descendant of the family of Shafers that figured largely in the earlier history of Schoharie County. Her grandfather and her great-grandfather were prominent in the construction of the Lutheran church of Cobleskill, which some six years ago celebrated its centennial.

JAMES L. UTTER,[*] the leading farmer of Oak Hill, Durham, and owner, on a large scale, of Western real estate, was born at Oak Hill, on the spot where he now resides, on May 20, 1846, son of Isaac and Mary A. (Niles) Utter. The farm of which he is now the owner has been in his family for three generations, his great-grandfather, James Utter, a Revolutionary soldier, having settled here when the country around was a wilderness. He came here with his wife and son James from Saybrook, Conn., in the spring of 1783, and built a log cabin. Some years later, after he had cleared some land, he built a frame house, which stood until 1894, when it was burned.

The second James Utter was born in Saybrook, Conn., and came here with his mother on horseback. He was brought up on the farm, and in 1806 he built a house for himself where his grandson's house is now standing. He kept increasing his farm by buying adjoining land, and became a very prosperous man. In January, 1837, when he was only fifty-six years old, he slipped on the ice and broke his hip, and on the 19th of the month died from the effects. His wife, to whom he was married on November 26, 1805, bore him six children, none of whom are now living. Her maiden name was Elizabeth Post. She was a Presbyterian, and her husband was a Baptist.

Isaac Utter, above named, son of James, second, and Elizabeth, was born on December 19, 1808, and died on his sixty-fourth birthday. He always lived on the homestead, with the exception of four years which he spent elsewhere. He was interested in real estate in the West, particularly in Wisconsin, where he owned considerable land and held farms on mortgages. Politically, he was a Republican.

He was a liberal contributor to the Methodist church, of which both he and his wife were members; and for many years he was one of its most honored trustees. He took a prominent part in public affairs in the town, and was one of its Supervisors from the time of its incorporation. His wife, who was one of a family of ten children, was a daughter of Samuel Niles, who moved to Oak Hill when she was a young girl, and spent the remainder of his life here. Mrs. Utter resides with her son James, who is her only child.

Mr. James Utter's house, which is one of the finest in the county, was built by his father and himself and under their daily supervision. It was built entirely by the day, and is of the best possible workmanship. The son furnished the plans and gave suggestions for interior decorating and finishing. The decorations were made from exclusive designs, and are really works of art. There are twenty large and fully furnished rooms, some of them measuring fourteen by fifteen feet.

Mr. Utter was educated in the common schools, Greenville Academy, and a select school in Durham. After his father's death he then became proprietor of the homestead estate, which consisted of a hundred and ten acres. Since then he has bought some forty acres adjoining and eighty more on the mountain. He keeps seven horses and twenty-three head of cattle of Jersey stock, and makes butter for the New York markets. He cuts a large amount of hay, the annual crop sometimes reaching eighty tons; and, though he has built two new barns recently, he is still often obliged to stack some of it out of doors. He keeps two men employed the year through. Mr. Utter is a proficient carpenter himself, and has built a number of the buildings on his place, though others he hired built. His tenant house, near his own residence, is an example of his own workmanship.

In 1883 Mr. Utter went into the enterprise of buying land in the West, and he has continued to buy until he now has about seven thousand acres there. Of this he tills some six hundred acres, raising large crops of corn, wheat, and oats. In looking after his interests he has made many trips West, particularly to Dakota and Michigan, where his land is situated. He is one of the directors in the North American Loan and Trust Company of New York City, which has a paid-up capital of over half a million and a surplus fund of a hundred thousand dollars.

Mr. Utter married in 1871 Dora Kelsey, only child of Hiram Kelsey, a leading farmer of Albany County. Although he is an ardent Republican and takes active part in all political matters, attending State and county conventions as delegate, he refuses to accept public office. He is a member of the Methodist church, while Mrs. Utter is a Baptist. For many years he has been a church trustee. Mr. Utter is a hard worker, and everything about his place is kept in the best of repair. He is one of the best known men in the county.

HENRY C. GETTER,* of Middleburg, N.Y., one of the leading lawyers of Schoharie County, was born on June 16, 1857. His father, David Getter, was born in Schoharie. His grandfather Getter, who was a native of Germany, came to this country when a boy, and settled at Central Bridge, Schoharie. He was an expert handicraftsman, and followed the trades of gunsmith and clock-maker. A large number of clocks made by him are still in running order. He lived to be ninety-eight years of age, and his mental faculties were well preserved to the last. His wife attained the age of ninety-three.

David Getter grew to manhood at Central Bridge, where he was born, and in his youth learned the trade of blacksmith. Coming to Middleburg when he was of age, he set up his forge, and, starting in business for himself, continued actively engaged over fifty years. For a long period his was the only smithy in the town. He was an abolitionist and a Republican in politics. His vote was the only one cast for Fremont in his district, and four years later he was one of three to vote for Abraham Lincoln. A reader and a thinker, he was highly respected as a man of sterling integrity and sound judgment, as well as of strong convictions and more than average self-reliance. In religion he was a devoted Methodist, for twenty years superintendent of the Sunday-school and for thirty-five years class leader. His house was a home for Methodist ministers who came that way, and many a weary circuit rider there found shelter and refreshment. David Getter married Harriet Efner, daughter of Harvey Efner, formerly of Palmer, Monroe County. She is still living, being now past eighty years of age. Her father lived to the age of ninety-three years, and was then next to the oldest Free Mason in the State. Mrs. Getter has three children now living; namely, Harvey, Jerome, and Henry C. Two — Charles and Madison — are deceased.

Henry C. Getter obtained his early education in the common schools, and at a private school taught by Professor James Edmondson, now principal of a college in Missouri. He studied law with Messrs. Sandford & Thorn, was admitted to the bar, and then went to Kalamazoo, Mich., and was there for a time with Briggs & Burroughs. Returning East, he formed in 1883 a partnership with William H. Engle, which still continues, this law firm being now the oldest in the county and Mr. Engle the oldest lawyer in the State. Besides doing a large amount of office work, they have an extensive practice in the various courts of the State, including the Court of Appeals.

Mr. Getter married Mary E., daughter of Albert Sawyer and grand-daughter of Dr. Moses Sawyer, formerly of Fulton. Her father was a farmer in Fulton. He died at the age of thirty-seven, leaving two children. Mr. and Mrs. Getter have one child, Jennie L., who is now in the high school. Mr. Getter resided in Fulton up to 1897, when he removed to Middleburg.

Mr. Getter is a Republican in politics. He has been candidate for District Attorney, for County Judge, and for Supervisor, and has assisted to reduce the Democratic majority in the county. He is a member of the I. O. O. F. of Middleburg. Mrs. Getter attends the Methodist church, and he contributes to its support.

W. J. BREWSTER, M.D.,* of North Blenheim, N.Y., was born in Scotland, Albany County, January 8, 1863, son of William J. and Margaret (Ramsey) Brewster. On the paternal side he traces his ancestry, we are told, to Elder William Brewster, of the

"Mayflower" and Plymouth Colony. His grandfather, who was born in 1795, and died in 1841, operated a carding-mill in Schoharie County. His grandmother Brewster's maiden name was Silence Gallup.

William J. Brewster, the Doctor's father, was born in Albany County, in February, 1839. His education was completed at Schoharie Academy; and he taught school for a number of years in Schoharie County, where he also engaged in farming. His wife, Margaret, was the daughter of a prominent farmer and leading public official of Gilboa, who was of Scotch descent. Dr. Brewster's parents were members of the Reformed Church of Gallupville, and his father took much interest in church matters. He died April 13, 1883.

W. J. Brewster obtained his elementary education in the common schools, pursued more advanced studies at Schoharie Academy, and then by teaching school earned money enough to enable him to take the course at the Normal School, where he was graduated. His medical studies were begun under a private instructor, and continued at the University Medical College and at Bellevue Hospital Medical College. He took special courses in the laboratory, and a very thorough course in surgery. He was graduated a Doctor of Medicine in 1890, and then went to North Stratford, Coos County, N.H., where he was in practice till his health failed. After a season of rest and recuperation he came in 1897 to North Blenheim, where he is now settled. He is a well-educated physician, and has a good country practice. While in New Hampshire he was a specialist in orthopedic surgery, in which he has done some remarkable work. He was a Health Officer in New Hampshire, and served also as County Coroner. He was a member of Coos County (New Hampshire) Medical Society, being later a member of the Schoharie County Society. He is a member of Schoharie Valley Lodge, F. & A. M., No. 491. He has written valuable papers for various medical journals. He is a Republican in politics.

Dr. Brewster married Emily E. Earle, of Valleyfield, Province of Quebec, Canada, and has one child.

JAMES FROST,* formerly a prominent citizen of Mariahville, in the town of Duanesburg, N.Y., was born in Washington County, this State, August 4, 1783, son of Lot and Temperance (Semen) Frost. He was a descendant in the fifth generation of William Frost, first, a native of Hampshire, England, and a Quaker, who came to America and settled in Boston, but on account of the religious intolerance of that time was obliged to seek a home elsewhere, and accordingly removed to Long Island. He married Rebecca, daughter of Nicholas Wright. William Frost, second, the next in line of descent, who was born on Long Island about the year 1647, and resided there until his death, married Hannah Trior.

Benjamin Frost, son of William, second, and grandfather of the subject of this sketch, was born June 9, 1719, and spent the greater part of his active life in Dutchess County, New York. He married Rose Springer. Their son Lot, father of James, was born in Dutchess County, March 1, 1744. He was a resident for some years of Washington County, whence he moved to Duanesburg, taking up his residence on Quaker Street, a locality settled by the Friends' Society at an early date, and which is still known by that name. His wife, Temperance, was born on August 30, 1744.

James Frost accompanied his parents from Washington County to Duanesburg. He received a good education, and taught school in his younger days, but relinquished that occupation to become a surveyor, in which capacity he performed much work of an important character. He projected and completed a plank road from Albany to Fort Hunter, and drafted one of the earlier maps of Schenectady County. In 1833-34 he surveyed the new line between Canada and New York State, as well as the greater part of Clinton, Essex, and Franklin Counties, then a wilderness. With his associates he camped out for weeks and months at a time. At night the wolves howled around them, and were kept at bay only by fires. That section of the State, the Adirondack region, is now a famous place of resort in summer. In 1819 he began a survey of the east shore of the Hudson River, under the direction of the Surveyor General, traversing the river by sloop and making numerous soundings. He also surveyed the ground for the second railroad built in the United States, that between Albany and Schenectady, and surveyed and made maps of all old Schoharie, besides other territory. In 1835 he surveyed lands in Elizabethtown (now Elizabeth City), N.J., belonging to Messrs. Conner, Bryant & Crane of that place, and Clark and others of New York, and made maps of the city. Subsequently, removing from Quaker Street, to the northerly part of the town of Duanesburg, about two miles west of Mariahville, he engaged in farming, and also conducted a general store. Possessing an unusual amount of energy and ability, which made him especially eligible to the public service, he took a leading part in town affairs, was particularly interested in educational matters, acted as a Justice of the Peace for many years, and was a member of the Assembly three terms. Politically, he was a stanch supporter of the Whig party. Though reared a Quaker, he was liberal in his religious opinions, and in his later years favored the Universalist belief. He died at his home in Mariahville, December 23, 1851, and his death was the cause of general regret.

James Frost married Mary Marsh, who was born in Canaan, Conn., October 24, 1787, daughter of Silas Marsh. She was a good business woman, and rendered valuable assistance to her husband by carrying on the store while he was absent on surveying trips. She became the mother of ten children — five sons and five daughters - - all of whom grew to maturity, and two are living, namely: General D. M. Frost, a graduate of the United States Military Academy at West Point, and now a prominent resident of St. Louis, Mo.; and Miss M. Louise Frost. General Frost had a large family of girls, three of whom married English noblemen. One of them is now living in Paris. The others are in England. Miss M. Louise Frost, who is a lady of superior attainments, resides at the homestead during summer, and passes her winters in the South. The other children of James and Mary (Marsh) Frost were: Caroline, Adelia D., Silas W., Rosanna, James, William M., John S., and Phœbe A. The mother died August 18, 1864. The sons nearly all studied and followed engineering. John S., who was a lawyer, died in 1857.

JOHN H. PUTNAM, who carries on farming and market gardening in Niskayuna, was born in this town, June 15, 1816. His parents, Harmon and Margaret (Wheaton) Putnam, were natives of this county. His paternal grandfather, John Putnam, was an early settler here and a noted hunter in his day. He afterward resided in various places, and died in Greene, Chenango County, at an advanced age.

Harmon Putnam, the father, followed the carpenter's trade during his active period. He was married in Niskayuna, which was thenceforward his place of residence. He was a reliable workman, and as an honest, industrious citizen he stood high in the estimation of the entire community. He died at the age of sixty years. Margaret Wheaton Putnam, his wife, died at the age of twenty-seven. She was the mother of four children, of whom John H., the subject of this sketch, was the first-born, and is the only one living.

Reuben and Jacob died young, and the other died in infancy.

John H. Putnam was educated in the town schools of Niskayuna. At an early age he began work as an assistant on the farm he now occupies, which was then owned by one John Clark, and he afterward worked for other farmers in the neighborhood. When seventeen years old he began an apprenticeship at the carpenter's trade, which was his occupation for thirty years, or until 1864. In 1876 he bought his present farm of seventy acres, which he has greatly improved, and has since been engaged in general farming.

On February 28, 1839, Mr. Putnam was joined in marriage with Mary Ann Van Vranken, of Niskayuna, daughter of Jacob Van Vranken and a representative of an old family of this town. Mr. and Mrs. Putnam have one son living, Jacob, who was born January 1, 1846, and is engaged in farming with his father. He married Gertrude McChessen, and has four children — John, Margaret A., Julia, and Lena.

Since the breaking out of the Southern rebellion in April, 1861, Mr. Putnam has voted with the Republican party. He has served with ability as Supervisor and Town Clerk, each two terms. He was Highway Commissioner five years, and has been a Justice of the Peace. He is a Master Mason and one of the oldest members of St. George Lodge, No. 6, F. & A. M., of Schenectady, having joined the order in 1855. Mr. and Mrs. Putnam are members of the Dutch Reformed church.

MADISON YOUNG,* for a number of years a prominent figure in the public affairs of Carlisle, Schoharie County, N.Y., was born in this town, September 20, 1846, son of Benjamin and Lana (Van Vaulkenburgh) Young. His great-grandfather was Peter Young, a German, who came here from Hudson, N.Y., as a pioneer, and acquired possession of two separate tracts of land, the whole amounting to three hundred and ten acres. His log cabin stood about twenty-five rods west of the Rock Schoolhouse. He was a successful farmer, and his property, which was unencumbered at the time of his death, he divided among his children.

Matthias Young, Madison Young's grandfather, whose birth took place January 20, 1763, was the first white child born in Carlisle. Receiving a share of his father's property, he erected a frame house, and carried on general farming until his death, which occurred May 21, 1822. He was actively interested in political and religious affairs, held some of the important town offices, and was one of the leading members of the Dutch Reformed church. He married Helena Patria, who was of German descent, and she died March 14, 1824. They were the parents of five children; namely, Solomon, Benjamin, Richard, Margaret, and Lana. The great-grandfather served in the war of the Revolution, and the grandfather in that of 1812.

Benjamin Young, Madison Young's father, was born October 20, 1800. He succeeded to the possession of about eighty acres of his father's property when a young man, and cultivated his farm energetically for the rest of his life. He died in October, 1869. He was the father of six children: Helena, wife of J. Rose; Margaret, wife of Demosthenes Young; Sarah M., who married Adam Cole; Eva A., widow of Abraham Burnstein; Madison, the subject of this sketch; and Frances M., wife of E. C. Grantier.

Madison Young acquired a district-school education, and his aptitude for learning enabled him to attain unusual proficiency in his studies. He assisted in carrying on the home farm until after the death of his father, when he turned his attention to educational work, and taught school with marked success during the following eighteen years, with the exception of one term, the greater part of the time being spent in this and the adjacent localities. For the first term of teaching he received one dollar per day, after that two dollars a day, very few then receiving so high a salary. Finally becoming tired of the arduous as well as monotonous duties of a pedagogue, he resumed farming at the homestead, which contains about eighty acres of well-improved land; and, though not inclined to force its yielding power, he nevertheless raises excellent crops.

As one of the foremost leaders of the Democratic party in this section, he has long maintained a wide influence in public affairs, and enjoys the confidence of all voters irrespective of politics. His long and faithful service to the county was characterized by a judicious expenditure of public funds and an earnest desire to promote the best interests of the people. As chairman of the Committees on Printing and on Ratio and Apportionment during his two years as Supervisor, he greatly reduced the expenses of these departments, and by close figuring was able to effect considerable retrenchment in other branches of the service.

Mr. Young married for his first wife Elizabeth Brounnaghin and for his second Nettie Hilsinger. He has no children. In his religious views he is liberal.

WILLIAM H. NEVILLE,* a representative citizen of Middleburg, N.Y., and a man of varied business interests, was born in the house which is now his home on August 6, 1867, son of Jacob and Jane E. (Shafer) Neville. His grandfather, William Neville, was a pioneer settler in Sharon, and died there at an advanced age, leaving a large family.

Jacob Neville, one of the youngest of the children of William, was born in Sharon on August 21, 1827, and died in Middleburg in 1891. He was for many years closely identified with the growth of this town, and was one of the leaders in every worthy enterprise started here. His boyhood days were passed on the farm in Sharon, and early in life he assisted in the family support. His career in mercantile affairs began at the time he went into a store in Sharon Hill as clerk. At twenty-three years of age he came to Middleburg and entered the general merchandise store of the old firm of Becker & Beckman. So valuable did he make himself in the conduct of the business that upon the retirement of Mr. Beckman he became a partner in the concern, which thereupon assumed the name of Becker, Neville & Co. They were the leading merchants of the town, and had a large trade in all the surrounding country. In time Mr. Becker sold his interest in the business to Mr. Hoag, and the firm name became Neville & Hoag. Later Mr. Hoag sold out to Mr. J. L. Engel, and still later a brother of the latter, Mr. A. B. Engel, was admitted to partnership. The business was then continued up to 1889 under the name of Neville, Engel & Co. Upon Mr. Neville's retirement in 1889, the firm became Engel Brothers, and as such has continued in business to the present time.

Among the various enterprises in the accomplishment of which Jacob Neville was an important factor may be mentioned the following: the Middleburg & Schoharie Railroad; the First National Bank and later the bank building; and the Union school-house building, which is one of the finest in the county. He was a large stockholder in the railroad organization, and was a director and the vice-president until his death. He was also a director in the bank as long as he lived. Politically, he was a Democrat, and frequent appeals were made to him to accept public office. From 1885 to 1889, under Mr. Cleveland's administration, he was Postmaster of Middleburg; and, had not his death prevented, his friends would undoubtedly have elected him to the Assembly for the session of 1892-93. He was for many years an Elder in the Lutheran church, and generously assisted the church both by financial and by moral support.

His marriage occurred in January, 1864. His wife was the daughter of William and Maria (Gridley) Shafer, and grand-daughter of Joseph Gridley, who was one of Washington's body-guard. William Shafer was born in Blenheim, and was a lifelong resident there. He owned a number of dwelling-houses and farms, and dealt quite extensively in real estate, besides carrying on general farming. As a business man he was very successful. He died at the age of eighty-two. His wife, who died at the age of sixty-four, was a native of Middleburg. Of the four children born to them three are living, namely: Mrs. Neville, who resides with her son on the farm settled by her ancestors; Margaret, who is the wife of George Brockway, of Chicago; and Nancy. The last named married A. J. Freneyer, of Albany, who for many years managed the Freneyer House in Middleburg.

William H. Neville obtained his education in the public schools of Middleburg and at Albany Academy. Leaving the latter after four years of study there, he entered the post-office, his father then being Postmaster, and for the succeeding four years he had practical charge of the office. Upon the expiration of his father's term he went into the store as clerk, and afterward he went to Albany as clerk in the insurance office of W. C. Rose. Still later he became interested in the Brandow Printing Company, of Albany, but when the plant was burned he returned to Middleburg, where he took charge of his father's affairs until the death of the latter. Shortly after this event the son bought the Middleburg *Gazette*, of which he continued to be the proprietor for three years. Since selling out in 1895, he has occupied himself with looking after his own and his mother's real estate interests, and in doing some general farming and hop-raising. As he has a large real estate property, including a number of farms, he has little chance to be idle. He also retains an interest in the Brandow Printing Company, which has been reorganized since the fire. Besides this he is a stockholder in the Middleburg & Schoharie Railroad, in the projected road to Catskill, and in the National Bank. He is a director in the Middleburg Telephone Company and treasurer of the high school. For three years he was Village Clerk, and for a number of years he served on the Board of Education. Politically, he is a Democrat, and for two years was a member of the county committee.

Mr. Neville was married on June 22, 1893, to Maud E. Lewis, who was born in Gilboa. She is the daughter of Oscar and Agnes (Strickland) Lewis. Her father is now one of the most prominent stock farmers in Conesville. Mrs. Neville's two brothers, Messrs. Frank and Raymond Lewis, are interested in the stock farm in company with their father. Mrs. Neville graduated from the Normal School, and taught before her marriage in the grammar school in Middleburg. She is the mother of one son, Donald. Mrs. Neville is a member of the Lutheran church, and her husband is an attendant of the Sunday services.

Mr. Neville belongs to the Masonic organizations here; to La Bastile Lodge, No. 494, I. O. O. F., and Encampment No. 129; also to the order of Red Men. He has been Chief Patriarch of the encampment for one year.

CHARLES MANN,* one of the most able and progressive agriculturists of Schoharie County, owns and occupies a well-appointed farm in Fulton, not far from the village of Breakabeen. He was born in this town, November 2, 1856. He is a son of the late Almon Mann, and comes of hardy New England stock, his grandfather, Thomas Mann, having been born and bred in Vermont. From his hillside home in the Green Mountains Thomas removed to Albany County, New York, while yet a young man, and in the newer country cleared and partly improved a farm. Coming then to Schoharie County from Berne, he spent his remaining days in Fulton, living until eighty-six years old.

Almon Mann was born in Berne, N.Y., but removed with his parents to Fulton when a boy, and was there reared to man's estate. After completing his education, he worked as a farm laborer until ready to settle in life, when he bought land, which he cultivated some years. Prior to his death, however, at the age of sixty-six years, he removed to the village of Breakabeen. A consistent member of the Methodist Episcopal church, he held many of the offices in that organization, and was connected with its Sunday-school. His wife, whose maiden name was Maria Chapman, is living at Breakabeen, an active woman of sixty-four years. She was born in Fulton, the daughter of Jacob Chapman. She is a sister of William W. Chapman, whose sketch may be found on another page of this volume. She has twelve children, as follows: Alice, living in Amsterdam; Jacob H., who has been School Commissioner of Schoharie nine years; Theron H.; Charles; Rose E.; Wellington; Lilly; Irving; Julia; Hattie; Josiah; and Manley B.

Charles Mann acquired his early education in Fulton and Middleburg. After leaving the parental roof he made his home with an uncle, and for three or more terms taught school, a part of the time being thus employed in Richmondville. On marrying he bought and took possession of his present farm of one hundred and fifty acres, formerly known as the Burgh farm, where he has since been profitably engaged in general farming and dairying. In the latter industry he is very successful, having a well-selected herd of Guernsey and Jersey cattle. On the estate he has made improvements of an excellent character, having brought the larger part of the land to a high state of cultivation, erected nearly all the buildings on the place, and furnished it with the latest approved modern farm machinery and implements. He has built a silo, which he considers a good investment for a dairy farmer, and he uses a separator in his dairy. Mr. Mann reads the leading journals devoted to agriculture, and he is himself a frequent contributor to the home and agricultural departments of various papers, including the New York *Homestead* and the Utica *Press*. He is an active member of the New York State Grange, in which he has served as lecturer several terms. In July, 1898, he passed the required examinations for a milk expert in Albany. In politics he is an unswerving Democrat, and has been nominated as Assessor. A valued member of the Lutheran Church of Breakabeen, he has held the position of treasurer and secretary, and for many years has been superintendent of the Sunday-school connected with it.

In 1879 Mr. Mann married Miss Bertha Terpening, who was born in Princetown, Schenectady County, daughter of Henry H. Terpening, a farmer of that town. Mr. and Mrs. Mann have four children.

STANTON OSTERHOUT,* one of the stirring farmers of Carlisle, Schoharie County, was born in this town, May 20, 1852, son of Jacob and Betsey E. (Kniskern) Osterhout. His paternal grandfather, Abraham Osterhout, a native of Holland, immigrated to New York when young, and coming from Dutchess County, this State, to West Carlisle, settled upon a tract of land containing about two hundred and fifty acres. A sturdy pioneer, he improved his land into a good farm, and he took an active part in the affairs of the Dutch Reformed church in his neighborhood. He was twice married, and by both of his wives had children. Those of his second union were: Jacob A., George, Chauncey, Sarah, and Catherine. George, who was quite active in political affairs, died in 1862, aged forty-five years. Chauncey, who was engaged in business in Cobleskill, died in 1872. Sarah is the widow of David P. Brown. Catherine, who married J. J. Brown, died in 1878.

Jacob A. Osterhout, Stanton Osterhout's father, was a lifelong resident of Carlisle. After his father's death he and one of his brothers bought the homestead. He was one of the first farmers in the town to engage in the raising of hops, which he produced quite extensively, and he also made a specialty of hay and grain. He owned about four hundred acres of land. He was prominent and influential in town and county politics, took a conspicuous part in the various conventions, but would not accept office. His religious preference was for the Dutch Reformed church. He was the father of seven children, namely: Josiah; Stanton, the subject of this sketch; Wilson; Alfred; Albert; Elmira; and Melissa. Josiah died at the age of eighteen; Melissa married Daniel Mickle; Elmira married Aaron Young; Alfred is residing at the homestead; and the others are engaged in farming in this town.

Stanton Osterhout was educated in the district school. He assisted his father in farming until after his marriage, when he purchased the property known as the Young estate, which was formerly owned by his father. This farm, which originally consisted of one hundred and fifty-five acres, he has enlarged by the addition of adjoining land. He divides his time between dairy farming and the cultivation of hops. He keeps from twenty-five to thirty head of

Holstein cattle, besides other blooded stock, and is a member of the American Holstein Association.

He has served as Supervisor for at least two terms, was chairman of the Committees on Printing, Town Accounts, and Equalization, and by judicious management succeeded in making a considerable reduction in public expenditures. He has served as Highway Commissioner one year, and upon the Democratic County Committee several terms. He was instrumental in establishing the Farmers' Insurance Company of Seward, Carlisle, and Cobleskill; was one of the organizers, and is director and treasurer, of the Hop Insurance Company; is local agent for the Sharon, Carlisle, and Seward Insurance companies, and for the hop company.

Mr. Osterhout married Josephine Hilsinger, daughter of William Hilsinger. They have had three children — Orson, Elva, and Emory. Elva married Homer Karher. Orson died July 11, 1891, aged twenty years and seven months.

Mr. Osterhout belongs to Cobleskill Lodge, No. 394, is vice-president of the local agricultural society, a charter member of the grange, and a member of other organizations. He attends the Dutch Reformed church, but contributes liberally toward the support of other religious denominations.

JOSEPH B. GRAHAM,* ex-Mayor of Schenectady, N.Y., was born in Rossie, St. Lawrence County, this State, September 27, 1830, son of William and Janet (Fairbairn) Graham. His father was born in Wigton, near Carlisle, England, June 6, 1806, and his mother was a native of Scotland.

Joseph Graham, the grandfather of Joseph B., was born in Wigton about the year 1767. He was a saddler by trade, and carried on business there until meeting with reverses. In April, 1819, he sailed from Liverpool with his wife and eleven children, landing at Quebec in the following June. With his small means he purchased a tract of wild land in Wilna, Jefferson County, N.Y., and with the assistance of his five sturdy sons he cleared a good farm, upon which he resided for the rest of his life. He died in 1841, and his wife, who survived him, died in Lowville, N.Y., on her eightieth birthday, while visiting her daughter. They had five sons and six daughters. One of the latter, who was taken ill while on the passage from England, died soon after landing. The first and third sons settled near St. Catherine's, Canada. The others located in this State, married, and reared large families. All lived to an advanced age, and Margaret, the youngest, died in Carthage, N.Y., at the age of eighty years. The grandparents were members of the Church of England, but, through the influence of the itinerant Methodist preachers who visited the outlying districts in those early days, their children were converted to that faith.

William Graham, the father, was educated in England, and was an apt scholar, especially in mathematics. When nineteen years old he began teaching school in the Scotch settlement near Wilna, but his principal business was the furnishing of plans and specifications to contractors for heavy mason work, bridge building, and so forth. He was a highly intelligent, well-read man, particularly fond of biography and history, and is said to have predicted that slavery in the South would ultimately cause a civil war. He died November 3, 1858. Jeanette, his first wife, whom he married in 1829, was a daughter of James and Mary (Bell) Fairbairn, who came from the neighborhood of Glasgow, Scotland, in 1818, and settled in Rossie, N.Y. They were industrious farming people and sturdy pioneers. They reared one son and five daughters. William Graham by his first marriage was the father of eight children, of whom Joseph B., the subject of this sketch, was the eldest. All are living except James, the second-born, who died suddenly in May, 1894, aged sixty-two years, leaving two children. The mother died in 1852, aged forty-two years. By a second marriage William Graham had three daughters.

Joseph B. Graham resided with his maternal grandparents from his fifth to his tenth year, and, as they spoke the Scotch dialect, he learned it to perfection. He began his education in the district schools, and was fitted for college at the Wesleyan Seminary, Gouverneur, N.Y. In order to procure funds for the completion of his studies, he taught in the common schools until 1854, when he entered Union College, where he was graduated with honors in 1858. After teaching classics and mathematics at the Stillwater Academy for a time, he came to Schenectady, and in company with Mr. F. A. Young was engaged for the succeeding eight years in mercantile business, dealing in books, stationery, wall papers, pianofortes, and other musical instruments. Selling his interest to his partner, he was out of business for about six years, and then engaged in the dry-goods trade as a member of the firm of T. H. Reeves & Co., from which he withdrew some seven years later. He was for a number of years extensively engaged in the real estate business, and, although his activity in that line has somewhat diminished of late, he still owns a large amount of valuable city property, which is occupied by thirty or more tenants. He resides in a substantial house at 6 Nott Terrace, which he built twenty-seven years ago.

Mr. Graham is a director of the Union National Bank. In 1879 he became a member of the Mutual Relief Society, under certificate No. 212; he was a member of its Board of Directors for six years; was chairman of the Reserve Fund Committee and of the committee appointed to revise the by-laws; and at the annual convention in 1883 he was unanimously elected vice-president. His connection with the society has been marked by an unusually clear conception of and a conscientious regard for its business interests, and he is considered one of its most valued officials. He was twice elected to the Common Council, has been a member of the Boards of Health and Education, and as Mayor of the city in 1879-80 he managed the municipal affairs in a business-like manner.

On August 8, 1858, Mr. Graham was united in marriage with Cornelia L. White, of this county, daughter of Andrew and Cornelia (De Forest) White. Her father was a native of the north of Ireland, and her mother belonged to an old Dutch family of this city. She died in 1878, and in 1880 he married for his second wife Sarah E. Hagaman, also of a well-known Dutch family, daughter of Joseph J. and Elizabeth M. Hagaman. He was the father of three children by his first union, namely: Jennie, who died at the age of five; William, who died at the age of one year and six months; and Edward White Graham, who married Abbie Craver, and is now residing in Denver, Col. One child, Mary Hagaman, by his second marriage, is living with her parents.

Mr. Graham is an active member of the Methodist Episcopal church, which he has served in an official capacity. He was prominently identified with the building of the present edifice, which was completed in 1874, at a cost of eighty thousand dollars, and is a liberal contributor toward its support. He is a member of Union College Chapter of the Phi Beta Kappa Society; has been a trustee of the Troy Conference Academy, Poultney, Vt., continuously since 1874; and has been president of the board since 1878. He possesses and highly prizes a small writing-desk which was purchased in England for five guineas by his grandfather, who in April, 1819, gave it to his son William. In it are some rare specimens of drawings executed by his father when a lad of thirteen years, and also some letters received from the father by the son while in college. Mr. Graham received this heirloom from his father in November, 1858, just before his father's death.

JAMES C. McWILLIAMS, an able farmer and enterprising insurance agent of Prattsville, was born in Kortright, Delaware County, August 4, 1845, son of Joseph S. and Mary Ann (Kilpatrick) McWilliams. His parents were both natives of that town, and he is of Scotch descent. Joseph S. McWilliams learned the blacksmith's trade, which he followed until turning his attention to farming; and he was engaged in the latter occupation at the time of his death, which occurred October 27, 1869, at the age of fifty-seven years. He was an upright, conscientious man, who possessed considerable natural ability, and he acquired success in his calling. In politics he was a Republican. He and his wife, Mary Ann McWilliams, were members of the Presbyterian church. They had two sons: John B., who is no longer living; and James C., the subject of this sketch. The mother died May 19, 1890, aged seventy-four years. John B. McWilliams enlisted for service in the Civil War while under age, and was rejected on that account, but when old enough he re-enlisted in Company K, One Hundred and Twentieth Regiment, New York Volunteers, of which he became Orderly Sergeant. He died in the army at the age of twenty-one years.

James C. McWilliams started in life for

himself at the age of sixteen as clerk in the general store of G. C. Fenn, with whom he remained four years. After residing at Red Falls, N.Y., for a time, he became a travelling salesman for a Utica cigar firm, and a year later he went to New York City, where he secured a clerkship in a dry-goods store. He was subsequently in the employ of J. S. Conover, dealer in grates and fenders. After residing in the metropolis about five years, he came to Prattsville, where for the next seven years he was engaged in the cooperage business. Selling out in 1893, he was placed in charge of the post-office, and, being appointed Postmaster by President Cleveland, he continued to serve the community in that capacity until 1897. He is now local agent for several large insurance companies; and he also carries on a small farm, which he devotes to market gardening. He is quite extensively engaged in raising bees, and sells a large quantity of honey annually. Politically, he is a Democrat. He has been a Justice of the Peace for twelve consecutive years, was for a number of years Inspector of Elections, served two terms on the special license board, and was nominated by his party for the presidency of the village, which he declined to accept. He is sincerely esteemed as a high-minded, public-spirited citizen.

In 1869 Mr. McWilliams was united in marriage with Elizabeth Decker, his first wife, a native of Roxbury, N.Y., daughter of Lorin and Sally Ann Decker. Mr. Decker was a prosperous farmer and a life-long resident of that town. She died, leaving one son, William J., a farmer and market gardener, who married Mary Churchill. For his second wife Mr. James C. McWilliams married Ella Miller, a native of Cairo, N.Y., daughter of Seymour Miller. Her father was for years a widely-known hotel-keeper. At one time he was proprietor of the Prattsville House; and, previous to coming here, he kept hotels in Cairo, Windham, and other places. The children of this union are James E. and Marie.

Mr. McWilliams was made a Mason over thirty years ago, and is now one of the leading members of Oasis Lodge, in which he has occupied all the important chairs, having been its Worshipful Master for six years in succession. The family attend the Methodist Episcopal church.

CHARLES K. FRAZIER, M.D., an able and progressive physician of Cobleskill, Schoharie County, was born in this town, October 17, 1850. He is the son of the late Dr. David Frazier, who was here engaged in the practice of medicine for forty-seven consecutive years. His great-grandfather Frazier came to Cobleskill from Germany in 1776, being one of the early settlers of this part of the county. He was here engaged as a tiller of the soil the remainder of his days, and here his son John, the father of the elder Doctor, was born and reared. John Frazier was born in that part of Cobleskill that is now known as Richmondville, and, having succeeded to the occupation of his father, he was engaged in agricultural pursuits throughout the active period of his life of seventy-eight years.

David Frazier obtained his elementary education in the common schools of this town, and was graduated from the Schoharie and Albany Medical Schools. Settling in Cobleskill, he practised his profession with unusual success, having an extensive patronage, and being by far the best-known physician within a radius of twenty miles. He was very influential in local affairs, and besides being one of the members of the first Board of Town Trustees, a position which he filled several years, and Supervisor of the town three terms, he was superintendent of schools a number of years, and also Coroner. In politics he was true to the principles in which he was reared, and zealously supported the Democratic party. He died in 1894, aged seventy-five years. His wife, Susanna Jenkins, was born and educated in Dover, England, from whence she came with her parents to New York State when a girl. She died September 25, 1897, aged eighty-three years, leaving three children, namely: Elizabeth; Charles K., the special subject of this sketch; and Frances, wife of the Rev. George Muller. Both parents were members of the Lutheran church.

Charles K. Frazier received his early education in the public schools of Cobleskill, and after taking a course of study at the Albany Academy he read medicine a while with his father and with Dr. Armsby, of Albany. He was graduated from the Albany Medical College in 1873, and spent his first year of practice in Albany. He subsequently practised two years each in Waverly, Tioga County, N.Y., and Big Flats, Chemung County, not far from Elmira. In 1878 he returned to Cobleskill, and in the time that has since intervened he has built up a large and lucrative practice.

He is a sound Democrat, and was formerly quite active in political circles and a regular attendant of primaries and local conventions. In 1877 he was a delegate to the State convention that nominated Horatio Seymour for governor, and which, on Seymour's refusal of the proffered chair, reconvened at Saratoga, and nominated Robinson, the successful candidate. He has served as Town Clerk, and, having been appointed Coroner to fill out an unexpired term by his old-time friend, Governor David B. Hill, he has since held the position, having been re-elected for a term of four years in 1891 and again re-elected for another term in 1895. He is a member of the Schoharie Medical Society, and since 1895 has been its president.

In 1874 Dr. Frazier married Miss Rosalia L. Camp, daughter of Nathan Camp, a prominent citizen of Campville, Tioga County, where he still resides. Dr. and Mrs. Frazier have one child, Nellie.

MRS. MARY J. MULFORD,* proprietor of the Mountain Summit House, Tannersville, is a native of New York City. Her parents, John and Mary (Corson) Braden, were natives of Ireland, but came to America prior to their marriage. Arriving in New York at the age of nineteen, her father secured a position in a store. He subsequently came to Tannersville in the employ of the Edwards Tannery Company, remaining with that concern until it went out of business. After following various occupations, Mr. Braden turned his attention to farming, upon the property now owned and occupied by his daughter, Mrs. Mulford. His death occurred here at the age of seventy years. To him and his wife, Mary, were born three children — Margaret, Elizabeth, and Mary J., the subject of this sketch. Margaret resides with her sister in Hunter; and Elizabeth, who is the wife of William Stewart, is living in Sullivan County. The mother died at sixty-seven. The parents were Presbyterians.

Mary J. Braden in her girlhood attended the common schools, acquiring therein a practical knowledge of several branches of study, which have since been useful to her in a business way. In 1868 she became the wife of Samuel S. Mulford, who was born in Harpersfield, Delaware County, son of a prosperous farmer of the same name. Mr. Mulford was well educated, and when a young man he taught schools in Delaware, Schoharie, and Greene Counties. After his marriage he was engaged in the hotel business in Cairo, this county, for a short time, and, going from that town to Gilboa, Schoharie County, he conducted a stage line plying between Windham and Catskill. Relinquishing the latter enterprise, he came to Hunter, where he began the improvement of the Braden farm for summer resort purposes by first removing the old dwelling, which he replaced with a more commodious building containing accommodations for a number of guests. The success of the venture made necessary an enlargement of the house, the addition being completed in 1891, the year in which he died. He was then fifty-six years old. Mr. Mulford was widely and favorably known throughout this section as an able business man and a public-spirited citizen, ever displaying an active interest in the political, moral, and religious welfare of the community. He served as a Supervisor for a number of years, was School Commissioner for two terms of two years each, and he was an earnest supporter of the Democratic party. His judgment in public affairs was much sought after and followed. Perceiving the need of a permanent religious organization in this village, he was mainly instrumental in causing one to be established, subscribing liberally toward the erection of a church. He was a member of the Masonic order, and had occupied some of the important chairs in the Blue Lodge at Saugerties. Samuel S. Mulford was the father of three children, namely: William, Maud, and Francis, all of whom are now assisting in carrying on the hotel. William married Carrie McGee, and has four children.

After the death of her husband Mrs. Mulford became manager as well as proprietor of the hotel, and in these capacities has displayed her ability by successfully conducting both the business and domestic departments. The Mountain Summit House, which is a pleasant and healthful summer home, occupies a sightly location upon elevated ground. It has ample accommodations for two hundred guests, and that their comforts are well provided for is manifested by the large number who enjoy its hospitality during the summer and autumn months. Though not a member of any religious denomination, Mrs. Mulford is a generous contributor toward the support of religious work. She is highly esteemed for her many estimable qualities.

OSCAR H. SHANNON,* a Civil War veteran, was born in Schenectady, where he now resides, August 29, 1848, son of Thomas T. and Lucy C. (Geer) Shannon. The father was a native of Glenville, N.Y. His great-grandfather Shannon, and his great-grandfather Tull served in the Continental army during the Revolutionary War.

Having completed his education, Oscar H. Shannon at the age of fifteen enlisted in the Seventy-seventh Regiment, New York Volunteers, with which he served until the close of the Rebellion, and participated in the siege of Petersburg. After his discharge he went to sea as engineer's storekeeper on the steamship "Henry Chauncy," and was absent about one year, during which time he visited South America. Upon his return to Schenectady he served an apprenticeship at the tinsmith's trade, which he followed as a journeyman previous to opening an establishment on his own account, and he subsequently carried on a successful business for about fifteen years. Joining the National Guard, he served for some time as Lieutenant in a company of the Eighty-third Regiment, and assisted in organizing two other companies, one of which, the Washburn Continentals, formerly the Stanford Hose Company, withdrew in a body from the Schenectady Fire Department to become the Stanford Cadets. He was promoted from the rank of First Lieutenant to that of Captain of the company, and its present name was suggested by him. The Washburn Continentals were mustered into the National Guard during the war with Spain as Company F, Second Regiment. He was also one of the principal organizers of a company composed entirely of Civil War veterans, which flourished for a time as originally made up; but the veterans were compelled by old age to withdraw one by one, and their places were filled by young recruits. This company, of which he was First Lieutenant for five years, was mustered into service during the late war as Company E, Second Regiment.

Mr. Shannon married Mary A. Langdon, of Schenectady, daughter of John Langdon. He has one daughter, Bernice L., who is now the wife of Andrew T. Branion, of New York City.

Mr. Shannon belongs to St. Paul's Lodge, No. 17, I. O. O. F., and is a Past Commander of Harsfall Post, No. 90, G. A. R. In 1871 he joined Julian Lodge, Knights of Pythias, which was afterward disbanded, but prior to the surrender of its charter he withdrew for the purpose of organizing the Mohawk Valley Lodge at Fort Plain, and was its first Chancellor. He was representative to the Grand

Lodge in 1897, and was Deputy Grand Chancellor. He organized Loyal Lodge, No. 384, in 1896; was formerly Chief of Staff of the New York Brigade, Uniform Rank, with the rank of Colonel; received his Grand Lodge degrees during the present year; and was appointed assistant organizer of the Endowment Rank by Past Grand Chancellor and Supreme Representative William Ledew, his jurisdiction covering the entire State of New York outside of the metropolis. Mr. Shannon is now a member of Schenectady Lodge, to which he was admitted by card.

R EVILO COBB,* a well-to-do farmer of Ashland, N.Y., was born in Windham, Greene County, March 4, 1821, son of Simon and Eunice (Lewis) Cobb. His father came here from Connecticut as a pioneer, and cleared off a tract of land, which he improved into a good farm. He was an early schoolmaster in this locality, and figured quite prominently in the growth and development of the town. He died at the age of fifty-five years. Simon Cobb and his wife, Eunice, were the parents of ten children. Three of the four now living are: Revilo, Edwin, and Sidney. The mother died at the age of seventy-two.

Revilo Cobb was reared upon the homestead farm, and was educated in Windham. His boyhood was spent in a log house, and his clothing, like that of other children of this locality at that time, was made from home-raised wool and flax, which were spun, woven, and made up by the deft hands of his mother. When a young man he turned his attention to agriculture, and tilled the soil of one farm for a period of thirty-eight years. In 1888 he moved to his present farm of fifty acres, which is admirably located and unusually fertile. His principal efforts are devoted to the care of a well-equipped dairy. He was formerly an extensive sheep-raiser, and in that, as well as in dairy farming, he has, through his energy, perseverance, and sound judgment, realized excellent financial results. He still possesses the strength and agility of a much younger man, and attends to his every-day duties with the same activity that has for years been one of his chief characteristics. In politics he is a Democrat.

Mr. Cobb married Louisa Barlow, who was born in Ashland, daughter of Alanson Barlow. Her father spent his active life upon a farm in this town, and died at the age of seventy-seven years. Mrs. Cobb died at the age of seventy-six. She was the mother of but one child, George A., who was born in Ashland, October 28, 1850. Revilo Cobb acted as a vestryman of the Episcopal church for a number of years, and his wife was a member.

George A. Cobb completed his education in West Windham, and taught school a number of terms in different places. He took charge of the homestead farm when his father left it, and he carried it on until 1894, when he relinquished it in order to assist his father. In 1878 George A. Cobb married Elizabeth Sutton, who was born in Windham, N.Y., daughter of Aden and Elizabeth (Cook) Sutton. Her father was a native of Schoharie County, and her mother was born in Windham, daughter of Ichabod Cook. Aden and Elizabeth C. Sutton were the parents of four children, namely: Elizabeth, wife of George A. Cobb; Polly, wife of Henry Sutton; Ella, who married H. D. Martin; and Dr. I. F. Sutton, a physician, who died at the age of thirty-two years. Aden Sutton married for his second wife Theresa Cook, who died at the age of thirty-seven years, leaving a daughter Ursula. The latter married I. C. Lee, a merchant of this town, and is no longer living. The father died at the age of seventy-two years. He belonged to the Methodist Episcopal church, in which he was at one time a class leader, choir director, and steward.

George A. Cobb is a Democrat in politics, and takes an active interest in public affairs. He was one of the organizers of the local grange, Patrons of Husbandry, and is its present Master. Mr. and Mrs. George A. Cobb have one daughter, Hattie. They attend the Methodist Episcopal church.

INDEX.

BIOGRAPHICAL.

A.

	PAGE
Adams, Edward	350
Akeley, Frank	175
Albro, William H.	242
Alverson, James K.	416
Anderson, George W.	205
Avery, Benjamin H.	388

B.

Baldwin, Andrew G.	53
Baldwin, William H.	305
Barrup, Charles E.	417
Bassler, Wellington E.	209
Beard, Franklin P.	75
Becker, Harmon	20
Beekman, Dow	89
Beekman, Duryea	88
Bellinger, George W.	169
Benham, John T.	37
Bestle, Rudolph	208
Bice, Marshall D.	306
Billings, Ernest E.	368
Bloodgood, Clarence E.	359
Boens, Louis A.	158
Boorn, Clarence M.	320
Botsford, Henry T.	19
Boughton, Seymour	33
Bradt, John	260
Bradt, Nicholas	69
Brewster, W. J.	420
Bruce, Elbert O.	45
Burgett, William W.	215
Burhans, Judson	308
Burnett, Charles S.	140
Burtis, John H., Jr.	400

C.

Campbell, John D.	52
Campbell, William L.	240
Cary, John S.	157
Case, James M.	307
Casper, Frank L.	200
Chambers, David	302
Chapman, Mrs. Elda B.	273
Chapman, Frank A.	296
Chapman, William W.	370
Chase, Albert	265
Chase, Emory A.	276
Clapper, Franklin	410
Clark, A. W.	354
Clute, Bartholomew H.	156
Cobb, Revilo	436
Coffin, P. Gardiner	407
Cole, Loren P.	324
Conover, John M.	117
Courter, Stanton	293
Crapser, Wallace W.	377
Curtis, Stephen A.	22

D.

Daley, James B.	228
Danforth, George L.	71
Decker, William H.	189
Defandorf, Levi M.	395
De Forest, Henry S.	161
Dibbell, Renwick	13
Dickinson, Charles	83
Dodge, Egbert B.	314
Dormady, Thomas	37
Duncker, Jeremiah	226

E.

Elliott, Robert	225
Empie, John G.	193
Eisenmenger, Frederick	212
Enders, David	181

F.

Farquher, Arthur H.	385
Faulkner, George H.	149
Ferguson, Alonzo	183
Ferguson, John A.	180
Ferrier, Thomas E.	111
Flanagan, James H.	259
Ford, Edwin L.	136
Fowler, Charles	237
Fox, George L.	144
France, Frank H.	413
France, John H.	171
Frazee, Frederick L.	79
Frazier, Charles K.	432
Frisbie, Daniel D.	299
Frisbie, Grandison N.	17
Fromer, Jacob	258
Frost, James	421

G.

Gara, Hugh B.	144
Gaylord, John W.	405
Getter, Henry C.	419
Gifford, Edward A.	345
Goodsell, Elmer E.	32
Gordon, John A.	132
Graham, Joseph B.	429
Granby, William	137

INDEX

	PAGE
Gray, John H.	54
Green, Nelson O.	70
Griswold, John A.	230
Gulfin, Andrew J.	12

H.

	PAGE
Hager, Edwin D.	248
Hallock, Stephen P.	286
Hamlin, William S.	95
Haner, George	27
Hartt, Edgar	336
Hartt, John G.	337
Hinman, Chauncey W.	363
Hinman, David M.	307
Hitchcock, Dwight B.	291
Hoagland, Page T.	270
Howe, Eugene E.	288
Hubbell, Richtmyer	40
Hunting, Ambrose R.	250

J.

	PAGE
Jackson, Edgar	415
Jenkins, Daniel W.	235
Jeralds, Thomas W.	90

K.

	PAGE
Kelley, Solomon	259
Kerr, Albert L.	341
Kilmer, Thomas J.	118
Kilts, Jacob L.	80
Kipp, Herbert	170
Kline, Andrew J.	198
Kniffen, John B.	167
Kniskern, William B.	323
Kohring, William	87
Kreiger, Elmer E.	182

L.

	PAGE
Lackey, Michael, Jr.	255
Lape, Simeon	29
Larkin, Willard	355
Lasher, George	44
Lehman, Parke C.	108
Leonard, Duncan M.	328
Liddle, Andrew G.	103

	PAGE
Lomax, Howard E.	378
Loudon, Stephen	257

M.

	PAGE
MacMillen, Alexander	173
Magee, Peter	311
Maginnis, John	390
Malcolm, Joseph	25
Mann, Charles	427
Markham, Convas E.	411
Mattice, Garret W.	149
Mayham, Stephen I.	125
McCabe, Charles P.	317
McMillan, Andrew J.	31
McWilliams, James C.	431
Mead, Joel H.	375
Mead, William H.	218
Mulford, Mrs. Mary J.	433
Myers, John A.	211

N.

	PAGE
Neville, William H.	425
Newell, John A.	48
Nichols, Charles E.	60
Nichols, Charles E. (of Catskill)	151

O.

	PAGE
Odell, Herbert L.	146
O'Hara, Barnard	373
O'Hara, Michael	131
Olmstead, Henry F.	65
O'Neil, Hugh	192
Osterhout, Stanton	428

P.

	PAGE
Pelham, Elmer E.	349
Pettingill, Haman P.	122
Pitcher, Charles W.	176
Platner, Benjamin F.	384
Platner, William C.	384
Potter, Thomas R.	14
Putman, Joseph	166
Putnam, John H.	423

R.

	PAGE
Ramsey, Charles H.	351
Raymond, Andrew V. V.	349
Rector, Christian	320
Rifenbark, Hiram	253
Rivenburg, Willard T.	234
Roe, John	199
Rose, Eli	330
Rosekraus, Albert G.	338
Rossman, John	219

S.

	PAGE
Sage, Sylvester B.	221
Salsbergh, William	130
Schermerhorn, Simon J.	22
Searles, Frank R.	399
Selden, Robert	47
Shafer, William D.	191
Shannon, Oscar H.	435
Shelmandine, Lewis	63
Showers, Cyrus	39
Showers, Isaac	85
Sias, Solomon	101
Slater, David T.	327
Smeallie, William J.	388
Smith, Chauncey	162
Snyder, J. Augustus	275
Snyder, Jacob M.	283
Staley, James S.	129
Stanley, Peter I.	280
Stead, James	393
Sternberg, John H.	164
Stevens, Emory	404
Stevens, James	97
Stewart, William H.	202
Straub, Frank N.	56

T.

	PAGE
Tallmadge, Benjamin I.	263
Terpening, Ira M.	106
Thorpe, William E.	380
Tinning, Archibald	55
Treadwell, La Grand I.	364

U.

	PAGE
Utter, Israel P.	127
Utter, James L.	418

INDEX

V.

Name	Page
Van Bergen, Henry	138
Vanderbilt, William S.	266
Vanderpoel, Andrew J.	187
Van Dreser, Henry	96
Van Eps, Peter V.	66
Van Loan, Jane	93
Van Loan, Walton	77
Van Schaick, Joseph W.	285
Van Valkenburgh, Jacob	342
Van Wagenen, Jared	207
Van Zandt, Henry C.	34
Voss, Charles	104
Vroman, Dow F.	361

W.

Name	Page
Waddell, James W.	143
Waddell, William T.	63
Wakeman, Alonzo	197
Wasson, William A.	61
Weidman, Charles E.	222
West, Noah D.	114
Wilber, Kirby	76
Wilson, Mrs. Julia A.	238
Winegard, Richard	154
Woodworth, Lucius A.	294
Wyatt, James T.	367

Y.

Name	Page
Yates, Austin A.	9
Young, J. Edward	38
Young, Madison	424

Z.

Name	Page
Zelie, Luther	313

PORTRAITS.

Name	Page	Name	Page	Name	Page
Albro, William H.	243	Griswold, John A.	231	Rose, Eli	331
Anderson, George W.	204	Hitchcock, Dwight B.	290	Rose, Mrs. Eli	333
Baldwin, William H.	304	Hubbell, Richtmyer	41	Sias, Solomon	100
Beard, Franklin P.	74	Jeralds, Thomas W.	91	Stanley, Peter I.	281
Bellinger, George W.	faces 169	Kerr, Albert L.	340	Straub, Frank X.	57
Bloodgood, Clarence E.	358	Kilmer, Thomas J.	119	Thorpe, William E.	381
Bradt, John	261	Maginnis, John	391	Vanderbilt, William S.	267
Burtis, John H., Jr.	401	Malcolm, Joseph	24	Vanderpoel, Andrew J.	186
De Forest, Henry S.	160	Mattice, Garret W.	148	Van Eps, Peter V.	67
Dickinson, Charles	82	Mayham, Stephen L.	124	Van Zandt, Henry C.	35
Dodge, Egbert B.	315	Newell, John A.	49	Waddell, James W.	142
Eisenmenger, Frederick	213	O'Hara, Barnard	372	Wakeman, Alonzo	196
Ferrier, Thomas E.	110	Pitcher, Charles W.	177	Weidman, Charles E.	223
Frisbie, Daniel D.	298	Raymond, Andrew V. V.	348	Wyatt, James T.	366
Frisbie, Grandison N.	16	Rector, Christian	321	Yates, Austin A.	8
Gordon, John A.	133	Rifenbark, Hiram	252		

www.ingramcontent.com/pod-product-compliance
Lightning Source LLC
Chambersburg PA
CBHW051723300426
44115CB00007B/443